PRAISE FOR *AMERICAN WASTELAND:*

"While the very best way to end the food hardship now faced by 49 million Americans would be to increase wages and expand the federal safety net, doing more to recover excess food could play an important role in feeding more hungry Americans and filling in the gaps when those other efforts fall short. Jonathan Bloom's fact-filled book is an important wake-up call and prod to action."

—Joel Berg, Executive Director, New York City Coalition Against Hunger, author of *All You Can Eat: How Hungry is America?*, and former USDA Coordinator of Food Recovery and Gleaning

"How is it that America can be dumping so much food, yet still be overweight? It seems that something is askew, and Bloom's work uncovers it eloquently and with great insight. Bloom reminds us that good stewardship of our resources is not only easy, it is the key for us to thrive."

—Jeff Barrie, Documentary Filmmaker, Kilowatt Ours

"A fascinating read that explores the full depth of food waste from every angle. *American Wasteland* is chock full of research showing how essential it is that we strive to raise awareness that food is not trash—it has no place in landfills. Bloom also addresses composting, touching upon its many economic, social, and environmental benefits."

—Wayne E. King Sr., President, U.S. Composting Council

"Food isn't just gas for the body; it binds us together as a people and it's the key to our future. *American Wasteland* is a bold call to arms, providing shocking examples of waste (most of it preventable), as well as strategies to divert that food back into communities, insuring that NO food goes to waste, and no citizen goes hungry."

—Robert L.E. Egger, President, D.C. Central Kitchen/ Campus Kitchens Project/V3 Campaign

"As much about the food we eat as it is about the food we discard, *American Wasteland* draws our attention to a culture of excess and wastefulness and the threats that this cultural mindset poses economically, environmentally and ethically. Bloom challenges us to open our eyes and engage ourselves in an issue that we cannot ignore."

—Josh Viertel, President, Slow Food USA

"Bloom does a thorough job identifying places in the food chain where food is wasted—food that could feed the hungry instead. *American Wasteland* is an excellent read for anyone who wants to know how surplus and scarcity can exist in the same country or in the same city."

—Jilly Stephens, Executive Director of City Harvest

American Wasteland

American Wasteland

How America Throws Away Nearly Half of Its Food
(and What We Can Do About It)

Jonathan Bloom

Da Capo
LIFE
LONG

A MEMBER OF THE PERSEUS BOOKS GROUP

Copyright © 2010 by Jonathan Bloom

Set in Dante by the Perseus Books Group

Cataloging-in-Publication data for this book is available from the Library of Congress.
ISBN: 978-0-7382-1364-4

First Da Capo Press edition 2010
Published by Da Capo Press
A Member of the Perseus Books Group
www.dacapopress.com

Note: The information in this book is true and complete to the best of our knowledge. This book is intended only as an informative guide for those wishing to know more about health issues. In no way is this book intended to replace, countermand, or conflict with the advice given to you by your own physician. The ultimate decision concerning care should be made between you and your doctor. We strongly recommend you follow his or her advice. Information in this book is general and is offered with no guarantees on the part of the authors or Da Capo Press. The authors and publisher disclaim all liability in connection with the use of this book.

Da Capo Press books are available at special discounts for bulk purchases in the U.S. by corporations, institutions, and other organizations. For more information, please contact the Special Markets Department at the Perseus Books Group, 2300 Chestnut Street, Suite 200, Philadelphia, PA, 19103, or call (800) 810-4145, ext. 5000, or e-mail special.markets@perseusbooks.com.

10 9 8 7 6 5 4 3 2

TO EMILY,

*without whom this book would not exist
and the sun would not rise.*

TO BRUCE,

*without whom this book would have been finished sooner,
but for whom I count my lucky stars.*

CONTENTS

Twelve

If I Were the King of the Forest: Big Changes 291

INTRODUCTION

A forsaken orange sits in a Raleigh, North Carolina, parking lot.

PHOTO BY JONATHAN BLOOM

Every day, America wastes enough food to fill the Rose Bowl. Yes, *that* Rose Bowl—the 90,000-seat football stadium in Pasadena, California. Of course, that's if we had an inclination to truck the nation's excess food to California for a memorable but messy publicity stunt.[1]

As a nation, we grow and raise more than 590 billion pounds of food each year.[2] And depending on whom you ask, we squander between *a quarter and a half* of all the food produced in the United States.[3] Even using the more conservative figure would mean that 160 billion pounds of food are squandered annually—more than enough, that is, to fill the Rose Bowl to the brim. With the high-end estimate, the Rose Bowl would almost be filled twice over.

If those numbers don't hit home, consider that the average American creates almost 5 pounds of trash per day.[4] Since, on average, 12 percent of what we throw away is or once was edible, we can estimate that each one of us discards half a pound of food per day. That adds up to an annual total of 197 pounds of food per person. Ominously, Americans' per capita food waste has increased by 50 percent since 1974.[5]

How we reached the point where most people waste more than their body weight—or at least the average American body-weight—each year in food is a complicated tale.[6] In short, Americans' gradual shift from a rural, farming life to an urban, nonagricultural one removed us from the sources of our food. Our once iron-clad guarantee of inheriting generations of food wisdom became less so, as busier lives forced many of us to leave the kitchen or spend less time there. Convenience began to trump homemade, and eating out drew level with dining in. We have higher standards for our meals, but diminished knowledge about how to maximize our use of food. Many of us don't even trust our noses to judge when an item has gone bad. Yet, our awareness of pathogens has multiplied, and we apply safety rules to food with the same zealous caution that we apply to allergies, kids walking to school, and most everything in modern life.

Certainly, some food loss is unavoidable. For example, there are many potential pitfalls, such as harsh weather, disease, and insects invading farmers' fields, that are outside of our control. And then there's storage loss, spoilage, and mechanical malfunctions. I classify all of the above factors as loss, not waste (also omitted when I use the term "waste" are inedible discards like peels, scraps, pits, and bones). Broadly speaking, I consider food "wasted" when an edible item goes unconsumed as a result of human action or inaction. There is culpability in waste. Whether it's from an individual's choice, a business mistake, or a government policy, most food waste stems from decisions made somewhere from farm to fork. A grower doesn't harvest a field in response to a crop's lowered price. Grocers throw away imperfect produce to satisfy their (and, as consumers, our) obsession with freshness. We allow groceries to rot in our refrigerators while we eat out, and when at restaurants we order 1,500-calorie entrées only to leave them half eaten.

We're not going to revert to an agrarian society anytime soon, but that doesn't mean we can't have a greater appreciation of our food. While completely eliminating food waste may be impossible, reducing it isn't. Improvements are needed at all steps of the food chain, but most importantly at the part that involves us. Buying wisely, and maximizing our food use once it's in our possession, would go a long way toward minimizing that daily Rose Bowl–sized pile of waste.

My fascination with wasted food started in the sweltering lair of one of America's oldest food-recovery groups, D.C. Central Kitchen, in 2005.[7] I'd been cruising through most of my twenties as an increasingly food-focused journalist, but I hadn't quite found my niche. That summer day in our nation's capital, my task was to man an industrial-sized vat of pasta. This was not a plum assignment in a building without air conditioning. Yet the job's mindlessness granted me time to look around while I stirred the spaghetti with an oar. I noticed a variety of foods that somebody hadn't wanted. And it was all good stuff, too. We're talking about racks of lamb, ribs, and nice vegetables. Such abundance, all waiting for redistribution to the hungry.

What was the story? Where did these foods come from? Why were they cast away? And what happens in cities that lack such food-recovery organizations?

My curiosity about these questions led me to investigate the extent of food waste in America. I declined a traditional journalism job after graduation in order to focus on food waste—even if it made future meals with friends and family a touch uncomfortable. I launched a blog (WastedFood.com) in late 2006. Along the way, I began to be interviewed and was invited to give talks on the subject. It's an odd thing to call oneself a food-waste expert, but life's funny like that.

But there's more to it. I've always had a sense that food was not something to be wasted. Ours was not a house where one had to clean one's plate, but my brother and I certainly had to try everything. It was a place where all shapes and sizes of leftovers were saved, whether we were eating in or out. Chinese food containers accompanied us home from every meal at Chef Chang's or Lotus Flower. And having a leftover smorgasbord night was not uncommon.

Outside the kitchen door of my childhood home, a Victorian built in the 1890s, sits a hole with a cover operated by a foot pedal. The mauve-colored lid is akin to a foot-operated trash can. There's good reason for the similarity—it was where our predecessors dumped their food scraps for a local pig farmer to collect. As a kid, I had no idea what this contraption was for; it was just a nuisance during driveway basketball games. Looking back, though, I suppose the topic of food waste has been with me all along.

Less symbolic and more important, I grew up watching my Grandma Bloom eat. A teenager during the Depression, she'd get every morsel of meat from chicken drumsticks and, on New Year's Eve, lobster legs. On the other side of the family, Grandma Abby has another method for avoiding waste: attempting to serve all that she's prepared with her loving brand of "persistent hospitality." Anyone familiar with the Jewish Grandmother Code of Conduct will understand that this means she relentlessly pushes food on guests. And in his day, if there was anything left on your plate, Grandpa Jack made it disappear.

Growing up the son of second-generation Americans in Yankee Massachusetts, I was destined for thrift. The majority of immigrants to this country brought and continue to bring a culture of thrift that's less a choice than a necessity. That includes the Anglo Saxon settlers who arrived in the seventeenth century. Their habits, the vestiges of which still pervade the Northeast as "Yankee culture," were nothing if not practical and thrifty. If you've ever seen a New Englander make pot-scrubbing powder from eggshells, or breadcrumbs from stale bread, you know that many of us delight in avoiding waste.

I'm also a bit of a cheapskate (although, to be fair, I prefer the term "pragmatic")—and I love both preparing and eating food. I abhor the thought of food going to waste, both because it's anathema to my cheap, er, practical, soul and because it's a horrible fate for edibles that could otherwise help feed those who go without or just make something delicious. And after learning more about the resources that go into growing crops and raising livestock and the environmental impact of landfilling food, seeing those goods squandered frustrates me even more.

Despite all of my attention to the topic, I still waste food. Some items in our house go bad before my wife and I can use them (I'm looking right at you, cilantro bunch). Other foods get buried and forsaken in the fridge. And occasionally—with a dash of guilt—I toss something that just doesn't taste good. Okay, fine—it's more like a dollop than a dash.

Two years ago, when I was working at an anaerobic digestion company in Raleigh, North Carolina, an odd sight stopped me in my tracks as I walked across the parking lot one morning: an abandoned orange. In an otherwise immaculate strip of asphalt—because it was one of those places that contracted landscapers to leaf-blow the parking lot weekly—it was not hard to spot. I was transfixed. I returned to my car and got my camera to take pictures of this forsaken fruit. I couldn't imagine who would throw out what appeared to be a perfectly good orange. The exterior was a little dirty, but that's why oranges have skin. And I guessed that the spot of grime came courtesy of the asphalt. So what did I do? What would anyone who was blogging about food waste do? I ate it. And it was fine.

In addition to wondering who would discard a perfectly good orange, I couldn't imagine who would drop it onto the ground. Because, with the exception of cigarette butts, we just don't see people leave their trash behind as much these days as we did, say, twenty years ago. Collectively, we decided it was an unpleasant behavior and directly and indirectly set about to curtail it. Putting a name on the behavior—"littering"—helped. The Pennsylvania Resources Council created the "litterbug" idea in the early 1950s and allowed others to use it, and publicity campaigns followed.[8] States made it worth our while to turn in bottles and cans, and eventually counties and municipalities made it much, much easier to recycle through curbside collection.

Today, seeing someone drop a can on the ground or even in the regular trash is rare, but few passersby would bat an eyelash if you threw away half of a banana. A common misconception is that food automatically returns to the soil. But although it does not seem as harmful as inorganic trash, food waste, in truth, is more damaging than most other litter. Organic materials (such as foods) are the ones that release greenhouse gases into the environment as they decompose.

Food waste isn't considered problematic because, for the most part, it isn't considered at all. It's easy to ignore because it's both common and customary. William Rathje, director of the erstwhile Garbage Project, a University of Arizona study that examined America's trash habits for more than thirty years, told me that food waste and its consequences go largely unnoticed. Why? Because it doesn't pile up like old newspapers; it just goes *away*, either down the disposal or into the trash.[9] Yet, once you start looking for it, you can't miss the abandoned appetizers and squandered sandwiches.

Whenever the topic of food waste comes up in a conversation I'm having—after the awkwardness passes, if there's eating involved—most everyone has an intense reaction. Regardless of their take on the subject, each person has a strategy, an anecdote, or a question. I have yet to meet somebody who is pro–food waste, but many aren't convinced that it's important. And a good number of people, regardless of how they respond, don't *behave* as if it matters much.

But food waste matters. A lot. Wasting food has harmful environmental, economic, and ethical consequences. That's why we can't afford to ignore it anymore. You may see that orange and think that it's just one piece of fruit. True. But what if all 130 million households in America tossed out that amount or more of food each day?[10] We'd need a pretty big bowl to contain all that squandered food. Something about the size of the Rose Bowl.

In the coming pages, I'll take you to abandoned harvests, pristine supermarket produce sections, and restaurants where abundance is always on the menu. We'll end up close to home, well, actually, in your home. Because, as we'll see, wasted food occurs there, and all around us. Still, we remain blissfully unaware of it.

You may be amazed by how freely and easily we dispose of food, from farm to fork. But it can be equally amazing how freely and easily we can diminish our vast squandering. To achieve that feat, though, we need to fully understand and acknowledge the scope of the problem.

A team of pickers harvests iceberg lettuce in Salinas, California.

PHOTO BY JONATHAN BLOOM

chapter 1

Waste from Farm to Fork

I recognize the right and duty of this generation to develop and use our natural resources; but I do not recognize the right to waste them, or to rob, by wasteful use, the generations that come after us.

—TEDDY ROOSEVELT

Salad Days

"Welcome to Salinas, Salad Bowl to the World." The weathered sign along Highway 101 greets visitors to this California ag town with that humble claim. In case the endless rows of lettuce crowding the road don't communicate the Salinas Valley's focus, businesses like Vegetable Growers Supply and the Rain Store (irrigation) probably will. And the massive packing plants of Taylor Farms, Fresh Express, and River Ranch Fresh Foods certainly will.

Leafy greens of all varieties line the finger-shaped valley from the foothills of the Gabilan Range to the edge of the Santa Lucia Range. Not surprisingly, the majority of America's lettuce is grown in Monterey County. In reality, that means Salinas and its surrounding fields. There, oil-laden fertilizers, pesticides, and thousands of gallons of water are called upon to bring seeds to green fruition.

One can even find salad greens at the Crazy Horse Canyon Landfill. When I visited the now-closed landfill, an inch of shredded lettuce obscured the ground like a dusting of green snow. Atop the mountain of trash, Robert Correa oversaw the delivery of 200 tons of excess, rejected, or misbagged produce every day until the landfill's closure in 2009. The dump closed because it was full, an outcome hastened by that ceaseless supply of green waste.

"It's a slow day for ag waste," Correa told me during a visit to Crazy Horse, but we were still crunching lettuce with almost every step. Here, lettuce that was still perfectly good—crispy, even—had been thrown away for various reasons. It may have been damaged in the warehouse, or maybe it sat for too long to withstand shipping. Regardless, the majority of it was edible at the time it was dumped at Crazy Horse. While we were walking around, I spotted some lettuce and spinach still in the plastic tubs that you'd find stacked in the supermarket cold case.

I observed lettuce-harvesting up close one early autumn day on a press tour organized as part of Salute to Agriculture, an event celebrating the city's farming accomplishments. As advertised, the tour provided an "unprecedented opportunity to actually see how the fresh and flavorful produce and wine from the world-famous Salinas Valley is produced and processed." We visited a field of one of the largest growers in the area, Ocean Mist Farms, and saw a crew of Latino pickers in jeans and baseball hats laboring among rows of lettuce. Anglo and Latino supervisors observed the work in outfits straight out of a Wrangler ad.

The harvesters, both men and women, toiled behind a 40-foot-wide rolling contraption that served as a mobile assembly line. The wheeled vessel carried flattened cardboard boxes and plastic bags; workers, in pairs, used these to create cases of wrapped lettuce that would eventually land at supermarkets. The harvesting rig sailed through the rows, with workers picking under the Mexican flag that adorned the vessel. The teams of two picked, cleaned, bagged, and boxed the iceberg.

Without looking down, pickers squeezed each head for a split second. The ones that didn't feel right were not harvested, leaving what looked like perfect lettuces in the rig's wake. While the workers are paid a "piece rate" based on the total number of cartons they pack, they also know that their work must pass scrutiny. In order to receive credit for their labor, they must make sure the lettuce will withstand random inspections done at the cooling shed. They scrawl their number on each box so that their work can be traced back to them. Given the dual priorities of speed and quality, the workers don't stop to check a head of lettuce twice. If it doesn't feel perfect, or it's the wrong size or shape, it's left in the field.

That's the way their supervisor, Art Barrientos, wants it. Barrientos, Ocean Mist's VP of harvesting, with more than thirty years of service and an easy smile, explained to us tour visitors how the grower's quality assurances start in the field. "You better not be putting anything we don't want in the box," said Barrientos. "If it doesn't meet our standard, it stays in the field. That's our model."

When I asked what was wrong with the bypassed heads of lettuce, Barrientos picked one up to illustrate its shortcomings. He squeezed it a few times and guessed that some rot had set in. Slicing it in half with his handy paring knife, he held open two pristine, icy green halves. "Hmm," he said. He couldn't say why this one wasn't picked.

Yes, Barrientos could have grabbed a lettuce that was clearly rotten. The point is, he didn't. On a random inspection of castaway lettuce, he came up with a perfect head.

Our Stretched Food Chain

It's not as if growers want to leave healthy food in the field. Every pound of produce is potential revenue, and that lettuce left to rot in the fields likely means lost profits. But in addition to wanting to ensure quality, growers ask their pickers to be selective in the field because they know the lettuce has a long way to travel. Some heads go cross-country, and others even farther. The average U.S. supermarket produce item travels 1,500 miles before it arrives at its destination.[1] A tiny bit of decay at the time of harvest could mean a rotten head by the time the shipment reaches the grocery store.

All produce companies want to ensure that a vegetable picked today will not just be edible, but enticing, on vendors' shelves. Hence, a head of lettuce that is perfectly good now—but shows signs that it could be less than ideal in two weeks—won't be picked. From a freshness perspective, the producer wants it to be the same kind of produce you'd hope to find at a farmers market. Joe Pezzini, the vice president of operations at Ocean Mist, told me their that these time constraints determined their policy. "There's a seventeen-day shelf life for iceberg, if the cold chain is maintained," he told me over breakfast at my Salinas hotel. "You can't store it and hope the market improves, like with corn."

On the Salute to Agriculture tour, I was told that Ocean Mist harvests 97 to 98 percent of its crop. From what I saw on my one-day visit, that estimate seemed optimistic, at best. Whatever their actual rate, the word around Salinas is that Ocean Mist is one of the most efficient farms in the area. That word comes from John Inman, an agricultural consultant who has worked in Salinas agriculture since 1965 and whose business card bears the nickname "Mr. Equipment." He puts the average harvest rate industry-wide at 85 to 90 percent and says that lettuce is among the most efficiently harvested crops in the valley. The cycle of planting and harvesting (or not harvesting, as the case may be) continues unabated nearly year-round.

Pezzini declined to estimate the percentage of unharvested lettuce, but he did concede that it's more than he'd like. "It's fair to say that in any given field, in any acre, there are some good heads that could be eaten," said Pezzini, who has been at Ocean Mist for more than twenty-five years. "They might have some blemishes or something that the market doesn't want, but all in all there's produce out there that could be consumed. The pressure from the market is pretty acute. We're all out there trying to create perfect produce."

At Ocean Mist, when I was observing, it seemed that about one out of every five heads remained in the field. However, using a conservative estimate of 90 percent harvested, we can make some rough calculations. Since growers in the Salinas Valley produced 153,495 acres of lettuce in 2007, that's the equivalent of not harvesting 15,350 acres,[2] or leaving more than 13 million pounds of lettuce in the field. And that's just lettuce.

The heads of iceberg that do make it out of the field are trucked to a climate-controlled storage facility—the cooling shed—where the lettuce is inspected and chilled to bring its core temperature down. An array of 18-wheelers connect to numbered loading bays to begin what can be a cross-country journey to grocery-chain distribution centers or wholesale warehouses.

Often called "reefer" trucks, these refrigerated tractor trailers don't carry pot. Rather, they haul just about every kind of produce grown in the valley. The trucks and their refrigeration units guzzle diesel. Since most truckers operate independently from growers and receivers, skimping on the refrigeration was an occasional practice not too long ago. Since cutting back on cooling can disrupt the "cold chain" and cause the lettuce to break down sooner, most growers have instituted preventive measures to ensure adequate, consistent refrigeration. Still, trucks and their refrigerated units break down from time to time. Although nobody has calculated the amount of produce lost for this reason, it's another pitfall that leads to waste, as are crashes. Accidents caused by weary truckers or careless commuters can render cargo worthless or prompt delays that jeopardize shipments.

Most shipments of lettuce go to distribution centers for grocery stores such as Kroger, Safeway, and Whole Foods as well as to Target, Costco, Walmart, and other superstores. In addition, some trucks head for wholesale "terminal markets" that supply smaller grocery stores and restaurants. Whole Foods' South Region—which includes Georgia, North Carolina, South Carolina, Alabama, Tennessee, and part of Florida—receives most of its lettuce from those Salinas fields. The shipments arrive at the chain's Braselton, Georgia, facility, 40 minutes outside of Atlanta. The 100,000-square-foot South Distribution Center handles produce, meats, and frozen foods in addition to dry groceries.

There, as at all endpoints, the product is inspected once it arrives to ensure that it's in satisfactory condition. Items need to be in pretty darn good shape, as they still can sit in the facility for four to six days and then must last on the shelf and in customers' homes. The inspection guidelines should be the same for all stores because the U.S. Department of Agriculture (USDA) provides standards for all agricultural products. For each pallet of product, inspectors look into a few boxes to make sure the produce makes the grade. Yet some stores may be more stringent than others.

Since most iceberg lettuce comes wrapped in plastic bags, inspectors will open a representative sample and, as with most commodities, slice a couple of heads open. "A few are sacrificed," said Alex Rilko, who oversees all buying at Whole Foods' South Distribution Center.

Each shipment is scored based on the USDA guidelines. If it doesn't reach a certain score, the store can reject it. And with so much that can go wrong, there doesn't tend to be any grade inflation. Rilko explained that when inspectors check shipments of iceberg at the Whole Foods' distribution center, they are looking for soft heads, insects, too much trimming, not enough trimming, leaves starting to break or split, too much dirt, heads that are opening, worm damage, mechanical damage, overall injury, lack of freshness, the wrong temperature (taken by laser or probe to see if the truck was too warm), the wrong size, discoloration of the "ribs" (the centers of the leaves) or other parts, dark and scabbed "butts" where the head was cut from the stem, freeze damage, "spotting" (from insect damage), and "tip burn" (from too much wind or sun).

And that list of possible maladies is not all that long or unusual for produce. When you're at the mercy of the elements, there are many hazards, no matter the type of crop. Rilko noted that the only two products that get much leeway are cherries and potatoes, which can be a bit banged up. "The rest are all real close to each other; they're all pretty strict," he said.

When they find signs of damage, they'll peek into a few more cases before rejecting the load. "A few times a week we have problems with product that comes in the door. And when you're rejecting something you're usually rejecting a lot of it," Rilko said.

If the payload doesn't pass muster, it remains the property of the sender. Whether the truck belongs to that company or not, the driver now has a dilemma: He must find a taker for the rejected contents. A significant portion of the load is fine, but grocery stores that have paid for first-rate produce aren't going to take the time to sort through each box. The produce company then must scramble to find someone who will. It may try to find a wholesaler, or perhaps a lower-tier grocer who has the time and inclination to go through the cases. That is increasingly rare, though, as few stores accept second-tier goods. And should the company find a buyer, it won't get much for the items. Without a purchaser, it may opt to donate the load to a food bank—usually quite happy to separate the good from the bad—and receive a tax write-off.

All the while, though, the clock is ticking. Produce sitting on the loading dock isn't getting any better and requires diesel to keep it cool. Drivers don't have much time to spare, as they're either due to pick up another load for the return trip or are hoping to get home, pronto. That pressure, along with being unfamiliar with local food banks, hinders donations. Drivers occasionally choose to "waste it." If a portion of the load is declined, they may discard it in the store's Dumpster; a rejected truckload may require a trip to the landfill.

Once the boxed lettuce is accepted at the supermarket's distribution center, the inventory having been checked and assessed and found worthy, it may sit there for a day or two before being trucked to individual stores. Because this journey tends to be shorter than the one from the packing facility, there are fewer crates lost along the way. Still, it can take the delivery trucks as long as eight hours to travel from a distribution center to the stores that are farthest away on a given route.

When a shipment arrives in acceptable condition at the supermarket, there are still more potential pitfalls. In hot weather, deliveries can sit too long on the loading dock, or stay in the trailer too long after the refrigeration unit is turned off. When I worked at a supermarket in 2006—conducting research for this book—the arrival of a "truck" prompted an all-hands-on-deck approach. You dropped what you were doing to make sure all the items got to the refrigerated areas quickly. Yet, that urgency may not be the norm.

Handling errors are a reality at supermarkets. From my experience, maneuvering a pallet with hundreds of pounds of food, shrink wrapped and stacked about 10 feet high, is easier said than done. Steering a hydraulic pallet jack is akin to pushing a shopping cart with a bum wheel. Piloting such a contraption to the right storage area without crashing into other pallets of groceries, sending too many co-workers scrambling, or running into walls, which seem to jump out at you from nowhere, takes some doing.

After being unloaded, lettuce goes to the "walk-in" (aka refrigerator), where it can sit for days, depending on inventory levels. It's difficult to maintain the right level of product, and store managers would rather sacrifice their firstborn than run out of an item. Seeing an empty display is jarring—and rare. As you'd guess, the result of a system where managers pride themselves on a never-ending supply is that overstocking is a frequent problem, and it increases the produce's sitting time. All the while, the lettuce's biological clock is ticking, its "sell-by" date steadily approaching. Where I worked, we would rejuvenate the unwrapped red-leaf and romaine lettuces by "perking," or soaking, them before putting them out. This extended the shelf life by cleansing lettuce of leaf-threatening parasites. Iceberg, being wrapped, missed out on this life-extending wash.

There are dangers once the produce reaches the shelf, too. If produce isn't rotated properly, it will meet a premature demise. Rotation includes putting the freshest produce in the back or bottom so that shoppers buy the oldest first; it also means rotating individual pieces of produce so they don't get soft on one side. Both practices require vigilance on the part of produce department employees. But that kind of conscientiousness isn't universal, to put it kindly, especially near the end of a shift.

Furthermore, in choosing a head of lettuce, customers may shake, squeeze, and do God knows what with the product. All that poking, prodding, and sniffing accumulates, and at the end of the day, the remaining items may look like they've been mauled. Depending on the store, they may be pulled and thrown away, donated to a food bank, or placed on a sale rack. This in-store damage isn't as common a problem for iceberg lettuce, which is fairly hardy and usually wrapped in plastic, as it is for many other types of produce. More dangerous, perhaps, is the temptation for clerks to refill the display by shooting the orbs of iceberg onto the shelf as if it were a carnival game. Not that I did this—what with being all-consumed by avoiding food waste—but even I had to fight the urge. Even during a careful restocking of iceberg, heads had a habit of falling to the floor, likely sustaining some damage.

And the dangers for lettuce aren't confined to the produce department. As anyone who's ever been grocery shopping can attest, some absent-minded cashiers handle produce as if they're paid a bonus for ruining it. Can you tell that this is a pet peeve of mine?

No matter how the damage occurs, these dinged lettuces ultimately go bad faster than unharmed ones. While there's a commonsense appeal to that principle, it also has a scientific explanation, as Angela Fraser, a food-safety expert at Clemson University, explained. "Whenever you damage a food, you create openings," Fraser said. "When you damage that outer layer, any contaminant—bacteria, mold, parasites, viruses—can invade the inside of the produce and will cause it to spoil more quickly. So handle it gently."

Perishables like produce face still more perils on the journey home. A bus or subway ride is fraught with bruising threats. On hot days, many of us place our perishables into sun-baked cars that may or may not have effective air conditioning. And then there's the post-supermarket errand that takes longer than expected while your groceries heat up. Fraser voiced the accepted wisdom on food safety: "We generally recommend that after you purchase a perishable food, it's best to get it into the refrigerator within one to two hours."

However long it takes, the iceberg lettuce eventually makes it into our homes. Once it does, the main danger is neglect. As I write this, there's an old head of iceberg currently sitting in my produce drawer. I bought it to make B.L.T. sandwiches for some guests. But since I don't normally have lettuce in my sandwiches or enjoy iceberg in salads, it now faces a familiar, American ending. I haven't looked at it in two weeks and I've used nary a leaf in more than a month. I don't want to eat any more of it, but, out of guilt, I want to throw it out even less. So there it sits. My behavior is not atypical. An estimated 32 percent of fresh vegetables in supermarkets, restaurants, and households is wasted.[3]

Shoppers often buy fresh food with the best of intentions, but they seem to be in denial about their daily schedules. For a family with two working parents or a single adult logging long hours, preparing meals at home is less of a given than it used to be. Habits have changed, largely because of our busier lifestyles. In 2007, Americans spent 44 percent of their food dollars at restaurants or food stands of one kind or another instead of grocery stores and food markets.[4] Whether we have food delivered, order takeout, or eat out, it often means not using the perishables in our fridge.

Those familiar decisions—bypassing the chicken thighs we may have bought a few days ago because they were on sale, and ordering a pizza instead—have an impact. It means that we'll squander the time, effort, money, and fossil fuels that were expended to grow, process, and transport that chicken. When we don't eat our head of lettuce, the environmental cost of growing it will go for naught, as the food won't nourish anyone. Instead, it'll probably be fed to a land-fill like the one in Salinas, where its rotting will emit methane, a greenhouse gas twenty-five times more harmful than carbon dioxide. With global warming, we're reaping what we sow.

A Numbers Problem

Generally speaking, there is limited data on U.S. food waste. And what we do know about it isn't pretty: Two separate sources estimate that America wastes roughly half of its food.[5] The most recent calculations, from a 2009 study, suggested that we squander 40 percent of available calories.[6] The last time the Department of Agriculture studied the topic was 1997, when it estimated that we waste 27 percent of available food. And even the authors of that study admitted that their waste findings were likely too low, as they didn't include "preharvest, on-the-farm and farm-to-retail losses," owing to a lack of data.[7]

There are few studies on food waste partly because there just aren't that many people who want to tally unharvested lettuces—or any other kind of wasted food. There has been little imperative or political will to size up how much food we squander—until now. Plus, waste can be difficult to measure. It's much easier to count what is harvested than what isn't. Because waste disappears quickly in most parts of the food chain, it's that much harder to tabulate.

By that same logic, there is even less data on liquid waste. That's mostly because drink waste is elusive and even harder to measure than squandered food. That's why you won't see any discussion of beverages in the following chapters. (Also, I must confess, I'm more interested in food than I am in drink.) Besides, if we really knew how much coffee was dumped—if there was such a way to quantify such a statistic—our collective heads might explode.

But milk is in a separate category, given its role in nourishing children. In 1995, the USDA estimated that milk had the second-highest loss rate of any food item: About a third of it isn't consumed.[8] That year, 16 billion pounds of milk were wasted. That's the equivalent of every American pouring an 8-ounce glass of milk every day, then not drinking a third of it. And that doesn't include the amount lost at school lunches or to milk mustaches.

Looking Ahead

As we saw earlier, waste occurs at all stages of the food chain. Surprisingly, wasted food cuts across most socioeconomic distinctions. It is not specific to certain states, cities, or towns, although some municipalities are better at reducing or recycling food waste. Neither color nor creed is a useful indicator of how wasteful people are with food. To a certain extent, wasting food is universal. We've all done it, probably even today.

Partly because food waste is so pervasive, it's not something we can ever solve completely. There won't be any declarations of victory or "Mission Accomplished" banners. Yet, instead of being discouraged by the status quo, we can view our national food-waste habit as an opportunity. By trimming our waste and recovering the low-hanging fruit (literally and figuratively!), we can help feed hungry Americans, bolster our economy, combat global warming, and make our society that much more ethical.

A passive methane vent slowly releases methane from a landfill in Chapel Hill, North Carolina.

chapter 2

Does Food Waste Really Matter? Why You Should Care

There are at least four natural resources that have fueled our industrial food system that are now in steep decline: energy, climate, water, and soil.

—FREDERICK KIRSCHENMANN, FARMER AND
DISTINGUISHED FELLOW, LEOPOLD CENTER FOR
SUSTAINABLE AGRICULTURE, IOWA STATE UNIVERSITY

alking up the side of a capped landfill is not an unpleasant activity. Nor should it be, as many old landfill sites are now recreational areas. Just be sure not to dig those tent stakes in too deep.

The original portion of North Carolina's Orange Regional Landfill, called the "north side," is now a 45-acre hill covered in dirt and a layer of green weeds. If you didn't know that a combination of household and commercial waste created the slope, you might call it bucolic. And you probably wouldn't have any clue of its substructure were it not for a series of what look like six-foot-tall candy-canes dotting the flattened top of the hill. These forty-five shafts, however, don't have stripes; they're gray and hollow. Indeed, they're pipes. When the wind blows in your direction, you get a whiff of their purpose: a faint smell of natural gas, just like those scratch-and-sniff warning stickers.

These pipes, also called "passive vents," sit atop holes drilled in every acre and filled with gravel that encourage the landfill gases to escape evenly, instead of building up and causing fires or explosions. The word "passive" is indicative of the county's approach. This portion of the Orange Regional Landfill, in Chapel Hill, North Carolina, closed in 1995, collected plenty of waste during its twenty-three-year lifespan. Yet, it is not large enough to require a mandatory landfill-gas collection system under Environmental Protection Agency (EPA) standards. Orange County, like most landfill owners not required to act, declined to install any kind of expensive gas-collection equipment, instead choosing that ever more popular option: nothing.

Orange County is not some environmentally unaware backwater. It's one of the more progressive places in the South, having adopted curbside recycling in 1989, and it now pays for restaurants, supermarkets, and schools to compost their food scraps through a private company. The town of Chapel Hill amended its zoning laws to green-light the state's first gold-certified building in the Leadership in Energy and Environmental Design (LEED) standard developed by the U.S. Green Building Council. Orange County is home to the forward-thinking University of North Carolina at Chapel Hill and the nearby enclave of Carrboro, the first North Carolina municipality to elect an openly gay mayor. Yet, it's also home to a decent-sized landfill.

To be fair, the county installed a gas-collection system across the street at the active portion of the landfill in 2007 (although that was after allowing that section's greenhouse gases to escape since it opened in 2000). There's even talk of harnessing the gas there to create energy in the near future. And well there should be, because there's plenty of energy-rich food in those hills.

Because Orange County has a high recycling rate and an abundance of restaurants, its landfill has a higher percentage of food waste than the average U.S. landfill. As more recyclables are sent elsewhere, food becomes a larger portion of what's left. Food waste makes up about 25 percent of Orange Regional's contents, said Blair Pollock, solid-waste planner at Orange County Solid Waste Department.[1] The county only subsidizes composting for its larger restaurants, and the county's rate of food waste disposal is only increasing. From 1995 to 2005, food's proportion of both the residential and commercial waste streams doubled.[2] And did I mention that food creates most of the methane in a landfill?

Burying a Problem

The majority of food discarded today ends up in a landfill, with its associated problems. Unfortunately, we seldom think about the effects of our food once it's gone because, well, it's gone. Then, it's somebody else's problem. "There's a misconception among the people. They think that throwing away food or organic materials is environmentally benign," said Jan Lundqvist, author of an influential waste study and a professor of water and environmental studies at Sweden's Linkoping University. "But it depends on how food is being disposed."

Food scraps are the second-largest component of the national waste stream, making up 19 percent of what we dump into landfills.[3] (And the landfill figures don't include the food we shoot down the garbage disposal, which can be up to three times what we put in the trash and has its own consequences.[4]) As anyone with a mailbox can understand, paper is the most common landfill stuffer, despite our significant recycling rate. Food's proportion of the waste stream, or, dare I say, the foodprint, steadily increased as we have recycled other materials at higher and higher rates. By contrast, we barely recycle, or compost, any of our food. As a result, while food is 13 percent of all materials discarded, it's 18 percent of whats dumped into landfills (after factoring in recycling).[5]

And whereas our landfilling of food is on the rise—the rate doubled from 1980 to 2007—our pitiful rate of composting has dropped.[6] From 1995 to 1999, composting, according to the EPA, dipped a bit.[7] Since the turn of the millennium, this rate has increased slightly, but even with all the focus on increasing aware-ness of environmental issues, it hasn't exactly taken off. In 2000, we composted 2.5 percent of food discards.[8] In 2008, the rate was a strikingly similar 2.5 per-cent. Meanwhile, the overall recycling rate has done nothing but increase, climb-ing by 400 percent from 1989 to 1999.[9]

As previously mentioned, the average American sends more than half a pound of food to the landfill each day.[10] Good riddance and bon voyage, right? Yes, except that we're stashing pockets of greenhouse gases in the ground as little surprises for the next generation. Not all surprises are welcome. Food buried in a landfill today could still be emitting gas twenty years from now.

What does all this mean? In a word: methane.

Methane Mishegas

When solid waste rots in a landfill, it emits methane. And (with apologies to Adam Sandler) if trapping heat in our atmosphere was cool, methane would be Miles Davis.[11] Although methane is nowhere near as common as carbon dioxide, it's much more harmful. Methane has been found to trap heat far more effectively than carbon dioxide, with estimates of its "global warming poten-tial"(GWP) 21 to 25 times more than that of CO_2 over a 100-year period. In other words, sending food to the landfill aids global warming in a major way.

Landfills are the second leading source of human-related methane emissions in the United States.[12] They accounted for 23 percent of all methane emissions in 2007, and, of all materials, food has the highest rate of methane yield.[13] (The largest anthropogenic source is enteric fermentation, or, as you might call it, livestock belching and flatulence.)

True, landfill methane emissions are not our most dire environmental prob-lem; it is the ninth-largest source of greenhouse gas.[14] Still, food waste is an em-inently fixable problem. It would be much easier to prevent paper and food from reaching the landfill than to keep vehicles off the road and out of the sky, num-bers two and five in impact, respectively. (Increased paper and food recycling and wide-scale adoption of alternative fuels and public transport would be nice compromises, though.)

In 1996, the EPA began to require gas-collection systems at the largest land-fills. The most common solution was to install "wells," or long pipes reaching into the mass of waste, to collect the gases. Today, progressive landfills then convert that captured methane into energy and, sometimes, renewable energy credits (RECs).

Today, more than half of all landfills are still just letting their methane escape. Typically, the reason is that they do not meet the EPA's definition of "large"— which is 2.5 million metric tons.[15] Because the small and medium-sized landfills aren't forced to collect methane, they don't. Those systems are expensive. As a result, 61 percent of all landfill gases generated in 2003 occurred at landfills without gas wells.[16] The Orange Regional Landfill is a prime example. In fact, it's among the worst-case scenarios—a landfill just under the tonnage cutoff point with a high percentage of food waste.

And even landfills that collect greenhouse gases miss a large amount of methane. Published estimates of how much methane escapes range from 25 to 50 percent.[17] Mort Barlaz, who completed the EPA's Waste Reduction Model (WARM) projections, was nice enough to "run a model" for me on emissions from food waste. He found that over the life of a typical landfill, a collection system would miss 38 to 45 percent of the methane being emitted.

Of the landfills that capture methane, slightly more than half simply burn it off. This "flaring" destroys the methane, but it creates the less harmful carbon dioxide in the process. At landfills this kind of emission isn't counted as adding carbon to the environment because it's considered to be preexisting, or biogenic, carbon. The other landfills that capture methane harness it to create energy, but these projects are not cheap. Despite the costs, the number of waste-to-energy plants is increasing, thanks to the allure of renewable energy credits and energy companies' increasingly enticing rates for bulk purchases of renewable energy.

Barlaz told me that, on average, landfills don't start collecting gas until they've been accepting waste for a year or two. The exact percentage of methane escaping during that window of opportunity is unknown, but Barlaz estimated it at 30 percent of the methane a food item will emit during its entire rotting process. In Salinas, California, Crazy Horse Canyon Landfill received great amounts of agricultural excess during its seventy-plus years in operation, but it only received a gas-collection system after it closed, in April 2009.[18]

In addition to aiding global warming, methane stinks. Air pollution can have more than one meaning. Sending more food to the landfill lowers the quality of life for neighbors of the landfill. And as environmental justice advocates will tell you, landfills are predominantly located in areas with poverty and/or people of color. More than just being unpleasant, these odors can cause or exacerbate respiratory problems such as asthma.

Landfull

Groundwater pollution is another perk of landfilling food. Older landfills are dreadful in this regard, often with no liner between the seeping, toxic ooze and our drinking supply. Newer landfills must have a liner, and most do a decent job of keeping this "leachate" out of groundwater. But nobody is sure how long these liners—often a layer of clay—will last. If they falter, that leachate, caused by rain picking up various substances as it trickles through the trash, will find the holes. Those not employed by waste management companies acknowledge that, one way or another, landfills will eventually leak.[19]

No matter how you slice it, we're sending far too much food to the land-fill—and that has dire long- and short-term consequences. In a nation with ro-botic vacuums and phones that can give us directions, we're essentially using a Stone Age solution—digging a hole in the ground and dumping stuff in it—to handle our waste. The authors of the Natural Resources Defense Council study "Is Landfill Gas Green Energy?" didn't mince words in analyzing the overall effect of landfills: "At best, the Environmental Protection Agency's cur-rent landfill regulations merely postpone the inevitable damage landfills will cause," they wrote. "Landfills are simply unsustainable, and therefore so is LFG [landfill gas]."

Americans make up less than 5 percent of the world's population, but we supply almost a quarter of global greenhouse-gas emissions. Making matters worse, we're terrible at "recycling" our food waste. Large-scale composting in America is all too rare. American cities and towns, however, are increasingly re-alizing the beauty of turning food waste into a useful soil amendment that re-circulates nutrients into the growing of new foods (of which, about half will be wasted, but I digress). Some Americans are even learning about worm com-posting, and in addition, a fraction of Americans still feed scraps to hogs or other animals (such as goats). From bacon to goat's milk to soil-enhancing poop, there are inherent benefits for humankind resulting from these methods. Equally important, composting eliminates methane emissions, as food decomposes aerobically (as long as the pile is turned).

Barring a reduction in food waste or a widespread adoption of composting—reuse doesn't quite apply here—government agencies can alleviate the landfill problem. Municipalities, for example, can examine the progressive process of anaerobic digestion (AD) with an eye toward using it for energy production. That technology, now commonly used to process sewage sludge, harnesses the methane formed when bacteria consume food in a tank. Unlike landfill waste-to-energy systems, AD doesn't allow nearly half of the methane to escape, as the process occurs in an enclosed vessel. AD has been slow to catch on because of its upfront costs, but the technology, common in Europe, is beginning to make inroads domestically. In July 2009, a Bay Area utility company became the first facility in the United States to convert postconsumer food waste to energy through AD. (I'll go into more detail on this technology in Chapter 10.)

Squandered Resources

To fully understand the environmental impact of food waste, we must consider the resources that go into growing, harvesting, processing, transporting, and even cooking our food. Creating the meal on our plates is an energy-sapping, environment-impacting process. Wasting that food squanders our supply of water, depletes our soil's nutrients, and wastes the fossil fuels that are used throughout the food chain.

We grow about twice as much food as we need, but at a heavy cost—American agriculture currently uses about 10 percent of the nation's energy supply.[20] When you lump distribution with production, our food represents 17 percent of total American energy use.[21] We're inefficient in creating our food, with some items real resource hogs. It takes 8 calories of energy to grow every edible calorie of corn, for example,[22] and beef has a whopping 35-to-1 calorie ratio.[23] But no pressure to finish or take home that steak or anything.

Energy is required at all stages of the food chain. We even use energy—via our refrigerators—to keep our food from spoiling. When you add refrigeration to the energy needed to cook, the average American home invests more of its energy dollars in food than it does in anything besides heating and cooling the home itself (refrigerators use an average of 10,270 kcal of energy per person per day).[24] In 2000, University of Michigan researchers found that it took an average of 7.3 units of fossil-fuel energy to produce, process, transport, and store 1 unit of food energy.[25] Then again, that statistic becomes less surprising when you consider the inputs required at every stage of the food chain. Processing alone can be quite resource intensive. In a true sign of why it's evil, instant coffee requires the most processing energy per kilogram. The bad news for all of us is that chocolate is second (providing another reason, as if you needed one, not to waste it).[26]

Chemical fertilizers also require a great deal of energy to produce, and large-scale commercial farms now use these chemicals almost exclusively (as opposed to organic fertilizers). In fact, synthesizing nitrogen and natural gas into fertilizer accounts for 40 percent of the food system's energy use, making it the largest user of fossil fuels in the food chain.[27] In addition to the energy implications, the liberal application of fertilizer and pesticides depletes the soil and causes the nitrogen runoff responsible for that charming 7,000-square-mile Gulf of Mexico dead zone.[28] It has reached the point where the EPA is considering limiting fertilizer use. These practices are made all the more galling by the fact that humans have had a perfectly feasible soil enhancer for eons—manure. Yet, when you move from multifaceted farms to the monoculture approach, livestock are separated from the crops, and the manure is no longer so conveniently located. Manure is heavier, too, and thus more expensive to transport than chemical fertilizer.

Oil pervades agriculture's energy use. Today's crude approach to farming relies on petroleum at all levels, from making fertilizer to fueling the machines that plant, harvest, and ship our foods. About 400 gallons of oil are expended to feed one person for a year, roughly equivalent to thirty-three car refuelings.[29] Food transport represents more than 20 percent of all U.S. goods shipped.[30] The average food item travels 1,500 miles before it's eaten (or thrown away).[31] And oil shows up in unexpected places—for example, it powers irrigation systems. The USDA has estimated that making our irrigation systems just 10 percent more efficient would save 80 million gallons of diesel, not to mention countless gallons of water.[32]

Down the Drain

Ah yes, water. Let's not forget about that. American agriculture swigs water at an alarming rate. Farm uses, both animal- and crop-related, represent 90 percent of U.S. consumptive water use, a statistic that should put lawn watering guilt in perspective.[33] To reach that amount, we're diverting rivers and pumping water from aquifers faster than they can replenish themselves. In that sense, we're "mining" our water resources in a way that's anything but sustainable.[34] Waste makes it even less so.

While people living and farming in nonarid climates have long taken this resource for granted, they are coming to realize just how valuable it is. Without water, today's agricultural system wouldn't work, as one-third of the world's crops come from irrigated, not rain-fed, systems. As with energy, some of our food choices are less than efficient when it comes to water use. Taking into account the water used to grow the grains fed to cattle, it takes 15 tons of water to produce 2.2 pounds of red meat.[35] To then waste such a large proportion of our food means we're squandering all that water. And that's the main conceit of Jan Lundqvist's research.

In addition to teaching at Sweden's Linkoping University, Lundqvist is a senior scientific adviser at the Stockholm International Water Institute (SIWI). He came to my attention as a lead author of the 2008 SIWI report "Saving Water: From Field to Fork—Curbing Losses and Wastage in the Food Chain." Given its bent, it comes as no surprise that SIWI studies food waste: If you're interested in water conservation, you have to be interested in food waste. "I see them as very much intertwined," said Lundqvist, who told me that he tries to avoid food waste by not purchasing too much at once or blindly following best-by dates. "If we can reduce losses in food, we can cut the amount of water wasted. I hope that our 'luxury habit' of throwing away part of the food we buy will decrease as people learn about the environmental implications."

Soil depletion occurs almost any time you farm. You're using the soil's nutrients, enriched by centuries of decomposing plants, to grow crops. The more you deplete the soil, the more you need fertilizers, and a vicious cycle is set in motion. Soil erosion, exacerbated by row crops, is also part of the cycle. And overgrazing and clearing forests to make way for fields isn't helpful. The United

States is losing soil ten times faster than it can replenish itself. In just the past forty years, 30 percent of the world's arable land has become unfit for farming due to erosion. In short, our full-steam-ahead approach to agriculture, including increased watering and liberal fertilizer use, accelerates topsoil loss.[36]

If we're going to exhaust our soil, we may as well use the material we grow. Trimming waste would slow demand for more farmland, which would in turn reduce soil depletion and prevent erosion. More of our fields would have a chance to lay fallow. Since it takes hundreds of years to create an inch of topsoil, this wouldn't allow the soil levels to regenerate, but it would slow the rate of depletion.

And, as Tristram Stuart pointed out in *Waste*, the increased demand created by our waste launches an unhappy chain of events. Added demand for certain grains, partly for ethanol, increases commodity prices. That prompts opportunists in developing nations to create more arable land. In Brazil, that usually means cutting down rain forests. In Kenya, it meant draining and plowing the Tana River Delta, ruining the habitat of hundreds of species, including fishermen.[37]

And that demand is artificial, stimulated by a policy of maximum production with its accompanying subsidies. U.S. production is not driven by consumption. If it was, we wouldn't create twice as much food as we need. There are gluts in many commodity crops, and, increasingly, in corn. The abundance of inedible corn grown for the purpose of producing ethanol doesn't help the American poor; it has only hogged arable land, helping to spark increased food prices. And when surplus crops are shipped abroad to poorer nations, they undercut the ability of local farmers in those countries to make a living, as they can't compete on price with foods heavily subsidized by Uncle Sam.

In sum, we're wasting resources by growing too much stuff, which causes soil depletion, which in turn requires us to use more fertilizers (and fossil-fuel resources) to maintain yields. Meanwhile, we're speeding up erosion and using up our precious aquifers. There are newer seeds that don't require as much water or fertilizer, but for the most part, the cycle continues. The better we understand this scenario, the less likely we are to squander food.

Some people are trying to do something about our squandered resources. One such guy is Albany, California, restaurateur Aaron French, chef at the

Sunny Side Café. In addition to going to lengths to reduce waste in his restaurant, French also writes a column under the handle The Eco-Chef. When I met French, I asked him why he tries to avoid waste. "It's just the right thing to do," said French. "It really hurts me to see food brought all this way—with all the associated carbon effects—and then discarded. I compost, but even now it's not going directly into that food cycle, not fertilizing crops. All our problems come from not doing what we're supposed to—putting it back in the food cycle."

Yet, one suspects, most chefs aren't quite as eco-conscious. Perhaps they would be if they paid as close attention to the restaurant's stinky, rotting output as they do to their appetizing, fresh input.

Hauling (Is a) Waste

In addition to the landfill emissions—all that methane—we're creating more problems when we transport our waste from state to state. The long-distance hauling spews air pollution in the form of smog-forming compounds, particulate matter, and toxic chemicals. And a full quarter of the trash we bury or burn every year has crossed a state line.[38] Between 1995 and 2005, interstate shipments of trash more than doubled, with Pennsylvania, Michigan, and Virginia becoming key dumping grounds.[39] The Keystone State, in particular, received nearly one-fifth of the total waste shipped between states in 2005.[40] In 2008, Pennsylvania received waste from twenty-four states, including Colorado, Florida, Mississippi, and Nevada.[41] It even received 542 tons of waste from Puerto Rico.

These days, interstate waste is usually shipped by 18-wheelers averaging 4 to 7 miles per gallon. That's pretty abysmal, especially when considering that most of the 169 million tons of waste thrown out could have been recycled.[42] Plus, because food waste is about 70 percent water, this shipping is far less efficient than it could be.[43] Commercial food operations or municipalities could use simple "pulpers," machines that dewater (and lighten) waste, to reduce fuel consumption.

In processing New York City's waste alone, garbage trucks make 250,000 trips throughout the city and the same number of long hauls out of state.[44] Now consider that the average garbage truck, with its frequent stops and idling, gets about 3 miles per gallon.[45] Where I live, in Durham, North Carolina, the city collects the solid waste and ships it to a landfill outside of Lawrenceville,

Virginia, as Durham's own landfill closed in the mid-1990s. It's a 154-mile round trip.

American landfills are filling up or reaching their mandated closing dates, and fewer new ones are being constructed, mostly because it's incredibly difficult to site a new landfill (in short, because of the whole "Not in My Backyard" thing). When they are built, new landfills tend to be farther from population centers (and the waste), requiring more fuel consumption from hauling. The number of U.S. landfills dropped by 78 percent from 1988 to 2007.[46] Yet, as their numbers shrink, their average size increases.[47] America's average landfill is growing, just like our farms. So-called "mega-landfills" dot the economically depressed, Rust Belt states of Pennsylvania, Michigan, Indiana, and Ohio. Communities receive a share of the landfill's revenues, but that cash influx comes at a price. Landfills create decades of work for a few, but they bring centuries of environmental impact for all.

Tightening the Belt

Go outside and turn on your car. Don't ask questions, just do it. Now walk away. You heard me, just leave it running. Set your watch for thirty minutes. When that time is up, you can turn off your car.

While no sane person would let their car idle for a half hour, it burns through the same amount of money that we squander each day in wasted food (based on 2009 gas prices).[48]

Here's an even more evocative image: Just take $2,200 in cash and flush it down the toilet. Better yet, dump it into the garbage disposal—it'd be more fitting. That amount is how much the average family of four loses in wasted food each year.[49] That's based on a 25 percent loss rate, what Garbage Project founder William Rathje gave me as his estimate for the amount of food we throw out or put down the garbage disposal. If, however, you want to be more conservative, then use the more commonly cited 15 percent rate of waste, which would yield about $1,350.[50] In either case, imagine having that cash on hand to invest or spend. At the very least, it would buy a heck of a lot of compost bins!

That lost money, "opportunity cost" to those who survived Econ 101, is one way to view food waste through economics' steely lens. It assigns a value to our waste, and, if you're like most humans, this can encourage waste avoidance. It's money that could be in your bank account rather than the store's. Grocers, of course, aren't too concerned with this problem, because our discarded food often means we've spent more than we needed to at their store. That's not a dig at grocers—there'll be plenty of time for that in Chapter 7—and I'm not saying grocers deliberately prompt waste, just that they have a direct incentive to help you not avoid it. From that perspective, I tend to view any supermarket promotion with a bushel of skepticism.

Whether you squander $2,200 annually or not—and it's been shown that people tend to underestimate their own profligacy—food waste likely has a significant impact on your budget. Your groceries are "sunk costs." You've spent your money on that food, and now you either use it or squander its value. This inefficient use of goods represents a "market failure": There is no way to resell the items you've already bought. You can't sell off that extra pound of meat that you bought "just to be on the safe side." Food's perishability and our social norms preclude a secondary market for household foods. Craigslist has created many new markets, but this isn't one of them. Even with shelf-stable foods, I haven't heard of any peer-to-peer food selling.

Although we can't sell our unwanted food like a used car, we can each trim thousands of dollars from our household budgets by reducing our food waste. Unfortunately, that will require us to make a few changes in how we shop—and I mean more than remembering to bring those reusable grocery bags into the store. "I think that the obvious task would be to try to convince or stimulate consumers to reduce their wastage," said Lundqvist, the Swedish water expert. "It's in their own economic interest. It doesn't make much sense to pay for a lot of food, carry it home and then throw it away while it's perfectly good to eat. It doesn't make sense."

Yet we do that—not just occasionally, but over and over again. Basic economic principles do not explain our food choices. Why does food prompt such irrational behavior? Our need to eat and food's perishable nature separates it from other goods. But is it really that different?

On a macroeconomic level, our waste throughout the food chain spurs price increases. If less food were wasted, we wouldn't need to grow as much, which would lower input costs. To keep up with the anticipated waste, we've had to grow more crops, depleting the soil at a faster rate, requiring more fertilizer, pesticides, and irrigation, all of which come at a price, making food more expensive (and doing a number on the environment).

Someone has to pay for these increased costs, and, for the most part, it isn't the farmer, the processor, or the retailer. It's you and me. Consumers are subsidizing the waste throughout the food chain, as it is built into the price of goods, said Dave Swenson, an economist with Iowa State University's Leopold Center for Sustainable Agriculture. "The consumer pays for the commodity they get plus all that got lost along the way, going back to the farmer," said Swenson. "At the point at which it gets too expensive, we stop buying something."

Though few of us are aware of this relationship between waste and prices, it isn't exactly news. A 1977 General Accounting Office report to Congress spelled it out quite clearly: "Consumers ultimately bear the cost of losses in the form of higher prices. This is due to factoring anticipated loss into cost and hence, the pricing structure."[51]

The cost in dollars is not easy to tally. At the retail level, where waste occurs at tens of thousands of supermarket and restaurant locations, the losses quickly add up, but few grocers keep track of waste as a separate entity. It's just buried within the term "shrink," which also includes theft and damage. And at restaurants, waste is just part of the equation for "food cost." As long as enough entrées are sold, kitchen and storage loss can be ignored. One thing is certain, though: The majority of all this preconsumer waste ends up costing us. It's also an unnecessary drain on the economy.

Opportunity cost—that lost chance to pursue an alternative course—means potentially twice the waste. What isn't used and what could have been used are both lost. "If you're doing one thing, it comes at the expense of not doing something else," Swenson said. "What other things could we do with this land and these resources that are now going to grow corn?"

To gain further perspective, I put down my economics textbook and met face-to-face with an actual economist. Fortunately, I'm good friends with the son of a Nobel Laureate in Economics. I've known Amartya Sen, the Thomas W. Lamont University Professor at Harvard's Economics Department and 1998 Nobel Prize winner, since my college days and actually lived for a year with his son Kabir in the family's Harvard Square home. In a chat at a Cambridge restaurant, Sen noted that the resources wasted in growing and transporting today's food such great distances is a more significant problem than the food left on our plates. Later, he flashed his blend of insight and wit in discussing the irrational behavior surrounding food waste. "Buying three shirts and then throwing one away would be regarded as unorthodox behavior. But buying a sandwich and eating half and throwing the other half away is not," Sen said over his salad.

Waste Adds Up

I'd love to put a government-issued or peer-reviewed dollar figure on American food waste. Unfortunately, there hasn't been an all-inclusive look at U.S. food loss since 1997's "Estimating and Addressing America's Food Losses." Produced by the USDA's Economic Research Service (ERS), the study remains the most up-to-date federal review of food waste ever completed. And unfortunately, there isn't likely to be another one anytime soon. Brian Wansink, who headed the USDA's Center for Nutrition Policy and Promotion from 2007 to 2009, told me that studying food waste didn't exactly top the department's to-do list. "I think there are so many bigger fish to fry, I think they don't see it as a big priority now," said Wansink, who has returned to his post as director of the Cornell Food and Brand Lab.

Calculator in hand, I'm prepared to step into that void. Assessing the cost of our waste requires determining how much food we actually have. Using the ERS' food availability data for 2007, the most recent set available, I calculated that we produced 591.4 billion pounds of food (believe it or not, the ERS doesn't have this total already figured for you; you have to tally the different food categories).[52] Using the conservative 27 percent waste estimate from that 1997 USDA report, the United States chain wastes 160 billion pounds of food annually.[53] That's right, we produce almost half a billion pounds of food waste per day.

Given that amount, what's the actual cost? Former University of Arizona anthropology researcher Timothy Jones, who specializes in food waste, estimated it was "at least $100 billion" in a July 2005 article, in which he concluded that we squander around 100 billion pounds. If we go on the rough estimate of $1 per pound of food wasted, which I've heard used elsewhere as well, that would mean a loss of $160 billion dollars a year.

To put that in perspective, that's more than the GDP of Hungary, New Zealand, or Peru.[54] But does that amount really matter? Again, opportunity cost comes into play. What else could our nation put that money toward? For sure, some waste is unavoidable and it will never be eliminated. But if we dedicated our collective effort to the topic, we could certainly halve it. That $80 billion would be spread among farmers, processors, retailers, restaurants, and, mostly, consumers. And I doubt there would be many complaints from anyone about taking a portion of that pot.

Another way to view food waste is as a real waste of taxpayer money. The 1977 General Accounting Office report's title really says it all: "Food Waste: An Opportunity to Improve Resource Use." Under the heading "Plate Waste Results in Substantial Losses of Federal Funds," the GAO calculated that $267.5 million in federal funds were squandered. The study arrived at that number by applying the USDA's estimate at the time, a 15 percent loss rate, to the $1.8 billion in federal funds used to purchase food for various federal food programs, such as the National School Lunch Program (NSLP), the school breakfast program, summer feeding, commodity grants for elderly feeding, and direct distribution to institutions.

Employing that same method with the 2008 NSLP cost of $9.3 billion, we can estimate that today's plate waste from the program costs $1.4 billion.[55] That's not to say that this entire sum could be recouped, because there will always be some waste. Yet, some estimates of school lunch waste are even greater. Ethan Bergman, a professor of food science and nutrition at Central Washington University, found that elementary-school students waste more than a quarter of their food, which would put NSLP losses at more than $2 billion.

The Triple Bottom Line on Waste

LeanPath sells one product. The Portland, Oregon, company's ValuWaste System is a digital scale with an attached touch screen that wouldn't look out of place in *Star Wars*. The accompanying software helps commercial-kitchen managers recognize and reduce waste. It's intended for schools, hospitals, restaurants, and other institutions, where kitchen staff members are instructed to use the gadget to weigh and then classify the food they're throwing away. The ValuWaste software then provides data about what is being wasted and why, allowing managers to better manage their inventories and improve their bottom line.

ValuWaste provides a decent estimate on the cost of commercial-kitchen waste. Using the system and client feedback, founder and president Andrew

Shakman has found that kitchens waste between 4 and 10 percent of all food purchased. In some extreme cases they squander as much as 15 percent. It's important to note that this represents only kitchen, or preconsumer, waste, and does not include the food squandered by diners. This waste—from overproduction, spoilage, expiration, trimmings, burned items, catering leftovers, and contamination—provides a glimpse of the potential savings for large kitchens that trim their food waste.

Several examples from LeanPath clients illustrate how kitchens' ValuWaste analyses translate into dollars and cents. In a *Baltimore Business Journal* article, a spokesperson for Baltimore's Sinai Hospital said the administrators expected to save $100,000 annually by trimming 2 percent of the hospital's food budget.[56] North Memorial HealthCare in Minneapolis saved nearly $50,000 in its first year using the system, 2006.[57] That same year, the hospital halved its preconsumer waste total, and waste and expenses at the institution have continued to decrease since then.

Quite simply: When commercial kitchens waste food before it's served or even cooked, they reduce their profits. And those unused items, as well as whatever consumers discard, merge to form another cost—waste removal. This expense includes both hauling and the landfill gate charge, known as the "tipping fee" or "tip fee," and varies widely from state to state. While one would think that all restaurants would save money by sending food waste to commercial composters, keep in mind that in some states, composting is more expensive than the no-effort, knee-jerk method of throwing everything away. The hauling distances for the two options often determine which is cheaper.

The expense of collecting and disposing of food waste is a significant portion of its real cost. Trimming the total amount of waste created reduces the price of disposal. That's usually the case regardless of whether a business or institution is charged for trash removal by weight or by frequency of removal, or "pulls." Walter Thurnhofer, director of food and nutrition at the University of Washington Medical Center in Seattle, told me that the hospital saw great savings when it first began composting in the spring of 2007. Two and a half years later, the hospital's kitchen staff and restaurant customers were diverting 200 tons of food scraps and biodegradable cups and plates annually to a nearby composting operation, that charged $40 per ton. Compare that to the $135 per ton landfill disposal rate, and you find that the hospital saves almost $20,000 annually.

"It's kind of doing the right thing and saving money at the same time. So it's a win-win," said Thurnhofer, who oversees food and dining at the hospital. "It's a bit of a challenge because you have to educate people on what they can and can't compost. But once people get the hang of it, it's not too bad."

Because food waste is wet, heavy stuff, diverting it can save money. The suburban Boston grocery chain Roche Brothers trimmed 40 percent from its waste bill by diverting organics from their waste.[58] Two of its stores each saved $60,000 in 2003 through avoided disposal costs.[59] When all its factors are considered, food waste is expensive. It would be even more so if American food wasn't historically cheap. That's why, when LeanPath's Shakman pitches a new client, he discusses the environmental benefits, but focuses on the bottom line. "We lead with saving money," said Shakman. "The driver for people, the thing that gets them to actually move and make something happen, is still economic."

While money is a major character in the story of waste—both as a cause and as an effect—there's one more player—ethics. Dave Swenson, the Leopold Center economist, discussed the problem with placing economics above all. "Economics has a lot of trouble reconciling its solutions with 'the way of the ought,'" he said. "In other words, how ought we behave? An economist says we should behave rationally. But a homeless outreach coordinator would have a different response. So there's a fundamental battle there. There are truly limits to what economists can inform us about, because, ultimately, we're human beings who interact on a social basis. Economics is just one tool for interpreting human behavior. It's not *the* tool."

Discarded Morals

Anna Williams, who is eighty-nine, comes to the Seymour Center in Chapel Hill, North Carolina, most days to eat lunch, socialize, play dominoes, and, occasionally, take a class. Recently, she's been enjoying the one on jewelry making. Williams, deferentially referred to as "Miss Anna" by the staff, grew up in rural Chatham County. Like most families in the county, her people farmed. As with most farming families of the Depression era, they didn't have much. And like most African American families in the South, they learned to be self-reliant.

It comes as little surprise, then, that with eleven siblings, the concept of "food waste" was foreign to Williams. "I don't remember much about the Depression," she said. "It was sort of hard for my daddy to feed us all. There were twelve of us. We had it, whatever there was to eat. My daddy farmed. He grew beans, corn, cotton, peas, cane, and other vegetables. You had to eat quickly and get back to the field. No food was wasted, not with twelve of us."

Williams, in jeans, a red floral print blouse, and loafers, recalls learning to can food to "put it up" for the winter. All edibles had a purpose, and waste wasn't in the vocabulary. "We raised hogs and chickens, too. But there were no food scraps left to feed them."

She also raised six children of her own, and can't remember ever having much to save for later. That's why she finds it strange to be confronted with waste so often, especially at the buffet restaurants she occasionally frequents as a treat with her family. When I asked Williams how she felt when she sees food being thrown out today, she responded, "I wish I had some of that food when I was growing up."

One doesn't have to have grown up in a large African American family in the South during the Depression, though, to see a generational gap in attitudes toward food waste. Senior citizens of all income levels and backgrounds remember a time when food was regarded as something to be used completely. The leftovers were used for later meals, chicken bones were boiled to make broth, and even the string from the butcher wraps were saved for later use.

Florene Funk, enjoying a pot roast lunch (of which she didn't leave a crumb) at the same senior center as Williams, was born on Easter Sunday in 1924 and grew up in the working-class town of Mebane, North Carolina, one county over from Williams's girlhood home. Funk's father owned a grocery store and meat market with a chicken coop behind the store. "We also had a backyard cow, but lived a block and a half from town. A vegetable garden, too," said Funk, clad in a white cardigan and pants and wearing dark sunglasses, which she occasionally removed to reveal deep blue eyes. "During the Depression, every night my father would bring home food that didn't sell and mother would can it up. She'd be up late Saturday night doing that."

That experience stayed with her. She employed those values as a homemaker in Greensboro, raising two sons, and remains frugal today, living on her own in a townhouse near one of her sons. "I don't waste food as an adult. I really don't know why. I wonder if it was because I was a Depression child," said Funk, who remembers Franklin Delano Roosevelt's inauguration speech and hobos begging for food at her back door. "But we certainly didn't go without."

In pondering the topic of food waste over her slice of pecan pie, Funk vacillated between tough love and compassion. At one point, she struck a hard line: "What this country needs is a good Depression. Then people would appreciate the food and not waste it."

In the end, though, empathy seemed to triumph. "I don't think food is distributed fairly," Funk said. "It's too bad there's a lot of hunger and there is a lot of waste in the world. But that's normal—everyone feels that way, don't they?"

Later, when I asked Funk why it mattered whether we wasted food, she contemplated the question as if considering why the sky is blue. With her answer, Funk underscored how ingrained avoiding waste used to be, how squandering food was just not done. "I'm not sure why one cares about it, but you do," she said.

On Ethics

When I began this research, I knew it was wrong to waste food, I just couldn't tell you why. Or at least, I couldn't make a coherent ethical argument against it. After researching the topic for a few years, I was confident that the environmental consequences alone made it immoral to waste food. Building an ethical case against waste without mentioning methane, however, was a bit more difficult. I had a sense that there was more to it than that—that the number of Americans who don't have enough to eat made it unethical to waste food, for example— but I wasn't quite sure how to express that idea. How should the argument be framed? To better understand all the facets of waste's moral implications, I sought (and continue to seek) others' views.

With that motive, I called Paul Root Wolpe, director of the Emory Center for Ethics at Emory University in Atlanta. Wolpe grew up as a rabbi's son outside of Philadelphia. Two of his three brothers followed in their father's footsteps, prompting Wolpe to joke that he's the black sheep of the family—"I just became an ethicist."

Wolpe said that he wouldn't go so far as to classify wasting food as shameful, but that he did think it was "morally wrong." His logic sounded downright rabbinical. "The reason that it's wrong to waste food is because it leads to what the Western religious world calls 'the hardening of the heart,'" Wolpe said. "To treat food cavalierly leads to a lack of appreciation of the importance of food, of the fact that some go without it, of the suffering of animals that the carnivores among us are willing to tolerate to eat our food. It shows such a profound lack of appreciation for all that eating food represents."

I spoke with Tony Campolo, a pastor and a sociology professor at Eastern University in St. Davids, Pennsylvania. Campolo is also an author with a strong social-justice bent, and he advised Bill Clinton on spiritual matters during some of his harder times. Given that skillset, I figured Campolo's insight would pass muster. He called our squandering of food irresponsible, but not surprising. "When you talk about wasting food, you're talking about a society that wastes everything," said Campolo. "It's almost as though food is just one symptom of the overall problem."

Certainly, many of the ethical implications surrounding food waste stem from the idea that millions of Americans—and a billion people around the world—don't get enough to eat. Some even starve. Alice Waters is someone who appreciates and even reveres food. She not only started Chez Panisse, the influential Berkeley, California, eatery, she's a founding foodie of America's locavore culinary scene. She also established the Edible Schoolyard program at a local middle school to better connect kids with their food. When I asked Waters for her take on the juxtaposition of waste and hunger, she told me, "It's shameful to be wasteful around food when someone else is hungry. And I think we all know it."

When we waste food that is nourishing and possibly even tasty, I'd call that a shame. But is it shameful? That question leads us to one of the dominant associations we have with food waste—the often-maligned dinner-table commandment: "Clean your plate, there are children starving in (pick a country)." That notion is a thorny one. It invites guilt to the dinner table, which is never a good thing. It also implies a linear relationship between the two ideas, when it's anything but. The notion that you could somehow help hungry people far away with what's on your plate makes no sense. Getting that food to a developing nation is, to put it nicely, logistically challenged. Amartya Sen called it "an unrobust thought" and advised against overeating in a misguided attempt to help others.

Yet, there's something to associating unfinished food with hunger, morally speaking. The essence of "clean your plate" remains meaningful—value your food. As does the secondary message—Don't forget that some people don't get enough to eat. The problem comes when the two are linked too closely. Perhaps separating these messages is the answer; we could all stand to be reminded to respect our food and think of those less fortunate.

That's not to condone the outright wasting of food (rest assured!), but to hopefully be more thoughtful with it. Being thankful for our food, and possibly making donations of time or money to a charity, is a more useful approach than feeling guilty or mythically linking plate waste with those in need. As Campolo told me, we should be aware of the suffering of others, but also act in our own lives. "It's not a simple problem. We can't just ship our excess food over to India," Campolo said. "But I think, symbolically, being more responsible with our food should start in our own homes."

Wolpe agreed that even though our dinners may not feed those in need, our behavior still matters. "The reverence for our food—even if you have plenty of it—is important because it's a constant reminder of the preciousness of food," Wolpe said. "Maybe the result of that is that we'll write a bigger check. That Oxfam would have more money to feed the hungry. Not only is that a more effective way of handling hunger, it's also truer."

When I spoke with Ron Sider, another Eastern University professor and theologian, he went a few steps beyond merely advocating respect for our food supply. Sider is director of the Sider Center of Ministry and Public Policy, president of the center's Evangelicals for Social Action, and author of a book entitled *Rich Christians in an Age of Hunger*. Citing widespread starvation, poverty, and death around the world from preventable diseases, he came down hard on waste. "I think it's sinful. It's immoral to throw away and waste so much of the food we grow when other people are dying of starvation," Sider said.

Sin. That word brings us to an important territory for understanding the ethics of waste: religion. For Anna Williams, wasting food is wrong because it goes against her faith. She told me that the topic arises now and again at her church, Mt. Zion Baptist. "It comes up that it's a sin to throw away food. It's talked about in Sunday school and the preacher talks about it in his sermons. He tells 'em about how they should take care of food, and God created it for them, and if you read your Bible, it'll tell you about it," Williams said.

Getting Biblical with It

What, then, does that Bible say? There are many passages in the Old Testament, informing both Judaism and Christianity, that espouse an appreciation for making use of what remains after the harvest. They appear primarily as part of the discussion of gleaning, which forms part of the law of Moses that follows the giving of the Ten Commandments. Deuteronomy 24:21 (NIV) reads, "When you harvest the grapes in your vineyard, do not go over the vines again. Leave what remains for the alien, the fatherless and the widow."

In Leviticus 23:22 (NIV) the Lord issues similar, ahem, advice to farmers: "When you reap the harvest of your land, do not reap to the very edges of your field or gather the gleanings of your harvest. Leave them for the poor and the alien. I am the LORD your God."

In addition to teaching charity, these selections imply that we shouldn't squander our food, because others would love to have it.

Brother Jerry Smith, a sixty-one-year-old Franciscan monk and the executive director of the Capuchin Soup Kitchen in Detroit, agrees with that take. I asked him for the Christian view of food waste. He warmed up to the topic by talking about hunger. "The Scriptures are all about food and taking care of each other and feeding the hungry," said Smith, who has worked to alleviate hunger in both Detroit and Central America, where he was a missionary and a Peace Corps volunteer. "But it's also all about justice. In a world of scarcity, when one group wastes what could be the essence of life to another population, that's just really outrageous. There are lots of places in the Scriptures that talk about justice. That's not a huge leap to say it's wrong that one group can waste so badly, when another doesn't have what they need."

Sider believes that wasting food goes against Judeo-Christian teaching because it squanders our earthly gifts. "Christians and Jews certainly believe that this material world is a good gift from the Creator. God has given us this material world, and when we use the earth in wasteful ways, then we're not respecting the Creator. So it's important for us to respect the Creator by in fact not wasting the material world," Sider said.

More specific to Christianity, a notable New Testament passage from the Gospel of John teaches that Jesus could stretch food with the best of them. With only five small loaves and two little fish, Jesus fed more than 5,000 followers and *still* had leftovers. Most importantly, he told his supporters to save the remains. "When they had all had enough to eat, Jesus said to his disciples, 'Gather the pieces that are left over. Let nothing be wasted'" (John 6:12 [NIV]).

Sider finds further support for his argument against waste from a central tenet of Christianity—Jesus taking a human form. "I think the most profound Christian affirmation of the goodness of the material world is the incarnation," said Sider. "That God became flesh and actually took on a human body. That's an amazing affirmation of the goodness of the material world. It strengthens any kind of argument that we shouldn't waste the material world."

Sider also told me that he finds food waste wrong from both an environmental and a social-justice standpoint. "When some of us overeat and harm our bodies by being too fat and also waste food, we're doing it at a time when some are desperately hungry," said Sider, seventy. "The primary reason we should not waste is to spend less money on food we throw away so we have more money to share with poor people."

In Judaism, the prohibition against wasting or unnecessarily destroying anything of value comes from the Talmudic concept of *bal tashchit*, which translates directly to "thou shalt not destroy," but is sometimes interpreted as "thou shalt not waste."[60] This idea, which forms the basis of Jewish environmentalism, stems from Deuteronomy 20:19–20 (NIV): "When you lay siege to a city for a long time, fighting against it to capture it, do not destroy [*lo tashchit*] its trees by putting an ax to them, because you can eat their fruit. Do not cut them down. Are the trees of the field people, that you should besiege them? However, you may cut down trees that you know are not fruit trees and use them to build siege works until the city at war with you falls."

So the next time you're laying siege to a city, don't fell fruit-bearing trees, because that wouldn't be right. Invading armies in those times apparently regularly destroyed orchards, vineyards, and fields to demoralize their enemies, but God forbade it and took the time to explain that to Moses. In pondering that passage,

Talmudic scholars divined a general prohibition against waste. To them, the commandment of *bal tashchit* was serious business. To wit, the Talmudic version of the "Clean Your Plate" edict was that "Jews should be taught when very young that it is a sin to waste even small amounts of food."[61]

Avoiding waste in general is the way to respect the earth and God's creation, wrote Rabbi Samson Raphael Hirsch, a nineteenth-century German. "Regard things as God's property and use them with a sense of responsibility for wise human purposes. Destroy nothing! Waste nothing!"[62]

The word "destroy" arises frequently in discussions of *bal tashchit*, but I hadn't considered that verb in the context of food waste until reading the following excerpt from the Jewish laws related to marriage and family life: "Whoever breaks vessels or tears garments, or destroys a building, or clogs up a fountain, or destroys food violates the prohibition of bal tash'chit."[63]

Just as avoiding food destruction is one way to honor God's creations, so is pursuing thrift. Rabbi Hirsch expanded on the concept of demolition: "Destruction does not only mean making something purposely unfit for its designated use; it also means trying to obtain a certain aim by making use of more things and more valuable things when fewer and less valuable ones would suffice."[64]

While the idea of *bal tashchit* has long informed a general sense of stewardship over the earth, it became a rallying point for Jewish environmentalists in the 1970s. More recently, in response to those who would wonder if environmentalism is worth the trouble, the Jewish Nature Center wrote on its website: "We practice bal tashchit for one reason—because it is the right way to live. And what each of us must learn is that we change the world by changing ourselves. Then we let the change spread outward—to our children, our loved ones, our friends, our business partners and co-workers—and so on and so on until one day the unimaginable becomes reality."[65]

I couldn't write a more cogent argument for why you should care about food waste and why one person's actions make a difference. On the latter point, imagine what would happen if everyone did his or her best not to waste food. The sentiment, as the Jewish Nature Center pointed out, would spread. Unfortunately, the opposite also occurs: One person wasting leads to another doing the same. One individual or family influences another, and pretty soon a community becomes more profligate. Before long, this behavior influences an entire culture.

Islam's take on food waste is even clearer, if that's possible. No scholar is needed to interpret this line of the Koran: "O Children of Adam! Wear your beautiful apparel at every time and place of prayer: eat and drink: But waste not by excess, for Allah loveth not the wasters."[66]

Another passage from the Koran repeats that last line, albeit with more detail preceding it on food cultivation. "It is He Who produceth gardens, with trellises and without, and dates, and tilth with produce of all kinds, and olives and pomegranates, similar (in kind) and different (in variety): eat of their fruit in their season, but render the dues that are proper on the day that the harvest is gathered. But waste not by excess: for Allah loveth not the wasters."[67]

That passage brings up an important point, which must be stressed: Avoiding waste doesn't mean we can't enjoy the fruits of the earth. "I think it's important when we talk about wasting food not to give the impression that the answer is asceticism," Sider said. "The Christian view is that the world is good, we are called to delight in it, to dance, rejoice and celebrate in the material world. It's not that we shouldn't have a Thanksgiving feast. That's an appropriate way of celebrating the material world. But what's wrong is throwing away a third of that Thanksgiving feast. You can use that for the next week."

In the idea of karma, common to Hinduism, Buddhism, and several other Eastern religions, wasting food is a real no-no. In Hinduism, specifically, all food is to be revered because it is a manifestation of the Supreme Being. There are shunned foods, but in general, it is treated as sacred.[68] Sanskrit scripture says, "*annam parabrahma swaroopam*," or roughly, "Food is a manifestation of the Supreme Being."[69] Because food is a gift from God, it should be treated with great respect. Buddhism, at least the version of it found in Japan, informs the Okinawan cultural habit of *hara hachi bu*. The idea is that you eat until you're 80 percent full (it translates literally to "stomach 80 percent"), and avoid taking too much food.[70] In addition to preventing overconsumption, the habit suggests a healthy respect for food and an aversion to waste.

A Final Thought

The ethicist Wolpe raised his two children to eat kosher, in the Jewish tradition. Yet, he had other motives, too. "There's a religious reason to it, but more than that, it gives them a reverence for food. It changes your approach to food. You have to eat more intentionally. If you didn't keep kosher, eating can be done with much less thought," said Wolpe, who noted that keeping kosher was just one vehicle for teaching children to think about what they eat.

Wolpe also emphasized that reducing waste was important, but shouldn't be taken to the extreme. "If you have three peas left on your plate, you haven't committed some egregious moral transgression," he said. "No person can buy exactly and only what they need. There's always going to be some kind of waste."

That thought contains undeniable common sense, but also a risk, which Wolpe recognized. By that logic, we could conclude that we don't need to worry about our household food waste because it occurs on such a small scale—that we're off the hook, ethically speaking, for our waste. With so many environmental messages floating around, we already face myriad green pressures. We have to get the right lightbulbs, use eco-friendly cleaning products, trim our gas usage, use cloth shopping bags, and more. So-called green fatigue often occurs. When it does, it's tempting to ask: "Why should I bother?" While I don't believe we should feel guilty for wasting food, I do think we should strive to avoid it as much as is humanly possible. We can be mindful of all that went into growing, shipping, and preparing our food and remember that there are those who go without enough to eat. Then, we should act accordingly.

Roy and Diane Collins, who have experienced homelessness, outside their new abode in Chapel Hill, North Carolina.

PHOTO BY JONATHAN BLOOM

chapter 3

The Disgrace of Plenty: The Coexistence of Hunger and Food Waste

There is food for everyone on this planet, but not everyone eats.
—CARLO PETRINI, FOUNDER OF THE SLOW FOOD MOVEMENT

Hunger never saw bad bread.
—BENJAMIN FRANKLIN

A lbert Drapeau marched down the Champs Elysées with the First Army after helping to liberate Paris in August 1944. Three months later, once the fighting had shifted to Germany's forests, he fell captive to the enemy. The infantryman spent six months in prison camps until Germany surrendered in May 1945. During that spell, daily rations for the prisoners were one-sixth of a loaf of bread and what they called "grass soup."[1] Even before capture, Drapeau's surrounded unit was drinking rainwater and foraging for food. While a P.O.W., he dropped to 125 pounds from his prewar weight of 165.

The *Providence Journal*, the major newspaper of Drapeau's native Rhode Island, interviewed him a few years before he died in May 2007 for a series on World War II veterans. From his words, it was clear that Drapeau's P.O.W. privations had a lasting impact. He told the paper: "To this day I detest the sight of food being wasted. The sight of hungry people, particularly young children, bothers me. Whenever possible I volunteer some time to help the hungry in soup kitchens. Having been hungry for only a few months was an experience I will carry with me forever."

When I spoke with Drapeau's daughter, Kitty Holt, she said that her father had passed along those views in his own way. "When we were growing up, he would just give us a look if we didn't eat any food. He never said, 'I was a P.O.W. and didn't eat.' But, oh yeah, we knew what that look meant," said Holt, who is forty-one.

And Holt's mother held similar views and acted upon them. "My mother was the cook at our school when I was growing up. They were supposed to throw leftovers out, but she couldn't do it," Holt said. "I'm probably going to get her arrested for saying this . . . she brought it home. So we'd often have what we had for lunch for dinner."

Now that Holt has her own family, she has maintained those ways, for the most part. "My husband and I, we don't put too much on our plates. If we want more, we go back and get more. I try not to cook too much—so there isn't much left over. I think that's something [my dad] taught us," said Holt, who lives in Scituate, Massachusetts, and is director of research at Plan USA, an international child charity.

Holt said that she and her husband have a few other tricks for avoiding waste, too. They always serve their three children, who range from six to ten years old, so they don't pile on the food. The kids are always welcome to take seconds if they're still hungry, and the two oldest usually do. The family's medium-sized plates help keep the reasonable portions in perspective. Whether eating at home or, in rare cases, at a restaurant, Holt saves the leftovers and either freezes them or serves them the next day. She used to make her kids clean their plates, but doesn't anymore. "I don't want them to have any food issues," Holt said.

Hunger in America: Then and Now

We're used to hearing about a grandparent or an elderly American who was changed by hunger. The details may differ from Drapeau's tale—substitute the immigrant experience or the Great Depression for World War II, maybe—but the main idea doesn't. Yet, we tend to gloss over this suffering as we focus on happier, up-by-the-bootstraps stories. Hunger has been part of our country's experience, but not part of its narrative.

Dating back to early attempts at colonization and westward expansion, hunger has been present throughout American history. It was there in the early days of European settlement, as those in the Roanoke Colony—also called the Lost Colony—almost certainly experienced hunger, if not starvation (although their fate is unknown). Two decades later, almost 90 percent of Jamestown colonists died during "the starving time" in the winter of 1609–1610. Hunger has been a common experience for immigrants from the sixteenth century to today. And it was not unusual during the Depression, when the Great Plains became a giant Dust Bowl.

For some Americans, hunger is far from an antiquated notion; it is reality. Today, more than 49 million Americans don't get enough to eat.[2] The USDA's euphemism for hunger is "food insecurity," which the department defines as having "limited or uncertain availability of nutritionally adequate and safe foods or limited or uncertain ability to acquire acceptable foods in socially acceptable ways."[3] In 2008, 15 percent of Americans didn't have enough to eat at some point during the year.[4] Even worse, 22 percent of American children live in food-insecure homes.[5] Roughly speaking, these numbers have remained steady for the past ten years.[6] And a 2009 study found that half of American youth will live in a household that uses food stamps at some point during their childhood.[7]

In case you're confused, we're still talking about the United States—you know, the wealthiest nation in the history of the world. That's not the only incongruity at work here. Our sustenance status quo is warped: Millions of Americans go hungry while we waste a prodigious amount of food. To an outsider, or perhaps a child, it must seem strange that hunger and food waste can coexist. Frankly, it *is* strange. Just as it's odd that hunger and obesity can reside in the same home—and even the same person. Welcome to America!

Roy and Diane's Story

While many Americans are hungry today, their stories are rarely told in months other than November and December. Judging from the saga of Roy and Diane Collins, that may well be because those tales are not pleasant. Alcohol fueled the Collinses' descent into poverty and hunger. And it was a sharp fall. In 2004, only a few years removed from a comfortable existence operating a family-care home facility that they built in rural Cedar Grove, North Carolina, the couple was squatting in an abandoned house in a rough part of Durham. It had no running water or electricity, and the heart of the North Carolina summer was fast approaching. They were tired, hot, scared, dirty, and, most of all, hungry.

The couple had been booted from the city's primary homeless shelter, Urban Ministries, after Roy was accused of stealing his roommate's hat—a charge he said was as "ridiculous" as it sounds. Without a steady place to sleep, they alternated between hospital waiting rooms, church benches, and anywhere that looked safe and somewhat dry. That phase lasted four or five months, Diane said, but "it seemed like a lifetime."

At the time, Roy, who has a muscle enzyme deficiency and has had muscles removed from both of his legs, was wheelchair bound. Every day, Diane, forty-eight, pushed Roy, forty-two, through the city while they searched for food and a place to stay that night. The couple, who have been married for twenty-seven years, had noticed an abandoned house on East Main Street in their wanderings. One day, at wit's end, they snuck in and collapsed. "I had to push him in 108 to 110 degree weather on the streets of Durham 'til we run upon something that we could sneak into and just totally die for a while," Diane said.

Exhausted and scared, they only ventured out to collect Roy's medication from a downtown clinic. At a certain point, the hunger became unbearable.

Diane had noticed an older African American woman on their new street who seemed sympathetic, in part because she ran a family-care center from her home. "One day I got tired of being hungry. I walked up the street and knocked on her door," Diane told me. "I said 'Do you have any bread or *anything*? Me and my husband are starving to death.' Of course I was crying. She said 'Lord, yes.' One thing led to another and, while we were still there, we could pop in and she'd give us a little of this and a little of that. We was eating salmon out of a can, sharing it together. We was eating corn out of a can and drinking water or whatever she could give us."

The Collinses had to ration what their kindly neighbor, Evelyn, gave them because she didn't have much to spare. But it was enough. "If it hadn't have been for this woman," whose last name they never knew, "we'd have absolutely starved to death," Diane said. "That was the hardest thing I ever been through. I even hate thinking about it."

After a caring social worker helped them gain entrance into a more stable situation at the Inter-Faith Council (IFC) Shelter in neighboring Chapel Hill, the couple began to right themselves. Diane secured a job at the local K&W Cafeteria, taking advantage of the town's free buses to commute to work. They saved up enough money to get themselves out of the shelter and into a $350 a month apartment. Diane later became a cashier at a nearby Food Lion supermarket.

Yet, leaving the shelter's three daily meals was difficult, and they struggled. "Sometimes we would eat just peanut butter, peanut butter, peanut butter. That's all we had. Or she would cook a big pot of beans and we'd eat on it all week," said Roy, a former bodybuilder with a thick goatee, a camouflage Chevy hat, and a quiet way.

The Collinses collected a bag of groceries every month from the IFC Shelter, which also functions as a food bank, and a local church helped them from time to time. But there were occasions when paying the power bill had to come before buying groceries. At times, hunger brought Diane to the point where she had to panhandle, which she despised. Over three years, though, between her jobs and Roy's state disability check, the couple managed to set aside enough money to move to a nicer place.

Today, Roy and Diane are back on their feet, as they like to say. Neither of them has had a drink in five years. The couple lives in what can only be called a pastoral trailer park. One home down, their street dead-ends at a cow pasture.

Their gray, corrugated-metal, single-wide trailer has new wall-to-wall carpeting and Asian fans and flamingo figurines as decorations. When I visited, potted mums and an autumnal "Welcome" flag decorated the wooden front porch. A white 1990s Mazda Protégé, which the couple bought for $400 from one of Diane's supermarket co-workers who was returning to Mexico, sat in the driveway.

The Collinses tend to stay at home as much as possible. Diane cooks most of their meals, with meatloaf, stuffed green peppers, chicken casserole, and spaghetti appearing most often. They'll buy fish and shrimp when they're on sale. Yet, they haven't forgotten what it means to go without. Roy and Diane both said that they find it maddening to see food going to waste. He occasionally returns to the IFC Shelter to eat lunch, but he notes that a policy change there has resulted in more food going uneaten. When he stayed at the shelter, they used to allow seconds during meals, but now they scrape the food into the trash instead. "It's just a shame to see them throw that food away when people would eat it, especially when many of the guys are on medication that makes them eat a lot," Roy said. "It's beaucoups of food. It's probably about one or two pans a day. Salad, bread, meat—everything."

Diane now works at an assisted-living facility. She said she sees "unbelievable" amounts of food wasted every day at work. "It burns me up," said Diane, a self-described "talker," her short, brown ponytail bobbing with her words. "I think it should be in The Book under sins, one of the Ten Commandments. It should at least be the eleventh commandment. 'Do not waste food.' I mean point blank. It should be a sin. I don't think God ever thought we would do it so he didn't feel any need to put it in there. I think he thought we would have enough sense not to do that."

The Root of the Problem: Distribution

America has both a significant quantity of hungry citizens and wasted food. The question is, can we minimize the former by tapping the latter? The authors of a USDA study, "Estimating and Addressing America's Food Losses," thought that we could. In 1997, they wrote that we could feed 20 million Americans if we recovered a quarter of what we wasted. Yet, a more recent estimate by Kevin

Hall, a researcher at the National Institute of Health, found that a quarter of the food we squander would provide three meals per day for 43 million people.[8] What's more, it would yield enough to lift 430 million Americans, if that many existed, out of hunger.[9]

Thus, we could easily feed every hungry citizen if we rescued a portion of our waste and redistributed it. That raises two questions: Could this actually happen, and if so, what would it look like?

These questions are being answered around the United States every day by food-recovery groups, such as Sacramento's Senior Gleaners. Often these organizations redistribute our abundance through the work of volunteers like Eddie Heard. Heard, eighty-one, grew up in Mississippi, where being African American brought its challenges. In case that wasn't hard enough, he came of age during the Great Depression. Heard still remembers when cotton dropped to 3 cents a pound in 1933. He was seven. That year, he started plowing fields, and the next, he sold their homegrown greens—mustards, turnips, and some collards—on the way to school. He didn't experience hunger, but he saw it. "In my household, we grew lots of food. We were taught not to waste and to look after your neighbors by bringing them some," Heard said. "We'd give peas or beans to a family that didn't have a garden or didn't recover from the drought."

A career as a U.S. Navy mechanic brought him to California and left him comfortable financially. Yet, he still thinks of those who go without, and volunteers five or six days a week with Senior Gleaners, a group devoted to recovering food that would otherwise go to waste.

I accompanied Heard, a short man in beat-up slacks, suspenders, and Velcro sneakers, on a gleaning outing to a home just outside of Sacramento to recover grapes from a backyard arbor. After picking enough to make a year's vintage, Heard noticed a nearby fig tree in a prodigious spell. Figs littered the ground. We left with 159 pounds of grapes to be distributed to area homeless shelters and 9 pounds of figs that Heard planned to enjoy at home with his wife, after using their food dehydrator.

"When I see it going to waste, that upsets me. It's really not right," Heard told me. That's a sentiment shared by those who lived through the Depression or World War II, when food was rationed. It's also a common agrarian view, found among those who work hard to produce food. Yet, as our population has become less rural, there are fewer Americans connected to the land and, not coincidentally, fewer who think twice about scraping a plate of food into the trash.

On the other side of the country, the Hale family lives on a leafy cul-de-sac in Carrboro, North Carolina. An overturned recycling bin and a GMC Yukon XL sport utility vehicle share the driveway. The Hales have four children, ranging from ages two to sixteen. They try to eat together most nights, but Tae Kwon Do and piano lessons don't often allow them all to be there. They eat out about twice a week.

The night I visited with them, thirteen-year-old Davis rose from the dinner table and placed his half-eaten bowl of chicken ravioli on the counter near the sink. He opened the gleaming aluminum freezer door, extracted a half-gallon of Breyer's mint chocolate chip, filled a white bowl with three scoops of ice cream, and then microwaved it for about a minute—a habit he picked up from his grandfather.

Five minutes later, Davis's homemade ice-cream soup had vanished and his bowl of ravioli was in the garbage disposal. It's a regular occurrence, said his mother, Amanda Hale. "I'm not real big on forcing them to eat it all," she said. "But they can't have a bowl of ice cream if they haven't eaten a little of dinner."

A few minutes later, Amanda spooned the leftover ravioli from the pot into a clear plastic container. She wasn't sure if it would be eaten or not. Her husband, Mike, who works as a curriculum consultant at an education software company, takes leftovers about once a week for lunch. "I'm not big on leftovers," Amanda said. "I try to get him to take them to work."

Mike Hale eats out most days at work, but will bring leftovers if he's planning to use his lunch hour to exercise. Without any prompting, Mike assessed their food discard habits. "We probably waste about what most people do," he guessed.

Redistributing Our Plenty

Today, food banks and food-rescue groups recover vast amounts of food. But to fundamentally change the landscape of American hunger, we need to examine all facets of the food chain and concentrate our efforts on the areas with the potential to yield the most.

Farms usually do have a surplus, but it's often unharvested and, thus, hard to access. Food manufacturers have massive amounts of assembly-line excess, but it's not always in readily usable forms. For instance, when workers on the line at a North Carolina soup factory see a spotty potato, they knock it off the conveyor belt, but also end up knocking off everything around it, too, because of the operation's quick pace. Supermarkets are a great source for food recovery, but even their volume pales in comparison to wholesale loss. For sheer bang for the buck, excess food from wholesalers is our best bet for reducing hunger.

Harnessing this perishable wholesale surplus brings a real challenge, though—namely, how do we get that food to those in need? Distribution, or, more accurately, redistribution, is the real difficulty; indeed, it can make acquiring the excess food to begin with look simple (and it's not). That's another way of saying that some recovered foods don't reach America's hungry due to geography and perishability.

Every year, the Wilson-Batiz Borderland Food Bank in Nogales, Arizona, receives such massive amounts of produce that it has trouble unloading it all. The food bank is located near the U.S.-Mexico border crossing, where the majority of Mexican and Central American produce is imported. When truckloads of fruits and vegetables don't meet wholesalers' quality standards, many of them know to contact Wilson-Batiz executive director Yolanda Soto. As a result, the nonprofit routinely collects 30 to 35 million pounds of donated food per year.

The majority of it comes during the winter, when imports increase. While distribution of these perishables is Soto's main challenge throughout the year, it becomes acute in the colder months. She keeps a list of potential takers and sends out mass e-mails whenever she has an abundance of goods. "Unfortunately, there's more product than the organizations will take," Soto said. "In December, January and February I end up dumping about 50 percent of what we have."

In March 2007, that meant the Wilson-Batiz Food Bank had to discard 1.5 million pounds of donated tomatoes because Soto couldn't find takers before the shipment went bad. And it's not as if Soto only asks local groups. After Arizona food charities have received their fill, she e-mails a national network of food banks, essentially saying "send a truck and it's yours." They've supplied tomatoes to organizations as far away as New York and Canada. More often than not, however, distance, in the form of freight cost, is a stumbling block. That's especially true when diesel prices are high.

Ag Against Hunger, a nonprofit that recovers food from massive growers in California's Salinas Valley, has the same problem, only with domestic crops. It can only distribute so much, as the vegetable population dwarfs the human one in that part of the state. Executive Director Abby Taylor-Silva told me that receiving such large quantities of each product can make redistribution difficult. "One thing that makes it hard to get rid of big loads like that is that food banks want a variety of products," said Taylor-Silva. "They won't take more than six to eight pallets of one thing."

Brother Jerry Smith, the Franciscan monk who runs the Capuchin Soup Kitchen in Detroit, echoed the sentiment that redistribution is the major challenge in reducing hunger. "There's probably enough food in the world to provide everyone a healthy, good meal. It's the mechanics—the logistical stuff to get it to people who needed it—and the political will to make it available to everybody," he said.

Some go further than Smith, omitting the doubt from the statement. That's certainly true in the United States, where the percentage of waste—conservatively estimated at a quarter of our food—easily outpaces the 15 percent national hunger rate. But it's true globally, too. The Stockholm International Water Institute's study on food and water loss found that we produce enough food to feed the estimated 860 million hungry people worldwide.[10] The problem is that we squander so much at all levels of the food chain. "The amount of food produced on farmers' fields is much more than is necessary for a healthy, productive and active life for the global population," concluded the SIWI report. "Clearly, distribution of food is a problem—many are hungry, while at the same time many overeat. A hidden problem is that farmers have to supply food to take care of both our necessary consumption and our wasteful habits."[11]

As Smith mentioned, if we set our minds to maximizing food efficiency, we would overcome our distributional challenges. The political will to use our excess food existed in the not-so-distant past. In the 1990s, the federal government, via the USDA, showed an unprecedented desire and aptitude to put our food surplus to use. The three years from 1996 to 1998 marked the first and only time that our federal government has employed someone whose job was to encourage the recovery of America's potential food waste. As the USDA's coordinator of food recovery and gleaning, Joel Berg encouraged farmers to donate unsold crops and/or allow gleaners to recover what they hadn't already harvested.

The Federal Food-Recovery Guy

I met with Berg, now the director of the New York City Coalition Against Hunger (NYCCAH), on a rainy November morning. The downtown office sits on the fourth floor of a nondescript building squeezed between Yip's Restaurant and Candy Plus, two doors down from a Burger King. Above the door on the inside of Berg's office, a sign reads "3,647,595 lbs." Berg explained that that was one year's worth of food donations when he was the gleaning coordinator.

With his trim beard, quick eyes, and quicker sentences, Berg recounted the federal food-recovery heyday. "There were at least hundreds of federal employees working on it part-time, but I was the one person whose full-time job was focusing on food recovery—in history," said Berg. "Archimedes said, 'give me a lever big enough and I can move the world.' If you know how to use the federal government as a lever, you can get a lot done."

I'd say that the aforementioned 3.6 million pounds qualifies as "a lot." Berg was working on food-recovery projects—but not gleaning—through the USDA's section of AmeriCorps when Dan Glickman was appointed secretary of agriculture. After hearing that Glickman had a real passion for food recovery, Berg nominated himself for a new position to tackle it. "When Dan Glickman came to the department, he said I'm interested in this issue," Berg said. "And no one really worked on it. And so I, being entrepreneurial and a suckup and wanting to help the American people—not necessarily in that order—said, hey, we have an AmeriCorps program, why don't we do gleaning through the AmeriCorps program?"

Glickman bought in and created the USDA Food Recovery and Gleaning Initiative. And just like that, the Department of Agriculture became an active proponent of food recovery. They pushed growers to consider donating crops and held Food Recovery Roundtables, where Glickman brought stakeholders together and declared 1996 "The Summer of Gleaning." That summer, Ameri-Corps members organized twenty-two food-recovery projects. Later, the USDA published *A Citizen's Guide to Food Recovery* to help businesses, nonprofits, individuals, and local governments recover food. They also operated a toll-free number (1-800-GLEAN-IT) to disseminate food-recovery information.

All the while, Berg was pulling the strings. Much of his work included combating misgivings about food donation. Despite most states having liability protection for donors, it took a federal act—the Good Samaritan Food Donation Act—to soothe farm and restaurant owners' donation fears. Berg also named state gleaning coordinators and convinced USDA employees and cooperative extension agents to spread the word on food recovery. Glickman sent a memo to all the USDA department heads instructing them to make food donation happen within their agencies. Berg even helped get the department's field offices to donate food or otherwise contribute: "The USDA has thirty different agencies and my job was to figure out how every one of them could help," Berg said.

Harnessing the vast waste of the federal government apparatus became easier when President Clinton signed an executive memo directing all federal agencies to donate food or participate in recovery where they could. Emblematic of this attitude shift, the Agricultural Marketing Service, which helps market U.S. agricultural goods, began donating food samples after grading them (Grade A, etc.). Previously, they just threw them out.

Berg found that many schools were confused about what to do with their cafeteria excess, and he clarified their options. "There was a controversy where the Department of Education was telling people to throw out their food, and I came and testified and said 'No, you can donate it,'" he said. "The USDA had never ever told schools they couldn't donate their stuff, but there was sort of an urban myth that we had."

The idea of feeding the hungry with food that would otherwise be discarded seems like a universal, apolitical idea. But Berg, a Clinton appointee, found out that there is no such thing. "When I left, I gave the Bush administration this whole long memo on how they could continue this, rename it the faith-based initiative—because many of the groups I work with were fundamental Christian groups—and they totally blew it off," Berg said.

Making a dent in America's hunger will require a return to government involvement, this time with a bit more private-sector cooperation—and no small amount of public outcry to kick those two into action. While the heady days of USDA-encouraged gleaning and food recovery ended in 2001, along with tenure, they provide reason for optimism that we can reduce waste and curb hunger. I take comfort in knowing that there is a precedent for federal action on food waste. That in the recent past, our leaders recognized that we were squandering resources that could go a long way toward meeting the basic food needs of our citizens. Those needs have not decreased, nor has the amount of excess food.

Guerrilla Giving: Redistributing Food, One Plate at a Time

Where our government has failed, a few individuals have stepped in to redistribute food to the hungry—from their own plates. Several grassroots, small-scale efforts have illustrated that it's possible to simultaneously take a bite out of hunger and waste. While these individual efforts don't have a significant effect on the scope of American hunger, they're still helpful. (There are also many nonprofit food-recovery groups that do make a major impact, and we'll deal with these efforts in Chapter 9, as they deserve their own discussion.)

With individual donations, there are some limitations. Health codes prohibit us from donating food from our plates through official channels. Yet, that doesn't stop some from channeling their leftovers to those in need through novel methods I lump together as "guerrilla giving." These donations tend to be restaurant remains, not foods we save at home, mostly because when we leave a restaurant with a doggie bag, we're already "out" and our leftovers are neatly packaged. Being in an urban setting, where the hungry are more visible, helps, too. Whether or not these people, often homeless, want to eat your leftovers is another question.

These impromptu donations can be as simple as locating someone who looks hungry, or offering food in response to a beggar asking for money. Yet, there have been a few attempts to make random donations less so. In New York City, a Parsons student design group called Nohaus Solutions established a mechanism to prompt community food donations, making what was called the "FoodBox" by hand-painting a deserted newspaper dispenser to evoke a red-and-white-checked tablecloth.[12] The box, lined in tin foil, was a repository for doggie bags and other impromptu donations for a few years. It even had a mailbox flag that donors raised after dropping off food. Part art project, part social experiment, part donation strategy, the box was still sitting on 14th Street at 6th Avenue in 2010, but it had fallen into stickered-over, graffiti-covered disrepair.

Without having heard of the New York FoodBox, Craighton Berman, a Chicago designer, drew up a prototype attempting to spread the same idea of converting old newspaper boxes—the ones for free papers—into receptacles for leftovers. When he put his cartoonish rendering on the photo-sharing website Flickr, it received mostly positive feedback. While the problem of the boxes becoming dirty and unsanitary would have to be solved for the idea to be truly feasible, projects like these would fill a need. Many people see hungry or homeless people daily, and at the same time they often have leftovers they aren't going to eat but don't want to discard. The food-box idea provides a venue for merging those two sentiments.

Some neighborhoods have established other venues for plate donations. One such community solution existed in Cinnamon Cooper's old Chicago neighborhood. A bus stop outside of her Uptown apartment building housed what was known as "The Giveaway Bench." With many single-room-occupancy units and halfway homes in the area, there was no shortage of takers for the donations, edible and otherwise. Because many of these residents didn't have access to a kitchen, Cooper said, donations seldom went unclaimed for more than a few hours.

Cooper had noticed that shoes and socks were sometimes left on the bench, but she didn't know about the food component of this small giving program until observing a couple leaving their pizza box there—no small sacrifice in a city of such quality pies. Cooper began doing the same with her leftovers when she knew she wouldn't get to them, even asking the restaurant for plastic utensils to include in her doggie bag. "There isn't any food bank in the city that would take your leftover pizza or spaghetti and meatballs and give it to anyone, for health-code reasons," said Cooper, thirty-eight, who works in textbook publishing. "The bench made it easier for me to take something that I knew was useful, but I couldn't use, and give it anonymously to someone who could use it immediately."

Cooper moved to another part of the city in 2003, and as a result, no longer participates in this informal effort. But when she was in the area recently, she noticed that the bench was still serving the same purpose. Also still in existence is a slightly less geographically specific donation idea publicized by the founders of a San Francisco branding and marketing firm. In June 2007, Axel Albin and Josh Kamler took an observed Bay Area behavior—leaving leftovers atop a garbage can—and made it a verb: "replate." They publicized the idea by creating a website (Replate.org), and dubbing the whole thing an "open source food activism project in which you may already be participating."

Albin and Kamler, who run the design firm Language in Common, are the Che and Fidel of guerrilla giving. With Replate, they created a clever logo using cutlery to form the recycling triangle and put the idea online. Reactions were varied. Many objected on the ground that Replate and other "leave it and hope" ideas can be public-health threats. Vermin, winged or otherwise, might get to these donations before people do. And then there's the risk that the food will have gone bad before anyone finds it, which is why, on my blog, I proposed—with tongue firmly in cheek—trash-top, solar-powered refrigerator units. Sharing partially eaten food could also spread illnesses—it's not exactly what the county health department would recommend during flu season. And this food-leaving idea may be more about guilt avoidance than doing good. Albin said that, ideally, we would all eat our own leftovers and then contribute unopened food or money to charities.

Replated items do reach their intended recipients quickly in urban areas. Albin told me that most donations in downtown San Francisco are claimed in two to five minutes (he has done some sleuthy observing). More importantly, though, the idea and the site get people thinking and talking. "It's not really meant to be a solution for hunger or food waste, it's more meant to be a provocation. We wanted to spark conversations, and those will lead to real change," said Albin.

Yet, since there are some who won't or can't make use of their leftovers, replating is better than doing nothing. If people are going to dig through the trash for a bite to eat, we may as well make it more accessible and sanitary. Of course, I wouldn't want this idea to stand in the way of actual change, a view Albin shares. "A more real solution is restaurants serving more reasonable portions. Or some reorganization of social services so people aren't hungry," Albin said. "Boxing up your leftovers and getting it to a homeless person isn't changing anything—it's making one person's night better."

Some objections to Replate may stem from guilt, as it reminds us that we discard so much food when so many are hungry, or that when we do get a doggie bag, we may walk past hungry people and then let our leftovers rot in our refrigerators. Another criticism is that the idea condones a fear of the homeless. Then again, maybe that's just a realistic approach. "People are afraid of things they don't know. They may not know poverty or hunger," Albin said. "And we didn't want that to be a barrier to replating. If you don't want to talk to a homeless person, you can still get food to them."

Some online chatters have theorized that the anonymity of replating is actually better for the homeless than more formal meal handouts, as it allows them to keep their pride. I'm not sure how much stock to put in that sentiment, but I do know a hungry person can always turn down your offer. And since the food is going to go to waste anyway, why not replate it? Still, I'm guessing that there's a higher likelihood of leftover food being eaten when would-be donors aren't afraid of interacting with a homeless person and simply give their food to them

Egg in a Box is a donation idea that proposes that very tactic. More a donation recipe than a strategy, it encourages placing a hard-boiled egg in a box of leftover rice, then finding a hungry person to donate it to, along with a spoon and a napkin. Egg in a Box co-creator Elizabeth Berlinger, a thirty-two-year-old Ph.D. candidate in English, has considered simply leaving the food, but she prefers the hand-delivered approach. "I think human contact adds something naturally to an experience. Explaining the food opens up interesting kinds of conversation. And logic would say that there's a better chance that the food would be eaten if you hand them the food, because you know it's been received," Berlinger said. "Some might want the process to be anonymous. Then again, if someone doesn't know what's in the food, they may be less likely to eat it. Also, if they don't know how long it's been out there . . . "

The Egg in a Box practice requires a bit more time and effort than simply dropping off leftovers as you walk out of a restaurant, but not much more. You couldn't call hard-boiling an egg difficult or expensive. And finding a willing taker—while it may bring some puzzled looks—shouldn't be too hard for urban dwellers. "I would say 90 percent of the time, the response is positive. It's more unusual than your average leftovers, so we end up explaining what's inside the box. There's usually a moment of interest. It's like . . . 'Oh!' and then a thanks or a nod," Berlinger said.

Growing up on the Upper West Side, Berlinger and her sibling and Egg in a Box partner Gabrielle considered nearby Ollie's Chinese restaurant their second kitchen. Today, in their respective lives, both still order Chinese about once a week. That means a glut of leftovers, especially rice. In November 2007, it hit them. "We were sitting at the kitchen table one night about two years ago, trying to concoct dinner out of leftovers in the fridge. As usual, we had about four extra boxes of rice," said Berlinger. "On a whim, we threw a couple of eggs into a skillet with the rice and some spices and, voila!—the idea dawned on us that adding eggs to leftover rice was a quick and easy route to a tasty and nutritious meal. We had always wanted to reuse our extra rice, so we realized that giving away the box with a hard-boiled egg inside might be just the thing."

After a bit of tinkering, the duo launched a website (Egginabox.com) in January 2008 that's part blog, part simple recipe, part call to action. Through the site, the idea has expanded. Berlinger has heard that some donors "soup up" their boxes with "the standard Chinese food trio" of soy, duck, and hot mustard sauces, Indian takeout sauces, or even a deviled egg instead of a plain one. The sisters stress that the practice isn't specific to Chinese rice. As of this writing, though, they hadn't adopted my suggestion of implementing "Egg Drop Boxes" throughout the city.

A Simple Plan

Collectively, Americans have an unhealthy—some might even call it dysfunctional—relationship with food. We produce nearly twice the amount of calories we need, yet millions of Americans don't get enough to eat.[13] We waste nearly half of what we produce, and we're dangerously overweight. Our excessive waste is both an indicator and a symptom of this unhealthy relationship. There's an uneven distribution of food, and it's due in part to our affinity for abundance.

If we, as a culture, valued our food more, it would yield less unused food, reducing our excess, and, by extension, our hunger. And it would go a long way toward reforming our problematic approach to food. While making lasting changes is harder than doing nothing, what's the alternative? The status quo isn't quite cutting it. We have an embarrassing level of hunger for such a wealthy nation, an obesity crisis that threatens to drain our capital and human resources, and a habit of squandering food that is severe enough to harm our already fragile environment.

As our population grows, food will become scarcer. With the United Nations projecting that the world population will exceed 9 billion by 2050, economists, agricultural planners, and politicians are busy arguing about how we'll feed ourselves.[14] Making better use of the food we already produce has to be part of the solution. Yet, I seldom hear this mentioned in the dialogue. If we as a species—all 9 billion of us—plan to survive, we'll have to be more prudent with our food. Fortunately, there's evidence that this cultural shift has already begun.

This 1943 World War II propaganda poster linked avoiding waste with aiding the war effort.

IMAGE COURTESY OF THE NEW HAMPSHIRE
STATE LIBRARY COLLECTION

chapter 4

A Culture of Waste: Our Fall from Thrift and Our Imminent Return

For all our technological sophistication, Americans are not that different from those who inhabited most of the world's other great (and ostentatious) civilizations. Our social history fits rather neatly into the broader cycles of rise and decline that other peoples have experienced before us. Over time, grand civilizations have moved from efficient scavenging to conspicuous consumption and then back again the scavenger's efficiency.

—WILLIAM RATHJE AND CULLEN MURPHY, *RUBBISH!*

*Consumption lies at the heart of American life and economic
health, and intrinsic to consumption is garbage.*
—HEATHER ROGERS, *GONE TOMORROW*

Quitman County is one of the poorest counties in the poorest state in America—Mississippi. In 2007, 50 percent of the county's children lived below the poverty line.[1] When Martin Luther King, Jr., and his close friend and associate Ralph Abernathy were looking for a place to start the Mule Train march associated with the 1968 Poor People's Campaign, they chose Marks, Quitman's county seat. Abernathy later recalled that when he and King first visited Marks, King began to cry after watching a schoolteacher split an apple among four students to create what would be their lunch.[2]

I pulled into the elementary school parking lot in neighboring Lambert, Mississippi, on a cold February day in 2010. It wasn't hard to find the school because there isn't much else on Highway 3. Nevertheless, the red lettering on the white, wooden sign out front was conclusive: "Quitman County Elementary School: Where Hope Begins and Dreams Come True." Behind the one-story brick school, located in the heart of the Mississippi Delta, there's a dilapidated basketball court which not only lacks rims, but backboards. Only the basket supports are still standing. A graveyard borders the court. On the building's side, three pieces of brightly colored playground equipment stand out. Across the street from the school, there's a church.

I was in Lambert to experience lunch in a struggling school. As the "Say No to Drugs" clock above the kitchen entrance neared 11 A.M., the students, in their uniform of khakis and polo shirts, queued outside the door. Trays of that day's lunch were already assembled and waiting. Filing through the serving line, each child selected one of the trays, arranged with four corn-dog nuggets (six for the older students), a cookie, a serving of corn niblets, and a 4-ounce cup of peach slices. The only choice was white or chocolate milk and whether or not to buy a bag of Cheetos for 50 cents. In Quitman County, virtually all of the students get free lunch through the National School Lunch Program.

The cafeteria doubles as an auditorium and gym. A stage laden with book report posterboards and a red curtain overlooks the floor of gray plastic tables with attached pod-like seats. A painted-on panther snarls from the white and gray cinderblock walls. As a boy spilled his milk, the janitor I was chatting with lamented the color choice of the white tile floor.

I sat down with a table of seven boys and girls from one of the pre-kindergarten classes. The four- and five-year-olds were more interested in each other than their trays. Five of them peeled the batter from their corn dogs. Six of the seven didn't touch their corn. And five didn't even eat their chocolate chip cookie. The students' nibbling made more sense, though, when I learned that they had eaten their free breakfast at 9 A.M. upon arriving at school. It was only 10:40. As their ten to fifteen minutes of eating time elapsed, their teacher took their trays and dumped the contents into the gray, rolling trash can. Inside it, milk cartons mingled with corn, peaches, and breading, a medley of yellow, orange, and golden brown. And I'm still recovering from the sight of so many trashed cookies.

The lunch times were staggered, so there was a continuous flow of children entering and leaving the cafeteria. I next joined a group of first graders and their teaching assistant, Joe Ann McDonald. This group didn't do much better than the not-so-hungry pre-K class. When I asked McDonald, who is seventy-five and has been at the school for twenty-four years, about lunch waste, she didn't miss a beat: "It hurts my feelings. Good food's going to the garbage and other people are starving to death," she said. "Most of the food goes in the garbage because it's food they don't like."

One of the boys at our table asked "Miss McDonald" if he could eat his Cheetos. She said he could if he had a few more bites of corn. McDonald has been known to occasionally take food from students' trays before they dump it. She told me about her own school experience at a church in Liberty, Mississippi, where children of all ages were mixed together. "When we were young, there were no free lunches. There was no such thing as a cafeteria before I was in eighth grade," said McDonald, who raised fourteen children and also works afternoons at the post office.

As the eating and the lunch period waned, the first graders formed a line to dump their Styrofoam trays into the trash. There was more food on most of the trays than had gone into the students' bellies.

McDonald haad eight siblings and grew up in Liberty, where her grandparents had been slaves. Prior to working at the elementary school, she spent twenty-six years at Head Start. She began in 1960. "When I started working there, food was valued by the children like it was when I was a child. Now, it's different. It's really different."

School Squanderings

Ethan Bergman, a professor in the Department of Health and Human Performance at Central Washington University, studied waste at four elementary schools in poor neighborhoods in Yakima, Washington, where 90 percent of the students qualified for free lunch. He found that even at the most economical school, students still wasted a quarter of their food. At another, it was more like 40 percent. "On the days they're serving broccoli or cauliflower, you look in the garbage and it's all green or white," Bergman said.

Viewed from another perspective, school food waste—be it in Mississippi, Washington, or anywhere in between—is wonderful. It indicates that all children have access to food to eat, thanks to the National School Lunch Program. The worse news is what the government, through its paltry funding—less than $1.50 per pupil per meal—and dubious decisions, determines is fit to eat.[3] For example, the corn and peaches in the Mississippi lunch were both from cans. And then there were the corn-dog nuggets, hardly a nutritious choice. By throwing cheap, unhealthy offerings at our kids, we devalue food. It introduces them to our culture of waste, as they learn that food is something to be discarded. Even the poorest of schoolchildren in the United States—for whom hunger is familiar—learn to throw away trays of food.

The paltry time allowed for students to eat is another factor with school waste. A study conducted by Mary Jane Getlinger, a nutritionist at the University of Illinois–Chicago, with first, second, and third graders in Rockford, Illinois, noted that the lunch period was fifteen minutes.[4] A teacher I spoke with in Mississippi noted that her students had between ten and fifteen minutes. That's not a lot of time to get your lunch, eat, socialize, and clear your tray. Central Washington's Bergman compared students who had twenty-minute lunches to those with thirty minutes and found that the first group ate 10 to 15 percent less food.

The manner in which schools serve food also affects waste. Some schools still require students to take all the items, even if they don't want them. This was the model in practice at Quitman County Elementary. Most schools now employ what is called the "offer vs. serve provision" (OVS) to allow for some student choice.[5] With that strategy, students are still required to take the entrée and the milk, but they can decline one or two other items. And they are encouraged to take all five.[6] In a 1996 General Accounting Office (GAO) report, the second most common reason for waste (after attention on recess) was that the students "do not like that food."[7] The few schools in the National School Lunch Program that allow students to serve themselves have lower plate waste. Also, a few nutritionists I've spoken with wondered how often choice actually occurs.

One way to greatly reduce school food waste is to have lunch follow recess. The Rockford, Illinois, study found that waste dropped 30 percent when students ate lunch second.[8] This shouldn't come as a surprise to anyone who has attended elementary school. Finishing lunch just can't compete with bursting outside for recess. I know nothing short of dessert—and not the kind served by school districts—would have kept me inside at that age. In addition, some students may not be that hungry before noon, and pre-recess lunches mean late-morning lunches in many districts. The median first lunch period in the 1996 GAO report began at 11:00 A.M.[9]

Besides, all that running, climbing, and swinging during recess helps students work up an appetite. At the very least, they tend not to be as distracted at lunch when they've already played. The GAO report polled cafeteria managers on the reasons for plate waste. The number one answer was "Attention on recess, free time, socializing."[10] So why, then, do only 5 percent of elementary schools have lunch after recess?[11]

My hunch is that school administrators don't see avoiding food waste as important enough to warrant changing their schedule. Certainly, tradition plays a role in keeping the school day as it is. And we can't discount the sway of inertia. Yet, as Ethan Bergman noted, the primary barrier to mainstream recess-before-lunch adoption is that researchers have not linked increased food consumption (and less waste) with improved student performance in the afternoons. Still, the numbers on waste reduction speak for themselves. A culture that doesn't condone waste lengthens lunch periods, finds a way to have kids eat after 11 A.M., and/or holds recess before lunch. By continuing the status quo, we're teaching kids that it's acceptable to waste food.

Outside of the school setting, the same holds true. We're modeling waste for our kids when we scrape leftovers into the garbage disposal or decline to take food home from a restaurant. And children, quick learners that they are, absorb these lessons on food's minimal value. It's easier for today's children to waste food because they're so removed from its origins. They are less likely to value what they're served because it's not something that was planted, watered, nursed, harvested, and prepared before their eyes—or with their help. It's a disposable commodity to be tossed, just like any other item. Yet, when kids know where their food comes from or have a role in growing or cooking what they eat—either at home or at school—they're much less likely to squander it.

Food's Roots—Beyond the Supermarket

In 1995, after being quoted on the depressing use of land at a middle school in her neighborhood in Berkeley, California, Alice Waters received an offer from that school's principal: Help us change its culture. And so Waters, chef and owner of Chez Panisse, agreed to assist the school with what she knew—food. And that's how Martin Luther King, Jr., Middle School came to have a lush, one-acre garden that nourishes both its students and its curriculum, and the Edible Schoolyard program came to be.

Waters argues that the reason students often don't enjoy vegetables and other fresh foods is that they feel no connection to them. Yet, gardening and cooking reconnect kids to what they eat and, in so doing, makes them waste less. Their lunches come from items that they cultivated and prepared themselves, they're not mysterious commodities. "When children grow food and cook it, they eat it, all of it," said Waters. "And they like to be in the kitchen and at the table. It's a ritual that is in everyone's genes. It's just part of us. We've been disconnected from it, but as soon as we get back to the kitchen, we get reconnected very quickly."

This holds true for adults, too. We are much less likely to waste food we prepared ourselves, or that we know our loved one did, than we are to squander something we grabbed from the deli counter at the supermarket. As Waters put it, in universal terms: "You are less likely to waste the food that you know where it came from."

Reestablishing that connection would go a long way toward countering this statistic: The two most commonly wasted school-lunch foods in the 1996 report were cooked and raw vegetables.[12] The study found that an astounding 42 percent of cooked veggies were wasted.[13] That could be partly because canned or frozen vegetables dominate over fresh ones in schools. As a result, lunch ladies and men must contend with the dreaded mushiness factor.

Increasingly, children don't even recognize "real" or "whole" foods. They can't identify the plant, tree, or bush that produced what's on their plates. How can they, when they're so unaware of their food's origins? For the Mississippi students I sat with in Quitman County, being so far removed from the food chain is ironic, because they inhabit some of the most fertile land on the planet. Yet, what's planted isn't food, it's a source of income. Cotton fills the fields that mingle with their towns, with soybeans as the other crop. And with fewer folks having backyard vegetable gardens or livestock, most of these children don't think of food as something grown or raised. That's a far cry from Joe Ann Mc-Donald's day. She remembers gathering eggs, raising hogs, and pumping water for the mules, sometimes at the expense of going to school.

Our separation from the sources of our food is by no means specific to Mississippi, to children, or to Mississippi children. Over the past century Americans have experienced a continued physical, intellectual, and psychological distancing from farms. For many children—and plenty of adults—food does not come from the ground; it arrives magically in bright frozen packages, from a delivery man's car, or on polystyrene trays. Fewer, larger farms now produce our food. And despite our growing population, the number of farms in the United States shrunk by 70 percent from 1935 to 1997.[14] The average acreage more than tripled over that same period. Not only are we not growing our own food, we're farther away from those who are.

That distance from the production of crops and raising of livestock hinders our food knowledge. At the same time, a main driver of urbanization is that fewer Americans are farming, mostly because they've been priced out by larger operations. That shift in geography and occupations has both occurred parallel to and aided our transformation from a culture of thrift to one of waste.

In her 2007 book *Little Heathens*, Mildred Armstrong Kalish wrote about growing up on an Iowa farm during the 1930s. At one point, she described cleaning a severed hog's head to make head cheese. Using a toothbrush, she removed all the dirt from its teeth. Kalish and her siblings used baking soda to clean the grime from its ears and lips. Fortunately for them, the adults had already scraped off the hog's hair. Looking back on the chore, Kalish wondered, "Can you see a five- to ten-year-old child of today turning to such a task?"

Can you even imagine an *adult* doing it today? True, this is an extreme example of using the entire animal. And yes, it occurred on a farm during the Depression. Yet, our day-to-day food experience has changed so drastically that it is unrecognizable to the Americans who toiled on the land just a few generations ago. Cleaning a pig's decapitated head has almost nothing in common with pushing the start button on the microwave to heat a package of Pigs in a Blanket. Even less shocking tasks from "back in the day" are almost never done at home these days. For example, when was the last time you shelled walnuts or made your own bread crumbs?

A Culture of Abundance

Each week, it seems, my regular supermarket adds a new variety of store-baked bread and tempts us shoppers with samples. Last week it was something called a "filone." Before that it was a cheddar jalapeño loaf. The last time I was there, I counted thirty varieties of fresh-baked bread. The names vary, from boules to baguettes to batards. Come closing time, though, they're all called trash. The regular bread-counter woman told me that twice a week, a nonprofit collects the extras. But the other days, she logs the number of loaves and then tosses them. The amount remaining varies from day to day, which explains why this problem persists. The store doesn't sell day-old bread, and they have to make room for the next day's batch.

With such choice comes waste. Because stores refuse to run out of anything—they view it as driving customers to their competitors—they feel compelled to have the full lineup of thirty breads available from the time they open their doors until closing time. And that ensures a surplus at the end of the day.

In addition to variety, abundance dominates today's food culture. Although we are beginning to see inklings of change, this has been the case since shortly after World War II. And as with choice, abundance brings waste. When there's a wealth of goods, not everything can be chosen. Given how we stock our supermarkets, fridges, and restaurant menus, it can't be. The inevitable waste is somewhat palatable only because there's plenty more.

When we grew and raised the majority of our own food, we worked hard for our bounty. People had to till the soil, sow seeds, care for the crops through continual watering and weeding, and finally harvest the fruit of their labor. Today, there's an abundance to be had with minimal effort. It's all just a swipe of a card away at the supermarket or superstore. We can enjoy our plenty even if we can't actually afford it—simply by going into credit-card debt.

American excess fully arrived when chemical fertilizers and pesticides became commonplace after World War II. As use of these fertility boosters picked up in the 1950s, so did farm yields. And the average annual commercial fertilizer use for 1960–1969 was more than triple that used in 1930–1939.[15] Earl Butz, U.S. secretary of agriculture from 1971 to 1976, steered the nation toward maximum production. Encouraging farmers to increase yield and sell the surplus overseas prompted the harmful culture surrounding food that persists today. The increased supply reduced prices, and increasingly, cheap food prompted the attitude that we didn't have to worry about waste. All of this contributed to a devaluing of food. Making matters worse, we began exporting our subsidized goods, destabilizing foreign markets by undercutting their prices.

Once mass production of food became a reality, these attitudes slowly trickled into our supermarkets and our subconscience. With that excess at every turn, America transitioned from a grow-your-own, ration-adhering nation to a culture of excess. Food countercultures have come and gone, but they've just been garnishes to the main course of choice and abundance at any cost. After years of rationing and deprivation from both the war and the Depression, postwar Americans simply consumed, not bothering to think twice about the results.

The 1980s catering scene, as described by Robert Egger, the founder of the food-recovery group D.C. Central Kitchen, epitomized that scenario. "In the 1980s, if you wanted to make money you went into catering," Egger said. "Once food leaves the catering shop, it's not supposed to come back. It's already paid for and the fridges are full with tomorrow's food. Back then there were no federal limitations on lobbying. There was a wealth of other people's money. No one cared about excess, it was just 'Bring us as much roast beef and shrimp as you can.'"

Egger, who was working in food service at the time, had a front-row seat for this long-running show of waste. When he resolved to put the extra food to a better use, he realized just how massive the amounts were. "People would call me at 1 A.M.—I had a pager—they'd say, 'Dude, we've got 15 legs of lamb, 3 suckling pigs, 14 pans of strawberries,' and I'd say, 'Dude I'm on my way,'" said Egger. "One night I got six steamship rounds of beef. That's 150 pounds of beef. They're the big carving hunk you see at events. Each one could do a stew for 150."

While this 1980s Gordon Gekko "greed is good" era has long passed, the culinary excess has remained. The catering business, specifically, and the food industry in general may not be as extravagant now as it was then, but the sheer prevalence of food is still extreme. And food or "food-like products" are sold just about everywhere these days—at gas stations, pharmacies, even Home Depot and Bed, Bath and Beyond.[16] When some people I know drink too much, they use the euphemism that they were "overserved." While they're obviously being facetious, the average American restaurant patron could use that term in all seriousness.

Lost Foodways

Our separation from the production of food has helped erode our food knowledge, and, accordingly, our kitchen confidence. We throw out foods when we're not sure if they're good. We're perplexed by "use-by" and "sell-by" dates and often make no distinction between the two. We're not sure how long to cook items. Preserving and canning may be enjoying a resurgence, but the people now doing it have to take a class or read about it online. It's just not common knowledge the way it used to be, by necessity.

Often, we opt not to keep leftovers, and when we do save them, they ultimately end up in the trash later. We may not want to eat them, we may lack the knowhow to create new meals with leftovers, or we may not know how long they stay good. In a 2009 survey on restaurant leftovers, 34 percent of diners said what they wanted most in their doggie-bag packaging was an indicator for "when the food is no longer safe to consume."[17] And 43 percent of respondents sought instructions explaining how best to reheat the items. While such tips in doggie bags would help solve part of the food-waste problem, shouldn't it be self-evident when the food is no longer good and how it should be reheated?

We're now more obsessed with food than ever, and yet the popularity of cookbooks and "how-to" TV shows is partly a result of this lost food knowledge. Despite the massive technological advantage of refrigeration, we squander more food than our ancestors. If their ghosts could talk, they'd call us wasteful.

Our food choices are now seemingly limitless, both in eating out and cooking at home. Accordingly, the question "What's for dinner?" is unprecedentedly interesting and daunting, as Michael Pollan noted in *The Omnivore's Dilemma*. Our food culture sure has changed. Anna Williams, the elderly woman from rural North Carolina we met in Chapter 2, did not eat out while growing up. Ever. "The first time I ate at a restaurant I was grown and married. I know I was!" Williams said.

Certainly, American cuisine has improved, and the expanded range of ingredients and cuisines available has enhanced the national palate. Yet, our fundamental food skills have diminished. While more Americans know how to make crème brulée now—and own the silly blowtorch to finish it—fewer would be able tell you how to separate cream from milk. And far fewer would have ever done so. Similarly, how many of us have defeathered a chicken? My hand isn't raised; I have plucked not a feather.

Despite our increased attention to cooking and consuming, our food culture is out of sync. Many of us, often subconsciously, practice a form of conspicuous consumption with our food. Only it's not about how much we can consume, but how much is prepared. At gatherings, parties, and other events, we communicate prosperity or show hospitality by cooking copious amounts of food. The worst sin a caterer can commit is to have too little food. "Caterers never run out. They can't. That's why they plan 10 to 15 percent over, because they'll never work again if they run out. Empty tables are death for a caterer," said Aaron French, the Sunny Side Café's chef.

I've heard estimates on the amount of intentional catering excess that range from 5 to 30 percent. And a similar phenomenon often occurs in our homes, especially when we have visitors. I once planned the menu for some dinner guests so precisely that everyone was satisfied but nothing remained in the serving bowls. Yet, it felt as if my wife and I had been rude. Across cultures, there's interplay between serving too much and not finishing your plate—all in the name of custom and politeness. Somewhere in my cultural training, I learned that if there are no extras, you're a poor host (sometimes literally and figuratively). And I don't think I'm alone in holding that value. While having some extra food has always been nice, the definition of hospitality has seemingly been rewritten to include having far too much.

Bigger Is Better

I was manning the register at McDonald's when an older gent walked in and greeted me crisply. His neat outfit matched his tone. "Do you have any burgers that are regular-sized?" He specifically asked for one smaller than the Quarter-pounder patties, and he was in luck, because this McDonald's did still serve the original "Cheeseburger" and "Hamburger." Not that you'd know it, because they're not among the—count 'em—fourteen items pictured on the menu board. In fact, neither is even listed on the menu. What was featured prominently, in the oft-perused Dollar Menu, was the McDouble (a double cheeseburger with only one slice of cheese). Why pay $1.09 for a single-pattied sandwich when you can get twice the meat for $1.00?

In the short time I worked at the restaurant to gain insight for this book, I was surprised by how McDonald's steers us to consume more. Sure, there's the much-publicized option to Super-Size, I mean, "go large," with your value meal. But a recent promotion at the restaurant put all sizes of drinks at $1. If that's not leading consumers to the largest option, I'm not sure what is. In response to its competitors flaunting their sandwiches' heft, McDonald's recently added burgers that are one-third of a pound, besting their own Quarter Pounder. The elderly man whose order I took was among a select few I encountered who wanted a plain old cheeseburger. I can count on two hands the number of orders for Cheeseburgers I heard while working at The Arches. And it felt like every other person ordered a McDouble.

At many full-service restaurants, increased portions often go uneaten. Not so in fast-food land. One of my duties at McDonald's was to compress the garbage with a metal tool, and I rarely saw any uneaten food in the trash. (Trust me, I looked.) And the food on offer at most fast-food establishments is so harmful for people's health that I *almost* wish they would have left some uneaten. Then again—especially given the carbon footprint of beef—if you're going to order fast-food sandwiches, you may as well enjoy it. Yet, what these bigger burgers have done is redefine what's normal when eating out.

Super-sized meals are no longer specific to fast food. In recent years, seemingly everything in the food industry, from portions to plates, has swelled except for our common sense. In their 2002 paper examining the link between expanding portion sizes and our obesity epidemic, Lisa Young and Marion Nestle found that identical dessert and cookie recipes in the 1964 and 1997 editions of the *Joy of Cooking* specified fewer servings in the 1997 edition, meaning that portions were expected to be larger.[18] Portions even increased again in the period between the 1997 and 2006 versions of the book, illustrating our continually changing consumption norms. A waffle recipe that yielded twelve servings in 1997 made six in 2006, but the amounts of the ingredients didn't increase. The serving size literally doubled because the authors were expecting us to serve larger portions. It's probably a decent guess.

Young and Nestle found that portion sizes began to rise in the 1970s, but "increased sharply" in the '80s and continued to climb in the '90s. They pointed to a more competitive market for restaurants and food producers that led to using larger offerings as a selling point. "Our data indicate that the sizes of current marketplace foods almost universally exceed the sizes of those offered in the past," Young and Nestle wrote.

In that same paper, Young and Nestle also compared the average size of other kinds of foods from 1982 to 2002. The results were not pretty. The average bagel used to be 3 inches in diameter, but that has doubled to 6 inches.[19] The standard muffin size has almost tripled, while a portion of popcorn actually has tripled.[20] In the past ten years, we've seen regular soda containers jump from 12 to 20 ounces. And the average cookie—somewhat cartoonishly—has ballooned to 700 percent of its 1982 size. At least Cookie Monster is happy.

These large portions often induce waste. Just as often, they prompt overeating. Saving some for later is a better option, but it's not always desired or possible. In those situations, we're put in a position where we either have to waste food or eat too much. "When there was a small amount of food on your plate, you ate it all," said Chez Panisse's Alice Waters. "I'm so opposed to having portions put on my plate that are way too big and feeling like I have to eat it all."

Americans have recalibrated their assumptions about portion sizes. How much is enough? When does eating turn into overeating? We have different answers to these questions now than we did just ten or twenty years ago. And we have different responses to most of our other food-related questions as well. How many items and how much of each should be available at the supermarket? How big should that store be? The new answers to most of these questions encourage food waste.

One change that prompts both overeating and waste is the prevalence of giant warehouse retailers such as Costco and Sam's Club. These discount clubs can be anything but. Through the bulk packages of many food items, they're selling us waste. Want some dinner rolls for tonight's meal? How about a 36-pack? If you're in the mood for pork chops, hopefully you're hungry. Costco only sells packages of nine. Spinach is only offered in a 40-ounce bag the size of my pillow. It's either 4 pounds of strawberries or nothing. There are no half-gallons of milk, unless you want to buy a pack of three, which kind of defeats the purpose of buying that size. And if cottage cheese or sour cream is on your list, you'll have to work hard to finish either 3-pound tub.

At these stores, it's one size fits all—extra large. On a research visit (I don't shop there), I didn't see a shrink-wrapped package of seafood or meat less than 2 pounds.[21] The store surely helps larger families and shrewd homemakers who repackage and freeze some items or only buy nonperishables. But that doesn't work for many foods sold in bulk.

Whether it's at a restaurant, grocery store, or catered event, one principle dominates the food industry. As chef Aaron French put it: "You want more for your money, that's the American way. Few people want less for more."

Area and Volume

To contain this abundance, we tend to purchase massive plates and bowls. In fact, the surface area of the average dinner plate expanded by 36 percent between 1960 and 2007.[22] A possibly apocryphal story is telling nonetheless: At an antique fair, a young couple asked a dealer if he had any more of those beautiful dinner plates they'd found. There was just one problem—they were serving plates. This shift encourages waste, as Brian Wansink, bestselling author, food psychologist, and director of the Cornell Food and Brand Lab, told me that Americans use the plate as a visual cue for how much to eat.

Most of us eat based on external signals, such as how much food remains in our bowl, rather than internal ones, such as whether we feel full. We tend to leave behind the same proportion of food—an average of 8 percent of what we serve ourselves, and more when we're served by others, according to Wansink— regardless of plate size. Some of us determine how much to consume based on cultural rules. For instance, I've heard some people say that it's uncouth to clean your plate. But for others, the opposite is true: If you don't eat everything, you are somehow being ungrateful or taking food away from people who are starving. For whatever reason, "We eat the volume we want, not the calories we want," Wansink wrote in his book *Mindless Eating*.

Wansink proved this theory in a deliciously devious study: He served college students Campbell's Soup in bowls refilled through a surreptitious tube under the table. Because the majority of us eat to a visual indication—until we've finished the bowl, or we're half-way done, for example—and that indication was never reached, those with the refilling bowls ate 73 percent more soup than those with standard bowls.[23]

When the plates are large, as they often are these days, that means both more overeating and more food waste (when we don't save the leftovers). Leaving behind a set proportion on a large plate yields more waste than doing the same with a smaller serving. Wansink and his Cornell cronies launched a Web campaign in 2008 to combat overeating and waste. The Small Plate Movement urges us to downsize to a 10-incher for at least a month. The site tells us that switching from a 12-inch to a 10-inch plate will mean eating 22 percent fewer calories.[24] It would also reduce the amount we waste.

Time Is Money

I visited a 7-Eleven store in Boston recently to peruse the offerings. For those in the mood for turkey on the go, there were eight choices, from sandwiches to subs to wraps, with different options within each category. There was smoked turkey or regular, and jack, cheddar, Swiss, or American cheese. All told, there were twenty-one sandwich choices, most of which were ticking toward their 11:59 P.M. expiration, as their "enjoy by" label specified. There were packages of crudités with ranch or hummus dip and three kinds of salads. For those feeling fruity, there were apple slices with peanut butter, mixed fruit, and summer fruit salad, although the difference between those last two was unclear. I visited during the daytime, with the majority of pre-made items set to be thrown out that night if they didn't sell.

With all these prepared-food choices comes waste. Items without preservatives, while healthier, have shorter shelf lives and fall victim to the "best by" shelf culling. Then again, items occasionally slip through the cracks. At the 7-Eleven in the Jamaica Plain section of Boston, two packages of chicken macaroni salad with an expiration date of two days before, and two from one day before, remained on the shelf. I also noticed that the newer Italian cold-cut subs were in front of the older ones, a poor arrangement, as any supermarket employee could tell you. This was all before I got kicked out for suspiciously jotting down these details.

In the past five years, convenience stores have begun to expand their fresh food offerings to compensate for slumping profits. They are transitioning from being gas stations with packaged snacks to being food and drink purveyors that sell gas. Food is prepared on-site at 80 percent of all convenience stores, said Jeff Lenard, director of communications at the National Association of Convenience Stores. In addition to rotating hot dogs, convenience stores now serve items such as taquitos, fresh fruit, store-made subs, breakfast sandwiches, and, yes, sushi. The increased perishable offerings mean that more food is wasted, especially when raw fish is involved. "We're seeing more stores in the West Coast offer sushi. Sushi obviously is either good or not good," Lenard said.

We expect convenience stores to have fresh food available all day. And when an establishment promises to have fresh food and drink ready at any hour, it will throw out a fair amount of product. That expectation, coupled with the increase in prepared foods, leads to a staggering amount of waste. Timothy Jones, the former University of Arizona anthropology researcher who has studied loss throughout the food chain, found that convenience stores waste 26 percent of their product, by far the highest percentage of the sector. Nationwide, that means more than 5 million pounds of food every day.

Lenard likens that number to that of a start-up restaurant planning for a full house while they're still trying to figure out demand. Still, whether convenience stores are testing out their formats or not, their waste is a decision. They accept waste in exchange for growing sales. "Anybody would like to minimize food waste," said Lenard. "But to sell more stuff—like more fresh fruit—you end up increasing waste. That's the way it works."

The added convenience-store offerings are just one of the many signs of a dramatic shift in our collective food consciousness. We're all extremely busy or at least feel that way. In two-working-parent families, and single-parent ones, too, there's not much time for preparing homemade, healthy meals. If we're not picking the kids up from day care or tap dance class, we're making one last business call. Sometimes both occur simultaneously.

In this social climate, convenience takes on more importance. In some families, time trumps cost. In others, speed is more important than the quality of the food. Technomic, a food-industry research and consulting firm, conducted a survey in October 2009 asking consumers what they found most appealing about leftovers. The leading reason—that leftovers represented "one less meal to prepare"—topped "good value" and enjoying "restaurant-quality food at home."[25]

Breakfasts now come in bar form, wrapped in plastic for on-the-go eating. Packed lunches are often the same. Lunchables had become a $750 million cash cow by 2005.[26] For those who do plan to assemble their own sandwiches and want to mix turkey and ham, Oscar Meyer is happy to sell us—at a premium compared to separate packages of turkey and ham—a package with alternating slices of each. And as I write this, I'm eating an individually wrapped granola bar that I purchased because it's so easy to grab one on the way out the door.

We've been welcoming shortcuts into our kitchens for decades, whether it was Campbell's Soups or boxes of Jell-O Pudding, which became available at the turn of the twentieth century. Yet, now, the sheer volume of so-called convenience items at the grocery store is astounding. The prepared-food sections at most supermarkets are, well, super. No matter the section, though, it's hard to think of a food item that you can't buy pre-made at the grocery store today, from hardboiled eggs to shredded chicken and crisped bacon to pork barbecue. There are even individually wrapped baking potatoes for those without the time to break out the tin foil.

This shift in values prompts waste because it devalues food. We cherish efficiency over the food itself. And the sheer volume of these items illustrates how thoroughly we've moved toward convenience. In some cases the trend directly causes waste, as with the convenience-store sandwiches that go unpurchased or the container of sliced peppers that rapidly fades.

Of all these ready-to-eat offerings, though, my least favorite is the pre-assembled peanut-butter-and-jelly sandwich. Ignoring the fact that these are ridiculous and possibly a sign of the apocalypse, they epitomize our obsession with expediency. Smuckers, the jelly people, make a version called Uncrustables, essentially a PB&J with the crusts cut off, that you keep in the freezer. Their marketing materials really nail the zeitgeist: "Work. School. Piano lessons. Soccer games. At Smucker's, we know how busy your life has become . . . so we created a few more ways to help make your life simple again. Now you can enjoy the great taste of *Smucker's* anytime, anywhere!" PB&J Jamz is another, slightly funkier maker of frozen sandwiches. Apparently, the jar of swirled peanut butter and jelly wasn't enough of a time-saver.

Forming a Culture of Thrift

When I tell people that I write about food waste, most relay an incident related to the topic. It might be something they've witnessed, something they heard about, or even something they've done themselves. Some express contrition for their wasteful ways, as if I'm a priest behind a screen. Others are quick to explain why it doesn't matter. Regardless of their take, everyone has a strong reaction.

I have a few theories on why that's so. For starters, discarding an item without using it for its intended purpose feels odd. Food isn't just any item. When we hunted and foraged for sustenance, food was tenuous, and even after humans began farming 12,000 years ago, weather, pests, and poor storage meant that starvation was a real possibility. Today, it's not much of a threat for most of us, but I'd argue that we retain a bit of that instinctual sense that food isn't a given.

In America, frugality is embedded in our history, and thus, our character. In some respects, it is a latent aspect of our culture, but it's still there. The first Americans have a rich tradition of thrift dating back to Pre-Columbian times. American Indians were resourceful with their crops and game, using all parts of the animals they hunted (and were appalled by the white man's skin-only approach). The first European colonists were parsimonious by necessity. Crossing the ocean to a mysterious land with just the supplies their ships could hold must have been daunting. And once they arrived, they had to stretch their goods as long as possible to survive brutal winters, farming failures, great illness, and a time before Walmart.

Jamestown was the first European settlement to survive, but four out of five people there died from starvation from 1609 to 1610.[27] In some cases, entire colonies didn't make it. Before Jamestown, eighteen European attempts at North American settlements, including the famed Roanoke, failed.[28] And others wouldn't have lasted without help from their American Indian neighbors. In these seminal times in the forging of what would later be an American people and culture, food's availability was questionable.

The Written Record: Cookbooks

The Frugal Colonial Housewife, a 1772 work by Susannah Carter, illustrated Americans' resourcefulness and, yes, frugality. Judging from Carter's recipes, American colonists ate all parts of their animals. We're talking everything. There's a recipe for making jelly from a buck's horns (Hart's Horn Jelly) and four ways to prepare calf's head: boiled, fricasseed, as a hash, and in a pie. In addition to fricassee of tripe, Carter discussed Umble Pie, which includes the heart, liver, and entrails of a deer. It's not hard to imagine how the term "humble pie" evolved from this treat. Umble Pie, like Kalish's pig cleaning, shows just how little we use of the animals we eat today. That said, I'm grateful that boiled cod's head, another recipe in the book, is no longer common in my native Massachusetts.

Lydia Maria Francis Child's the *Frugal American Housewife*, first published in 1828, provides a glimpse at the thrift to which homemakers aspired in that era. The book went through twelve editions and was "an extremely popular manual for homemakers," according to the book's page on Amazon.com, an admittedly biased source. The book offered down-to-earth advice for improving home economy, like this passage on pig buckets and grease saving: "Look frequently to the pails, to see that nothing is thrown to the pigs which should have been in the grease-pot. Look to the grease-pot, and see that nothing is there which might have served to nourish your own family, or a poorer one."

Child illuminated the hardships of keeping food from spoiling in a time before refrigerators. "If you live in the city where it is always easy to procure provisions, be careful and not buy too much for your daily wants, while the weather is warm," Child wrote. She also recommended some tricks for making the most of leftovers: "Have all the good bits of vegetables and meat collected after dinner, and minced before they are set away; that they may be in readiness to make a little savoury mince for supper or breakfast."

Child essentially espoused a zero-waste approach back when that concept was a way of life. It was just common sense, not a way to be more environmentally friendly. Yet, slap on a new cover and include an eco-conscious introduction, and the book could be a modern one. In fact, small publishers issued three new paperback versions in 2009—its copyright has expired—and there are four versions available as e-books.

The Nineteenth and Twentieth Centuries

Like the colonists, westward settlers had to be frugal because they weren't sure how long their journey would last. Pioneer wagon trains, essentially really long road trips, required wise use of rations. As anyone who's played the old computer game *Oregon Trail* knows all too well, squandering food brought disastrous results. Furthermore, the continual arrival of immigrants in America has meant a steady influx of thrift. Most newcomers have arrived on these shores short on funds, necessitating a shrewd use of their food supply. And immigrant frugality continues to this day, with only the languages and cultural specifics shifting.

The mobilization leading up to U.S. involvement in World War I brought the first widespread push to influence how Americans treated their food. Mostly, this came in the form of propaganda posters encouraging culinary thrift.[29] A 1917 U.S. Food Administration poster was notable for its starkness: "Food—Don't Waste It," the poster warned. It provided surprisingly current rationales for this reprimand as well: "Buy it with thought, cook it with care, use less wheat & meat, buy local foods, serve just enough and use what is left."[30] My favorite poster, produced by the administration in 1918, features a basket of produce above the silhouettes of American troops on horseback: "Food is Ammunition— Don't waste it."

Another one, "Food Will Win the War," depicted immigrants approaching the Statue of Liberty by ship. It called for "those who came here seeking freedom" to "help preserve it" by not eating wheat. "Wheat is needed for the Allies," the poster proclaimed. Yet, it's the last line that I find most poignant: "Waste Nothing." And it doesn't seem like a suggestion. Finally, if guilt is your thing, you'll appreciate the directness of the one that read: "Don't Waste Food While Others Starve."[31]

Sandwiched between two world wars, the economic hardships of the Great Depression solidified America's culture of thrift and exhibited our culinary ingenuity. Boiled milkweed pods? Cooking with cattails? Potato candy? Sure enough. And then there were the soups: coffee, pretzel, sour grass, and that famous Depression soup—1/3 cup ketchup and 2/3 cup boiling water.[32] Pat Box, now eighty-nine, told the *Los Angeles Times* that she remembered scraping bakers' barrels for residue of sugar or cocoa as a child.[33]

Food was just not wasted in the 1930s. Not when nearly everyone was struggling just to survive. The 1996 book *Dining During the Depression*, edited by Karen Thibodeau, illustrates this mindset through recipes submitted by folks who lived through the period. What the recipes may lack in enticing names—Corn Bread– Tomato Goop, Depression-Style Mush—they make up for in creativity. Fried locust blooms had nothing to do with the insects; rather, the recipe makes use of the honey locust tree. Three other entrées—Poor Man's Steak, P'or Soles, and Hobo Stew—fit the spirit and budget of the times. The same can be said for making syrup by boiling corn cobs.

World War II rationing appealed to and expanded this ever-present sense of frugality. Each member of the family, including babies and children, received a ration book with stamps.[34] Meats, canned fish, cheeses, canned milk, and canned produce were rationed from March 1943 to November 1945.[35] Most Americans learned to make do with less. Then again, some turned to the black market, where meat and sugar were the most commonly traded items.[36] But people were much less likely to squander beef when they were only allowed to buy a finite amount of it or when they knew that acquiring it illicitly was their only other option.

American war propaganda portrayed waste as unpatriotic and even beneficial to our enemies. In 1943, the Office of War Information (OWI) produced a series of posters to hammer home that point.[37] The most common one read much like its World War I predecessor, saying, "Food is a Weapon—Don't Waste it!" It included another line that was music to my ears: "Buy Wisely—Cook Carefully—Eat it All." The OWI told citizens how to stretch their rations with its "Plant a Victory Garden" posters and how to avoid waste through its "Can All You Can" message. Rumor has it that the "Can It" slogan was a close second choice, while in reality, a World War I poster from the National War Garden Commission did advise citizens to "Can vegetables, fruit and The Kaiser, too."[38]

These posters aimed to make Americans feel that their scrimping could help the war effort. And even after the war ended, one reason to be food savvy persisted—hunger. A 1946 Department of Agriculture poster carried this message: "Am I Proud! I'm fighting famine . . . by canning food at home."[39] From that message and the 1918 poster "Don't Waste Food While Others Starve!" it's a short leap to "Clean your plate, there are starving children in China."

In postwar America, Baby Boomers had a divided experience. Parents who had known or at least witnessed hunger in the 1930s and 40s, or had lived through rationing, could react in one of two ways. They could make their children clean their plates, reminding them that there were less fortunate people in this world, or they could celebrate the war's end and relish American abundance by allowing their kids to eat only what they wanted. The latter won.

Ultimately, all of the enforced frugality spurred a movement away from thrift. After two world wars and the Great Depression, it must have been a relief to buy and consume food without thinking of propaganda. No longer was it patriotic to plan and eat sensible-sized meals. Nor was it economically necessary to do so, as food prices came to represent a lower share of personal income. After an initial postwar increase, food became less expensive every year. By 1957, it was 22 percent cheaper than it had been in 1947. And food costs in 1967 were 40 percent less than they had been in 1947. It's not that food prices dropped, necessarily, but that incomes rose while prices stayed relatively stable. And food's percentage of disposable income represents an indication of its true cost.

In those formative moments for the American character, however, necessity had required frugality. And these humble beginnings have had a lasting effect. I know, I know: How enduring can these values really be if we've strayed from them? My point is that they're still with us, as most of us feel a nagging guilt when we throw away that freezer-burned chicken or out-of-date beef. I'm sure we can all imagine one of our older relatives shaking their heads at such impracticality.

Despite the dominant culture of waste, there are plenty of Americans upholding our rich tradition of thrift (and chances are good that many readers of this book fit that category). What's even more encouraging is that in some circles, we are just beginning to see American thrift return to a more mainstream station. It's an organic reaction to the economic woes of the late 2000s and the mounting environmental threats and against the excess and waste common to much of the second half of the twentieth century.

Different Generations

Treva Mitchell lives in Indianapolis, but grew up in the 1960s on a farm in north central Indiana. It was Benton County, to be precise, where "if you stand on a tuna can, you can see for miles," as Mitchell tells it. Her nearest neighbor was a good bike ride away, but she remembers pedaling the whole distance "just to get spit on" by the boy in that family, partly because he was "the only other person not older than dirt around," and partly because she liked him.

I spoke with Mitchell by phone after exchanging e-mails. She felt like an old friend after a few minutes. Mitchell, née Treva Schluttenhofer, was the youngest of five kids living on a 550-acre grain farm. Her father, Cyril Schluttenhofer, grew corn, wheat, and soybeans, and he grumbled about the price of all three. The family was largely self-sufficient, with livestock, fruit trees, and a vegetable garden where they grew "just about everything." The family raised Angus cattle, sheep, goats, and chickens for their own consumption. "I remember my mom would whirl the chicken around her head like a lasso about three times, then put her foot on the body and wrench its neck up. And that was dinner," said Mitchell.

As was common then in that part of Indiana, Mitchell learned to drive when she was nine, and by age twelve she'd had her first wreck. By that point, she already knew how to process beef cows. The family slaughtered, cleaned, and butchered its beef, and the children played a vital role. "We did it all—from the 'bleed out' to writing the name of the cut on the package before we put it in the freezer. That was my job, since I was the youngest," said Mitchell.

In earlier days, the family had kept goats for their milk. That habit faded before Mitchell's time, and her mother stopped raising chickens when she was nine. Mitchell recalls going into town to buy milk, chicken, and, as she got older, things like Fruit Loops. Still, they ate a somewhat limited cuisine. "I had spaghetti for first time when I was seventeen or something crazy like that. It was not a product they carried at the IGA in Fowler," said Mitchell.

Mitchell's parents were married in 1933 and saved for about fifteen years before they could buy the land that became their farm. Her dad sharecropped and worked at a factory in Lafayette. Her mom, Clara, took in laundry and mending. With money tight, the "clean your plate" ethic was present, but not overt. "It was implied, but not strictly enforced, because whatever you didn't eat, someone else would. Usually my dad."

Any remaining food went to the family mutt, for whom they didn't buy dog food. But there wasn't much, because the children learned to appreciate what was on their plates. "My dad made food," Mitchell said. "That's what he did for a living. My mom and dad both came from huge families where you didn't get a lot of food." They had also lived through the Depression. "Food was respected. Our dog was skinny," she added.

The family learned early on what went into the cost of store-bought food. "At the dinner table, my dad would be like 'You spent 79 cents on Corn Flakes, when I'm only getting $1.35 per bushel?' And you could probably get about 200 boxes of Corn Flakes out of a bushel. There was this ongoing conversation of the market prices versus the prices for the products they make with them." Yet, Mitchell and her siblings learned that purchased and home-grown food each had a certain value, whether it was the time, energy, and resources that went into producing what they raised or the money that bought it at the store.

Mitchell and her siblings also learned to get the most out of food by watching their parents. She remembers her mom making what she called "Last of the

Garden," an end-of-summer, chutney-like concoction made by combining and pickling whatever scraggly veggies were left hanging, including lima beans, green beans, and corn. The results must have been tasty, as Mitchell recalls eating it straight out of the jar. Her father would save the crumbs from the bottom of potato chip bags and cracker boxes and then mash the assortment together to make breading. Today, Mitchell does the same with her crumbs. And she creates so much breading that she'll often give some to friends.

Pass It Down

Mitchell is proud that her kids have absorbed the lessons that she and her husband have tried to teach them about valuing what they have. If her sons don't want everything on their plates, they offer the remains to others in the family or save them for later. "If I fix pork chops, never would it ever cross their mind to throw it away. They'll ask if anyone wants it, and if dad doesn't want it, we'll put it in the fridge," Mitchell said. "Of course, it'll probably end up in a meatloaf. That makes me happy."

If Mitchell's kids break something, they pay for it with their own money. The same rule applies to food. She recalled her oldest son, Austin, leaving open a bag of chips overnight when he was eight. They got soggy and lost their crunch. "We made him get his 99 cents and buy a bag the next time we went to the store," Mitchell said. "He got in line in front of me—it was a separate transaction. Of course, those [crunchless] chips went into the stuff I turn into breading. But I didn't tell him that."

Mitchell's sons are surely learning from observing some of her other habits, too. She stores vegetable leftovers in a quart-sized container in the freezer. When it's full, she makes a vegetable soup. Mitchell also purees leftovers and sneaks them into dinners. "Anything with a sauce, you can get it in there. All the stuff you don't want recognizable, you run it through the Cuisinart," Mitchell said. "There have been a couple of times when a kid has been picking through the sauce and found some greens in it. I just played dumb—'What's that doing there?'"

Mitchell, who estimates that she feeds her family of four on $40 each week, has even made potato peelings soup. "It has a bit of an earthy flavor to it, but it's good," Mitchell said, appreciating her pun. "You just gotta make sure you clean them well."

Although she has been an urban dweller since 1979, Mitchell is still surprised by her neighbors' distance from their food. She recently taught a canning class at her house and was taken aback when visitors had no idea what an okra plant looked like. "There are so many people here who have no idea where food comes from. And I don't think that's specific to here, it's probably true across the U.S.," she said.

Mitchell's father was fond of the saying, "Use it up, wear it out, make it do, or do without." This unattributed, often unsolicited advice is listed as an anonymous "New England maxim" in *Bartlett's Familiar Quotations*. Regardless of its origins, though, the phrase gained new life during the Great Depression and World War II. It even appeared, minus the "do without," in a World War II–era poster of a woman mending her husband's pants while he, amusingly, mowed the lawn in his underwear.[40] Subsequently, the phrase lived on in Mitchell's house when she was growing up: "Dad—he'd say that constantly. It was like a mantra," she said. "My sisters and I would roll our eyes, but all of us have done the same thing with our families."

A Return to Thrift

I first heard of the aphorism quoted above in a comment left on my blog by Katy Wolk-Stanley, a Portland, Oregon, labor and delivery nurse who blogs as The Non-Consumer Advocate. She signed her comment, and all subsequent ones, with "use it up, wear it out, make it do, or do without." Wolk-Stanley also includes the phrase as part of her e-mail signature. When I asked, she told me she considers it her motto. In her life, the saying has meant less clutter and—yes—less food waste.

Wolk-Stanley started her site to help others enjoy the important things in life by living on less income. Before she chose this mission, she had always been a frugal person and good with money, but she had her weaknesses. "I was a recreational shopper. I'd be at the 75 percent off table and having to find something because it was such a good deal. I'd buy that plastic bathroom storage unit that I didn't know I needed five minutes ago."

Then, in December 2006, she read a short newspaper article on the Compact, an online pledge not to buy anything new for a year, with a few notable exceptions, such as food, toilet paper, and a few other staples. She was intrigued, but didn't feel ready to commit to a year. She decided to try it for a month in January 2007. The experiment took, and she has been forgoing new purchases ever since.

Not that she's a zealot. Wolk-Stanley breaks the Compact occasionally, in situations when she feels it's "not a time to get up on my soapbox." For instance, Wolk-Stanley recently bought new items for her son to bring as gifts to his Japanese exchange hosts. And because her husband and children are not beholden to the idea, they bought a new cordless phone when their existing one died. But that was only after repeated attempts—involving a soldering iron—at fixing their old one. Still, she has remained remarkably free from new purchases for more than three years.

And she's not alone. The Compact, which began in 2006, now has more than 10,000 members on its Yahoo Group. Before it was a movement, it was just an agreement struck up between ten friends in—where else?—San Francisco. Taking its name from the Mayflower Compact, and using the ideals of living for the greater good that the Pilgrims espoused it as a guide, these middle-class twenty-somethings agreed to put their wallets away for a year. The idea was threefold: to counteract the negative impacts of the disposable consumer culture, to simplify their lives, and to reduce personal clutter and waste.

Through her participation in the Compact, Wolk-Stanley has dramatically changed her food habits. Her general anticonsumerism sparked kitchen thrift. She's altered how she serves and prepares food and has issued multiple "Waste No Food Challenges" on her blog.[41] Before she began this shift, she cooked massive amounts of food with the idea of maximizing her efforts by having plenty of leftovers. It's a sound theory, but in reality, her family of four would usually end up tossing the majority of the remains into the compost bin. Even freezing the food leftovers just delayed the squandering. These days, Wolk-Stanley only cooks enough to have leftovers for a single meal. To trim her sons' plate waste, she serves them less. In addition, Wolk-Stanley shops with a keen eye on avoiding waste. From buying smaller onions to just the right amount of deli meat needed, her shopping strategy has brought a sparser refrigerator and a clearer conscience.

A Cultural Shift

The Compact—and Wolk-Stanley's blog inspired by it—are part of a burgeoning movement toward thrift and against waste. And unlike previous iterations, these Americans are choosing thrift rather than having it forced upon them. Of course, the recession that started in 2008 didn't hurt, either. Still, many of us are opting to darn socks and can vegetables more because of environmental and cultural realities than economic ones. Wolk-Stanley embodies this spirit in her blog bio: "I am a library patron, leftovers technician, Goodwill enthusiast, utility bill scholar, labor and delivery nurse, laundry hanger-upper, mother and citizen."

While this cultural shift draws upon earlier nonconsumption ideals in America, it is taking place in a twenty-first-century venue: the web. This discussion about reducing food waste mostly occurs in the peer-group world of the blogosphere. For instance, Wolk-Stanley posted her first Waste No Food Challenge in May 2008 and has followed with several more. Deanna Duke, a Seattle blogger better known as "Crunchy Chicken," issued a Food Waste Reduction Challenge in February 2009. And I've challenged visitors to my blog, Wasted Food, both to reduce their squandering and to want to read about food waste every day.

Kristen Cross, better known as "The Frugal Girl," posted a photo of her family's food waste in July 2008 on her blog. That month, after including an untouched cucumber in her photo, she wrote: "I'm particularly annoyed with myself about the cucumber. I'm ashamed to say how many cucumbers have perished in like manner while residing in my veggie drawer. . . . I seem to forget about them way too often."

A few months later, Cross launched a recurring feature called Food Waste Friday, in which she publishes a weekly photo report card of her family's fridge efficiency. She also encourages others to link to their own weekly waste tallies. The idea came about organically. "I think I probably thought of the idea one day when I was cleaning out the fridge. I'd often thought about how embarrassed I'd be if someone saw all my waste. I do remember thinking that if I knew someone was going to see my waste, I might be more inspired to use up my food!" said Cross, thirty-one, who manages to blog daily while homeschooling her four children, moonlighting as a professional photographer, baking her own bread, and occasionally teaching piano.

As Cross's "cheerfully living on less" tagline exemplifies, frugality is in. Though it's not a formal, self-conceptualized movement, there's a cultural shift nonetheless. Print and television journalists produce pieces about how to reduce waste, and some restaurateurs, tired of seeing how much goes in the Dumpster, are reducing portion sizes (and sometimes prices). Even canning is enjoying a renaissance, as Treva Mitchell can attest. A book called *The New Frugality*, published in December 2009, preaches that less can be more, financially. And, of course, there are the frugal blogs that dot the web. The ones specifically related to being frugal with food, such as Premeditated Leftovers, Stuff on Rice, and Not Made of Money, are prompting a sea change in our approach to saving leftovers and using up our cabinet castaways and refrigerator refugees.

These bloggers are the vanguard of social change. By writing candidly about their goal of avoiding waste, they make it more likely that the average American will eat a food item one or two days past its expiration date. They are nudging the social barometer further toward composting, too. The recycling fanatics of twenty years ago often elicited a rolling of eyes, but they paved the way for mainstream adoption of recycling. Today, a full 60 percent of Americans have access to curbside recycling, and that number is growing.[42] Perhaps in twenty years we will be saying the same about food-waste recycling. We have a long way to go, but these efforts are already bearing fruit. In October 2009, San Francisco made composting mandatory for all households and businesses. Seattle followed suit in March of that year for single-family homes. If the composting trend, or, even better, a food-waste reduction program, progresses as quickly as recycling has, the change would be astounding. In 1989, 8 percent of solid waste was recycled. Ten years later, the percentage had increased fourfold.[43]

For the Dogs: Leftover Culture

Don't believe me that we're at the cusp of a cultural shift in food waste reduction? You have to look closely, but it's there. Rather than let their food go to waste, many are choosing to give it away. Community-specific sites like Craigslist and Freecycle prompt reuse by linking sellers and donors with takers. Cross, for example, has given away cucumbers, hot peppers, and cilantro that she knew she wouldn't use both to friends and strangers via Freecycle.

Yet, our burgeoning cultural shift away from waste can really be seen in our handling of restaurant leftovers. Taking restaurant leftovers home has gradually become much more mainstream over the past fifteen years. In the early 1990s, comedian Jerry Seinfeld had a bit that referenced the embarrassment of having to ask for a doggie bag. Yet by 2009, a survey by the food-research group Technomic found that eight in ten respondents either "always" or "sometimes" took home leftovers when they ate out.[44] The "sometimes" may be a bit more common, according to Cornell's Wansink, but what was once almost a pizza-specific behavior has become widespread.

Regardless, taking home leftovers is now the norm. This shift has been gradual, but it has certainly arrived. "Between the portion sizes having gone past large into obscene, and with the economy as it is, people don't have any qualms about taking things home," said Mat Mandeltort, a consultant at Technomic. "I paid for it, I'm taking it," is the attitude that has emerged.

On Valentine's Day 2009, the White House press corps photographed President Obama and his wife leaving the restaurant Table 52 in Chicago. Sure enough, First Lady Michelle Obama was carrying her dinner remains. First Family doggie bagging goes a long way toward legitimizing the practice. Perhaps even more impressive, though, was the endorsement from another American institution, *The Joy of Cooking*. Though the book now includes larger portion sizes than in the past, it at least suggests more ways to use the leftovers from the recipes. The index in the 2006 version lists sixty entries for leftovers, compared to three in the 1997 version.

As a further sign of increased acceptance of using leftovers, even Alice Waters, Chez Panisse's founder, whose schooling in French cooking framed her view of doggie-bagging as gauche, now supports the idea. "Any time people want to take food home, I give it to them without question. Whereas twenty-five years ago, I just thought those little bags for the dogs were unacceptable," Waters told me by phone. "I just thought it was impolite to take food home. Now I take food home and it's a lunch for my kids the next day."

Even the process of packing up doggie bags is now more overt than in the past, befitting our less formal culture. "It used to be that if you wanted to take something home, you asked the waiter and he would take it in the back, wrap it, and discreetly bring it back to you," said Mandeltort. "Now when you ask for leftovers, they throw the container at you and say 'Have at it.'"

Doggie bags, not surprisingly, got their name from diners taking home meat bones and scraps for their pets, but it evolved into a euphemism. Few would admit that they planned to eat their restaurant leftovers, so everyone pretended to be taking them to the family dog. Yet, why were we sheepish with the practice? Did we not want to appear to be thrifty? Or was there a sense that we would seem gluttonous if we wanted to make sure we got every bite? Some have a sense that the practice is dangerous from a food-safety standpoint. For whatever the reason, some still view taking leftovers home as "undignified," as one Massachusetts newspaper called the practice in a 2009 article.[45] The restaurant industry has latched onto our leftover-loving, using it to maintain business in harsh economic times. The previously mentioned Technomic research appeared in a monthly newsletter for restaurateurs, the *American Express Market Brief*. The writeup came to this conclusion: "In today's economy, it is fairly safe to assume that when diners leave a decent amount of food on their plates, they will want to take it home. Make sure your staff is well-versed in leftovers etiquette; they should always offer to get the containers or pack things up, rather than having to make customers ask and / or wait a long time to get the process going."[46]

Some restaurants even see leftovers as a selling point now. I'm on the e-mail list for my favorite eatery, Crook's Corner in Chapel Hill. Now this is a white linen, waiters in bow ties kind of place that was a semifinalist for a 2010 James Beard Award for Outstanding Restaurant. Their July e-mail newsletter included the following: "The Picnic Plate is piled high with cold fried chicken, old-fashioned mustard potato salad, tangy cukes & onions and a watermelon wedge. This is a big plate and like our other main courses there's enough food for lunch the next day."

Crook's Corner and other restaurants are hoping that if we take some of our meal home, we'll divide the price in half in our minds. The National Restaurant Association's Annika Stensson told me that this line of thinking has become quite popular. "Today's consumers want to get as much bang for their buck as they can. One way is to take part of your dinner home to enjoy for lunch the next day as you basically get a two-meals-in-one deal," said Stensson, the group's media relations director. "While the concept of a 'doggie bag' is not new, it has become commonplace for diners to request part of a meal to go and for restaurants to accommodate these requests."

While we've made strides on portion sizes and leftovers, we're not there yet. Overall, ours is still a culture of waste. To wit: the "Today and Tomorrow" promotion at Maggiano's Little Italy, where diners who order certain entrées are given another dish—for tomorrow—to take home at the end of their meal. This despite the fact that Maggiano's portions are gigantic—so large that they don't publish calorie information—and would do just fine as two meals anyway.[47] "Some say the recession is causing a new generation of Americans to eat a dish they've never eaten before: the leftover. 'Today & Tomorrow' re-invents the leftover, with a free meal that is world-class quality and made fresh daily to take home," said Steve Provost, senior vice president of marketing and brand strategy for Maggiano's, in a press release.

This thinking is questionable. Instead of encouraging leftover-taking, Maggiano's promotion will probably prompt diners not to box up what remains on their plate. Why would they, when they have another entire meal coming their way? Leftovers are not reinvented; they're likely forsaken.

Neither this promotion nor our general apathy toward waste should come as much of a surprise. After all, we squander food from field to fork, plow to plate. Changing such an ingrained dynamic can't occur overnight. Yet, it shouldn't take too long to overthrow our culture of waste. After all, it evolved in a short period of time, and we're already returning to our historically ingrained thrift. In moving our food ways forward, we can look backward for inspiration.

Unharvested pears gone to ground at Ivicevich Orchard in Lakeport, California.

PHOTO BY JONATHAN BLOOM

chapter 5

American Farms: Growing Waste, Selling Perfection

Without regret, with less and less interest in the disciplines of thrift and conservation, with, in fact, the assumption that this is the way of the world, our present agriculture wastes topsoil, water, fossil fuel, and human energy—to name only the most noticeable things. Consumers participate "innocently" or ignorantly in all these farm wastes and add to them wastes that are urban or consumptive in nature: mainly all the materials

and energy that go into unnecessary processing and packaging,
as well as tons of organic matter (highly valuable—and
certainly, in the long run, necessary—as fertilizer) that they
flush down their drains or throw out as garbage.

—WENDELL BERRY

A cucumber should be well-sliced, dressed with pepper and
vinegar, and then thrown out.

—SAMUEL JOHNSON, 18TH-CENTURY
ENGLISH AUTHOR AND POET

Outside an industrial shed carved from the woods of Virginia, a dump truck appeared. The hulking vehicle drove under a 20-foot-tall, green steel vat cantilevered out over the pavement and stopped. A minute later, a chute opened and a flow of oblong green objects tumbled out. The dump truck had parked under Parker Farms' "cull tower," which was filled with cucumbers. The cascade of cukes proceeded until it had filled the payload of the truck. What was happening? The vegetables weren't being collected to create an industrial-sized cold soup; nor would they be used in some kind of high-tech biofuel. Instead, they were being trucked to a nearby field to be dumped.

Cucumbers: The Straight and Narrow

In the beginning, there were two acres. Rod Parker launched Parker Farms in 1974 along with his father and brother on that bit of land in Clinton, Maryland, just down the road from Andrews Air Force Base and about 10 miles from the Capitol dome. What began as a "pick your own" operation with vegetables and berries had expanded to serve roadside stands and farmers markets a few years later. By 1976, the enterprise had swelled to 150 acres. Parker Farms slowly transitioned from direct sales to wholesale and by 1988 had built a packaging and cooling facility for their accumulated 500 acres.

Today, Parker Farms remains a family-run farm business, but it's a much larger one than it used to be. The Parkers have moved their headquarters across the Potomac to Virginia, roughly halfway between Washington, D.C., and Richmond. The Parkers still grow many of their own crops, but they also sort, process, and distribute vegetables from thirty Virginia growers and a few more out-of-state farms. They sell tomatoes, peppers, squash, cucumbers, and more to the fresh market and can truck an order overnight to any location on the East Coast. On their website, Parker Farms calls themselves "Growers/Packers/Shippers of Fine Vegetables."

Now, about that adjective: How fine is "fine"? Since Parker Farms grows specifically for the fresh market, or retail sales, what the Parkers ship has to look just right. A vegetable's taste comes a distant second to its appearance and size. As a result, fewer than half of the vegetables the Parkers grow leave the farm.

With cucumbers in particular, there are a number of reasons why they might not be considered presentable for sale. The winnowing begins in the field. Rod Parker, the farm's general manager, told me that at least half of the cucumbers aren't harvested. The experienced pickers know not to collect ones that are flawed for any one of a number of reasons. Cucumbers can be too curved, which hinders box packing and supermarket stacking. Those with a tiny white spot on one end—something that happens when the tip is buried and doesn't receive any sunlight—are also shunned. Finally, some cucumbers have small cracks that prevent them from aging well (but they would be fine if sold locally, where shelf life wasn't as vital).

The cukes that actually make it out of the field are brought inside the Oak Grove packing shed and loaded on a long conveyer belt. They're power-washed to remove the dirt and pesticides. Workers hand sort the vegetables, placing the "imperfect" ones on a separate conveyer belt headed to the steel holding tank, where they await the next dump truck. The majority of these sorting culls happen for purely superficial reasons. "I'd say 75 percent are edible. They're fine cukes to eat and have the same nutrition, but there's not much eye appeal to them," Parker told me.

The cucumbers that pass this hand grading face a final test in this vegetable judgment day—mechanical sizing. As the cucumbers are conveyed along, they come to a "drop sizer," a series of parallel, 5-foot pins that gradually become farther apart. The cucumbers that are too small for the market "drop" through to another belt routed for the green vat. They're either the right size or the wrong one; it's a black and white world for these green vegetables. In addition, there are places where workers can drop cucumbers on a discard belt all along the sorting line. These all eventually flow together, as the outcasts are routed directly to the cull tower.

At Parker Farms, workers sort cucumbers the day after they're picked, which happens about every four or five days during the harvest. On sorting days, Parker noted, they usually fill two dump-truck loads of culled cukes, with each one holding 15 to 20 tons. "You might do it a couple times a day," Parker said.

Recently, Parker started working with a few nonprofits, including D.C.'s Bread of the City, to try to get the product to those who would eat it. Yet, timing can be a real obstacle. "Sometimes we can do something about it," Parker said. "We do have connections with some gleaning outfits. That works well with potatoes and less perishable items. If there is a food bank standing there as those cucumbers come off the line, they can do something with them. But otherwise, the product line we carry is too perishable."

When donation can't be arranged, the rejected cucumbers are driven back to their fields or neighboring farms and dumped on the ground. They'll eventually be plowed back into the soil, like birds that never left the nest. "We dump thousands upon thousands of them every time we sort," said Parker. "It frustrates me. We didn't grow it to throw it away."

The Big Picture

The seminal 1997 USDA work "Estimating and Addressing America's Food Losses" provides our most comprehensive federal study on food waste to date. Sadly, though, it doesn't include farm waste—which is ironic and unfortunate for a Department of Agriculture study. Here's what the report, done by researchers with the USDA's Economic Research Service (ERS), does give us on agricultural waste: "Although ERS was not able to quantify food losses that occur on the farm or between the farm and retail levels, anecdotal evidence suggests that such losses can be significant for some commodities."[1] In other words, there's a whole bunch of farm loss; we just have no idea how big a bunch we're talking about.

Hence, we'll have to look elsewhere for a sector-wide estimate. In a 2005 article, the University of Arizona's Timothy Jones estimated that farm industry losses amounted to $20 billion.[2] Jones also found that losses were 29 percent in the citrus industry and 18 percent in the vegetable industry.[3] In addition, the policy brief by the Stockholm International Water Institute on how water loss is tied to food waste found that with field-grown crops, post-harvest losses alone amounted to 13 percent.[4]

Farm losses are higher with fruit and perishable vegetables than with the more stable commodity crops—corn, wheat, oats, sorghum, barley, rice, soybeans, and cotton (which can't be considered food, but the USDA tracks it). What the USDA does do well is provide long-term projections that compare the number of acres planted to those harvested for these eight crops. Tallying those 2008 estimates, one can deduce that 9 percent of the commodity crops planted in the United States aren't even harvested.

Farms, unlike other segments of the food chain, often have "loss" that isn't really "waste" (that is, food that's squandered through human error). Frost, hail, pests, and viruses all account for significant food loss. As any farmer knows, weather damage—from frost, drought, hail, or excessive rain—is a particularly acute threat to crops. Nick Ivicevich, a pear grower with almost fifty years of experience in the business, knows that all too well.

Ivicevich lives in a ranch-style home on a 56-acre orchard in Lake County, California. In addition to his own orchard, he has been temporarily overseeing his son's acres for the past few years. In 2008, frost was a major concern for growers in the area. While most farmers ward off frost damage by irrigating their fruit, Ivicevich's son's water pump failed, leading to severe freeze damage. The combination of mechanical problems and adverse weather meant that an orchard that normally yields 600 to 700 tons only produced 250 tons of salvageable pears. Then again, there's really no such thing as "normally" in farming.

Perfect Enough to Eat

Increasingly, there's a demand for perfect produce. While there have always been high-end shoppers and foodies (before they were called that) accustomed to pretty produce, that desire has spread. In many parts of the American food chain, appearance trumps taste. Acting on demands of the market, many growers have heartiness in mind, not taste, when they choose what varieties of a certain fruit or vegetable to grow. Julia Stewart, spokesperson for the Produce Marketing Association, attributes this trend partly to shifting geography. "As the agricultural base has gotten farther and farther from consumers, growers have to be sure that their produce can reach stores in good condition," Stewart said. "Growing varieties for storability and transportability happens more with softer, delicate fruit like tomatoes, berries, apples and pears."

Heartiness is so important because growers and wholesalers have had to become even more selective in recent years to match the rising expectations of stores and shoppers. And this superficiality is in no way specific to Parker Farms or cucumbers—it's industry-wide. In eastern North Carolina, Faison's Burch Farms grows sweet potatoes, greens, and cucumbers. Jimmy Burch, Sr., the farm's owner, agreed with Parker. "With cucumbers, we only get a 30 to 40 percent packout. The rest of it goes to the cattle or hogs," Burch said. "The market just wants the very best. We've trained people to be too picky. It's true with all the produce, it ain't just cucumbers."

Roughly 70 miles south, Nash Produce of Nashville, North Carolina, processes and ships mostly sweet potatoes, but also handles cantaloupe, watermelon, and cucumbers. Sweet potatoes may be the crop with the most variety accepted. I once found one at a supermarket that looked so much like a mouse that I flinched—before buying it with glee. Even with that tolerance, there's a wide variety of sweets that don't make the cut. Charles Edwards, a salesman at Nash who has sold produce for more than thirty-five years, lamented that shift. "It's become, in my opinion, far more selective. Everything is appearance, color, and attractiveness," said Edwards. "It's unfortunate because all products do not grow that way. We as a society are just spoiled by trying to just select the perfect. To some extent it's almost ridiculous. That we should take something a little misshapen or that has got a blemish on it and then throw it away."

Mark Reasons, the general manager of the Ocean Mist cooling facility in Salinas, California, blames these heightened expectations on a change in the grocery industry. "There used to be 'garbage markets' that didn't want to pay for top-quality produce. But retail has gotten so competitive, they all want top quality," said Reasons, who has been in the industry for more than forty years. "There used to be more of a range of quality in acceptable produce. Now it's much higher."

These enhanced grocery standards won't come as much of a surprise to anyone who has strolled through a U.S. supermarket in the past fifteen years. The average supermarket has become more upscale. As food culture, of brows high and low, has expanded, so has the need for immaculate produce. Instead of opening a can of green beans to round out a casserole, Americans are increasingly using fresh, not frozen, vegetables. Flawless fruits and vegetables are now expected. If we're going to bother to cook, we want it to look like it does on TV or in the magazines. And the displays at high-end retailers like Whole Foods and Wegman's—what many call "food porn"—raise our expectations. We've come to believe that perfect, uniform produce is normal.

The Enormity of Uniformity

In addition to attractiveness, supermarkets demand uniformity in both size and shape (and, more understandably, color and texture). Just as retailers won't take curved cucumbers, they reject straight bananas. Hence, round eggplants are shunned, as are oblong tomatoes. That is, if these items even make it off the farm. This superficiality means a waste of perfectly edible produce just because it may be an inch too short. Or too long. Or too thick. Or too thin. "When a retailer is featuring a certain size, the eye appeal is for everything looking pretty much the same," said Jack King, manager of national affairs at the California Farm Bureau.

Our fastidiousness has different effects with different fruits and vegetables. The outliers of many items, such as lettuce, aren't harvested, as we saw in Chapter 1. With some crops, everything is picked, but then the oddities are filtered out. From that point, there may or may not be a second run through. It depends on the labor situation and the market for that crop. After the first go-round, there are secondary markets for some crops. With apples, for example, there are alternate uses, such as jam, baby food, and juice. With some crops, like potatoes and tomatoes, the superficial culls are just thrown out if there isn't a proactive food-rescue group, such as Florida's Farm Share, to distribute unwanted food to those in need.

This selective harvesting can stem from practical considerations—for example, the standard boxes used to ship squash can only accommodate so large a zucchini.

Yet, that doesn't explain why smaller ones are omitted and alternate uses aren't found for the larger ones. Or why certain shapes are preferred over others. Humans and other animals find symmetry appealing, so it makes sense that we prefer our fruit that way. Yet, we also like to eat, and we like bargains. I'm confident that if you charged a fraction less for these nonuniform fruits and vegetables, they'd sell quite well. Actually, they already do at many a supermarket.

Who's to blame for all this superficial culling? Patricia Robbins, cofounder and chairman of Farm Share in Florida, points to wholesalers. "The companies that buy the product have a size and look they want," said Robbins. "They do not want a tomato that isn't perfectly shaped. If it has an indentation, that's considered a cull, and it's thrown away."

Yet, wholesalers say they're merely responding to supermarkets' wishes. In general, the demand for uniformity in produce trickles down the food chain, from shoppers to supermarkets to wholesalers. In addition to that downward demand, there's an upward passing of the buck. I've found that those in the food industry like to project blame for this phenomenon up the food chain. Farmers say their wholesalers only want a certain kind of product. Wholesalers say store managers only want pretty fruit. Store managers blame their picky customers.

Are we to blame for the increased emphasis on superficiality? Shoppers tend to base their view of an entire store on the appearance of the produce section. According to the 2008 U.S. Grocery Shopper Trends, a poll of more than 1,000 shoppers, the state of a store's produce is the most important factor for people when selecting their primary supermarket. "High-quality fruit and vegetables" topped the list, as 75 percent of respondents deemed it "very important."[5] That means that the availability of top-notch produce is more important to shoppers than low prices, store cleanliness, or convenience of location. And supermarket executives are well aware of this belief.

Although most shoppers do prefer perfect produce, I'd guess that those in the food industry overestimate shoppers' insistence on homogeneous foods. Many of us aren't put off by a curved cucumber or a straight banana. And a zucchini that was a bit longer than most buyers' specifications would be even less of a problem. After all, farmers markets and backyard gardening, both laden with eccentric produce, are growing in popularity. And these "natural-looking" fruits and vegetables have also seen a resurgence through the uptick in local foods. The reduced pesticide use and emphasis on heirloom varieties that many customers support often leads to some funky, delicious foods. In the early days of the organic food movement, the shoppers who frequented the natural food stores were quite tolerant of imperfection. With the renewed emphasis on local foods, more consumers are likely to find produce of the non-cookie-cutter variety acceptable, if not charming. Yet, our current system eliminates quirky produce (despite its inherent personality!).

Nick Ivicevich, the California pear grower, has experienced Americans' fruit fussiness from a few angles. In addition to his years of farm experience, Ivicevich once worked at a supermarket, where he was surprised by the produce department's emphasis on appearance over taste. He can also contrast Americans' preferences with the attitudes prevalent in the homeland of his adoptive parents, Croatia. "If you go back to Croatia, they load pears with a shovel. People have their paring knives and just carve out the bad spots," Ivicevich said. "Here, they gotta be perfect."

Secondary and tertiary markets exist for many crops as a way to utilize ones that aren't perfect. As with apples, pears are among the lucky fruits, with four possible destinations, based on appearance: fresh market, cannery, baby food, and juice. To determine the grade, most packing sheds employ a variety of methods, from a pressure tester to the oh-so-scientific eyeball test. With blemishes, they try to imagine gathering all of the blemishes into one spot. If that spot is smaller than a dime, it will go to the market. If not, that pear is headed to the cannery, on one condition: It has to split in half perfectly. If there isn't symmetry—which they test by seeing if the pear will stay standing—it's off to the baby food or juice factory.

These secondary markets vary for each crop, and the demand, as with the fresh market's, fluctuates with each harvest. The sweet-potato growers I spoke with mentioned the burgeoning markets for sweet-potato fries and chips, in addition to the traditional ones for pie filling and baby food. Yet, as reported in the *New York Times Magazine*, food processors don't want anything to do with white sweet potatoes.[6] Nobody, it seems, wants sweet-potato fries indistinguishable from French fries. As a result, it's supermarket or bust for these tubers. Unless, that is, they're purchased at a steep discount by the California Association of Food Banks, as the article described.

Canneries aren't really a second option for some crops, said Parker Farms' Rod Parker. Most cannery business is contracted ahead of time, and they have their particular growers they work with. That's why Parker, despite growing can-friendly crops like tomatoes, corn, and green beans at his Virginia farm, only sells for the fresh market. He said that's not unusual. "Very few people have their feet in both pots, here and in other regions," said Parker, who also noted that canneries tend to be pretty picky. "Canneries really don't accept a lesser quality. There's enough good product out there that people don't have to fool with the culls. And here in the United States we're affluent enough to be that way. Other countries may not be."

Size Matters

Though the industry seeks perfection with all produce, it emphasizes enormity with some items. Have you seen the size of oranges and onions lately? In most conventional grocery stores and supermarkets, the grapefruit are like small bowling balls, and the bananas seem particularly gorilla-sized. It's hard to find an apple that weighs less than half a pound. Some smaller ones are still available, but they're typically sold in 3- or 5-pound plastic or mesh bags. Those who only want a few are out of luck.

Not only are fruits bred for heft, they're harvested that way, too. With prices based on weight, it's no mystery why stores prefer and pay growers more for large produce. While heftier produce fetches a higher price, the focus on size also requires growers to spend more and to further tax our natural resources by using increasing amounts of water and fertilizer. These crops are like the *fois gras* of the fruit world. "They want the big size; they pay us more for them," said Ivicevich of pears. "But then you gotta fertilize more and water more."

Ivicevich noted that the larger fruits tend to taste worse, or less sweet, than the smaller ones. In addition, this Godzilla fruit prompts waste. The emphasis on enormity means smaller produce often isn't harvested. That's the case with California peaches. "We'll harvest for size first," said King. "Smaller ones are excellent fruit, but they don't meet the standards of retailers. If growers can— if they have the labor and the prices are right—they'll sell the smaller stuff to farmers markets or the secondary retail market or to Mexico. More often it doesn't happen. It's disced in [i.e., plowed under], fed to animals, or thrown away."

Our preference for larger fruit prompts us to waste when we can't finish an item. The less choice we have in produce size, the more we squander. Not everyone wants to eat a giant apple, onion, or cantaloupe. And Ivicevich finds the size of today's pears, even the ones he grows, a bit much. "I like the medium size," he said. "With the big ones, I can see a kid taking two bites and throwing it on the ground."

Stewart at the Produce Marketing Association experienced that very problem when her kids were younger. "I would hand them a big piece of fruit and they just wouldn't know what to do with it," said Stewart. "Or they'd eat a quarter of it and I'd have to throw the rest away. I ended up having to slice it up or give them smaller pieces of fruit."

Stewart, a ten-year veteran of the apple industry, noted that the size of apples at the supermarket has been increasing steadily. "The average size of apple on display at retail stores has trended upward in the last decade," she said. "That's probably generally true across the board."

Retailers, driven by price and aesthetics but not considering the waste-inducing effects, encourage growers to deliver larger and larger produce, Ivicevich lamented. "The supermarket produce buyers want what'll look best on the shelf. They think bigger looks better," he said.

Steve Lutz is the executive vice president of The Perishables Group, a consultancy whose clients are in the fresh food industry. Prior to that, he was the CEO of the Washington Apple Commission. Regarding the push for larger fruit, he noted that there's a balancing act. "If a customer is going to come in and buy four apples, it's better to sell them a larger apple than a smaller apple, assuming it's being sold by the pound. But you can go too far. Most apples are eaten as a snack—that's the number one usage. At what point does an apple shift from being a snack to a meal? And at what point does some of that snack get wasted because you can't eat it all?"

Those questions were bouncing around my head the next time I went to a supermarket. As I strolled into the produce section of The Fresh Market, a higher-end chain with eighty-six stores in seventeen states, I was pondering how we know when an apple is just too big. The answer I settled on evoked former

Supreme Court Justice Potter Stewart's test for pornography, included in a draft of a 1964 opinion: "I know it when I see it."[8]

I saw it. The apples, especially the Fujis and Granny Smiths, were huge. The cantaloupes were similarly sized, prompting a thirty-something woman in a black fleece vest to remark, unprompted, that they were like bowling balls. After I refocused on the apples, it was difficult to find the proverbial snack-sized one. Frustrated, yet amazed, I started to weigh particularly large ones. It only took me four tries to find a one-pounder (a "Gee Whiz" Fuji). The first three were seven-eighths of a pound. I think it's pretty safe to say that these apples had crossed into "meal" territory.

The USDA determines the serving sizes for all fruits and vegetables. An apple still counts as one serving, but that might just be outdated. The USDA publication *Dietary Guidelines for Americans* calls a "medium apple" one serving.[8] And a USDA worksheet aimed at helping children visualize serving sizes equates the standard apple with a tennis ball.[9] Well, the tennis-ball-sized apples are not easy to find. The best I did that day at The Fresh Market was a half-pound Jazz apple.

The nomenclature for apple sizes is based on how many fit into a standard 40-pound box. The larger the number, the smaller the apple. A "56" is about the size of a softball, a "100" is approximately baseball-sized, and a "125" is like a tennis ball, said Lutz. The consensus is that the average-sized apple is anywhere from a 100 to an 80, all a few sizes larger than the tennis ball–like "125." So it may be time to bump the apple up to two servings. After all, not every fruit is lumped into the one-serving category—peaches count as a half-serving, even though they, too, are getting larger.

When I worked at a supermarket produce department, the topic of produce size never came up. That was probably because, as you might guess, all the fruits were roughly the same size—big. While we did carry the five-pound bags of tennis ball–like apples, the smaller loose items (and the non-uniform ones) had already been weeded out.

Our preference for heft, however, just might be on the wane. Smaller cars are coming into vogue, and homeowners are realizing that paying to heat and cool a 4,000-square-foot house isn't all that fun (or environmentally friendly). Yet, America may be stuck with larger produce for some time. It can take years for consumer demand to filter down to growers and for them to react.

The first step toward making this change, however, is for shoppers to start asking for smaller items, provided that's what they want. Collective purchasing power can go a long way. Few would have imagined ten years ago that a Durham, North Carolina, Food Lion, a standard lower-middle-brow supermarket, not known for progressive policies, would stock cans of organic chick peas or have numerous aisles devoted to groceries enjoyed by the Latino community (and a few gringos). If shoppers seek out "regular"-sized produce and make their views known, we might slowly reverse this super-sizing trend. Buying direct from growers, at a farm, orchard, farm stand, or farmers market, is the easiest way to do that, as we can actually just voice our preference or choose the smaller ones. Either way, through our buying power, we can make our views known. And then perhaps shoppers won't have to face the choice of wasting half of their apple or saving it for later when it will be browned and half as appealing.

Left Hanging

When I visited Nick Ivicevich's Lakeport, California, home, he led me out his back door, past his down-at-the-heels swimming pool, and into his orchard, which had just been harvested the week before. After walking a few hundred feet between two rows of elderly, macabre trees, he stopped. Reaching up to a higher branch, he grabbed a pear. Ivicevich turned it over a few times in his hand, frowned, and tossed the fruit on the ground.

Ivicevich was attempting to show me why the remaining pears hadn't been picked. In his jeans, tinted glasses, and plain, navy blue T-shirt, Ivicevich, seventy-two, moved to the next tree and gazed up at the partially picked branches. He pulled down two pears, but they lacked the telltale "starring" marks on the bottom that indicate the frost damage he wanted to illustrate (other potential problems include stem bruising and wind damage, or "limb rub"). "These are fine," Ivicevich grumbled. He snatched another pair. "These too!"

Counting his son's acres, Ivicevich oversees 20,000 trees over three fields. Yet he still recognizes individual trees. He told me you could drop him anywhere in his orchard and he'd know right where he was. I believed him; he called out specific characteristics of some of the trees that day. But as we walked through the older part of the orchard, with trees dating back 120 years, Ivicevich only spotted healthy pears. "All these are perfect!" he said. He finally found an unhealthy example, but he was peeved to find so many good pears still on the tree, especially after having paid $120,000 to have the orchard harvested. "I hate to come out here because I see all the ones not picked," Ivicevich said. "It bugs me."

Ivicevich was annoyed, but not mad. When it's your forty-seventh harvest, when you've seen entire fields wiped out—by weather, pests, and viruses—it's hard to get too aggravated by harvesting shortcomings. Besides, this year's results weren't unusual. Ivicevich estimated that with 135 tons harvested, 5 tons are usually left in the field, and that this year was no different. Still, walking through the orchard, we noticed at least a few large, healthy-looking pears on every tree. Why had this happened? Were there no ladders available? Did Ivicevich have a particularly devout group of laborers this year, cognizant of the Old Testament command to leave part of a harvest for gleaners?

The long and, well, short of it is that many of the pickers aren't that tall. Ivicevich theorized that while that stature is a boon for the stooping specific to ground crops, it's not helpful when working on fruit trees. The shorter the worker, the more he (or she) will need to use a ladder to reach pears. Unfortunately, setting up the ladder and climbing up and down it clashes with pickers' main motivation: speed.

Based on how they're paid, workers may have an incentive to leave good fruit on the tree. As with the Salinas lettuce pickers, most agricultural laborers are paid on a "piece rate," or by the weight they harvest. By emphasizing pace, not thoroughness, growers can't be too surprised when the least accessible fruit goes unpicked. And paying "piscadores" by quantity will likely prompt some mishandling of fruit, given human nature.

Rushed harvesting does not mix well with the fragility of pears. Ivicevich cataloged the ways that pears can be damaged in the harvest. He told me that he's seen many workers drop pears into their waist-level baskets from above their heads, transforming the fruit into a missile. "What happens is that the stem can stab another pear," Ivicevich explained. "It bruises it and then after two months in cold storage, that'll be a rotten spot and can make the whole box rot."

While working too fast is one problem, carelessness is another. Ivicevich's main gripe was that today's pickers are sloppier than those of yesteryear. "A lot of times, they won't bother with ladders on the high trees. Or, when nobody is watching, they'll yank a branch or whack it with a ladder," Ivicevich said. "How do you supervise fifty guys trying to go as fast as they can?"

At first, I thought I detected a racist and/or elitist note in Ivicevich's complaints, given that his workers are almost exclusively young men from Mexico and Central America. Yet, I came to understand that his objection was more of a generational one. "The workers are like a bunch of kids, and they are!" Ivicevich told me as we sat in the shade by his weathered pool house. "They don't do a thorough job."

For Ivicevich to deride young Mexican workers as careless or unwilling to learn is one thing. To hear one of his longtime Mexican employees do the same is telling. While Ivicevich was showing me around his orchard, we ran into one of his former supervisors, Guillermo "Bill" Bernadino, who now works at the neighboring Skully Packing Company. When Bernadino saw us, he cut the engine on his tractor and smiled out from under a Skully Packing hat, happy to see his old boss. They spoke in Spanish about today's pickers. Ivicevich lamented how they just don't learn. "No quieren," Bernadino said. They don't want to. "No quieren," he repeated.

Available Hands Less Available

While workers' shortcomings cause waste with all hand-picked crops, they aren't as harmful as labor shortages. When the harvesting crew doesn't make it to your field, nothing is picked. And 100 percent of crops not reaped are wasted. U.S. farmers are increasingly finding that they don't have enough available hands come picking time. This is especially true for crops that must be hand harvested—mostly fruits and vegetables.

For some time, few Americans have wanted to pick crops. It's hard labor often done in high heat. Tree harvesting involves climbing ladders with a bag of up to 30 pounds of fruit in a basket slung over your neck. Dan Fazio, the director of employer services at the Washington Farm Bureau, has had to deal with this problem. "Nobody wants to be a migrant farmer anymore," Fazio said. "It's just not a very attractive way to make a living. It's hard work."

As a result, growers have long relied on migrant laborers who have often come to America from Mexico or Central America. Some migrant workers are in this country legally and some aren't. You've probably heard people say that without illegal aliens, our economy would collapse. I'm not sure about the entire economy, but the farm industry is a safe bet.

Reliable labor became harder to find after September 11, 2001, when America began to tighten its borders. "Things have been getting progressively worse since 9/11," said Dan Fazio. "With all this immigration stuff, we're facing all of this uncertainty with workers."

Yet there has been a low rumble of labor concerns that predates those events, mostly due to competition. "The shrinking workforce has been a trend line that's been happening for a while. All the attention to the border accelerated the trend a bit," said Jack King at the California Farm Bureau.

Steadier, better-paying construction work siphoned off many potential pickers until the recession hit. Despite decent wages—with "piece rates" usually working out to $10 to $15 per hour, or $20 for those who really hustle—farm pay doesn't match that of construction. Meanwhile, restaurant and hotel kitchens offer steadier, safer work in a workplace free from the elements and ladders. "Migrant workers are harder to find because many have found jobs in an industry that doesn't require migration—construction," said Fazio.

Despite the economic downturn curtailing construction work, laborers who have settled down have been slow to return to or seek migrant jobs. Labor shortages have caused problems in produce-heavy states like Washington. The state has 25,000 in-state farm workers, but its growers need three times that number to bring in their harvest. Washington growers must then find 50,000 workers willing to migrate from farm to farm and crop to crop. The Washington Farm Bureau has taken some novel approaches to this problem, including proposing a bill that would grant students free in-state college tuition for one quarter for each summer they worked in agriculture. "They're trying to get high school kids out there, housewives," Fazio said. "But none of them seems to be working because it's really hard work. Nobody wants to do it."

And with fewer laborers to go around, the help often doesn't arrive at the right time—they're too busy elsewhere. And that's no shock, given the fragile, time-sensitive picking progression. In California, for instance, pickers must transition from cherries or apricots to asparagus, then to peaches or plums, then pears. "There was a somewhat magical system that has worked over the years in California, with pickers moving from one crop to the next," said King. "Workers have almost a sixth sense on when to move on to the next crop."

Fazio says that these shortages aren't too bad with crops that have longer, more forgiving harvesting windows, such as oranges and tree nuts. Yet labor shortages frequently lead to pears being left on the trees. Picking pears when they're green and firm allows growers to keep them in cold storage for a few months. But if they ripen on the tree, well, you're screwed. They'll be too soft by the time they hit the stores. "With pears you only have a three- to four-week harvest window," King said. "If you don't have enough workers, or you're delayed starting, the harvest just sort of overwhelms you. And you have the entire year's investment riding on getting that crop in. That's really just a terrible situation to be in."

But that's the position in which Nick Ivicevich and most pear growers in Lake County found themselves in 2006. That year, Ivicevich had his best crop in as long as he could remember. And in strict accordance with Murphy's Law, that was the year pickers failed to arrive in time (weather had thrown off the harvest calendar for some fruits, so the time-honored progression of seasonal labor from one crop to another was off). An insurance agent who visited that year to update Ivicevich's file assessed his crop at 40 tons per acre. In a normal year, Ivicevich told me, he gets about 25 tons per acre. With harvesters in short supply, Ivicevich had to scramble to avoid a total loss. In the end, he guesses that he lost at least half of his crop that year.

The labor situation has deteriorated to the point where bumper crops aren't always desired with handpicked fruits and vegetables. That was the case with Washington apples in 2006. Fazio, in response to a question about the possibility of fruit going unpicked, uttered this incongruity: "This year we got lucky. We had really bad hail storms. We had a smaller crop, so it looks like we'll have just have enough labor to get the crop in." In other words, had that fall brought a regular-sized harvest or bigger, much of it would have ultimately gone to ground.

Still, the lack of a guaranteed labor force doesn't stop farmers from planting more than they'll likely need. Most growers do so to hedge against disaster, should disease, pests, or weather intervene. Planting more than they're likely to harvest or be able to sell is a perfectly normal response to the uncertainty of farming; it's just that it has consequences. "To a farmer, it's not natural to grow less," former Agriculture Secretary Dan Glickman told me when I asked him about possibly encouraging smaller yields. "Productivity is natural to agriculture. The more you produce, generally, the more you make."

Major League Mechanization

While farmers haven't altered their planting habits, because of the scarcity of labor, they have begun to consider other options. The recent labor shortages and the fear that they'll persist have been a boon for the makers of mechanized pickers. Growers and state farm bureaus are increasingly working with universities and companies like San Diego's Vision Robotics to develop mechanical harvesting devices to replace those fussy human pickers. Vision Robotics' CEO, Derek Morikawa, said that almost all fruit and vegetable industries are looking to mechanize their harvests. "One hundred percent of our participation with these industries is because they're concerned that labor will just not be available. It's not so much that they want to cut the cost of labor or cut it out of the equation," said Morikawa. "In the near future there's a real fear that labor is not going to be there when you need to pick your crop. If your labor isn't there—and it's a perishable crop—you're dead."

Machines have long replaced human and animal labor in agriculture, but the fruit industry advances are more recent and robo-centric. The Florida orange industry, where the majority of fruit is liquefied and, hence, can stand a little bruising, now uses them extensively. While they may look more like enemy contraptions from James Bond films than productive tools, they are quite efficient. Oxbo International makes a "shake and catch harvester" that can collect 1 million pounds of oranges in a single day, doing the work of 120 laborers.[10]

The final frontier in mechanization is to create machines capable of picking fruits and vegetables once thought too delicate for anything but human hands, to have robotic harvesting for the fresh market (our supermarkets). Toward that goal, Vision Robotics is working with engineers to develop "end effectors," or picking hands, that will look more like suction cups than robotic hands. The prototype operates by scanning and mapping the location of a tree's fruit before picking it with its multiple arms. After watching human pickers dump their 30-

pound bags of pears into a central bin, I have no trouble imagining a machine gentle enough for the job. Depending on whether you're picturing Robot B9, C-3PO, Johnny 5, or Wall-E, you may or may not agree.[11]

If this mechanization progresses, growers could see labor-related waste, be it from worker shortages or human error, dip. Yet, a less attractive byproduct of this mechanization is that there might be (evil) food scientists trying to grow a tomato tough enough to handle being machine-picked. Like the drive for perfect and large produce, this classic horse-before-the-cart idea is an example of profits trumping taste.

Vision Robotics is now developing mechanized harvesters for both the apple and orange industries. Morikawa projected they will be using robotic limbs to pick fresh-market fruits by 2015. When I spoke with him about the challenges specific to each fruit, I had to suppress a laugh when he said, in all earnestness, "Apples are very different than oranges." In all fairness, I was the one who'd just asked him, in the context of harvesting, to compare apples to oranges.

To Pick or Not to Pick

Mechanization will not bring an end to waste. There remains plenty of human error involved, from poor tractor operation to carelessness. A large problem at Nick Ivicevich's orchard came not from the harvesting, but from transporting some of the crop. As we walked, we came to a rotting mess of pears along the rutted dirt road between two stands of trees. He told me the driver spilled two bins—each with 1,000 pounds of fruit—because of reckless driving. "We tried to salvage some," Ivicevich said. "They were sent to juice. But that was about a $200 screw-up."

Farmers' decisions can also cause waste. The majority of on-farm squandering comes when crops simply aren't harvested. This tends to happen when the price for that crop would be less than the cost of harvesting, processing, and transporting it. Many call this conscious squandering "walk-bys," because farmers simply "walk by" instead of harvesting. I call it a waste.

Those in the nonprofit world of food recovery, who rescue unwanted food for the hungry, are keenly aware of walk-bys. People like Christy Porter, of California's Hidden Harvest, have to be, because they receive many of their donations from these fields. Some growers in the Death Valley area of the state will call Porter when they decide not to harvest an area. From that point, Porter has to scurry to find a crew to pick as much as possible. "There's a ratio in farmers' heads on what they want to get out of each crop," Porter said. "They know what they've put in for labor, seed, and water. They have a benchmark they're hoping to hit. Once they've made what they hoped to make, if it's diminishing returns after that point, they just leave it. Also, they have the next crop to plant."

Walk-bys aren't a rare occurrence, although their frequency fluctuates with the prices. Two years ago, strawberry prices plummeted, and Hidden Harvest received many donations and invitations to harvest berries. Yet these offers were impossible to keep up with, as the food-recovery group could only pick so many of them. Porter told me that the scent of strawberries filled the air as she drove through the valley, because so many growers just left their fields unharvested.

Contamination fears also prompt walk-bys. While limiting a bacteria outbreak is important, the means for doing so causes great amounts of waste. In September 2006, an *E. coli* outbreak in spinach swept the nation. California growers left entire fields of spinach unharvested, not because their crops were affected or suspected of being infected, but because prospects were bleak. "The market completely disappeared on spinach," Porter said. "Nobody was selling it."

As an aside, these outbreaks also lead to waste further down the food chain. I was working in the supermarket the day the *E. coli* news hit in 2006. We pulled all bags of spinach and salad mix with the potentially malevolent green. All told, I tossed 43 pounds of spinach in packages ranging from 5 to 9 ounces. And that was just at one store. Now consider that there are more than 35,000 supermarkets in the country.[12]

A similar story occurred two years later with the salmonella outbreak. When it first hit, officials identified tomatoes as the likely culprit, sending tomato sales tumbling. Then they weren't quite sure what was to blame, with onions and peppers cited as possible culprits. In the end, officials are pretty sure the contamination came from Serrano peppers in Mexico, although that's disputed. What's not debatable is that tomato sales, under the cloud of suspicion, took a dive. In June 2008, tomato sales plummeted 40 percent nationwide.[13] The United

Fresh Produce Association, the produce industry's leading trade association, estimated losses for U.S. tomato growers at $200 million.[14]

Health takes precedence over avoiding food waste, and the Food and Drug Administration (FDA) has a daunting responsibility to protect us all. Still, their incorrect judgment led to great losses of crops and income for tomato growers during what would have been their peak season. Tom Nassif, president and CEO of Western Growers, a cooperative association of farms in California and Arizona that produces about half of all produce grown in the United States, described the outbreak's effect on farmers to an interviewer from National Public Radio in July 2008: "Our folks are not harvesting; they're letting them rot on the vine or they're bulldozing plants in the fields in the hopes that they can plant something else that will let them recover some of the revenue that they've lost from tomatoes."

An even more frustrating problem than walk-bys is when crops are picked, but not sold. This kind of farm waste varies by region and crop. Sue Johnson-Langdon, director of the North Carolina Sweet Potato Commission, said that 25 to 30 percent of the sweet-potato crop isn't marketed. For many fruits and vegetables, an even higher percentage goes unsold. "Farmers, when they pick row crops like tomatoes, squash, green beans, zucchini, if they can sell 50 percent of what they farm, that's considered excellent," said Patricia Robbins at Farm Share.

In many farming operations, a significant amount of waste is unavoidable. It's simply a cost of doing business. That's especially true with strawberries. Think about how quickly strawberries go bad in your climate-controlled refrigerator and imagine what happens to them in a warm, sunny field. Then you'll have a decent idea of the scene at the self-pick strawberry patch operated by Vollmer Farm in Bunn, North Carolina. "They ripen quite fast from mid-May to late-May. That's when we get our glut," said John Vollmer, who owns the farm. "After Mother's Day, there is a definite tiredness of strawberries, and that's when we're coming into the peak growing season. If the fruit doesn't come off the plant, it creates a real mess out there. It's strawberry jam right in the field."

Vollmer invites gleaning groups to pick his excess crops partly because it aligns with his beliefs, but also because strawberry production will slow if the fruits aren't picked. "Any help we get from gleaners is helpful, rather than me paying for someone to pick it and dispose of it," Vollmer said.

What Commodity of Commodity Crops?

Walk-bys happen more frequently with hand-picked crops than with machine-gathered food, but they aren't unheard of with the latter. According to the National Agricultural Statistics Service (NASS), 57 percent of oats, 12 percent of wheat, and 9 percent of corn wasn't harvested in 2008.[15] And although labor for handpicked crops is certainly more expensive—it can account for as much as 65 percent of a farmer's total cost, said Johnson-Langdon—mechanical harvesting, too, has a price. Grain growers often have combine-harvester operators to pay, and should they own their own, it still takes plenty of time, effort, and diesel to power the machinery. These costs bring a hesitancy to harvest if the prices aren't there.

With commodity crops, much of the waste comes from storing the grains. According to 1974 Department of Agriculture data, storage losses amounted to 5 percent.[16] Today, the accepted loss estimate for grain storage is 5 to 10 percent, said Timothy Jones, the anthropologist who has been studying food waste for more than ten years. Spills accumulate throughout the process, from harvesting through the transfer of grain in and out of silos or storage bins. And the augers used to move grains crack a small amount of them, said Alan Baker, a USDA corn, oats, and barley specialist.

Storage losses are more common with corn than with most grains because it is harvested later in the year. Occasionally, that means that the corn will be too moist at the time it's stored. As I mentioned earlier, I don't consider weather-related loss to be true "waste." Unless, that is, it occurs as a result of farmers' decisions. Corn growers know that to prevent mold, they have to store their corn when it has a moisture content of about 15 percent. To achieve that, farmers have a choice: They can let the corn dry in the field, or they can harvest it a bit wetter than they'd like and use propane- or natural-gas-fueled bin dryers to get the corn to the right moisture level. There are consequences either way. Leaving the corn in the field too long could lead to greater loss if the weather turns. But the cost of using propane to dry crops is no mere drop in the bucket; it constitutes 5 percent of agriculture's energy use.[17]

Kevin Dhuyvetter, an extension farm management specialist in Kansas State University's Department of Agricultural Economics, explained the decision. "Field loss versus the cost of drying is what it boils down to," said Dhuyvetter. "With cost of propane and natural gas up, you'd rather not have to dry it yourself."

The choice reminds me of a corn-based conundrum many of us face: deciding when to press stop on a bag of microwave popcorn. In both scenarios, corn can be ruined if you get greedy and wait too long. So what do most growers do? They chance it by leaving their corn out longer. Dhuyvetter explained the rationale: "It's like gambling. Every year there's always that discussion. At what point are you better off harvesting and paying the cost of drying it than risk losing a whole bunch of your crop to weather? If people could predict the weather, it'd be a whole lot easier."

The stakes aren't all or nothing, though, as corn is hardy enough to withstand most cold weather. Some ears can even withstand the entire winter. Sometimes, as in North Dakota and Minnesota in the fall of 2008, they have no other choice. After a cold summer, many growers left their crop in the field to dry down. Yet, they faced an extremely wet fall that delayed field drying. In some cases, the corn was too wet for dryers, necessitating more waiting. Harvesting wasn't an option, as the growers didn't want to tear up their muddy fields. Then, in November, winter pounced on the northern plains, and it didn't leave until the spring thaw. At the end of November, when NASS performs its final harvest estimate for the year, more than 100,000 acres, or 30 percent of the crop, hadn't been harvested, said Earl Stabineau in the North Dakota NASS office.

Once the snow melted and the mud evaporated, farmers salvaged some, but not all, of the corn. During the winter, deer nibbled on it, and some stalks broke from the weight of the snow. Others sagged, "goosenecking" down near the ground while continuing to grow. When ears slump far enough, combines can't harvest them without risking picking up rocks, which can damage the million-dollar machines. As a result, a large amount of the harvest was lost—or wasted.

Unfortunately, we will never know how much of that remaining 30 percent made it through the winter.

NASS also conducts a survey in December, the end of the season, but it merely assesses whether farmers intended to harvest what is left out there, and almost everyone hopes to get what remains in the field. The 2008 harvest data therefore did not account for this truly "white corn" that had enjoyed the North Dakota winter. While the Peace Garden State growers who were not fortunate enough to harvest before November certainly felt the loss, their plight barely made a ripple in the reflecting pool of American agriculture. This kind of loss—resulting both from human decisions and the weather gods—is part of the farming landscape.

On-the-Farm Processing

Unharvested crops squander the financial and natural resources that go into growing a field, but at least the stuff left behind will be tilled into the soil, or "plowed under." While it seems unreasonable to leave perfectly edible food in the fields, "discing in" crops is better than harvesting them only to send them to a landfill because plowing under returns nutrients to the soil. Unfortunately, the increased demand for bagged and washed vegetables means that more food scraps are thrown away. While convenient, these "higher-value products" in effect shift the trim waste from households to the massive "grower/shippers," such as Earthbound Farms, Fresh Express, and Ocean Mist Farms in California's Salinas and Central Valleys. That's fine when grower/shippers find another use for these carrot peels and lettuce tops and bottoms, or compost them. Yet, when that doesn't happen, the local landfill is kept busy. The sheer concentration of trimmings and scraps is part of the problem, as with animal waste at livestock operations. Instead of a few outer leaves of lettuce in everyone's waste bin, compost pile, or garbage disposal, the local landfill gets a huge pile of green waste that will release methane when it "goes anaerobic."

The Salinas Valley Solid Waste Authority employs three drivers who do nothing but collect Dumpster loads of produce waste from producers. A grower/shipper may spend $15,000 to $20,000 per day in hauling and landfill fees, dumping eight or nine Dumpsters' worth of food waste. Each large grower may spend as much as $1 million on disposal costs for the nine-month growing season.

Edible vegetables end up at the same resting place as the scraps. Most of the pre-cut lettuce that is discarded consists of "overs" and "unders," greens that have been cut too big or too small. And then there are the factory miscues, such as the bags of salad mix and spinach that aren't cut by the sort line machine, leaving two or more bags connected. Given the speed of the operation and the labor costs, it's cheaper to toss both bags than to cut them by hand. Cesar Zuniga, field operations supervisor at the Sun Street Transfer Station in Salinas, where smaller loads of agricultural waste are brought to be sorted, said it isn't uncommon to see as many as ten interconnected bags in the trash.

Some higher-value produce is thrown away because of problems with bags' vacuum seal. And the fresh-cut industry's next level of offerings—including dips in snack-sized packs—faces more potential pitfalls. When some Chiquita Fruit Bites apple slices did not receive the accompanying portion of caramel dip, the whole batch ended up on the ground at the Sun Street Transfer Station, mingling with broken tiles, motor oil bottles, and rusty chairs.

"Ag waste keeps going up and up," said Zuniga, who has managed the Sun Street facility for thirteen years. "Salad processing just took off in the late '90s."

And processed produce makes grower/shippers more vigilant in inspecting and culling imperfections, because they have their name attached to their product and are keen to maintain their reputation. Selling unpackaged produce eases that pressure. All goods must meet certain standards, but they're higher for brand-stamped items. Ocean Mist's supervisor Art Barrientos voiced that ethic in explaining the company's modus operandi to a group visiting a lettuce field. "Anything that doesn't meet our measure of quality gets discarded," Barrientos said.

Finally, there are the so-called "sell-by" casualties. Knowing that they have to ship produce great distances, and that stores don't like to receive packaged produce less than a week before the sell-by date, manufacturers often throw away goods with as much as three weeks of life left in them. I wouldn't believe this waste inducer if I hadn't seen it myself with bags of spinach and lettuce at the Salinas waste transfer station.

Even though Zuniga's department depends on generating revenue from land-fill tipping fees, he'd prefer to see processors reduce their waste. "We like their money, but it's hard to permit a new landfill," Zuniga told me during a 2006 visit. Growers in Monterey County now send their waste elsewhere; Crazy Horse landfill closed in April 2009. While in operation, though, the Salinas dumping ground received about 200 tons of agricultural waste every day during the harvest season. In other words, area growers brought the equivalent of three M1 Abrams tanks daily to Crazy Horse—in vegetables! "We try to persuade them to cut waste, and they do it for a while, but then they go back to their old ways," Zuniga said. "I think they say, '$1 million, that's it?'"

On the opposite side of town from the Crazy Horse, I drove by a field of re-cently harvested romaine. I pulled over and had thoughts of hopping the irri-gation ditch to examine what was wrong with each head of lettuce (trespassing just to get a *look* has never seemed too malevolent to me). Then I noticed a man on a tractor pulling a tiller. I stayed and watched, mesmerized as the plow turned over both earth and lettuce. Ashes to ashes, lettuce to dust.

A Hooters in Raleigh, North Carolina, appeals to customers with the promise of hefty portion sizes.

PHOTO BY JONATHAN BLOOM

chapter 6

Waste on the Menu

Respect for food is a respect for life, for who we are and what we do.

—THOMAS KELLER, CHEF AT THE FRENCH LAUNDRY

lbany, California, came into being in 1908 when a group of shot-
gun-toting women halted the import of garbage from nearby
Berkeley. Apparently, the residents of Berkeley viewed their northern neighbors' unincorporated settlement as a dumping ground, which didn't
sit too well with those who lived in Albany. Before the incident, the Albany men
met to discuss their options. The women, still without a vote, took matters into
their own hands.

As horse-drawn garbage wagons approached what's now the intersection of
San Pablo and Buchanan, the women confronted the drivers with two shotguns
and a 22-caliber rifle.[1] The drivers—no fools—retreated back to Berkeley with
their garbage in tow. Emboldened by the women's defiance, the Albany residents incorporated their settlement shortly thereafter, making it an official city.
It's fitting, then, that less than a mile away, chef Aaron French today attempts
to prevent dumping in Albany. Only in his case, it's keeping food from being
thrown away at the Sunny Side Café.

French has created a menu with an eye on avoiding the food waste common
at most restaurants. For example, his breakfast and lunch café serves French
toast that's a bit thicker than usual. It's also round. The menu lists it as "Orange
French Toast made with poppy seed bread," but, upon questioning, French is
happy to divulge that customers are eating yesterday's hamburger buns.

Lest anyone get the wrong idea, these aren't generic, white burger rolls, but
locally baked, high-quality buns. French slices off a half-inch from the top and
bottom to allow the bread to soak up the batter, and, as I recall it, the dish
achieves a delicious, delicate flavor. Yet, when French began his bun-tastic tactic,
and it was clear that he was using rolls, customers complained about the French
toast's shape. "I think our culture teaches us—even in this day and age—that
reuse is somehow wrong or dirty. I'm not even sure they knew themselves why
they were making a big deal out of it," said French. "People equate newness
and freshness with being good. And something that's old with being bad, even
though with French toast, the fresher bread isn't as good. Dryness is better, especially when you're dipping it in batter and grilling it."

After some searching, French found a wooden griddle press to place atop the
buns—flattening them to look more like regular French toast. Après griddle
press, few customers really notice. "Aside from a few poppy seeds, you'd never

guess your orange French toast had been yesterday's hamburger bun," French said. "It's a little like French toast from Texas toast."

The idea of using old bread as French toast isn't revolutionary. After all, in France, the dish is called *pain perdu*—or lost bread. Perhaps a more apt name would be saved bread (*pain sauvé?*), as dipping it in eggs and then frying prevents the loaf from going for naught. Yet, as far as I know, the idea of using old hamburger buns to make this breakfast dish is original.

And the French toast is not the only measure chef French takes to minimize Sunny Side's food loss. Yesterday's baguettes become today's croutons, essential for the popular caesar salad. The café now offers fewer cheeses than it used to because French found that having so much variety led to waste. He can only order large amounts of cheese, and he found that he wasn't finishing most varieties before they became unusable. As a result, he's dropped goat cheese and mozzarella, leaving cheddar, jack, cream cheese, and Swiss. By limiting the selection, French has less cheese waste.

Also known by his nom de plume of "Eco-Chef," French writes a bi-weekly column for the *Oakland Tribune* and its network of newspapers on green eating. And he's the environment editor at the website Civil Eats. French's moniker stems from his college years at the University of California at San Diego (UCSD), where he cooked at the restaurant associated with a co-op in which he was a member. "The whole Eco-Chef thing comes from my time at the Ché Café. I was trying to get this anarchist punk vegan to recycle, and this dude said to me, 'What are you, some sort of eco-chef?'" French's peers meant the appellation as a derogatory term, but there was truth in it. While at UCSD, he spent a semester in Costa Rica, where he fell in love with the rain forest. After graduating, he did tropical field work around the globe for years as he worked toward a master's in ecology. In between biology jobs, French took cooking gigs to make money.

Yet, it wasn't until the mid-2000s that French began to see his old nickname in another light. "A couple years ago, I brought it back," French said. "People who knew me from before would say it's a good time to be an ecologist working in the food industry. A combination of a background in ecology and working with food went from being an oddity to being relevant. It's really serendipity. I don't claim to have planned that out."

French has, in fact, been "eco" since his young days growing up on a three-quarter-acre farm near Sacramento "when it wasn't cool like it is now" to be agrarian. He tended to rabbits, chickens, and vegetables as a boy, which gave him an appreciation for food. Living in remote cultures in Africa, Asia, and Latin America as a biologist furthered that appreciation. Avoiding food waste in his restaurant stems from his understanding of how our culinary choices affect the environment and animal populations.

French and his investors recently opened a second location in the former garbage-exporting hub of Berkeley, but he remains humble about his eco credentials. "In terms of the waste at the restaurant—I feel that most of what I do in that regard is common sense, or perhaps ancient wisdom—things that chefs a century ago wouldn't dream of NOT doing," French wrote in an e-mail. "Now, we have the option to be wasteful, and it takes a little extra work NOT to be, but I'm not reinventing the wheel, just looking back to the ways things were."

So why don't all restaurants find uses for yesterday's bread and strive to reduce their waste? Why would they knowingly throw out resources that cut into their bottom line twice, by increasing both their food costs and their waste-removal bill? Well, it's complicated.

Setting the Table

The quickest, but definitely not the easiest, way to assess the scale of restaurant food waste is to peek into an eatery's Dumpster at the end of the night. I'll spare you the smell, though, by providing a sense of just how prevalent food is in a restaurant's waste stream.

There are many estimates out there: Food can be anywhere from 30 to 70 percent of a restaurant's total waste stream.[2] Kevin Anderson, vice president of Missouri Organics, a Kansas City company that helps restaurants begin composting, said that the percentages varied so much because kitchens have different amounts of prep waste. Whether a restaurant receives boxes of shredded lettuce or whole heads makes a real difference. The same goes for ordering chicken breasts versus whole birds. When pressed for an estimate, though, Anderson said that food likely makes up 60 percent of the average sit-down restaurant's Dumpster contents. That also corresponds with the finding of WasteCap Wisconsin, a nonprofit group that helps Wisconsin companies reduce and recycle their solid waste, that 74 percent of restaurant waste is compostable. That includes food, paper, and cardboard, with the majority of the weight coming from food.[3]

There are two kinds of restaurant food waste. Kitchen waste includes foods prepared but not served, inventory casualties, and the inevitable "prep waste," or scraps. Fortunately, this waste source is largely in restaurant management's control and can be reduced or donated to food banks. The other restaurant waste stream comes from what diners don't finish. While this "plate waste" can't be donated, for obvious health-code reasons, it can be drastically reduced at most restaurants, as we'll discuss later.

The Center for Ecological Technology (CET) helps Massachusetts restaurants manage and minimize their waste. When its consultants talk with restaurant managers to give them an idea of how much they could save in reduced waste-hauling costs, they cite a half pound of waste per person per meal. It's just an estimate—and one that incorporates both kitchen and consumer waste—but Lorenzo Macaluso, a waste-management specialist at CET, has found it to be consistent across the restaurant continuum. "When I'm doing estimates for someone who's thinking of starting a composting program, that's where I start," said Macaluso of the half-pound-per-meal estimate. "Then I'll ask questions, like how they handle their vegetables. Do they buy peeled potatoes or trimmed lettuce? But I usually end up going with that half pound."

In 2002, when officials at the Massachusetts Department of Environmental Protection wanted to determine how much food waste all of the state's restaurants produced, they hired New Hampshire–based consulting firm Draper/Lennon to come up with an estimate. The firm used a formula to make this determination, multiplying the number of employees at each restaurant by 3,000 pounds per employee per year. In essence, the larger the restaurant, the more waste it would be expected to produce. A five-employee restaurant would theoretically produce 15,000 pounds per year. A ten-employee restaurant would create 30,000 pounds annually, or roughly three elephants' worth of waste.

Fast Food, Faster Waste

Today, few fast-food restaurants make unordered sandwiches simply to have them ready. Instead, they have all the parts prepared for quick assembly. These days, fast food is a little less so. At McDonald's, where I worked a register, the burgers and chicken patties and nuggets were cooked and then placed into neat little plastic drawers inside a heater unit. A card listed how long each item could sit before being served: an hour for the various chicken patties, 30 minutes for their squares of fish, and 20 minutes for nuggets and burgers.

The life span of French fries is even more fleeting. Fries are the mayflies of the food world, as a laminated card over the fryer station instructed that they could only sit for 7 minutes. The same card could be flipped over for the fried breakfast items—hash browns—which enjoy a 10-minute existence. Many customers feel that a fry that's anything but hot is unpleasant. I was surprised by how many of them indicated that they'd rather wait the 3 minutes and 7 seconds for the next batch than settle for the merely warm ones.

One evening while I was working, a middle-aged woman ordered two small fries and some other items. There were only enough fries for one order, which I scooped and placed under the keep-hot lights. When the new fries finished cooking, the manager bagged two new small fries and threw the older one in the trash right below the register. The manager said something about the fries being too cold. Not that he checked. Christine Andrews, food-safety director for the National Restaurant Association (NRA), told me that up to 10 percent of a fast-food restaurant's items are tossed because they've reached their time limit. The fast-food outlets that do still pre-make their sandwiches have a heavy waste toll. Textures and taste fade quickly, as buns get soggy, warm patties wilt the lettuce, and crispy fried items become less so.

Fast-food waste also stems from mistakes in ordering and order-taking. This can happen at any restaurant, but the sheer pace of the transaction and the muddled drive-thru audio make fast food more prone to these slip-ups. One evening, a friendly older woman amended her order after I'd already entered it into the system. By the time she decided she didn't want pickles or onions, her double burger was already made. So the first was tossed. My fellow burger-slingers could have opened the sandwich and removed these accoutrements, but that's not how they roll in the fast-food industry.

Mistakes at the register by yours truly, I'm sad to report, also led to waste. I'm sure I wasn't the first to mis-key orders, nor will I be the last. At one point, I pushed the button for a Grilled Chicken, instead of a Crispy Chicken, sandwich, which led to the demise of the former. I even wasted a decent amount of milkshake one night—a true shame—due to a sit-com-like caper of not knowing how to stop the vanilla flow (a co-worker told me it would turn itself off, which was not the case).

Preconsumer Kitchen Waste

We customers certainly waste plenty of food at restaurants. Yet, some food waste occurs without our help. Kitchen waste happens everywhere, no matter what chefs may say about their own establishments. The amounts vary greatly, though, depending on the chef and the restaurant. Also, it's worth noting that when restaurants order foods like peeled and sliced carrots, the trimmings from those items still exist, they've just become someone else's problem, further down the food chain.

As anyone who's seen the reality show *Hell's Kitchen* can attest, any toque-worthy chef knows waste is suicidal in the ultra-competitive restaurant business. Wasting food is one of the surest ways of keeping food costs high and running a restaurant out of business. Independent restaurants, where the line between success and failure is quite thin, are likely to be ultra-vigilant about waste (or at least they should be!). Fortunately, these independent operations make up less than half of the industry's sales.[4]

Even Berkeley's famed Chez Panisse, in no danger of folding, is conscious of the bottom line in avoiding waste. Yet, its employees also have some less pedestrian motivations for it. First, the use-it-all ethos of the French kitchen shuns waste. Second, waste is not sustainable in any sense of the word, as Chez Panisse Café sous chef Nathan Alderson explained: "We try not to waste because we do get such wonderful ingredients. They're all beautiful things." Yet, Alderson continued, "nobody wants to lose money. It's something that's definitely discussed in culinary school."

Chain restaurants, too, with their eyes increasingly on inefficiencies that affect the bottom line, have become more waste conscious, said Tom Miner, an analyst and principal at Technomic, the research and consulting firm that advises restaurants. "Food loss is always a business component," said Miner, who worked as a chef for fourteen years before spending the past fifteen years consulting. "Most restaurants are able to keep it at 2 to 3 percent of sales."

While Miner said restaurants are now better at avoiding food loss, it's important to note that kitchens aim to keep waste at only 2 to 3 percent of *sales*. That means they lose a greater percentage of their food *inventory*. When I asked Miner if there were some eateries that are less economical with their food, he replied, "Yes, but they don't stay in business very long."

Miner asserted another restaurant truism: The larger the menu, the larger the waste, as there are more ingredients to manage. By that logic, a hot-dog cart has it made. And In-N-Out Burger, where the only choices are how many patties and whether you want fries (okay, fine, and if you want your burger "Animal Style"), has an easy time maintaining its inventory. By contrast, The Cheesecake Factory doesn't do itself any favors by offering more than two hundred items.[5] This tactic—what I call the Cheesecake Corollary—is the opposite of Aaron French's strategy of fewer cheese choices on his menu. While most chains are more waste-conscious today than they used to be, they also face increased pressure to diversify their menus to provide "something for everyone."

And because they now face stiffer competition for customers' food dollars, many restaurants emphasize serving the freshest, prettiest, and tastiest entrées possible. That means there isn't much leeway with ingredients. "Most restaurants are not using the question of 'Is the food bad?' as an operating principle. Long before it becomes bad, it becomes not as competitive in flavor and texture as what they want to sell," Miner said.

When I asked Alderson, at Chez Panisse, if he had any suggestions for other restaurants, he had this simple advice: "Just buying what you're going to use. A lot of kitchens tend to buy too much."

Why would a restaurant purchase more food than it can use? A common reason is that the restaurant is new. Or there may be a new chef or manager, said Miner. "When there's a change in management, a lot of restaurants don't have a written trail on how much they're ordering," Miner said. "Often, the manager knows how much to order in their head. So when that manager leaves, sometimes they lose that knowledge."

Almost all of the top five hundred chains—about half the industry in dollar sales, according to Miner—harvest data from their point-of-sale systems. In that way, they can understand what's selling, what isn't, how much of certain items they need to produce, and, thus, how much they need to order. Of the remaining independents and small chains, only a quarter are doing that kind of data harvesting. That often leads to over-ordering, as the default amount is "plenty."

Plate Waste Aplenty

Those in the composting world call the stuff you and I leave behind at restaurants "plate waste." Anyone who's ever worked at a restaurant can attest to how much of it exists. Even though it had been more than ten years since he worked at a Ruby Tuesday in Birmingham, Alabama, Matt Knisley, a medical student I met while at the University of North Carolina, remembered just how much edible food he bused from tables there. In particular, he recalled being amazed by the number of diners who ordered a meal and either had just a few nibbles or didn't eat anything. "After a few weeks, I realized I was filling up a big trash can with food every hour," Knisley said. "It really struck me how much food was thrown away."

Brian Wansink, the director of the Cornell University Food and Brand Lab, found that diners leave an average of 17 percent of their meals uneaten. "Partly that's from the exaggerated serving sizes," Wansink said. "But you also get some unwanted side dishes. I wanted the pork chop, but got the cauliflower. Unfortunately, they get thrown away."

By contrast, letting diners choose exactly what items end up on their plates can trim restaurant waste. It's a simple concept: The more choice diners have in their meal, the fewer unwanted items they get. Hence, the less they'll leave uneaten. That's why French lets his customers pick their breakfast side: homefries, garlic-roasted tomatoes, vegetarian black beans, or a fruit cup. There's no sense in serving Brussels sprouts and parsnips alongside a steak if the customer doesn't like either. This tactic follows the example of that venerable southern tradition, "meat and three." In this culinary institution, the number connotes the quantity of deliciously unhealthy sides diners can pick.

In addition, there's a decent amount of uncertainty in many eating-out experiences. Unless we've been at the restaurant before, we're never quite sure how a dish will taste. We can pepper the waiter with questions, some of which might be answered adequately, but in the end, we're taking a chance, and sometimes, we're served a lot of something we turn out not to like. Unfortunately, we have little recourse here. There's no ice-cream-shop-style sampling at restaurants (Could I try a little of the pork shank?). At least none of the restaurant analysts or insiders I spoke with had ever heard of one.

Unclaimed Remains

Sarah Klepner, thirty-five, has spent her entire working life in food service, dating back to one day at a Burger King when she was fourteen ("I didn't like that job," she explained, deadpan). The Little Silver, New Jersey, resident moved on to a bagel shop, then a cafeteria while at Rutgers University, before graduating to a catering company and numerous other restaurants and settling at a New Jersey diner for three and a half years. She stopped working at the River's Edge Café in June 2009, but the amounts of food served and wasted there were fresh in her mind when we spoke a few months later.

At the "glorified diner," as Klepner called it, the amount of food served was comical—and sad. "The portions were massive. They were f'n massive," said Klepner. "That was how the prices were justified. A $10 omelet has to be pretty big."

Klepner recalled that the largest item on the menu, the round farmer's omelet, was about a foot across. "It was significantly larger than a Frisbee. Oftentimes, half of that would go in the garbage," said Klepner, who grew tired of tossing so much food. "I threw out enough food every day to feed a village. It drove me nuts that all this compost material went in the garbage."

Then again, Klepner didn't toss everything. The restaurant was mostly a breakfast/lunch joint, but served dinner Friday and Saturday nights. At those meals, servers brought a basket containing a half loaf of semolina bread about 8 to 10 inches long to each table. Diners left so much bread uneaten that, in addition to snacking on it during her shift, Klepner took some home and made bread pudding. The owner knew the staff saved bread because he would see them put it aside, and he didn't mind, partly because Klepner was shrewd enough to share some of her repurposed dessert with him.

Yet, the owner didn't approve of waiters eating the remains from diners' plates. Klepner calls this tactic "table diving," a play on the related art of Dumpster diving. In theory, waiters were supposed to buy food if they wanted to eat while working. But in practice, Klepner and a few co-workers would munch on diners' lunch and dinner remains or wrap them for later. "It was definitely something I didn't flaunt, but I'd eat uneaten food," Klepner said. "If there was a half of a sandwich, I'd eat it. If there was some salad, I'd go for that, too."

Klepner and her co-workers could even be quite selective in their table-diving because the restaurant's generous helpings meant most plates came back with plenty on them. She chuckled as she recalled an event that occurred toward the end of her days working at the café. An older woman asked to have a word with the owner, as she found the huge portions offensive. They came to an agreement—the owner was happy to serve the woman a smaller portion while allowing her to pay the full fare.

Out of Proportion

Jason Bissey is the head chef at Rue Cler, an independent bistro in Durham, North Carolina. Before that, though, he worked at an Italian restaurant—not a chain—where even the kitchen staff made fun of the portion sizes. "The joke motto at the restaurant I used to work at was, 'It might not be that good, but we give you a lot of it,'" Bissey said.

After scanning our food landscape, I've found that the same saying could be used at many a restaurant. A single entrée at some establishments pushes the limits of the *daily* recommended caloric intake. At 1,990 calories, Chili's Crispy Chicken Crisper Tacos just about fulfills the daily energy needs for most men and women.[6] No matter what you order, a three-course meal at Romano's Macaroni Grill is almost certain to top 2,000 calories. Choosing the chicken parmesan and New York cheesecake with caramel fudge sauce, though, would put you at an unfathomable 3,250 calories.

Maggiano's doesn't even list nutritional information and declined to provide it when I e-mailed the company's media contact. "Don't ask, don't tell" seems to be the policy at many restaurants when they're not required to disclose their meals' calorie information. They don't want to tell us the truth, and frankly, we often don't want to know.[7] With these calorically dense meals, the amount of "plate waste" really piles up.

Nutritionist Lisa Young's book *The Portion Teller* includes a fascinating appendix: a series of food-size-inflation time lines, tracing the always-expanding arc of the pizza and the concurrent growth of the candy bar, the French fry container, the hamburger, and the soda. McDonald's large fries, added to the menu in 1972, were 3.5 ounces. Today's large is 6.3 ounces.[8] In 2002, Jack in the Box beefed up its burgers by 66 percent without raising prices. Indeed, burger names at some fast-food chains are comically appalling: There's McDonald's Mega Mac, Burger King's Meaty-Cheesy-Bacony X-Treme Whopper, McDonald's defunct Big Xtra, and, at Sizzler, the—wait for it—Bigger, Better Burger.

Today's portions dwarf recommended serving sizes. In other words, we're eating too much—way too much. But what exactly is the difference between those two terms, portions and servings? Portions are what you put on your plate. Servings are a standard unit of measure and the amount the USDA recommends that you eat in one sitting. For example, nutritionists recommend eating a serving size of fish or meat, which is 3 ounces, or about the size of a deck of cards or the palm of a hand (yours, not Sasquatch's). Yet, so many restaurants serve Sasquatch-sized portions that you'd have a better chance of finding an actual deck of cards on the menu than a 3-ounce steak.

It's no shock that restaurants, where food is meant to be enjoyed, don't follow the letter of cardiology law. Yet, the degree to which they flout the prevailing wisdom is surprising (and saddening). Meanwhile, as we eat out more often, we're getting heavier and heavier. And chefs, if they're to be taken at their word, are blissfully unaware of their role in the problem. A 2007 study published in *Obesity*, a research journal affiliated with the Obesity Society, found that "although the majority of chefs (76 percent) thought their restaurant served 'regular' portions, when asked for specifics on certain foods (pasta and steak), the portions they reported were 2 to 4 times greater than are recommended in the US Dietary Guidelines."[9]

A Packed Restaurant (Landscape)

Why are portions so large? In a word: competition. The seeds of today's 1,500-calorie entrées were sown in the 1970s. As fast-food eateries flooded the nation, getting a cheap, quick meal became easy.[10] In the battle for customers, upping the amount served while only slightly increasing prices helped franchises gain attention. Later, larger portions were reactions against the "petit chic" dining scene of the late 1980s, when the nouvelle cuisine trend was fashionable. Back then, "you had a 12-inch plate with food you had to look for," said Rupert Spies, senior lecturer at the Cornell School of Hotel Administration.

The petit chic trend didn't last long because, as the economy soured in the early 1990s, value had become diners' priority. Restaurants found that larger portion sizes were a way to distinguish themselves.[11] And that has only continued. "It's a competitive environment," said Brian Wansink, director of the Cornell Food and Brand Lab. "There are lots of chains like Friday's, Chili's and O'Charley's that aren't tremendously differentiated except in value. Increasing portion sizes is a way to ask for more money in a competitive market because it's perceived as a better value."

That competition has prompted the restaurant-industry's version of an arms race. As in the Cold War, "mutually assured destruction" is the threat. But in this case the destruction—of our health—is actually occurring. And the economic downturn in the late 2000s has created an even more cutthroat restaurant landscape. The only way restaurants have been able to raise prices without losing customers has been to add more food to the plate. "There are certain costs you have to absorb to stay in business," Spies said. "One of those is having larger portions in order to compete with other businesses. Consumers expect that these days."

It's no surprise that we value volume. We're seduced by the "good deal" of large portions, even if we don't eat everything. Why buy the Gulp at 7-Eleven at 5 cents per ounce when you can buy the Big Gulp for 2.7 cents per ounce?[12] A 12-inch tuna sub at Subway is 100 percent larger than a six-incher, for only 47 percent more money.[13] Of course, as many a nutritionist has written, overeating and the resulting health problems it creates make these meals anything but a good deal.

There have always been establishments that have traded on the "bigger is better" or "more for less" motto (I'm looking right at you, Sizzler). The Cheesecake Factory, where eating one of their salads is like swimming against a strong tide, fulfills the former. Subway's $5 Footlong is ingenious in its ability to connote plenty and price in three words and ten characters. But forget 12 inches, how about 20? In downtown Boston, Al Capone's—home of the 20-inch sub, according to its literature—serves subs that size for about $9. There is a wrap option for about $7, but diners who want a sandwich have to order one as hefty as Al Capone's tax debt. And these giants are "normal" menu items, not a "we'll take your picture and give you a T-shirt if you finish it" side show.

How much can food retailers be blamed for the abundant waste in our nation's eateries? Well, today's giant portions leave us this choice: Overeat, waste food, or take the leftovers home. The third option is the obvious winner, but there are some occasions when taking leftovers home isn't possible. Perhaps we're traveling and have no refrigerator, or are not going straight home afterward. And some people just plain dislike leftovers. In those scenarios it's overeat or waste. Harm yourself or the environment. It's an unsustainable choice either way.

What can restaurateurs of all stripes do to reduce waste? In the short term, they can offer the choice of smaller portions. Allowing diners a bit of customization through portion sizes, providing at least the option of a sensibly sized meal will make diners and Dumpsters lighter and happier. As someone who enjoys eating, rest assured that I'm not proposing a return to the days of avant garde, sparse entrées. I'd settle for ones that don't weigh 2 pounds or have more than 1,500 calories. Since we love a good deal, the majority of us aren't going to accept a smaller meal for the same price, even if it comes served on a green plate with an accompanying "low carbon foodprint" sticker. A better plan is less for less.

A Small Idea

In March 2007, T.G.I. Friday's scaled down entrées and prices with its Right Portion, Right Price menu. Serving about two-thirds of an entrée for two-thirds the regular price proved so profitable that the chain made the promotion permanent a year later, said Amy Freshwater, vice president of corporate communications at Carlson Restaurants Worldwide, Friday's' parent company. "We consider the Right Portion, Right Price menu options to be wildly successful," Freshwater told me in an e-mail.

While the privately owned company wouldn't reveal specifics, it did say in a press release that in the promotion's first year, guest counts surpassed the industry average. To the restaurant's surprise, the average check "has also increased, due in part to the increase in appetizer and dessert sales," the company wrote in a press release.[14] That's important, as appetizers and desserts tend to be high-margin items, said Mat Mandeltort, another Technomic restaurant analyst. In addition, cheaper meals lure in the harder-to-get weeknight clientele.

In hindsight, the factors pointing to the success of "Right Portion" seem obvious. Especially given Brian Wansink's finding that diners don't notice when they're served as much as 20 percent less food.[15] Yet, the move was seen as a calculated gamble when it was launched. Ruby Tuesday's, which introduced smaller portions and began posting nutritional information in 2004, wasn't as lucky, and its promotion only lasted five months.[16] Healthy wasn't selling.

The timing was right for Friday's. The chain's leadership learned from customer surveys that a majority of people didn't want to bother with leftovers. The idea of paying a decent price to get an indecent amount of food was starting to lose its appeal. Those sentiments, combined with an increased emphasis on eating healthily—by not overeating—told Friday's' execs that they had an opportunity. "Research, independent and our own, suggested that the consumer was asking for this," said Freshwater. "There was one survey that received our attention: that 51 percent of respondents in a *Restaurants & Institutions* poll said portion sizes were too big. But there were also 49 percent who didn't feel that way. For us, it was about giving our guests a choice."

While the decision to launch the Right Portion, Right Price menu was revenue-driven, reduced waste has been a nice by-product. Missy Pizzonia has waited tables at T.G.I. Friday's for two years, both in Boston and Los Angeles. She told me that people ordering from the Right Portion menu seldom leave leftovers. Pizzonia, twenty-one, who now works at the Woodland Hills, California, location, estimated that almost half of her customers order from the Right Portion options.

Downsizing

Thanks to Friday's' success, the idea of "less for less" is spreading. "More and more operators in full service are offering the option of smaller portions. Smaller portions and less out of pocket," said Technomic's Mandeltort.

The sluggish economy has helped, but the way the idea is starting to be picked up by other chains is mostly a result of that restaurant-industry constant—mimicry.

"If other places have it, you need to have it," Mandeltort said. "That's why every-one offers the same thing."

"You're starting to see restaurants cutting back a bit on portions, not neces-sarily for health reasons—but to try to avoid the veto," Mandeltort said. "They don't want to lose an entire family if one person in the car objects. So you need to offer a small plate for when mom isn't hungry."

Eat'n Park may have the order of operations mixed up, but it seems to have its portion sizes moving in the right direction. The roadside restaurant chain debuted its self-explanatory "smaller portions at smaller prices" promotion in March 2008.[17] That same month, Au Bon Pain launched a new food line called Portions. The small plates—all with fewer than 200 calories—and available half sandwiches allow customers to mix and match their size and flavors, said Thomas John, Au Bon Pain's executive vice president of food and beverage. "I'm against telling customers that this is what the portion is, and if you can't eat it, pack it up or throw it away," John told me. "Our main effort was to give that flexibility, that choice to the customer."

Thankfully, Maggiano's Little Italy also offers scaled-down versions of its main entrées for less dough. And Buca di Beppo, a Minnesota-based chain, does the same. They list Buca Small and Buca Large options for all menu items, in-cluding sides, entrées, pastas, antipasti, salads, and—anticlimactically—pizzas. Sadly, the only thing Buca di Beppo restaurants don't offer smaller versions of is its desserts. That's unfortunate for diners' waists, but not for the restau-rants' waste, because we all know it's physically impossible to leave a dessert uneaten, and diners often share desserts anyway. As my brother Seth hypoth-esized when he was twelve, humans (or is it just Americans?) have a separate dessert stomach to fill, unaffected by how much we've consumed during the meal.

Even The Cheesecake Factory, that sultan of super-size, has launched a line of smaller plates. Of course, it being The Cheesecake Factory, these "small" plates aren't exactly microscopic. "It's a great value for folks who may not have as much money to dine out as they used to," Mark Mears, chief of marketing, told Reuters. "At the Cheesecake Factory, we don't really do anything small, so the portion sizes are actually pretty generous."[18]

Servings Sized Up

There's a thin line between serving too much and not enough. And it's one that Aaron French, the Eco-Chef at the Sunny Side Café, understands, both as an ecologist and an eater. "I've always been a big eater and I hate leaving a breakfast hungry," French told me. "I always found it a little insulting to get small portions, but there's that balance of giving enough that people are happy and not giving too much."

French has a novel approach. He cut the portion size of his homefries, but essentially has instituted free refills. The menu spells out the policy in the Low Carbon Efforts section: "To reduce food waste, we have reduced our standard portion of homefries. *Please ask your server for more complementary fries if you like.*"

This enlightened approach requires restaurateurs to trust that their customers won't abuse the privilege. Yet, French said fewer than a dozen diners per week ask for seconds. And he believes he's found that hard-to-achieve balance in how much he dishes out. "We adjusted—I was overdoing it, so I gave less," French said. "The people who asked for more were stoked because they're getting a good deal."

In addition to the motivation of matching their competition, restaurants serve copious amounts partly because they think we want it that way. In a 2007 study, researchers asked three hundred chefs what factors influenced portion sizes in their restaurants. The most important factor was the presentation—chefs want what they serve to appear generous.[19] Second was customer expectation, as 88 percent of chefs reported being affected by our anticipation of a whole lot of food. And they're right, to a certain extent. To our detriment, most of us do expect to be served more food than we'd care to eat. And so we are.

A typical restaurant meal has at least 60 percent more calories than the average home-cooked meal, according to the NPD Group, a market research firm.[20] Partly, that's because of restaurant food generally being less healthy, with more calories coming from fat and sugar. But it's also due to the sheer volume of food included in the meals. It's safe to say that we would prefer more to less, if the price was the same. But getting served an abundance of food isn't as important as chefs may think. A 2009 Technomic survey assessing "Consumers' Concept of Value at Restaurants" found that portion size was the least important factor, below price of meal, quality of items, and overall experience. So give us a little credit, chefs! Help us help ourselves by serving less food for less money.

Which Came First—the Portions or the Plates?

There's no chicken-and-egg conundrum with oversized plates and portions. Neither came first, said Brian Wansink. "They kind of happened parallel."

Even if we can't entirely blame portion sizes on them, today's restaurant plates—like our home versions—are just plain big. The average diameter of the ten best-selling round dinner plates on Amazon.com in August 2009 was 10.45 inches.[21] At Durham's Rue Cler, chef Jason Bissey uses 12-inch dinner plates. And chefs sure like to fill those plates. Bissey, in his cut-off camouflage cargo pants and blue T-shirt, told me how the restaurant fills up the plate to the band around the edge for entrées that aren't part of the prix fixe menu. "We're pretty generous with things here," Bissey said while enjoying a post-shift beer.

The aforementioned finding that 76 percent of chefs think they dish out "regular" portions may have something to do with how that menu item looks when served on today's Frisbee-sized plates. Yet, the chefs are right. Unfortunately, these giant portions have become normal. As with most things food- and psychology-related, Wansink has us covered. In one study, he tested small plates against big ones in a Chinese buffet setting. Diners who took large plates (10 inches) served themselves an average of 52 percent more food and wasted 135 percent more than those who selected smaller plates.[22] Those large-plate-takers wasted 14 percent of what they selected.

All You Can Waste

Plate size isn't the problem at Golden Corral—the national buffet chain has reasonable-sized crockery, but an excessive variety of offerings. I visited a Golden Corral near my home to get a firsthand look at the array of items. Upon entering the Durham restaurant, which is located across a massive parking lot from

Sam's Club and Target, I expected a sizable number of options. Yet, I wasn't prepared for six kinds of fried seafood and seven varieties of chicken.

The buffet stretched more than 100 feet, from The Greenhouse (the salad bar) to The Grillhouse (which had steaks and other proteins wrapped in bacon) to the Chocolate Fixation Station (an inaccuracy, as it satisfied all kinds of cravings). I counted 81 hot-bar choices, not including sauces and condiments. And then there were 52 salad-bar items and 29 dessert choices. To be fair, Golden Corral is not alone in offering that wide of a selection.

Predictably, the abundance on display prompted some poor choices. I tried to be disciplined, but I found it difficult to exercise restraint. In my first go-round, I filled my plate with fried tilapia, fried catfish, turnip greens, broccoli, a lasagna slice, baked carrots, cornbread stuffing, and a giant cheese biscuit. What was I thinking? Partly, I wasn't. I was just following my (misguided) instincts, as I had recently enjoyed these same foods at other, better restaurants. Or maybe I just have less restraint than most. Then again, my fellow "researcher" Matt selected a steak we both knew was a bad idea.

In addition to variety, the sheer limitlessness of the food makes it seem less valuable. We're much more likely to waste a piece of lukewarm *naan* at an Indian restaurant if we know there's a steaming canister of them on the buffet. Yet, if you'd ordered it from the menu at an extra cost, you'd be more likely to eat that lovely Indian bread.

The all-you-can-eat policy at buffets almost dooms us to waste food. The one-size-fits-all price incentivizes us to overeat so we feel we've gotten our money's worth. We take too much, then can't eat it all. In addition, buffets prompt the machine-gun method of food selection, where we try a little of everything. Bourbon chicken or teriyaki? Yes. As a result, we often wind up with plenty on our plates that doesn't suit our fancy, and we leave it for the waiter to clear. And because most eateries require a clean plate for every trip to the buffet, our slates are wiped clean with every return to the spread.

In addition to the between-rounds plate waste, there's the final-round squandering. Since few buffets allow you to take anything home, the food left when we call it quits is trashed. Some all-you-can-eat sushi restaurants, especially in Hong Kong and elsewhere in Asia, charge a penalty for leaving uneaten rolls.

The Nigerian restaurant Obalende Suya Express London charges a £2.50 fee for unfinished food, which the restaurant then donates to Oxfam. But in America, we deem it our right to waste. That's part of the reason Chinese buffets, Golden Corrals, and Sizzlers are so popular.

When I finally waved the white flag at Golden Corral, I had a cookie, a brownie, and some peach cobbler left on my plate. I was pretty sure what he'd say, but I decided to ask my waiter if I could have a box to take the desserts home. He said I could if I wanted to pay the $5.39 per pound take-out charge. He apologized, but said that otherwise customers would take advantage of the situation and load up their last plate. That makes perfect sense, but it's hard to accept a rule that results in so many items ending up in the trash.

My waiter also suggested that I could covertly wrap my cookie in a napkin, which, of course, I had already planned to do. But that doesn't work so well when your remains are candied yams or even cobbler. Given the impending dumping of these foods, it's tempting to sneak in a container to "liberate" foods toward the end of the night. Really tempting. So tempting that I may or may not have rescued some cut fruit on my next (and final) visit.

All Items at All Times

In addition to customers' excess, buffet waste comes from the hot bar itself. More specifically, from the compulsion to constantly restock the buffet and keep it full until closing time. The sheer act of having everything ready, as opposed to cooking foods to order, leads to waste. Any buffet worth its steam table regularly swaps out entrées and veggies that are reaching (or have long ago reached) the wrong texture. And buffets must be ready for that primal fear—a busload of customers near closing time. The need to keep the buffet filled even though the evening and the crowd is winding down yields waste at the end of the night.

I went to Golden Corral near closing time to see how the staff handled the hot-bar refilling toward the end of the night. At 9:10—less than an hour before the 10:00 closing—the grill guy finished cooking a teriyaki chicken batch. At 9:28, a cook refilled the corn on the cob. When I left at 10:15, a quarter of an hour after the official closing time, the buffet really didn't look much different from the way it looked when I'd entered at 8:40, except for the fact that someone was cleaning the chrome exhaust hood above the grill. I knew that none of the food left in the trays would be donated to food banks because, for health-code reasons, that's not allowed for food from open buffets. (You know those sneeze guards? They're not 100 percent effective.)

I asked the manager about their end-of-day practices and he said that while they might reuse some salad bar items that hadn't been sliced or cut, all the hot foods are thrown away. On that night, that included a whole cheese pizza, seven chicken breasts wrapped in bacon, six slices of lasagna, eight baked potatoes, thirteen Salisbury steak servings, and eleven fried chicken breasts. There were full trays of pot roast, mac and cheese, beef tips, broccoli, beef taco filling, tempura vegetables, and fried tilapia.

A Different Approach

Casey's Diner is a yellow boxcar that's 10 feet wide and 20 feet long. There's a large storage area added onto the back, but all of the eating and cooking takes place in those 200 square feet. There are ten stools at the counter; everyone else is forced to hover at one of the ledges in the rear or use the take-out window on the east end. The diner sits one street back from the main drag in suburban Natick, Massachusetts. You have to know it's there to find it, and once you do, you'll be pleased.

I grew up in the neighboring town and became familiar with the practices and patois of the place. For instance, when new customers enter, the ones already at the counter are expected to slide over if it helps the entering party sit together. Once seated, it's time to order a few franks, but only a rookie calls them anything but "dogs." You probably want your dogs "all-around," with ketchup, mustard, relish, and onions. And if you have your heart set on one or three of those delightfully steamed, yet crisp wieners, don't arrive too late. Casey's doesn't close until 8 P.M., but they sometimes sell out of hot dogs before then because the management would rather run out of food than freeze it. In fact, the diner doesn't even have a freezer. Casey's receives shipments every few days, ordering just about enough, but never more, to ensure peak taste. This tactic ensures freshness and prevents waste, which as a shoestring operation, they can't really afford.

This strategy wouldn't fly at many restaurants. Can you imagine going to order at Chili's or Red Robin and being told that they were out of burgers? It's almost inconceivable. That's partly because chain restaurants value perpetual availability at the expense of, among other things, heightened waste. Indeed, Au Bon Pain permits its stores to have $80 worth of leftovers (at inventory cost) each day to ensure that there are some items on the shelf up until closing.[23]

It's easier for independent, artisanal eateries to get away with running out of items than it is for chain restaurants, where customers expect the standard menu items to be available. Take Crook's Corner, a new South meets old South institution in Chapel Hill, North Carolina, for example. Bill Smith, the James Beard Award–nominated chef orders his ingredients the way Casey's does. "I sort of try to run out of things on Sunday night," said Smith. "I don't mind running out of things Sunday because we're closed Monday. Our menu changes every day, so I feel perfectly justified to say 'You should have come earlier.' Of course, a chain restaurant, for example, can't do that."

Aaron French has a similar strategy, albeit for a brunch- and lunch-oriented time frame. "When I have special items that are time-sensitive, I prefer to run out in the afternoon," French said. "If we run out at 2 when we close at 3, that's when I'm the happiest. That's when I know I've ordered right. If you come the last hour, you might just be out of luck."

Part of ordering accurately comes from knowing how many guests you'll have and what they'll order. That's easy at a place like Chez Panisse, which has a set menu and a static level of business—full. Just about every night, one hundred diners file into the cozy bistro for four courses of predetermined local cuisine. For their à la carte lunches, the restaurant's nearly forty years of experience helps the kitchen forecast how much food to purchase.

Most restaurants have a much harder time predicting demand than Chez Panisse. Many establishments have software to track trends across the years and seasons, but the sheer number of variables makes it tricky to accurately predict the volume of business. The economy, the traffic, the weather, and whether the home team wins all affect how many customers will show up. Some chefs, like Crook's Corner's Smith, go more by feel. "We have a pretty good sense of the number of customers we'll have. People ask me how I know and I'm not sure," said Smith. "I just do."

French has had a harder time figuring out demand at the Sunny Side Café. But that might be because he is determined to order as accurately as possible to trim his waste. "As with many places, we see a wild fluctuation in our customer base week to week. I can predict about 80 percent of the business flow, but that last 20 percent is what produces the waste," French e-mailed. "I have to be ready for the rushes that we get, but don't want to over-prep. So it's constantly a balancing act."

Left with Options

Predicting demand takes on greater or lesser importance depending on how restaurants handle their excess. Having extra food leaves a kitchen with some choices: re-serve the item, reuse it in another way, serve it to staff, donate it, compost it, or throw it away. The easiest path is the first option. There are certain items that can be served again the next day without a noticeable deterioration in quality. Soups, stews, casseroles, and meatloaf top that list. While Bissey was showing me Rue Cler's walk-in, a metal canister of soup with cling wrap caught my eye. The wrap had "Pot. Mushroom Soup 8-14" written on it. It was August 15, and Bissey said they planned to serve the soup for at least two more nights. He said they usually serve a soup for four days, just heating up enough of the batch for that night. "If you had to make soup every day, you'd go crazy," Bissey said.

Yet, most restaurants steer clear of re-serving food out of a sometimes-misguided concern for quality. They know that customers don't pay top dollar for leftover food. And there are no bakery-style "day-old" discounts in the restaurant world (at least until I launch my gastronomical empire). Chains, in particular, don't even reuse foods that could easily be served two or three days in a row. Maria Caranfa tracks the activities of more than six hundred restaurants for Mintel, a market research firm. She told me that one trend precludes another. "We've seen a really large increase in restaurants offering fresh foods. So it's not very advantageous for restaurants to tell diners they're serving yesterday's food," said Caranfa, director of Mintel Menu Insights. "You don't want to go into a restaurant and find out that they're re-serving yesterday's soup."

That leaves repurposing, a time-honored strategy with many applications. As Aaron French's French toast example shows, bread can be used in countless other ways, from panzanella to stuffing to bread pudding. While croutons and bread crumbs may be mundane, they're easy—the no-brainers of bread repurposing. Chicken has its own progression, from fresh-cooked to chicken salad to casseroles and soups.

Leftover proteins make nice additions to meatloaf and meatballs, a tactic perfected at San Francisco's A16. In what it calls Meatball Mondays, the Marina neighborhood Italian restaurant uses leftover prosciutto scraps and whatever else it has around to form the savory spheres. Most weeks, the meatballs include beef scraps, too, and they've also used duck, chicken, and lamb, chef Lily Shaw told me. The meatballs are only made once a week, so the staff stores up the scraps and trimmings for that day.

Shaw noted that A16 uses a 60/40 meat-to-bread ratio, which is more typical of the true Italian recipe for *polpettone*. That recipe not only helps the restaurant use up its old bread, then, but also stretches the meat. Shaw, who also mentioned that she uses day-old bread to make the restaurant's crostini and bruschetta, said that the Americanization of meatballs usually means, you guessed it, too much meat.

Unfortunately, repurposing, like reusing, is rarely seen at chain restaurants. Again, it's because they want customers to receive the freshest and tastiest food possible. Au Bon Pain's Thomas John told me that the chain doesn't repurpose or reuse anything the next day. That includes soups and baked goods, although the restaurant does sell the latter for half-price an hour before closing and tries to donate the remainders to food banks.

Another reason repurposing isn't common at chains is that it requires a certain amount of knowhow. Chances are, a kitchen with a cook wastes more than one with a chef. Rue Cler's Bissey washed dishes at a Denny's when he was in college. Reflecting back on his experience there, he couldn't believe how much they threw out. He attributed most of the waste to inflexibility. "If you're at Denny's, even if you're the kitchen manager, you're not making decisions about how much food to make," Bissey said. "At a Denny's, you're never allowed to run out of things."

At chains, the old "err on the side of caution" dynamic trumps the tailored approach. Although most chains have demand-predicting software, many of their managers are so new they may not be able to glean insights and act upon them. Inflexibility, whether from ignorance or powerlessness, spelled waste at the Denny's in Columbia, Missouri, where Bissey worked. "They wasted a terrible amount of food, mostly because they had systems that weren't malleable," Bissey said. "They prepared the same amount every night and they had to throw out things if they sat too long."

From one perspective, it's not hard to see why chains don't repurpose. They're running publicly traded companies that can't take chances on variables such as the skill or creativity of individual chefs. And their promise of uniformity precludes improvisation. A steak fajita at Applebee's not only has to taste great, it has to be the same in Anchorage and Albany.

Most of all, repurposing requires menu flexibility, which most chain restaurants lack. The majority of chains serve the same food every day and thus don't have the option of creating an entrée to use up excess food. Specials are rare, and when they happen, they're planned well in advance by headquarters and often done to test a potential menu item, said Caranfa. Chains just aren't as nimble as independent operations. New menu items take months of development— from board meetings to test-kitchen tinkering to focus groups to more tinkering. They certainly don't come from epiphanies had while peering into the walk-in fridge for ingredients and inspiration.

Menus à la Minute

While the downstairs bistro at Chez Panisse publishes its set menus a week in advance, the newer Chez Panisse Café upstairs is much more improvisational. In fact, when I met with Nathan Alderson after lunch, he hadn't yet written the menu for the next day. He said that he usually finishes it in the middle of dinner. "The meat is planned in advance, but otherwise I write the menu based on what we have. We put out more advanced copies of the menu, but that's more a rough guide."

The Tuesday I visited, the lunch salad featured rabbit shoulder that had appeared on the dinner menu on Saturday evening. The kitchen staff had preserved the meat by cooking it in fat (a confit). The restaurant is closed on Sundays, and that Monday had been Labor Day, but the rabbit waited patiently until Tuesday to become "Escarole with Devil's Gulch Ranch Rabbit."

Back East, when I had the privilege of browsing the walk-in fridge at Rue Cler, I asked Bissey what he saw when he opened its door. "I see a bunch of bundles of money with clocks. As the clock ticks, the value decreases," Bissey said. "Some of those clocks have a lot of time on them, some don't."

I asked Bissey to show me an example of repurposing in action. Peering out from underneath his University of Illinois cap at the ticking bundles, he found an ideal one: a mostly full tray of mashed potatoes from the previous night. The tray would have looked at home on any buffet line, but Rue Cler wouldn't serve them again, Bissey said, because reheated mashed potatoes get "gluey." After a bit of earlier brainstorming, he had decided to prepare a play on shepherd's pie. He planned to shape the starch into flattened cakes coated in Japanese bread crumbs, deep fry them, and place the results atop short ribs braised in a sauce of bacon, herbs, and *mirepoix* (chopped onions, celery, and carrots). Beat that, Denny's!

In another example of flexibility, the potato mushroom soup I saw in the walk-in got its start when Bissey saw a remaining canister of grilled mushrooms that had accompanied a braised pork entrée. Repurposing matches the cuisine at Rue Cler. "Rustic French cooking or French country cooking—the entire concept of it is frugality, really. You can take any dish and, at its core, it's about saving food," Bissey said. "Now, the great chefs know how to cook offal. But it used to be a peasant thing. That's what's fun—you're taking a whole history of frugality and turning it into something people will seek out."

Yet, knowhow and reuse aren't specific to French cuisine. At the Sunny Side Café, odds and ends go into omelets, but more often into specials. When I visited, French showed me the contents of his walk-in fridge, which is so tiny it's almost a misnomer. He wanted to see what perishables were calling out to be cooked. "Specials are a way to use up what I have. For example, now I have a little okra and some asparagus," French said, rooting around a bit. "These Mirabella eggplants. A small amount of lobster mushrooms. It'll be a great weekend to have a nice hash on the menu. I'll call it the East Bay Hash or something."

I asked Bissey what chefs call this practice of making specials from what remains. Borrowing my term out of necessity, he said, "Repurposing is so innate to the job there isn't really a word for it. We might say 'work it in.' But that's what we do. . . . If you're throwing away a lot of food, you're not doing your job."

Leftover Logic

When I was a kid, we always took home leftovers. The reason was simple: Why wouldn't you?! We'd paid for the food, so throwing it out seemed silly. And the food would make a great meal the next day. That's why I found it so illogical when I first heard someone say they didn't like leftovers.

When I visited the Hale family of Carrboro, North Carolina, to observe their eating habits, the father, Mike Hale, told me, "You can't save Mexican leftovers because they're no good the next day." As I scribbled down his words I looked at him like he had two heads—neither of them sensible. I gradually learned that Mike's opinion wasn't all that uncommon. Many people have either universal or cuisine-specific leftover biases.

Cornell's Brian Wansink told me that Hale is in the majority, but barely. Wansink has found that roughly 55 percent of major leftovers aren't taken home. At her Red Bank, New Jersey, restaurant, waitress Sarah Klepner felt that conspicuous nonconsumption was a factor. "The restaurant is in a ritzier area of this town and it's frequented by people who don't want to appear that they're in need. If you're asking for your leftovers, it means you need them, and they didn't want to appear that way," said Klepner. Along those lines, she noted that many customers asked to take food home, but neglected to remind her about their boxes when she forgot to bring them out.

Red Bank Café waiters were even trained not to bring up the question of doggie bags. "We were instructed in the orientation, don't offer to wrap the food," Klepner said. "They didn't want us to push it. They thought that it would offend people—making them feel bad for not eating all their food."

That question—"Do you want to take your leftovers?"—does put us on the spot. If we decline, we're basically saying, "No, throw it out." Maybe a better model, one that would save food and face for those concerned with looking gauche, is for wrapping remains to be the default. That way, waiters wouldn't ask a question as much as make a suggestion: "Let me box that up for you." Diners could still object, but the path of least resistance would yield leftovers.

For better or worse, consciously or subconsciously, I would guess that most of us are at least somewhat concerned about what others think of us, whether it's the people at our table or the neighboring ones. Maybe it's even the waiter. That's why Noodles & Company's strategy of leaving a stack of take-out boxes by the napkins and silverware is so neat. By making the to-go process self-service, they've removed a barrier to taking food home by allowing customers to circumvent any perceived judgment or condescension. Of course, this would be trickier at a full-service restaurant.

Finally, some of us forsake our leftovers because a restaurant meal has become less special than it used to be. For many Americans today, eating out is no treat—it's dinner. Cornell's Wansink remembers going to a restaurant just twice while growing up in Sioux City, Iowa, during the 1960s. And that specialness impacted the doggie bagging. "I would guess [restaurant] waste is higher than it used to be," Wansink said. "People used to bring leftovers home no matter what."

Kitchen Leftovers

Not all restaurants want to repurpose unserved food or are able to do so, but they can donate it. As we'll discuss further in Chapter 11, it's fairly easy for restaurants to donate their edible excess. It is not, however, easier than throwing it away. That unfortunate fact dooms many potential donations. Giving away food usually requires a tiny bit of effort—such as wrapping a tray, or setting aside some refrigerator space—as it's unlikely that you'll be able to find a nonprofit willing to pick up excess food right at a restaurant's closing time. It is even better done with a blast chiller to quickly cool food items to minimize their time in the bacteria—cue the Kenny Loggins—"danger zone."

In addition to that warm, fuzzy feeling that donating food brings, it can also yield tax breaks for donors. One barrier to action, though, is the fear of liability. Yet, the federal Bill Emerson Good Samaritan Act of 1996 protects those who give food in good faith. That means that unless a restaurant knowingly sends shelters bad food, there won't be any liability issues. There are also state Good Samaritan acts, yet some restaurants still decline to donate because they're unfamiliar with such shield laws. Far worse, though, some eateries feign ignorance about these protections when they don't want to bother.

One restaurant rationale for not donating that I've heard all too often is that they don't fear losing a lawsuit as much as having their name sullied in the media if an unfounded suit was filed. I find this excuse dubious, at best, though. Food-recovery veterans can't remember one such liability lawsuit, and that's not surprising—it'd be like suing Santa Claus. Still, in practice, many restaurants responsible to shareholders are reluctant to donate their excess. That's unfortunate, because they're more likely than the smaller operations to have excess, as they don't repurpose food or have flexible menus. Nancy Hahn, who runs the San Francisco food-recovery group Food Runners, said that the majority of restaurant donations come from independent eateries (with the Olive Garden a notable exception).

Restaurateurs would do well to consult with the Environmental Protection Agency's Food Waste Recovery Hierarchy.[24] The first objective is to reduce the amount of waste created. That's a noble goal, but it may be like reminding someone with a flat tire to avoid nails. The second item on the hierarchy is to feed people, which could include either donating leftovers or feeding restaurant workers a staff meal. Next is feeding animals. In other words, get the food to livestock. Pig farmers can essentially take anything, as they're required to cook the slop for thirty minutes anyway.

The final item on the hierarchy is composting. Most restaurants with a will to compost should be able to find a way to do so. Whether it's putting a bin out by the Dumpster or wherever there's room, or working with a commercial composter, there's probably a way to keep organics out of the waste stream. Diverting food from landfills brings environmental benefits for everyone, but also economic ones for restaurants. They can slash their waste-hauling bills when there's less trash to remove.

Certification under the Green Seal Environmental Standard for Restaurants and Food Services asks a few things of restaurateurs.[25] They must make a waste-reduction and management plan, have a waste audit done, reduce their overall waste, divert it from the landfill, donate what's edible, compost what's not, and recycle fats, oils, and greases. Given that rigorousness, the Green Seal program could really impact restaurant-industry norms, if becomes popular.

While it lacks Green Seal's rigorousness, the Boston-based Green Restaurant Association now requires reducing food waste or at least handling it properly.

Restaurants wishing to achieve the Green Restaurant Standard 4.0 must compost their preconsumer waste and send their used grease to make biodiesel or energy. And, though it's not required, making weekly donations to a food bank will net restaurants 5 points toward certification.[26] Offering portions at least 25 percent smaller than the regular portions for a reduced price, meanwhile, is worth 2.25 points.

Unfortunately, only a fraction of restaurants participate in either certification program. While a renewed emphasis on food waste reduction and recycling is spreading, it isn't exactly widespread. But we're getting there. Slowly.

Bagged salads thrown away after reaching their "sell-by" date.

PHOTO BY JONATHAN BLOOM

chapter 7

A Cold Case of Waste

A person buying ordinary products in a supermarket is in touch with his deepest emotions.

—JOHN KENNETH GALBRAITH

The great bargain of buying five pounds for $5 does not end up being so great if you eventually throw two pounds away.

—BRIAN WANSINK, FOOD PSYCHOLOGIST
AND AUTHOR OF *MINDLESS EATING*

M y first day of work in a supermarket produce department began
at 8 A.M. Ten minutes into it, I was throwing away food.

Orientation would come later, I was told; first we had to "cull"
all of the "out-of-code" products. That meant that another employee, Moises,
and I were to look through all the bagged produce and remove anything with a
"sell-by" date of that day or earlier. The manager handed me an apron—my
"Jon" nametag would also have to wait—and pointed me to the refrigerated
wall of packaged produce.

Yanking containers of cut fruit and washed lettuce from the cold case, I
couldn't ignore the obvious: These items were perfectly edible. I collected sliced
mushrooms, cut peppers, and diced onions. I pulled seven varieties of bagged
salads and veggie trays of crudités with dip included. Based on their container
weights, I tossed 24 pounds of packaged watermelon, pineapple, and cantaloupe
chunks that first morning. Most items would last about another week, and the
veggie trays actually had a printed "enjoy-by" date of four days past the "sell-
by" date, but store policy went by the latter.

Most of what I culled was pre-cut, pre-washed, and packaged. When produce
is sliced, diced, or chopped, it oxidizes (or "wounds," in industry terms) and
goes bad faster than if it were whole. Once these bags are opened, the count-
down starts in earnest. So long as the bag is sealed, the decay is slowed by "Modified Atmosphere Packaging" (MAP)—the bag is either vacuum sealed or mixed
with oxygen, carbon dioxide, carbon monoxide, and/or nitrogen so that the
"high-value produce" inside will last longer than it otherwise would. Thus, these
products will remain good well past their sell-by dates as long as their bags remain sealed. All of the packages I took off the shelves were not only edible but
tasty. Many were items that I would, and later did, eat.

While I worked on culling the pre-cut and wrapped produce, Moises combed
through the loose stuff for imperfect items. When he was done, his tray of
culled fruits and veggies looked like it could have restocked a restaurant buffet.
I headed to the back room, where Gary, the produce manager, was "crisping"
some lettuce, soaking them to revive the leaves after their cross-country journey.
I asked him what I should do with my cart full of out-of-code product, holding
out a sliver of hope that it would be used by the deli department or salvaged in
some other way.

Without looking up, he said, "Take it to the Dumpster."

Donning the Apron

After a few days, I'd been shown how to crisp the lettuce myself and did it regularly. But what was a food journalist doing washing dirt from lettuce as opposed to digging it up? Before taking the job as a produce associate, I'd never felt that I was getting the real story on waste when I spoke with grocery executives. I suspected that some were less than candid because they knew the whole truth would look bad. Others were honest but deluded. In the fall of 2006, I set out to investigate supermarket waste from within. I got an entry-level position at a regional grocery chain and worked there for three months. I'd be lying if I said that throwing away so much food as my first act of employment wasn't validating and somewhat satisfying. I'd researched food waste for more than a year at that point, and here I had found my white whale. I struggled to take it all in, jotting brief notes during breaks. Yet in that first hour, it was almost too much too soon. And then, when the thrill of the chase wore off, it was incredibly sad.

In earlier research, I had tagged along on numerous food-rescue missions with volunteers from nonprofit groups. On these supermarket runs, the shopping carts full of donations made me wonder what happened to all the unsellable but edible items at stores where there were no such recovery efforts. More precisely, the big question that puzzled me was why an industry with wafer-thin profit margins—an average of 1.84 percent net profit after taxes— and sophisticated demand-forecasting software, would still throw out tens of billions of dollars' worth of food each year.[1]

In the 1980s and 1990s, supermarkets made significant strides in efficiency. Today, according to Timothy Jones, a University of Arizona anthropology researcher, they are fairly efficient compared to other parts of the food chain, but they still waste millions of tons because they handle such massive quantities of food. Supermarkets have continued to grow, so even if they are wasting a smaller proportion of their food (which remains to be seen) they are producing more waste. In 2008, the median store size was 46,755 square feet, or one-third larger than the median size in 1994.[2] And that number will likely increase, as the supermarkets being built today average about 60,000 square feet.

Supermarkets' efficiencies have dipped in recent years. Stores have started offering more prepared food in hopes of fending off competition from restaurants, which are making inroads on the food dollar. While grocers enjoy higher margins on prepared foods, these items are rarely donated, because of liability and food-safety fears. Prepared-food sales increased 39 percent from 2000 to 2005. In 2007, Technomic Information Services estimated that supermarket prepared-food sales was a $25 billion market.[3]

It's difficult to find estimates of supermarket waste because, not surprisingly, chains aren't exactly forthcoming on the amount of edible food they discard. Yet, as any Dumpster diver will attest, there's plenty. We can gain insight from the fifteen-store Massachusetts chain Roche Brothers. The privately owned grocer performed a waste audit in three stores while it transitioned to organics recycling in the early 2000s. Roche found that *each store* created more than 800 pounds of food waste per day.[4] Furthermore, Dawn Reeves, manager of environmental sustainability for the southeastern chain Harris Teeter, told me that its average store produces 2 to 3 tons of food waste per week, which works out to 715 pounds daily.

We get a sense of the staggering amount of food waste produced by U.S. supermarkets when we consider that each outlet creates about 800 pounds of food waste daily and that there are more than 35,000 grocery stores in the country.[5] That means about 30 million pounds of food waste per day, equal to the weight of 4,500 Hummers.[6]

To be fair, not all of that ends up in Dumpsters. Most of the Roche Brothers stores and a few Harris Teeters compost their organic waste. Yet, while supermarket composting is growing, it is by far the exception to the norm—sending food to the landfill. And food donations vary greatly in variety and volume, even within a chain, as we'll see in Chapter 9.

The most recent government study on grocery waste is "Supermarket Loss Estimates for Fresh Fruit, Vegetables, Meat, Poultry and Seafood and Their Use in the ERS Loss-Adjusted Food Availability Data." Despite having one of the least catchy titles I've encountered, this USDA study is useful—and quite specific—in listing the loss ratio for many supermarket goods. We learn that 64 percent of mustard greens and 25 percent of veal is squandered, but only 4 percent of beef and chicken is tossed.[7] Prior to this study, the USDA simply estimated a 7 percent loss rate for all fruits and vegetables and 12 percent for meats, poultry, and seafood.[8] Unfortunately, however, the authors didn't attempt to calculate the total amount of food squandered in our grocery stores.

The Produce Pageant

Later on my first day of work, I had the pleasure of watching the *Entry Level Produce Associate Training Video*. It included this passage: "If you ever have a question about whether a product should be culled, remove it and discuss it with your manager." Whenever I'd ask my manager about an item, he'd invariably say, "Toss it." In other words, guilty until proven innocent.

By my fourth week at the supermarket, I wasn't any closer to finding answers as to why the grocery industry seemed so *fine* with food waste. Every day on the job, I threw out some pretty nice stuff. This was especially disheartening considering that what reached our store was the cream of the crop. Items that weren't the right size, shape, or color had already been weeded out. Whether by nature or by conditioning, consumers have come to expect sweet, ripe fruit like grapes year round. So wherever you live across our vast country, the store where you shop will have them. And unless you live in or near California, the grapes most likely will have traveled a long way, advancing through many hurdles, possibly from as far away as Chile.

Some smaller chains and independent grocers are more resourceful with their produce, but they are the exception these days. Graul's, a six-market chain in Maryland, is one of those exceptions. When Donna Taylor, the produce manager at the Cape Saint Claire Graul's produce department, said the store strives to throw away as little food as possible, she meant it. "There's stuff that's gonna be garbage. There just is," Taylor said. "But whatever can be used gets used. If there's something with a bad spot, we'll cut it up and use the parts we can."

As we talked, Taylor sliced open snack packs of Cool Cuts baby carrots that had just reached their sell-by date. She emptied a total of twenty-seven 2-ounce packages, each with a container of ranch dressing, into a large clear bag. Later, her employees would incorporate these perfectly good carrots into the store-made veggie trays, while ditching the ranch.

How else does Graul's utilize its culled produce? Mainly, they feed them into their salad bar and prepared-food offerings, or, as they call them, "signature items." When Taylor took over the produce department thirty-four years ago, she installed the first one, dill dip, in her first week. The store's in-house goods have expanded along with consumers' tastes. Today, the signature items have quite a following. And the store pushes these products with hand-written signs with lines like, "Invite Graul's Dips to your next party."

When I visited a Graul's in April 2009, they were selling their own fruit salad, crudités, boxed salads, four kinds of dips, and four varieties of dressings. Just about any fruit or vegetable that is culled from the open displays are re-purposed, Taylor explained. Packaged salads that reach their sell-by date replenish the salad bar. Celery that's not quite nice enough to sell as is goes into the chicken salad. When they consolidate two strawberry containers into one, the excess goes into fruit trays. When cartons of eggs have one or two cracked, they'll combine a couple of cartons or use the rest in the bakery or prepared-food departments.

Picky, Picky

Further into the cartoon-laden produce-associate training video, a green monster representing "shrink," the industry term for theft and waste, told us that "the rule of thumb when culling is to ask yourself if you would buy the product. If you wouldn't, then why would the customer?" You can't argue with that logic, but does that mean those items are now trash? I may not buy an apple with a small bruise when I can have an unblemished one for the same price. Yet, I might buy it for a discount. And certainly *someone* would eat that perfectly nutritious apple.

Everyone laments the loss of slightly imperfect food, but nobody wants to buy it—not when given a choice between that item and its flawless sibling. Most shoppers profess that they purchase food based on ripeness, smell, or taste, not appearance. Yet those in the food industry know that, for the most part, that's not the case. "People will say they'll take fruit that's a little rough, but in reality, they buy with their eyes," said Kevin Moffitt, president of the Northwest Pear Bureau. "The consumer says one thing and, frankly, does something different."

While American shoppers have always had a fairly discerning eye, their ex-pectations have increased even more in recent years as cooking has become a more pervasive part of our culture. Cooking shows litter the television; food blogs, with gorgeous photos, dot the Web; and foodie magazines of all stripes share space at grocery checkout counters with the gossip rags. "Celebrity chef" was not a job description fifteen years ago. Culinary school applications have swelled nationwide. These trends, in addition to the slow move away from frozen and canned to fresh and local, have brought aesthetics to the fore. Meanwhile, the branch of Foodiedom that doesn't garden or go to farmers markets wants its produce as pristine as possible.

Shoppers are also fussier because we're getting better-looking produce. "I think industry-wide, we get nicer stuff today," said Taylor, from her perch of thirty-plus years in the grocery business. "Shipping and trucking have improved, so the quality of produce is better."

On a recent shopping trip to a Harris Teeter supermarket, I noticed that the insides of the remaining ears of corn didn't look great, a real rarity. I asked the clerk if he had any more in the back, and he took a surprisingly long time to return. Upon arrival, he told me that he had been "preparing" the ears for the display. With the corn, not only had the associate removed some of the dirtier layers of the outer husk, but he had trimmed the silks atop each ear into a 1950s' flattop. My demand for pretty produce had brought a long wait because the corn had to look nice. In my defense, I was only concerned with the kernels and couldn't have cared less about the husk's appearance. But without communicating that, I got a nice taste of supermarket superficiality. On another occasion at the same store, I gawked as a produce associate used a vacuum hose to suck the crinkly, unkempt peels from a display of onions.

Grocery stores err in throwing away their slightly downtrodden food. From reading through the blogosphere and talking to many a frugal foodie, I know that there are plenty of us out there who would happily buy the homelier ears of corn for a discount. With that in mind, why not have a sale-produce rack for fruits and veggies that are still edible, but not as pristine as they once were? Supermarkets would avoid great amounts of wasted produce and squeeze some revenue from items for which they've already paid.

This isn't a new idea, as some stores already sell discounted produce. At the supermarket where I worked, we didn't have a dedicated area, per se, but whenever we put ripe bananas (mostly yellow with some black) on sale—for $0.29 instead of $0.49 per pound—they sold briskly. Some of the Harris Teeter stores I've visited have actual sale racks and some don't. At most supermarkets, you'd have to look very hard to find an asymmetrical apple, let alone any discounted

produce. Even Food Lion, not exactly a high-end retailer, abandoned sale produce shelves in the early 2000s. "We just want the produce department to look
at its peak freshness all the time," said Food Lion's corporate communications
manager, Jeff Lowrance. "We pull everything that doesn't look like it's at its
peak freshness."

Freshness—got it?! Stores are petrified that shoppers will associate their fruits
and vegetables with anything but that word, because numerous studies have
confirmed that shoppers' opinions of the produce department inform their view
of the entire supermarket. The U.S. Grocery Shopper Trends 2008 study indicated that "high-quality fruits and vegetables" was the most important factor
to customers when they were selecting their primary grocery store.[9] That means
that top-notch produce trumps low prices and clean stores. And that has been
true in three of the past four years of the study. Knowing that, supermarket executives do their best to ensure that shoppers find nothing but flawless items.

The Pornography of Perfect Food

Andre Agassi must have worked in a grocery store. In a series of ads for Canon
cameras, the erstwhile tennis glamour boy famously stated that "image is everything." Many would object to Agassi's thesis, but it seems to be the organizing
principle for supermarkets. This superficiality is seen in supermarket branding,
as chains redesign their logos to connote greener, happier practices. And they
create their built environment and displays in calculated ways.

Kevin Kelley is an L.A. architect who designs supermarkets and specializes
in how physical environments affect consumer behavior. A founding partner at
Shook Kelley, he has worked with Whole Foods, Kroger, Harris Teeter, and
many other supermarkets. Specifically, Kelley noted that the dairy and meat sections often feature pastoral tableaus to sooth our doubts about the origins of
products.[10] The seafood case always contains plenty of ice to connote freshness
and dispel our fears about the fickle nature of its contents. Yet, the ice doesn't
serve a real purpose since the case is already refrigerated. And the produce section usually has wicker baskets, wooden crates, and farm-stand-like carts. Lighting and music even have roles to play.

This overarching superficiality carries over to the food itself. The term "food porn" is sometimes associated with high-end retailers such as Whole Foods and Wegman's, particularly the former. The national, natural retailer has earned a reputation for sensational displays of meat, seafood, and most notably, of produce. Are they aesthetically pleasing? Do they drive up consumer expectations for produce appearance? Yes, in both cases. As a result, they doom less-perfect items to be discarded somewhere between the farm and the stocking of the store display.

The stakes have been raised, and traditional supermarkets have to keep up to risk losing customers. Honor Schauland, a campaign assistant at the Organic Consumers Association, a public-interest group that seeks health, justice, and sustainability, said that most stores now value appearance over taste. "Just taste one of those perfect, round red tomatoes you can get in any supermarket during the winter. It's like a pretend tomato," said Schauland, citing a classic example. "My grandma used to say, 'They look pretty, but it's like sticking your tongue out the car window.'"

Whole Foods does many things well. In the case of creating beautiful displays by only having flawless, uniform food, a little too well. To achieve this visual wizardry, its buyers are picky about what they buy and accept. This is true at most stores, but it seems that the standards at the Austin, Texas–based chain are a bit higher than the rest. As Whole Foods' website declares, "Our buyers around the country are very discerning about what they purchase, scouring the land for the very best products and sometimes turning away shipments at the door that are undersized or lacking in flavor." Of the produce that is accepted and stocked, employees are quick to pull imperfect items from the sales floor. What Whole Foods refers to as "rapid inventory turns," I call excessive culling.

Fortunately, many Whole Foods stores donate these quite edible foods to nonprofits. When I was out with the Cambridge, Massachusetts, food-recovery group Food for Free in 2007, we pulled up to the back of a local Whole Foods. In the commotion of unloading trucks and scurrying employees, we found a stack of boxes left for us to collect. I'm not exaggerating when I say that the two boxes of apples could have been going in the other direction—into the store to be put on shelves.

In one sense, this fine-toothed culling is wonderful, as the recipients of the donated apples would be getting some nice fruit. Yet, there are harmful by-products of this pickiness. It prompts excessive pre-store winnowing, and can be incredibly wasteful when grocers from the chain stores don't have nonprofits collecting their castoffs. It teaches us that imperfect is unacceptable.

Shopping Psychology

When I was working the closing shift at the supermarket, my instructions were to stack everything—be it bananas, peaches, or onions—three high before leaving. That way, when shoppers bought produce in the few hours after I left but before the store closed, there would still be plenty on the shelves when the store opened the next morning. My manager explained it to me thusly: Nobody wants to buy items if they think they are among the last few remaining. They want to see full, brimming bins.

In addition to freshness, produce departments go to great lengths to communicate plenty through their displays. This both echoes and reinforces our culture of abundance. On that topic, Paul Kneeland, vice president of produce and floral at New Jersey's Kings Super Markets, told *Produce Business*, "We . . . do higher displays in order to give a multi-dimensional look to the department. We want it to look like a mountainous produce department."

Having that much food out on the shelves often causes loss. Customers mishandle—some would say manhandle—or drop the stuff. If fruits stay in one position too long, they can bruise. Exposure to room temperature makes many fruits and vegetables look a bit tired. And, as we know, those tired and bruised ones are the ones that are promptly culled away.

Smarter stores achieve the same look of abundance without losing stock by "dummying out" displays by using space fillers. That means using props, essentially to take up space. The tactic provides that mountainous look without having the quality of the goods suffer from the weight of the stacking. My manager was pretty skilled in this art, often improvising by using an upside-down vegetable tray. Other stores have display tables that are already layered like a steppe pyramid.

As the Atlanta-based regional produce buyer for Whole Foods in the South, Alex Rilko is in charge of the fruits and vegetables for eighteen Whole Foods stores in five states. In addition to homogeneous, beautiful produce, Whole Foods aims for teeming displays, Rilko told me when I spoke to him in 2009. "Psychologically, a customer comes into a store—any store—and if the display is empty or looks picked through, it turns them off," said Rilko, who has worked in the grocery business for twenty-three years. "If there's an abundant supply of apples, you're gonna grab one."

Kelley, the designer of retail spaces, has studied shopping psychology for seventeen years. He's found that brimming displays work because they trigger an instinct from our primitive roots. "We're wired as humans to like bountifulness," said Kelley. "Our mind says—there's food here, we're not going to die. It's pretty exciting." That subconscious excitement often translates to sales.

The abundance imperative applies in all sections of the grocery store. Matthew Enis, fresh-market editor at *Supermarket News*, said that having plenty is a must, because the opposite will hurt sales. "You don't want to let the selection look sparse—that's one of the big faux pas in fresh foods. If you're in a bakery and there's one donut left—nobody wants to take the last donut."

The sight of empty space on shelves is not only unappealing, but frightening. It even feels vaguely un-American, both because it almost never occurs in U.S. supermarkets and because it evokes the tales we heard about Soviet Cold War–era shops. My manager instructed me to avoid empty spots on the shelf at all costs. If we were out of one kind of bagged salad, we would double up on the neighboring variety. If we were low on honeydew, that meant more space for cantaloupes.

In their book *Rubbish! The Archaeology of Garbage*, William Rathje and Cullen Murphy discuss a related phenomenon. Rathje, who oversaw the Garbage Project's household waste sorting in Arizona, remembered researching garbage during the 1973–1974 meat shortage in the United States. The authors had hypothesized, logically enough, that the shortage would lower the amount of beef they'd find in the garbage. Yet, they found that the opposite occurred: There was more meat than usual being thrown away. In fact, three times as much meat wound up in garbage bins than had been there before the shortage began. What happened? Rathje's hypothesis:

> When confronted with the widespread and sometimes alarmist coverage of the beef shortage in the local and national media, many people may have responded by buying up all the beef they could get their hands on, even if some of the cuts were unfamiliar. Of course, they didn't necessarily know how to cook some of those cuts in an appetizing way. More important, they didn't necessarily know how to store large amounts of meat for an extended period of time. The inevitable result in either case: greater waste.[11]

There is another lesson to glean from this finding: After growing accustomed to abundance, we don't behave rationally when it disappears.

Oopsy Dairy

Don and Mary Musitelli pulled into the alleyway behind the Trader Joe's in Capitola, California, in their 1980s Toyota pickup. They were there to recover food for the Santa Cruz–based nonprofit California Grey Bears. Usually they find a random assortment of Trader Joe's unsellables. On this day, that meant three crates of eggs, two loaves of bread, and a package of three shrink-wrapped red peppers, where "one is a little squishy," in Mary's words. There was also a package of artichokes, a partially ripped bag of penne pasta, and what she calls a "mystery can," which had lost its label. Trader Joe's outlets usually have fewer goods they can donate because they don't sell much loose produce or prepared goods. Plus, the quirky, Monrovia, California–based chain isn't afraid of selling out of items.

Yet, that day, as happens occasionally, there was a whole lot more. Seven cases packed with quarts of lowfat milk sat outside the back door. I was astounded that a store would have more than 200 pounds of milk it didn't need. The Musitellis, who've been volunteering at Grey Bears for twenty years, were less surprised.

As we went inside to collect a few other donations, I got to speak with Steve Keenan, the store supervisor. He explained that the person doing the ordering had mispunched the number of crates desired. The worker hit both the two and three keys, yielding twenty-three cases instead of the usual two. Knowing that they wouldn't be able to sell the milk before it reached its sell-by date, they donated it to Grey Bears. "It's part of the business," said Keenan. "It happens."

Ordering at Trader Joe's involves quickly entering the desired quantity for item after item. Employees seldom catch their mistakes, Keenan said. Plus, the store orders every section of the store every day, so there's plenty of number punching that can go awry.

That kind of mistake doesn't happen all the time, but it occurs more than stores would like. On a random Monday in February 2007, a truck from Raleigh's Inter-Faith Food Shuttle picked up seventy boxes of lettuce in perfect condition from a Harris Teeter that had over-ordered. Punching in numbers blindly with no double-checking is bound to lead to many misorders. "There's always going to be human error; it does happen a fair amount," said Michael Garry, the logistics editor at the trade publication *Supermarket News*.

Yet, the difficulty of forecasting customer demand also creates more waste, Garry said. It's not easy to predict demand for an entire 60,000-square-foot grocery store. As with restaurants, grocers have many variables to consider. The weather virtually dictates consumer shopping practices. And traffic, events, and competitors' promotions all influence demand.

Shrewd managers are essential for trimming loss. As far back as 1970, Edward McLaughlin, director of Cornell University's Food Industry Management Program, identified managers as the main obstacle to minimizing waste. Most stores provide managers with software to study sales patterns from years past in an effort to better predict demand for Thanksgiving turkeys and Fourth of July strawberries. Experienced managers who can utilize that technology and add their own experience to ordering are invaluable. "Skilled management is very important," said Mark Wiltamuth, retail food analyst at Morgan Stanley, who tracks grocers such as Albertson's, Krogers, Safeway, and Whole Foods. "If you're having a lot of turnover, that could explain problems with shrink."

Like farmers, grocers do not like to run out of a product, whether it's a holiday or not. While they try to be efficient in their ordering and avoid large inventories, they tend to aim for more rather than less. "Companies like to avoid out-of-stocks—they lead to missed sales," said Wiltamuth.

Accordingly, supermarket ordering errs on the side of excess. "You tend to order more," said Lance Parchment, a prepared-food assistant coordinator for Whole Foods' South Region. "For example, if you're selling five cases of something, you tend to buy seven. You definitely order a little more to maximize sales and allow for sampling."

Just Another Commodity

The first time I actually had to put edible fruits and vegetables in the Dumpster, I couldn't quite bring myself to do it. I set aside particularly fresh-looking foods next to the bin with the hope that a (human) forager would stumble upon them. And, truth be told, a few of those items did somehow manage to end up in my car at the end of many a shift.[12] Yet, I'd be lying if I said that throwing away perfectly good food didn't become easier. The bags of lettuce and bruised peppers started to become like any other disposable commodity.

No matter the reason, grocery workers throw away so much edible food that they become immune to the waste. Numerous supermarket workers I talked to spoke of this particular numbing effect. Lucy Davis, who worked in the bakery department at the Chapel Hill Whole Foods, lamented the loss, but she gradually stopped being repulsed by it. At a certain point, rotisserie chickens, boxes of cereal, and tomatoes cease being food and simply become garbage. As I learned firsthand, throwing away edible food is part of the job. For employees, taking out the trash—whether it includes moldy strawberries or ones simply past their "sell-by" date—is simply a task that stands between them and going home. Because they know their bosses won't let them take it home, grocery workers learn to forget this tossed food.

Yet, I couldn't stop thinking about it, both because of my obsession with waste and because it was so ludicrous. The height of absurdity occurred one day when I found two Granny Smith apples that a shopper had bagged and apparently decided not to buy. He or she left the bag atop the bell peppers. When I asked my manager Gary how to proceed, to my surprise, he told me to put them in my culling box. "Why couldn't they be resold?" I asked. After all, apples are handled and not purchased all the time at their display. Gary's response was that I should stop worrying about the apples and start restocking the peppers.

After that day, whenever I found fruits or vegetables in a bag, I just quietly placed them back with their display. In fact, I do the same today as an unpaid shopper (which is reason number 237 why I take so long at the supermarket).

Gary was so quick to condemn produce to the culling bin because he had ceased to view fruits and vegetables as foods that could nourish people. Instead, they were just product, disposable goods like any other. From that perspective, the mentality was "get it out of there," which he told me to do on numerous occasions. In the process of processing, displaying, and selling produce, some *will* be lost. And with that in mind, two apples are a drop in the, well, Dumpster.

As I mentioned, I was much less hesitant about throwing out edible food at the end of my time working at the store. I can only imagine how I would have felt after two years. Or the three decades Gary worked there (he has since passed away). My ad-hoc attempts to find takers by putting food beside the Dumpster weren't leading anywhere. So I redirected my efforts and tried to start a large-scale donation program. I still threw away the daily culled produce because it was part of the job. Ultimately, it was their property and they wanted it thrown away.

One evening when I was the last one working in the section, I dropped a case of zucchini in the store room. To my surprise and dismay, half of them snapped as if they were spring loaded. Nobody noticed this clumsiness-caused waste—at least nobody said anything to me—and we only had one other case of squash. That silence communicated just how much tolerance for loss exists in supermarkets. Later, my manager confirmed this leeway when he told me that our store budgeted for $12,000 worth of unsold produce each month. This includes items that have passed their expiration dates, lost their freshness, or are, I don't know, dropped.

While stores pay increasing lip service to reducing waste, and they don't enjoy throwing away money, supermarket executives see it as a cost of doing business. "There is a certain amount of waste inherent in the industry," said Michael Garry at *Supermarket News*. Perhaps, though, it's that cutting waste would require asking hard questions and implementing major changes that store leadership may not be prepared to make.

Confuse-By Dates

One time when I was shopping at a local supermarket, I noticed that half gallons of the store brand milk had a "sell-by" date on the carton, near the top. Yet the organic half gallons of the store brand milk simply had a date without any words preceding it. I had no idea whether that date was the last day consumers should drink the milk or the last day the store should display it. One case over, a package of Wellshire dry-rubbed, peppered bacon contained a "sell or freeze by" date. The neighboring product, the Coleman Natural hickory smoked bacon, had a "use or freeze by" date stamped onto the plastic. And beside that, the store-brand center-cut smokehouse bacon was back to the "sell or freeze by" label.

It's no wonder that dates on packages baffle consumers. We're constantly getting mixed messages, resulting both in confusion over the labeling terminology and uncertainty over how much stock to put in the dates. The same confusion occurs overseas. In June 2009, Britain's secretary for the environment, Hilary Benn, suggested that the UK government take action to clarify these types of labels. "Too many of us are putting things in the bin simply because we're not sure, we're confused by the label, or we're just playing safe," he told the *Telegraph* newspaper.[13] "This means we're throwing away thousands of tonnes of food every year completely unnecessarily—as part of our war on waste I want to improve the labels on our food so that when we buy a loaf of bread or a packet of cold meat, we know exactly how long it's safe to eat."

After recovering from the shock of having an elected official, let alone one on par with a U.S. cabinet member, discuss how to reduce food waste, I considered Benn's stance. After all, the main problem that he was railing against exists on both sides of the Atlantic—the lack of standard language surrounding expiration dates. In American retailing, our complex status quo includes terms such as "sell by," "sell or freeze by," "display until," "use by," "use or freeze by," "enjoy by," "best by" and "best before." I study food waste and it even confuses me from time to time.

Taking a step back, these labels fit into three main categories. The first kind of term, such as "sell-by," refers to the day after which the retailer should not sell food items. The second, as in "best by," represents the manufacturers' estimation of when an item won't be at peak freshness. After that date, the taste or texture may begin fading. The third, epitomized by "use by," is more stern. It represents, supposedly, the date after which the consumer shouldn't eat an item.

Unfortunately, many shoppers miss the nuances and treat these terms as interchangeable. They simply see a date that tells them when to toss an item. As Benn said, when individuals aren't sure whether something is still good, they'll often just discard it. Phil Lempert, a grocery industry expert and "consumerologist" who calls himself the Supermarket Guru, concurs. "Consumers are totally confused by sell-by and use-by dates, which is why one of the things we've pushed for for a number of years is to just have a use-by date," Lempert said.

Academics have reached similar conclusions. In their study *Food Discard Practices of Householders*, for example, Oregon State University professors Shirley Van Garde and Margy Woodburn asked participants to analyze whether packaged foods were edible. Van Garde and Woodburn, both in the university's Department of Foods and Nutrition, noted subjects responses and found that "householders in all age and income groups did not clearly understand package dating and need information as to its use."[14]

Date labels puzzle shoppers and retailers alike. When perusing some gorgonzola cheese that was on special, I noted that the store's sale sticker read "sell by" June 3, yet the manufacturer's label said "best by" that same date. At times, though, the cult of freshness, not confusion, prompts date label problems. Cindy Brickley, forty-nine, worked in the cheese department at the State College, Pennsylvania, Wegman's. She was taken aback the first time her boss instructed her to throw away prepackaged goods *before* their labeled date. "I guess there was something like a snob factor to it. Anything two or three days away from their sell-by dates, they'd take it off the shelf," Brickley said. "They were so worried that people would say 'Oh it's only few days from the date.' They'd almost preempt that by throwing it in the garbage."

Brickley noted that her department was conscientious about using custom-cut cheese scraps to make cheese spreads. It was the packaged goods like crème fraiche, linberger, and Boursin, however, that became sell-by victims. In one instance, she recalled throwing away twenty tubs of crème fraiche. "It felt terrible; there was absolutely nothing wrong with any of it," said Brickley, who worked at the store from 2004 to 2006. "It just seemed awfully wasteful. It shouldn't be surprising, but it was. The first time you see something like that happen it can be a real eye opener. As a customer, you think, oh, they'll put it on special or donate it to a food bank. But apparently that doesn't always happen. Sometimes it just goes in the trash."

Expiration Exasperation

Products at or past their sell-by dates have in no way gone bad. Instead they have passed the manufacturer's best estimate for when they ought to be sold. Shoppers should be able to take an item home on the sell-by date and still have a reasonable amount of time in which to eat it. The sell-by date is aimed at the merchant; as consumers, we'd be best served to ignore it if there's a second date on the package. These goods are the ideal candidates for donation to food pantries because, although they remain good, stores can't sell them after the sell-by date. Yet, many store managers treat these unsellables like Cinderella, thinking they'll transform into garbage at the stroke of midnight. That's not the case. "You can use food for a week past the sell-by times, if you store it properly," said Angela Fraser, a professor of retail and consumer food safety at Clemson University.

The sell-by date affords the shopper time to use the product. Understanding that can reduce waste. "They give a pretty generous window with the sell-by dates," said Steve Keenan, the Trader Joe's manager. "I've brought home out-of-code bread, and ten days later, it's fine. It's the lawyers—they've made everything difficult."

Of the two date labels aimed at consumers, "best by" is less severe. Essentially, as they're saying, this item would be best before the listed date. It's more about taste and quality than safety. Then again, even "use-by" dates, while more strict, aren't really about spoilage. Instead, they're cautious best guesses on when the item may start to be less than ideal. "Package dates are indications of quality, not safety," Fraser said. "There's a difference between safety and spoilage."

Even the USDA concedes the approximate nature of food dating. The department's Food Safety and Inspection Service website states, "'Use-by' dates usually refer to best quality and are not safety dates. But even if the date expires during home storage, a product should be safe, wholesome and of good quality—if handled properly and kept at 40°F or below."[15]

Yet, incredibly, the USDA doesn't even take its own advice. The paragraph of the previous quotation continues on to say "If product has a 'use-by' date, follow that date." Even stranger, after spelling out the difference between "use-by" and "sell-by" dates, the USDA site promptly ignores the distinction: "If product has a 'sell-by' date or no date, cook or freeze the product by the times on the chart [embedded on the page]."

Perhaps it's best to get our advice elsewhere. Taylor, at Graul's Market, is more succinct: "In produce, dates are suggestions," she said.

As I mentioned at the beginning of the chapter, the supermarket where I worked didn't even sell items up to their sell-by dates. By contrast, Graul's culls packaged produce items the morning after their expiration dates. So if the sell-by date is today, they take it off the shelf tomorrow morning, which makes perfect sense. After all, stores are supposed to sell it *by* the sell-by date.

Some stores reduce the price on nearly out-of-code items as their dates approach. That takes some foresight and organization; less organized stores may have trouble pulling out-of-code items weeks past their dates, let alone identifying what foods are approaching expiration dates. And given the massive inventories at large stores, sell-by markdowns are easier to manage and more common at smaller stores, such as Graul's. Taylor said her store usually offers discounts as the dates approach. "Something's better than nothing," she said.

Although stores try to be zealous about pulling items on or before their out-of-code dates, that's not easy to do. As of 2008, the average supermarket carried 46,852 different items.[16] On a recent trip to the store, I overheard a woman complaining at the customer service desk that she bought a package of fresh cheese ravioli that was twenty-three days past its sell-by date. I once found a can of baby food—a real no-no—seven months overdue. Given the number of products at the markets and the Sisyphean nature of managing that inventory, these slip-ups are inevitable. Yet, some food manufacturers take a proactive approach, hiring third parties to minimize their occurrence.

These third parties ensure that the store isn't displaying any of their items past their sell-by-dates and that they're receiving the shelf space they've paid for (via "slotting fees"). The former is done with excessive caution. Roy Cordes, of Hayward, California, works for Acosta, one of these independent companies hired by brands such as Duncan Hines and Swanson frozen foods. Based on the amounts that he takes from the displays throughout the East Bay area of California, Cordes estimated that supermarkets pull more than $2,300 worth of out-of-date goods per store every day. Some of these items, such as sliced bread, are taken back by their distributors for sale at discount stores. Others, usually bakery goods, are donated. But a large amount is simply thrown away. And that irks Cordes, who grew up during the World War II era, when discarding food was a major no-no.

Once Cordes finds out-of-code goods, the process varies, depending on the chain and even the store. Even though the food is edible, just not sellable, on its sell-by date, it is often put in the Dumpster. "I pull a lot of refrigerated pasta—the kind that's already cooked," said Cordes. "Some stores will itemize that and record the loss. With others, there's no system, it just goes directly into the garbage. They don't even want to look at it, they just throw it away."

Cordes told me that although federal law requires that infant formula be removed from the shelves sixty days before its use-by date, the Lucky supermarket chain pulls it ninety days out. While that might seem like a good idea—it's hard to argue against caution when it comes to babies—that extra cushion sends tons of perfectly good product to landfills.

Infant formula and some baby foods are the only items required by federal regulations to carry a "best-before" date.[17] Yet, virtually every supermarket item now carries a "use-by" or a "sell-by" date. Accordingly, what began as a badge of honor—to illustrate rigorous freshness standards—is now practically expected.

Expiration dates are not a negative thing, per se. Yet, they often beget excessive caution that causes unnecessary waste. This is especially true with nonperishable items. There's plenty of usable food thrown away in the "center of the store" due to expiration dates, especially given the preservatives in use today. Shelf-stable groceries such as cereal, tomato sauce, and cookies are tossed when they reach their sell-by dates, even though many of these goods wouldn't go bad for years. These days, everything has an expiration date—from bottled water—water!—to individual eggs.

While expiration-date waste hasn't been studied in the United States, a government-funded study in the United Kingdom found that Britons waste approximately 370,000 tons annually because of label date confusion.[18] That's about 5 percent of UK household food waste.[19] British and American food waste habits are similar enough that we can use that 5 percent figure as a decent esti-mate. What's more, that figure doesn't include date-related losses that occur earlier in the food chain (when some items aren't even shipped if they're too close to their sell-by dates).

The solution proposed by Hilary Benn and Phil Lempert—to obscure sell-by dates so consumers can't read them—is a sound one. Then again, maybe we'll soon see the day when all products have radio-frequency identification (RFID) tags and this problem will be moot. RFID tags are little transmitters that send out signals to a proximity reader. Essentially bar codes on steroids, they could do for grocery check-out what the EZ-Pass and similar transponders have done for tolls. As soon as they become a little cheaper, these tags could eliminate printed "pull dates" and the need for employees to check them. The German retailer METRO Group now uses RFID tags in its Future Store to warn workers when packages of meat are approaching their sell-by dates.[20] Say "Guten tag" to the future!

Until RFID prices dip, grocers will still need a way to determine how long to display items. Yet, it doesn't have to be a date printed on the package. Man-ufacturers could communicate this same information without confusing cus-tomers through "closed dating," which is already used on some products. This involves using either numbers or colors to represent days of the week, the way many packaged bread companies do with their twist ties or bag cinches.

We can certainly do better than the status quo. If nothing else, standardizing the language would alleviate some of the confusion. A more radical idea would be to ban sell-by dates altogether, as was proposed in Britain. Or we could re-quire two dates on packaged goods—a sell by and a use by, which might help consumers learn the difference. My cynical side thinks we'll see use-by dates stamped into rinds or added to those annoying fruit stickers before we see any changes to the existing expiration-date chaos.

Bundling Waste

Sell-by dates are not the only source of packaging-induced casualties. Lumping together multiple whole foods in one container also causes waste. Whenever produce is packaged together there is the possibility for what I call "waste by association." For example, the store where I worked carried 5-pound plastic bags of potatoes. One afternoon I came across a ripped bag. Not a problem, I figured, just add them to the loose potato display. Unfortunately, our store didn't sell loose white potatoes (only sweets and bliss). That meant the entire 5-pound bag wound up in the trash.

The same principle applied to the mesh bags of tangerines. One bad piece of citrus doomed the rest. The bags were stapled shut and while it would have been possible to add the healthy tangerines to another bag, that wasn't store policy. While some stores do combine bags, that requires at least two bags with some "bad apples." And in the bustle of the produce department, that kind of "above and beyond" effort is uncommon, though not unheard of. Of course, if avoiding waste were a priority, it wouldn't be too hard. In my situation, I threw away the two bad tangerines and took home the rest. They looked fine and, sure enough, tasted that way.

Although my store didn't encourage it, I found that one worker surreptitiously combined fruit packages. On my third day on the job, Moises, a Salvadoran who had been working there for six years, called me over to illustrate how to combine two plastic "clam shells" of mixed-quality cherry tomatoes into one good one, thus shattering my notion of the sanctity of packaged produce. We did this with containers of tomatoes, strawberries, blueberries, and raspberries. I was happy to adopt the practice to save food, but Moises said most of the other workers didn't do it.

By November, the changing season meant fewer loose fruits and vegetables. In addition to the boxes of clementines and bags of grapefruit, we sold shrink-wrapped packages of corn, with four ears in each set. They had been husked, meaning they'd fade quickly once opened, and sometimes before that. If one went bad, the rest were thrown out with it. We had a shrink-wrap tool in the back, but I never saw it used for anything but making Christmas-season fruit baskets.

Another problem with packaged produce is that it often prevents shoppers from getting the right amount. For instance, a shrink-wrapped tray of red, yellow, and green bell peppers is visually appealing, but this veritable veggie traffic light will force some shoppers to buy more than they need. In that way, stores and warehouse clubs are packaging waste. While it's a growing trend in produce, this problem also occurs at grocers without staffed butcher, seafood, or deli counters.

Bunched produce and large packages of meat provide a real challenge for those who live alone or are cooking for themselves. Food-savvy folks will say these people can freeze what they won't use. And that's true—for items that freeze well. But many of us forget about what's in our freezers until it's a frost-laden monstrosity. And why should we be forced to pay more upfront to get a surplus?

In general, the more choice, the less waste. Being able to buy foods in custom amounts helps prevent squandering. That's why I appreciate deli counters where you can ask for, say, four slices of provolone if you're planning to make four meatball subs. The same goes for farmers markets and produce departments that sell loose carrots, mushrooms, spinach, and other veggies instead of larger packages. Bulk bins offer another means for purchasing just the right amount, as long as we ignore the adjective in their name.

Contrastingly, there's the volume of goods that warehouse stores foist upon their customers. Although some of these items are not perishable, shopping at stores such as Costco and Sam's Club is especially problematic when they are. The massive containers are like food-waste time bombs. When that loss occurs, the vaunted per-item savings evaporate. Given the size of some of the packages, shoppers may have a hard time using up even the dry goods. For example, Costco sells twelve 12-ounce containers of honey (in bear shapes, of course) for a mere $45! It's a great deal, unless they (or you) expire before you use half of them.

I'm not a member of any of these discount stores, but on a research outing, I bristled at the bundling of perishables during a recent visit. Sure, this kind of shopping may make sense for larger families—think *Cheaper by the Dozen*. Or for an army. Yet, many items are waste traps for the average household, which now has a biology-defying 2.6 people.[21]

Judging a Food by Its Cover

Packaging also causes problems with hard (or "dry") groceries. Damage to a box or container often means goods are thrown away, even though the contents are fine. There are plenty of pitfalls: The shelf stocker may have sliced into a box or two of Grape Nuts while opening the case of twelve. Maybe the entire pallet-load was dinged in-transit or at the store while being unloaded. Or customers could have dropped the item, leaving a dent. The packaging on some of these groceries isn't "hard" enough. But fortunately, there are many groups willing to look past these superficialities to the untouched product within. When I visited the Senior Gleaners, a food recovery operation in Sacramento, California, I saw an entire warehouse-sized "salvage" room with pallets full of damaged boxes of crackers, granola bars, and cereal, all stacked and shrink-wrapped together.

There's a growing secondary market for goods with slightly damaged containers and out-of-date promotions. These are the limited-edition boxes that aren't quite limited enough in quantity, like the Olympic Wheaties a few weeks after the Games. Dented cans, too, are sent out, often to discount retailers such as Big Lots or Dollar General. For regular supermarkets, these may no longer be sellable items, but, as the secondary markets show, they're far from garbage.

Haste-Based Waste

Americans lead busier lives than ever before. We're working longer hours, and our leisure time is increasingly invaded by e-mail–equipped mobile devices. There are more households with either one parent or two working parents, and there is less time for making meals. Yet, many people still want to cook supper and are looking for any kind of shortcut they can get. The food industry has responded by supplying them with washed lettuce, peeled garlic, and sliced mushrooms. There are now bags of washed green beans that you just plop straight into the microwave, complete with an enclosed sauce. If we don't have to chop the onions and peppers for fajitas—great. A beef stew that doesn't require cubing potatoes and slicing carrots? Even better.

Our shrinking free time means growing sales for packaged produce that has been washed, peeled, cubed, or diced. This category, often called "higher-value produce," "value added," or "fresh cut," accounted for 22 percent of produce sales in 2008, according to the trade magazine *Progressive Grocer*.[22] This segment of the produce section has boomed since it came into existence in the late 1980s. By 2007, the fresh-cut market had $1.3 billion in annual revenue, not including prepackaged salads.²³ Baby carrots accounted for about half of those sales, which isn't too surprising, considering that they launched the fresh-cut movement.

Baby carrots began as a way to reduce waste—finding a use for the bumpy, crooked, and stubby carrots that any gardener would recognize. They are basically carrots cut into two-inch pieces and whittled down in an industrial peeler. The technique was invented in the 1960s, but languished. It wasn't until 1986, when a Bakersfield, California, grower named Mike Yurosek brought the product to market under the Bunny Luv label, that we began seeing these little carrots in the supermarkets. And once we did, we really took to them. Thanks largely to the convenience of not having to peel them, these minis prompted a carrot resurgence. Per capita carrot consumption almost doubled between 1986 and 1997.²⁴ Carrot sales have leveled a bit since then, but producers have turned to other fresh-cut produce to further boost veggie sales.

It's ironic that a method for making use of a waste product sparked an entire industry of fresh-cut produce that now creates more waste. As previously mentioned, any time you cut into a whole food, it speeds the decaying process. Peeling, slicing, and chopping decreases the natural defenses of a piece of fruit or a vegetable. It's like piercing its armor, said Trevor Suslow, an extension research specialist in postharvest quality and safety at the University of California at Davis. "The more wounding you inflict, the quicker it becomes unusable," Suslow said. "It starts chemical reactions in the fruit that responds to the wounding. It may not make it inedible as soon as it makes it cosmetically unappealing—turning brown or off-color."

That decline is likely to come in your refrigerator, not in the store, because of the aforementioned Modified Atmosphere Packaging (MAP) found in packages of lettuce, spinach, and most other processed vegetables. Packers seal bags of each product with different mixes of chemicals to achieve the desired goal: keeping the food from breaking down during shipment. "Packing lowers oxygen levels and elevates carbon dioxide that would prolong the items' shelf life, but it's still shorter than if it wasn't cut up," Suslow said.

Once you open that bag, though, the wounding brings a quick death—quicker, that is, than you'd see with a whole fruit or vegetable. Oxygen is the real enemy, as respiration speeds the product's decomposition, a word and process that food manufacturers strive to keep far from their goods. The convenience of higher-value produce comes at the cost of increased home food waste.

In addition, the fresh-cut boom has brought expiration date casualties to the produce department. Heads of lettuce aren't marked with any dates, but bags of salad mix sure are. Accordingly, 22 percent of the produce department's goods now face sell-by-date wastage in addition to the standard "it doesn't look so hot" culling.

The Cost of Convenience

Just as our busy lifestyle created the market for pre-cut produce, it has sparked an explosion of ready-to-eat foods at the supermarket. What began in the 1990s as a way to counter the Boston Market chicken fad has only accelerated in recent years. By 2008, 95 percent of supermarkets offered fresh, prepared foods for takeout.[25] There's a surprising amount of variety along the edges of most supermarkets: What was once the domain of rotisserie chicken and mashed potatoes now includes everything from apple-stuffed pork loin to roasted zucchini. That same 2008 report found that 23 percent of stores had a sushi station.

Supermarkets have steadily grown over the past decade, and as their footprints have ballooned, stores have devoted fewer and fewer square feet to the "center store" hard groceries, moving away from the many long rows that store designer Kelley called the "Model-T chassis"—an outdated "ingredient-based model" of shopping. Instead, the so-called "outside" of stores has expanded. Nothing's been moved outdoors; the term refers to the edges of the store, where prepared foods, deli counters, and bakery departments get more real estate, said Wade Hanson, a senior manager at Technomic. Supermarkets have been happy to chase this new form of food sales, as prepared foods have gross profits roughly twice as high as the percentage for traditional groceries, although they require more labor.[26]

And as the International Dairy-Deli-Bakery Association reminds us in its *What's in Store 2009* report, there are a growing number of self-serve bars.[27] Whereas the salad bar used to be the only supermarket self-service option for ready-to-eat items, many stores now have olive bars, chicken wing bars, taco bars, Asian food bars, and even dessert bars. As the report explains, "The size of food bars is expanding rapidly at many supermarket delis to meet the increased demand for an alternative to restaurants." This is significant, because unlike the foods behind a counter, because of the health codes anything put out on a self-service buffet cannot be donated or repurposed. A shopper might have sneezed in the *sag paneer*, or maybe a kid reached into the kalamata olives trying to replicate the haunted house jar-of-eyeballs experience.

"Home meal replacement" is the wooden, industry term for explaining supermarkets' new role in our lives—chefs. Stores such as Wegman's, Whole Foods, Central Market, and some of the newer Publix, Safeway, and Kroger stores have ramped up their offerings. Even a salt-of-the-earth chain like Food Lion has a line of "ON THE GO Bistro" foods ready for reheating that it advertises as "faster and less expensive than takeout." "Supermarkets had been losing market share to restaurants for some time," Hanson said. "When stores saw what consumers were asking for, they saw an opportunity. Instead of only having rotisserie chicken and take-and-bake pizza, if they have a variety of fresh options, they could succeed. It has almost made some supermarkets look and feel like a restaurant."

Phil Lempert predicts that in five years prepared foods will make up 50 percent of supermarkets' offerings. We're certainly headed that way now. Whole Foods is really blurring the line between restaurant and supermarket with a few of its newer stores. Whole Foods markets in Austin, Manhattan, Chicago, and the D.C. suburbs have multiple "mini restaurants," in-house eateries where shoppers/diners order custom-prepared meals. Whole Foods' prepared-foods Web page begins with a two-word paragraph warning us about the variety of offerings: "Prepare yourself." Still, I'm not sure I was prepared for the sheer variety of options I found in the Whole Foods Union Square shop in New York City.[28] Not only did it have an array of Mexican and Chinese hot food offerings, there was almost an entire hot-bar devoted to Indian food.

Indeed, the number of choices available at the prepared-foods section of any supermarket built in the past few years can be staggering. "It's not unheard of to have retailers offer two hundred varieties of entrees, sides, and other dishes," said Hanson, author of Technomic's *Retailer Meal Solutions* report. "When you have two hundred options, it's a real challenge to keep them all fresh. If you have that many items out, how many [inventory] turns do you have to do? What's the loss?"

It's a pretty simple equation: The more perishable food the store serves, the more waste it will have, said Edward McLaughlin, director of Cornell University's Food Industry Management Program. Today's beautiful prepared foods in the deli case become tonight's trash, or, in some cases, compost.

Amy Brooks is the food-waste coordinator for Brooks Contractor, both the largest retail food-waste collector in North Carolina and a family business. Every now and again she'll tag along on a collection run, peeking into the bins to ensure that customers are sending the right materials to be composted. Brooks said she sees plenty of entrées and side dishes in supermarkets' bins, plus the prep waste that went into making the prepared foods. Raleigh Whole Foods, for example, almost always fills twenty 64-gallon rolling bins for their every-other-day collection. "There's a lot of people who say, 'Wow, look at how much we've composted!' Well, there's another way to swing that around, to say look at how much you wasted," Brooks said.

I tend to be an off-hours food shopper. One night near 8:30 P.M., I was gathering a few salad bar ingredients at a Durham Harris Teeter. This particular store is open twenty-four hours a day, but its salad bar is not. As I was making my choices, an employee began "closing" the salad bar. When I'd finished, I'd watched in shocked silence as he dumped each individual bin into a rolling trash can. Even though on some level I knew it was coming, I found it almost unfathomable. It would be somewhat understandable if the contents had been dressed salads that would wilt by morning. But whole cherry tomatoes? Untouched olives? There were no distinctions made between the different foods. It was just trash.

Discarding everything from a salad bar makes sense from a legal standpoint. As discussed earlier, health codes prevent the donation or repurposing of anything on a self-service buffet. Many germs could have been introduced throughout the day. But from an ethical and empathetic perspective, it's maddening.

'Round and 'Round

It's strange to pay for something after having just watched its compatriots get thrown away. At 8:29 P.M., it's $4.99 per pound; at 8:31, it's garbage. But that salad-bar reality has also happened to me with rotisserie chickens. You're probably thinking I should shop earlier in the day. Well, unfortunately, stores throw away roasters all day long.

If you want to learn about food waste, ask the guy at a supermarket deli about his store's rotisserie chicken policy. Maybe include the phrase "peak freshness" in your question. When I inquired about the chicken policy at my local supermarket, the deli clerk, whose raspy voice and tired tone leant a certain grocery gravitas, told me that they marked down their chickens after they sat out for three hours, and threw them away after four.[29]

At another one of this chain's stores, a clerk assured me that rotisserie chickens go into the trash after sitting out for five hours. She likely thought this information would be reassuring, but I was taken aback. It's not often that I hear people admit to throwing away food, especially not stuff that could be repurposed. After all, some stores in this same chain make their chicken salad from rotisserie remains.

Although those birds may not taste as good as ones fresh from the oven, they're still safe to eat as long as they're kept at the right temperature. The reason individual stores can have different time limits on prepared meals is that regulations are often temperature-based. They also vary from state to state and county to county, with health departments using either time or temperature requirements, said Jon Kawaguchi, environmental health supervisor for Oregon's Multnomah County. "When stores toss things right at four hours even though it's at temperature, it might be a quality issue," said Kawaguchi. "For example, pizza. I can't put a pie under a warmer for four hours. It's gonna be cardboard. You either sell it or discard it in an hour."

Knowing their demand should help, but most stores don't seem to mind throwing out chickens so long as it means never running out. They must not mind, or they'd change their practices. Paul Robichaux, a former deli clerk at a Greensboro, North Carolina, Harris Teeter, said his department threw away about half of all the rotisserie chickens they cooked. Robichaux, who now lives in Washington, D.C., blamed the store's obsession with having birds available between 4 and 6 P.M. He also grumbled—still indignant a decade later—that employees were not allowed to eat any chicken without paying for it.

When Life Gives You Old Chickens . . .

There's a great way to reduce all this waste from prepared foods—use it else-where. Those rotisserie chickens can be used in chicken salads, pasta dishes, or soups. At Harris Teeter, cooked poultry is now reused in three different chicken salads available at the deli. The aptly named rotisserie chicken salad derives from roasters that have sat out for a while (if available) or ones straight from the oven. Either way, the store benefits from this mayo-based makeover, as the chicken salad sells for $6.99 per pound, a $3 markup from the whole bird's per pound price.[30] Costco does the same, making some chicken salads and chicken que-sadillas with unsold rotisserie roasters, said Technomic's Hanson. Repurposing chicken "is becoming more common because retailers are trying to figure out how to minimize that loss," said Hanson. "It mostly happens at retailers doing a significant amount of prep in the store. If food is prepared in a central com-missary, that obviously makes it more difficult."

In-store uses abound for ready-to-eat items. Like many grocers, Graul's Mar-ket redirects some unsold rotisserie into chicken salad. But more innovative is Graul's use of that in-store ubiquity—fresh-baked bread. Since stuffing is in de-mand around the holidays, employees chop and freeze some bread a few months in advance, and when the holidays arrive, they're ready to meet the demand. Other times, they make croutons or bread pudding. Graul's Donna Taylor said that other edible but unsellable items may end up in a soup: "We make soup in-house," Taylor said. "That can be a destination for the odds and ends. I mean, soup is pretty much anything you want it to be."

As with restaurants, this impromptu repurposing is easier to pull off at smaller or independent markets. Mom and pop operations have more freedom to operate and less lawyerly input. Accordingly, these local establishments aren't as restrained and can try things out, such as populating the salad bar with lettuce from packages at their sell-by date. Taylor used to trade notes with her sister when she worked at a Safeway. "There's a significant difference between chains and independents. Chains don't have any freedom. They can talk all they want, but the bottom line is individual stores in that chain are towing that line," Taylor said.

Yet, that doesn't mean larger chains can't make it their policy to save food. If an operation as large as Costco can repurpose their rotisserie chicken, anyone can. And the incentive should be strong—multiplying the new procedures by hundreds of stores would yield impressive chain-wide savings.

For stores unwilling or unable to reuse their chickens or other prepared foods, there's another way to avoid waste—donate it. Unfortunately, supermarkets shy away from donating ready-to-eat items. While it's not feasible for open-buffet items, with a little effort, anything served by staff could go to a soup kitchen. Instead of simply dumping the food in the trash, employees would just wrap and refrigerate the food they're not going to sell.

Wasted Dough, Bread

Bread and baked goods are by far the most commonly wasted foods at supermarkets. According to Timothy Jones's study at the University of Arizona, 9 percent of the bread that enters a grocery store is wasted. Packaged, bread-aisle loaves are pulled from shelves by their sell-by dates. And at that point—thanks to their abundant preservatives—these loaves are still perfectly edible. Yet, even more bread waste comes from store-baked loaves, which have fewer preservatives and count on freshness to lure buyers.

Supermarkets seem to have so much leavened excess it's as if they somehow bake day-old bread. Stores churn out baguettes, rolls, and loaves with what appears to be complete abandon—and little regard for actual demand. From their perspective, water and flour are pretty cheap, and, like all items made on-site, the baked goods have high profit margins. The same rule of excess applies to supermarket cakes, muffins, and pastries.

Grocers want their shoppers to know that there will be fresh bread available even when it's just a minute before closing time, and being sure of that is apparently worth having to throw out many loaves a day. Not only do stores not want to miss a sale, but they fear disappointing a customer and possibly sending that shopper to another store. At one supermarket I visited with the Inter-Faith Food Shuttle, we recovered thirty-five pounds of bread. And that was just one day's excess.

If I ran a supermarket, I'd suggest a revolutionary idea—stop baking so much stuff! A renewed emphasis on demand forecasting would help accomplish that. And selling yesterday's loaves at a discount wouldn't hurt, either. This change would require a fundamental shift in supermarket thinking; not having the store appear as fully stocked a few minutes before closing as during the middle of the day would become the new normal. And what better way to communicate freshness than having consumers see that your store had sold out of that day's danishes?

Don't Hate, Get Stores to Donate

Fortunately, at the time I worked at a supermarket, I was also helping a soup kitchen secure food donations. I spent much of my volunteer time at Inter-Faith Council (IFC) Community Kitchen calling supermarkets and institutional kitchens to find excess food. Accordingly, I knew that the IFC staff would be willing to collect my supermarket's fresh produce in their rickety white van.

Getting my employers to participate necessitated some hoop jumping, though. When I asked the store manager, he told me to "ask corporate." When I spoke with someone at the corporate headquarters, they told me it was up to the manager. That led to another round of messages and a letter or two. That avoidance and excuse making is common among supermarkets, Paul Eberhart, the IFC Community Kitchen coordinator, told me.

After moving beyond that buck-passing stage, I found that implementing food donations was not that difficult. For example, after some initial wrangling, we were able to institute a weekly pickup at my store. It didn't even require us produce workers to rummage through the culled produce. The IFC was more than happy to sort through the boxes to determine what they could and couldn't use.

What's more, donating food actually made life easier for the produce employees. It was harder to discard the culled items than to set it aside for donation, because the Dumpster was 50 yards and one annoying door past the spacious walk-in cooler. After a few weeks of donations, I asked my manager how he felt the collection was going. He seemed quite casual about the whole thing. It wasn't a big deal, he said. Exactly.

The IFC pickups from my supermarket ranged from two to six 20-pound boxes of loose fruit and vegetables and bagged salads. Occasionally, a supermarket staffer threw out the boxes by mistake. Eberhart called the typical yield "a hodgepodge, but a good hodgepodge." For example, one collection included pears, apples, oranges, berries, tomatoes, cucumbers, squash, zucchini, and some packaged fruit, including watermelon chunks. "Fruit is the key because I'm about to run out of fruit from cans," said Eberhart, who sports a tattoo of the cover art from Shel Silverstein's *Where the Sidewalk Ends* on his forearm. "And serving fresh fruit is always great."

The one thing my supermarket manager was adamant about was that I not be the one to pick up the food for the shelter. This stemmed from a fear of employee theft—that old "shrink" monster again. He said it would be a conflict of interest. And he was right, in a way. My goal of keeping food from the Dumpster would conflict with the store's apparent goal of filling it.

To be fair, America's supermarkets already donate large amounts of food to the hungry. The Food Marketing Institute (FMI) Survey of Supermarkets and Food Banks, published in 2005, painted a happy scene. Across chains of all sizes, 95 percent of respondents said they donated unsellable goods to food banks.[31] Yet, that likely includes some exaggeration. After all, it's easy for a supermarket manager, in a survey, to say that his or her store donates certain items. Yet, more important questions than *whether* a store is donating food are *how much* and *what kinds* of food they are giving. Most stores donate only a fraction of their unsellable food. Peter Clarke, codirector of the food-rescue adviser From the Wholesaler to the Hungry, based in Los Angeles, estimated that only 10 percent of the available edible food is recovered each year.[32]

In considering the types of foods donated, the FMI survey results aren't all that surprising. While 88 percent of respondents said that they gave dry groceries, only 51 percent give fresh produce and just 33 percent passed along deli items and fresh meat. Unfortunately, fresh fruits, vegetables, and proteins are the hardest items for food banks to get.

That's why it was so gratifying when my store started donating fresh, albeit blemished or misshapen, produce. Yet, fittingly, I never was able to convince the butcher department to donate. Still, I felt like I'd done my (admittedly minor) part. With each new store "turned," as Eberhart called getting a grocer to donate, we move one step closer to the day when food donation is the norm. As more and more stores "go green," or at least want to appear to be doing so, donating food should become an easier sell. The opportunity to simultaneously do the right thing environmentally, feed the hungry, and save money (via tax deductions and diminished waste-hauling costs) makes it seem like an easy decision. Of course, that doesn't necessarily mean it's likely to happen at all grocery stores—without our intervention.

What You Can Do

With so much excess built into supermarket operations, what impact can one person make (besides altering personal shopping habits)? You'd be surprised by the effect your dollars and voice can have. Buying oddly shaped or nonhomogeneous produce—if you can even find them—may prevent that store from blindly throwing them away in the future. And don't be bashful about telling the department manager that you're doing so. Similarly, asking store management about selling slightly blemished items and goods nearing their sell-by dates may convince stores that there's a (slightly discounted) market for these goods. Based on what I've seen from working and shopping at supermarkets and speaking with friends, there is. If a produce sale rack exists, buying these items communicates that thrift and avoiding waste are as important as the sanitized vision of peak freshness. Your words and deeds can remind supermarkets that they're discarding sound food and revenue.

Furthermore, ask the manager of your local store what they do with their edible but unsellable food. If they aren't currently donating it, you can tell them about the local soup kitchens, shelters, and food banks that would happily collect these goods. If they need persuading, I hope that by now you can make a compelling case. Don't forget to remind them that they're protected from liability.

If a store remains squeamish about donating, they can still do something positive with their food waste. They might be able to send it to a livestock farmer or a commercial composter, for example. If you're unable to convince a store to donate food to the hungry, you could provide the supermarket manager with a list of local livestock and composting operations. Landfilling food should only be the last resort.

Check Out

During my three-month stint at the supermarket, I worked diligently—as my one-month review attested. I observed plenty and asked many questions. I took the job because I wanted to understand where and why supermarket waste occurred. I also wanted to see this squandering firsthand—and I sure saw it. By doing this participatory research, though, I was complicit. While working, I threw away, by my estimates, nearly my own weight in food each day, enough to feed hundreds of people. After weeks of tossing mind-numbing amounts of food, it became easier to do, and by the end of my three-month term, I began to understand why food-industry executives see waste as unavoidable, even while stiffening my resolve to prove them wrong. There will always be some loss; it's just a reality of selling perishable items. Yet, there's great room for improvement.

To this day, every time I see a produce worker pulling items from the displays, I'm compelled to look at what he's removed. Next time you're at your grocer, I recommend doing the same. It's worth examining what ends up in the cull box. But beware: Seeing this perfectly good food that could nourish someone en route to the trash is exasperating. Especially when you realize that the only way to access these items is via the Dumpster.

A peek inside D. J. Waldow and Kristina Milan's refrigerator may look familiar to many of us.

PHOTO COURTESY OF D. J. WALDOW

chapter 8

Home Is Where the Waste Is

You ever have milk the day after the day? Scares the hell out of ya, doesn't it? The spoon is trembling as it comes out of the bowl. 'It's after the day! I'm takin' a big chance! I smelled it, you smelled it, what is it supposed to smell like? Smelled like milk to me!'

—JERRY SEINFELD

The most remarkable thing about my mother is that for thirty years she served the family nothing but leftovers. The original meal has never been found.

—CALVIN TRILLIN

*I*t was a typical Monday night on a quiet cul-de-sac in Durham, North Carolina. D. J. Waldow and his wife Kristina Milan had just finished a homemade dinner that each had helped prepare. What began with a baby spinach salad with feta, broccoli, and a homemade lemon–olive oil dressing concluded with a tangy Thai-style stir-fried chicken with basil atop jasmine rice. In between, they enjoyed a toasted Israeli couscous salad with mint, cucumber, and feta.

After dinner, Waldow, a thirty-three-year-old software-company executive, packed two lunch-sized containers of the night's chicken and rice and searched for a place to store them in the fridge. He combed through the crowded shelves, trying to clear an opening for tomorrow's lunch and the other leftovers from the meal. Meanwhile, Milan, thirty, a resident at UNC Hospitals, lamented that she'd had no other choice but to buy a large bunch of mint for the half-cup required in the couscous recipe. She held up the remainder of the bunch, an unpackaged collection of stems, held together with a twist. It could have supplied 5 cups. "We have a crapload of mint," Milan said. "We will not use all of that mint."

Waldow chimed in, frustrated at how parsley is sold. "You'll need a quarter of a cup and you have to get the biggest bundle of it," said Waldow. "I wish you could just get the amount you want."

While we talked about how hard it is to use up store-bought herbs before they go bad, Waldow began digging into the crisper drawer that doubles as an herb graveyard. He unearthed a collection of plastic herb containers, some robust, some wilted. And then Waldow pulled up an item concealed in a paper towel. Opening it up, he revealed a healthy collection of mint leaves. Waldow and Milan moaned in disbelief.

Sure, a bunch of mint is a relatively minor item. At $2.29, it was not terribly expensive, but a closer look at Waldow and Milan's refrigerator showed that the mint wasn't the only thing duplicated. It was a recurring problem as Waldow continued to look through the fridge. He discovered half of a red onion hiding in the butter drawer, which, much to Milan's consternation, Waldow had begun using for items other than butter—like their dog's ear medicine. Unfortunately, Waldow had just purchased another red onion. And the couple owned identical tubes of ground basil because Waldow bought a second without realizing they already had one.

To some extent, we all waste food in these ways. It seems innocuous, but the resulting costs accumulate for a family. And the environmental impact quickly mounts when multiplied by the 110 million American households.[1] Just as significant, though, is the mindset that home food-waste reveals.

Taking a Step Back

Waldow works in the same industry as my wife. I had come to know him a bit from a touch-football game and his prodigious Twitter feed. When I was looking for a representative, normal American couple to observe, he and his wife came to mind. I sought to interview them on their foodways because, in addition to being game to talk about their waste and letting me snoop around their fridge, they seemed perfectly regular. Although they may be a bit more gourmet than some—in fact, they subscribed to *Gourmet* (until it recently folded) and two other cooking magazines—they didn't dispute their normalness when I explained why I had essentially invited myself over for dinner.

Waldow and Milan, who knew about the thrust of this book beforehand, promised to behave exactly as they normally would while cooking and eating dinner.[2] They seemed to stay true to their word, or at least they weren't trying to cover up their waste.

The couple estimated that they spend $300 to $400 per month on groceries, but I'd guess it might be more. Waldow and Milan live comfortably, but not lavishly. They own their house and the requisite wall-mounted flat-screen television with digital cable. He has a Toyota Camry and she drives a Chevy Malibu. Like many Americans, they buy some of their food at Costco to save money, and Milan told me they can't afford as much organic or free-range foods as they'd like. They're certainly not extravagant people. When their fridge handle came loose three years ago, they used Shoe GOO to reconnect it—a solution that held until I temporarily broke it.

Another Step Back—The Big Picture

Household food waste is subtle and pervasive. Domestic losses are so persistent, it's almost easier to list ways we don't waste food than vice versa. The Cornell University Food and Brand Lab found that 93 percent of those polled bought things they never use.[3] Food is constantly going bad in our refrigerators, which serve as cleaner, colder trash bins. The situation in our freezers is similar, only with a slower, less smelly rate of decay. Waste is seldom, if ever, eliminated in the home.

It seems odd that we waste so much of our food despite the enhanced technology—in the form of refrigerators, freezers, vacuum sealers, green bags, and so on. Yet, these "aids" are part of the problem. We haven't had to worry about keeping food from going bad for so many generations that we don't think about it. We unload our hefty shopping haul into the refrigerator and freezer, then put it out of our minds. By the time we remember about a certain item, it's a smelly, gooey mess.

In a 2004 study, Timothy Jones found that household food waste represented $43 billion in squandered groceries.[4] A 1977 report to Congress by the comptroller general lends a less recent, more depressing look at the topic. Using the 1974 crop year, it put household food loss at 39 percent of the food produced for human consumption.[5]

The Garbage Project at the University of Arizona provides our best, longest-running study of home food-waste in modern America. From 1973 to 2005, the project employed student "garbologists" to pick through and categorize what Tucson residents discarded. They also conducted interviews to corroborate beliefs with practices. William Rathje ran the Garbage Project while an anthropology professor at the University of Arizona. In Rathje's 1992 book *Rubbish! The Archaeology of Garbage*, which discussed the project's conclusions, he wrote that "American families waste between 10 to 15 percent of the food they buy." In a 2006 phone conversation, he told me that the Garbage Project found hard (or mushy, as the case may be) evidence that 15 percent of the food entering homes is wasted. With either estimate, the costs of waste add up quickly. Using that higher, more recent estimate, and assuming that a family of four, shopping on what the USDA considers its low-cost plan, spends $175 per week on groceries, we can determine that that's the equivalent of wasting $26.25 every week, or $1,365 per year.

Yet, Rathje said that that figure did not account for the food that his "garbologists" couldn't count—the stuff fed down the garbage disposals of Tucson. Rathje, now affiliated with the Stanford Archaeology Center, devised a formula to account for the household food that's liquefied and sent to wastewater treatment plants. In short, he found that we discard another 10 percent in this manner. Thus, 25 percent of what we bring into our homes we throw away. Using the USDA figures, that would mean that a family of four squanders $43.75 per week and $2,275 annually.

Rathje's garbage-disposal formula seems downright conservative after talking with Michael Keleman of disposal maker InSinkerator. He pointed me to a report by an InSinkerator engineer finding that in homes with a garbage disposal, 75 percent of the food waste generated is sent down the drain.[6] Rathje's estimates don't seem too high in light of a recent study in the United Kingdom that found that Britons squandered one-third of the food entering their homes. And I have no reason to believe the British are more wasteful than Americans. In fact, I'm tempted to think the opposite is true. Limiting waste requires patience, effort, and food knowledge. While these used to be common American traits, that is less true today.

Home food-waste is universal. It does not break down neatly along economic lines—everyone wastes. In their 1987 study *Food Discard Practices of Householders*, Oregon State University professors Shirley Van Garde and Margy Woodburn concluded that "household income was not linearly related to the amount of discard."[7] Of the four income brackets in that study, people in the wealthiest group didn't throw away the most in any of the three categories. And, in fact, the lowest-income group discarded the most food that was "judged unsafe." A decade earlier, the 1977 comptroller general's report had stated that "the biggest food wasters are middle-income families, not the very rich or very poor."[8] The

Garbage Project found roughly the same amount of food waste in the trash cans of the wealthy and the poor, but determined that more went down the garbage disposals in the affluent homes.

The only reliable indicator of food waste is age. Those who lived through World War II tend to squander less. Van Garde and Woodburn found that the study participants older than sixty-five wasted about half as much as those in the other three age groups. And half of that eldest cohort said that past food shortages or their mothers' discard practices were "the one most influential factor" in their "household's discard patterns."[9] By contrast, Van Garde and Woodburn wrote, "the younger groups' perception of food as being disposable is probably also a large factor in their higher discard rates."

Our high standards cause much of our waste. We don't eat many items that are far from perfect, and we're even less likely to serve them to guests or our families. Van Garde and Woodburn showed householders three samples of iceberg lettuce. The first was pristine, the second had a slight browning on the base of an outer leaf, and the third had slight browning on the cut edges and outer leaves. They were all perfectly edible, but 40 percent of those queried said they'd only serve the first example in a sandwich. Sound familiar?

Out of Sight, Out of Mind

Sometimes we create our own trouble with our food. Even waste-obsessed folks like yours truly fall into seemingly obvious waste traps. For instance, losing track of an item. I recently bought a tub of hummus, a somewhat unusual purchase for us. After using it once, I put it back in the fridge on the bottom shelf. I'm sure you can see where this is going—it slowly got pushed backward, mostly by a large Tupperware container of leftovers. Because I don't usually eat hummus, I wasn't really looking for it. And because it wasn't in plain sight, I forgot about it. By the time I noticed the hummus, it had a thick layer of that pink mold on it that I don't mess with.

Clutter is another major cause of waste. Through messy or cramped pantries and fridges, much of our home food supply isn't visible. Losing sight of perishables means we end up not eating them and can even lead to duplicate purchases. That's certainly the case in the Waldow and Milan household. The night I visited there, Milan, who does most of the family's shopping, thought that they had some frozen Costco chicken breasts remaining from a bulk purchase. Yet, when she got home, she didn't see any of the individually sealed, two-breast packets. That prompted a hurried run to a local grocer. Later that night, though, Waldow found the missing package, buried at the back of the freezer. That oversight didn't lead to any food waste—just an extra trip to the store—but it's instructive.

That same night, Waldow had meant to cook a bunch of asparagus that wasn't getting any younger, but forgot to because he didn't see it in the crisper drawer. As is the most common design, Waldow and Milan have a refrigerator with the freezer on top (called a "top-mount" in fridgespeak). Waldow told me he laments the design of his fridge, as he can't see items in the crisper drawer because it's so low. To really find out what's in it, you have to make the effort to reach down and open the drawer, often just enough of a nuisance.

This is the case even when the drawer is made of clear plastic. My refrigerator, a black Frigidaire that came with the house my wife and I bought, is also a top-mount. Since I use the fridge roughly ten times more than I use the freezer, this is less than ideal. I stand north of 6 feet, but the refrigerator portion of the machine ends just shy of four. Standing directly in front of it, I can't see any of the top shelf and only half of the second shelf, because it's too tight of an angle. The sightlines for the bottom shelf are fine, but the bottom crisper drawers often remain shrouded in condensation and mystery. Seeing all that's in the fridge requires some bending and squatting. And that's before the aforementioned problem of clutter is taken into account. Or aging, aching backs and knees and failing memories. While we could be better at reducing our "out of sights," our refrigerators sometimes don't give us the best chance of succeeding.

Having the refrigerator on top would seem like the obvious solution. So why, then, were top-mount refrigerators even created? Bernard Nagengast, an engineering consultant and a refrigeration historian, said that that layout stemmed from practicality. "The reason freezer/fridges were designed that way was because that's the way ice boxes were designed. Cool air falls," said Nagengast, a consultant to the American Society of Heating, Refrigerating and Air-Conditioning Engineers on historical issues. "They followed the same approach. All of the earlier refrigerators had the freezing unit on top."

During the 1960s, once fans entered the equation, the "cool air falls" thing became less important. "When they put the fans in, it didn't matter where you put the freezer," said Nagengast, indicating that we then had the ability to direct cold air in any direction. Shortly thereafter, bottom-mount designs started arriving in showrooms. Yet, today, having the freezer on top remains the norm, a vestige of early fridge design.

Refrigerator manufacturers have periodically tried to phase out fridge waste. In the 1950s, General Electric sold a fridge with lazy-Susan shelves to tackle the "out of sight" issue. Nagengast isn't sure why that idea never caught on, and neither am I. Pull-out shelves are touted as one of today's perks, but they've existed since the 1930s. And refrigeration engineers previously attempted to slow foods' decay with biology. "There was a period of time—I'm not sure exactly when it was—when some manufacturers thought it was a good idea to put an ultraviolet light in the fridge to kill the bacteria to reduce food spoilage," said Nagengast. Today, some high-end fridge makers, such as Sub-Zero, have brought back this technology that, in their marketing-speak, "scrubs the air."[10]

To be clear, behavior, more than design, is at fault for most fridge food waste. Overcoming these visibility challenges shouldn't be too difficult. And since we're all different sizes, there's never going to be a perfect refrigerator design. The important thing is to be aware of areas that are hard to see or reach. And if you're buying a new fridge, consider what kind of unit best complements your height and habits.

We can take heart from knowing that we're not alone in our fridge squandering. Even refrigeration experts like Nagengast have food wasting away in their refrigerators. "I do lose stuff in my fridge. You forget about it and pretty soon it's nasty," said Nagengast. "Sometimes there might be a cup of yogurt or cottage cheese that gets stuck way in the back. Or a leftover we forget about. I would say that that's pretty much a universal problem."

Stuffed

More than the design of their fridge, the sheer amount of food crammed in their fridge induces waste for Waldow and Milan. After dinner, Waldow opened the (now) wobbly door to illustrate some of his points on their food habits. He indicated being pleased that he'd been able to clear out some items, but I couldn't imagine it much more full. There was hardly room for the night's leftovers.

To illustrate this volume of food, I later asked Waldow if he'd be kind enough to inventory their fridge for me. To my pleasant surprise, he agreed. After I interviewed them for this chapter, though, Waldow and Milan moved to Salt Lake City, where Milan is doing her residency. What follows is Waldow's inventory of their refrigerator, in his words, after eight months in their new home:

Top Shelf

- ✓ 2 Nestlé Coffee Mates (quart-size)—one sugar-free, one fat-free
- ✓ Sugar-free apricot preserves
- ✓ Grated parmesan cheese
- ✓ 16 oz. box baking soda
- ✓ Chunk of butter (originally from a stick, in a side-dish container)
- ✓ Gallon of 1% milk (expiring in ten days)
- ✓ Tropicana no-pulp, calcium-fortified orange juice (purchased as part of a 3-pack from Costco, expired three days ago)
- ✓ Buttermilk (used for a few baking recipes, expired a few weeks ago)
- ✓ Random can of Fresca
- ✓ A bit of rancid sour cream (promptly tossed)
- ✓ Swiss chard, fennel/anise, celery root (to be used later today for a soup recipe)

2nd Shelf

- ✓ Whole-wheat English muffins (opened, with 4 of the original 6 remaining)
- ✓ 64 oz. (4 lbs.) plain yogurt (from Costco—we normally eat a few per month)
- ✓ Philadelphia Garden Vegetable Cream Cheese (1/3 less fat)
- ✓ More sour cream (this one is still good)
- ✓ Brick of parmesan cheese (to be used in recipe later today)

- ✓ 1 lb. organic spring mix salad (from Costco)
- ✓ 30 oz. tub of hummus (purchased at least six months ago from Costco)
- ✓ Heavy whipping cream (expired more than a month ago—tossed down drain. Yuck!)
- ✓ Unopened bag of whole-wheat English muffins
- ✓ 4 jars of homemade jams (made by Kristina)

3rd Shelf

- ✓ Smucker's jam
- ✓ 5 random beers (Three are nonalcoholic ones from about two months ago when Kristina's father was in town. I keep most of the beer in the second fridge in the basement.)
- ✓ Loaf of whole-wheat bread (part of a 2-pack from Costco)
- ✓ 2 lb., 14 oz. tub of natural, unsweetened applesauce (Costco?)
- ✓ Leftovers from last night's dinner (Spanish chicken with chorizo and chick-peas) in Tupperware
- ✓ Tub of dip mixed in a sour-cream container
- ✓ 2 hard-boiled eggs (in a bowl)
- ✓ Tub of gorgonzola cheese (old, but isn't it always old?)
- ✓ 36-count of "homemade" corn tortillas (really old, cracking—tossed!)
- ✓ 1 lb. of bacon (to be used in tonight's soup)
- ✓ Breast of leftover chicken (in a Ziploc bag, recently defrosted)
- ✓ ½ an onion (in a bowl covered with Saran wrap, three days old)
- ✓ ¼ loaf of whole-wheat bread (part of a 2-pack from Costco)

4th Shelf

- ✓ Homemade jar of pickled ginger (a few months old)
- ✓ Bag of Craisins (old, but used on salads every so often)
- ✓ Unsealed bag of dried apricots (old, but not sure they go bad—every time I clean out the fridge I try to toss them, but Kristina says no)
- ✓ Unopened bag of honey-wheat premium bagels
- ✓ Tub of chive and onion cream cheese
- ✓ Package of turkey cold cuts (second half of 2-pack from Costco)
- ✓ Bunch of cilantro (to be used in soup later that day)

✓ Container of baby arugula (5 oz.) (from Costco, to be used later today)

✓ 15 oz. tub of Brummel & Brown Spread, Made with Yogurt (which we often buy in 2-packs from Costco)

✓ Red onion

✓ 2.6-lb. block of feta cheese (normally don't buy that much but am using it in a recipe; also use it on salads)

✓ Bag of 20 carrots (some for soup, others to snack on and use in salads)

✓ 3 large English cucumbers (for soup)

Produce Drawer

✓ 2 bags of pre-cut celery, 2½ lbs. each (from Costco, one for soup, the other for snacks and salads)

✓ ½ of an old carrot

✓ *Really* old bag of green onions—tossed!

✓ Limp, old, wilted celery (forgot we had it—tossed!)

✓ 1 pear in a bag (still good!)

✓ 2 pretty old apples (decided not to throw them out)

✓ Old, browning broccoli—tossed!

✓ 2 oranges in a bag

✓ Old, wilted, bad cilantro—tossed

✓ 5 packages of random herbs: thyme (2), rosemary, mint, basil

"Other" Drawer

✓ Bag of half-eaten flatbread (light)

✓ Half a bag of uncooked flour tortillas

✓ Half-empty bag of multi-grain, 94 percent fat-free tortillas (low in carbs)

✓ Bag of pita-pockets (1 remaining)

✓ Bag of 30 corn tortillas (about 25 remaining)

✓ Bag of Mexican-style grated cheese with four cheeses (used mostly for quesadillas)

✓ Block of Norwegian cheese (half-eaten)

✓ Pack of string cheese (from Costco)

✓ One random serving of string cheese

✓ Jarlsberg Swiss (only a few pieces left, in a Ziploc bag)

✓ Monterey Jack cheese (in a Ziploc bag, expired)

✓ 40% reduced-fat Mozzarella cheese (nearly gone, also in Ziploc)

✓ Small block of Jarlsberg (in Ziploc, expired a few weeks ago)

Side Door—Top shelf

✓ Eggs (10 remaining)

Side Door—1st shelf

✓ 24 oz. bottle of Hunt's Ketchup

✓ 20 oz. bottle of Heinz Ketchup

✓ 14 oz. bottle of Heinz Reduced Sugar Ketchup

✓ 23 oz. bottle Frank's Red Hot Original Cayenne Pepper Sauce

✓ 17 oz. bottle Sriracha Hot Chili Sauce

✓ 2 oz. bottle of Tabasco

✓ 10 oz. bottle Carolina Pepper Sauce (at least ten months old)

✓ Bottle of Volker's Bakery "Smokin' Viablo" hot sauce (purchased at Salt Lake City Farmers Market the previous summer)

✓ 10 oz. bottle Low-Sodium Kikkoman Soy Sauce

✓ 15 oz. bottle of A1 Steak Sauce (Original)

✓ 10 oz. bottle of A1 Steak Sauce (Sweet Hickory)

✓ 10 oz. Lea & Perrins Original Worcestershire Sauce

Side Door—2nd shelf

✓ 16 oz. Newman's Own salad dressing

✓ 32 oz. Cardini's Caesar dressing (part of 2-pack from Costco)

✓ 8 oz. can of grated parmesan cheese

✓ 10 oz. Nalley Sweet Relish (likely purchased for a recipe, but not used since)

✓ 8 oz. Grey Poupon Dijon Mustard

✓ 16 oz. Mezzetta deli-sliced hot pepper rings

✓ 12 oz. bottle of Framboise Lambic

Side Door—3rd shelf

✓ Kretschmer Wheat Germ

✓ 32 oz. Kraft Mayonnaise with Olive Oil. (Good marketing. Looked interesting so I bought. Tastes like crap so I just tossed!)

✓ 8 oz. French's Classic Yellow Mustard

✓ 32 oz. Claussen Kosher Dill Pickle Halves

✓ 1 lb., 8 oz., Classico Tomato & Basil Pasta Sauce

✓ 17.5 oz. Sugar-Free Hershey's Syrup

✓ 22 oz. Best Foods Light Mayonnaise

Side Door—Bottom Shelf

✓ 16 oz. Wild Harvest Chunky Salsa (old, old, old)

✓ 1 lb. Krinos Tahini (a teaspoon was used for one recipe)

✓ Jar of homemade cranberry sauce

✓ 16 oz. Better Than Bouillon Chicken Base

✓ 8 oz. Better Than Bouillon Beef Base

✓ 8 oz. Better Than Boullon Vegetable Base

Now that's a full fridge! Of course, Waldow and Milan certainly aren't alone in stuffing their fridge. Why do we do it? First, we're uncomfortable at the sight of anything approaching an empty fridge. And given that many of us have 20-plus cubic feet of fridge space to fill, once we do that, we're hard pressed to use all of our food before it goes bad. And that's if you remember what's in there. Or maybe it's just that we're able to keep more in it, so we do.

While I enjoy *New York Times'* food writer Mark Bittman's no-frills approach to food, I wholeheartedly disagree with one piece of his advice in his book *Food Matters.* Under the heading "Sane Shopping," Bittman steered readers down a questionable path: "Make sure your refrigerator is full at all times, mostly with fruits and vegetables. Keep bowls of fruit (vegetables, too) on the kitchen counter or dining room table—they're gorgeous, after all, and if you live with them, you'll eat them." Unless, that is, you buy so much that you can't.

In Bittman's defense, the New York City kitchen is partly to blame here. In a separate column, Bittman referred to his "moderate-size refrigerator," and on the *Times'* "Well" blog, he even wrote, "I think a big refrigerator is not that helpful. Stuff that's in the refrigerator shouldn't be in there all that long anyway."[11] With that in mind, I'm guessing that his version of keeping the fridge full is quite different than it would be for someone with a Sub-Zero, or even a Frigidaire. For those of us with a cavernous or even an average fridge, this strategy is a recipe for waste.

How big are our fridges? In 1992, the average refrigerator volume was 19.6 cubic feet. By 2002, it was 28.6 cubic feet.[12] Big-box retailer Lowe's, on its website, lists 185 top-mount refrigerators for sale, only 10 of which had less than 15 cubic feet of space to fill.[13] On a cultural note, I only realized just how large North American fridges are after living in New Zealand. Seinfeld was quite popular then, and I was surprised by the number of times I found myself in discussions with New Zealanders on the size of Jerry's fridge. While the appliance's heft wowed Kiwis, I'd never given it a second thought. The fridge just seemed normal. And it was, by our standards. When I later visited some homes in the United Kingdom and elsewhere in Europe, I was surprised to find what seemed to be glorified dorm fridges in many of the kitchens. (And that was in people's homes, not at the hotels.)

Bittman's goal is a noble one—encouraging readers to eat more fruits and vegetables. Yet, that can be accomplished without stuffing your fridge and having overflowing bowls of fruit sitting around. Waste need not be a cost of healthy eating. To avoid it, we just need to plan ahead a bit or shop more frequently. And avoid certain pitfalls in the store.

Shopping Begets Waste

D. J. Waldow had recently read an article in *Best Life* magazine about the healthy diet of a particular firefighter. Among other things, this fireman had recommended eating beets. That information was in the back of Waldow's mind the next time he went to the farmers market and, perhaps not surprisingly, he snapped up a fresh-looking bunch of beets. Two weeks later, the previously mundane, now somewhat exotic root vegetables were in the trash.

At first, Waldow forgot that he had the beets. He had planned to make them on the night I visited, but he only remembered that as he was looking through the fridge after dinner. Beets were hidden from view in the crisper drawer. He held them up and said, "I was gonna cook it tonight, but forgot. Now I'm gone 'til Friday and [Kristina] doesn't like beets. These are gonna go to waste." Yet, when he got back from his business trip, there was still plenty of time to eat them. The real problems were that he didn't have a plan for the beets and was reluctant to prepare them because he never had in the past. When I checked back with Waldow a few weeks later, he had a new reason for not eating them: "I didn't want my first time making beets to be with ones that were kinda old and wouldn't taste great," Waldow said.

As Waldow admitted with a chuckle, these beets were not an anomaly. He tends to be a sensory shopper and likes going on the weekend so he has time to poke around. Milan said he often returns with in-season produce, such as asparagus, or shellfish, which they turn into appetizers. "I'll have a list, but I definitely make impulse purchases," Waldow said. "I'll come home with three bags and Kristina will say 'What'd you impulse buy this time?'"

Supermarkets are designed to separate us from our money by goading us into these whim purchases. Upon entering the store, we're usually shuttled through the produce department, with its sights, scents, and anticipated tastes. Kevin Kelley, the L.A.-based architect who designs supermarkets, noted that the produce section almost always comes first in the store, traditionally in "corner one" of stores oriented for counter-clockwise shopping. While this might maximize sales, it isn't the best for customers. We're prone to buy more than we need and some items may begin to break down while in our carts, both from the time unrefrigerated and the bumps from other groceries. Increasingly, the prepared-food sections—with their even harder-to-resist savory scents—are also near the front. I tend to view supermarket layouts as a challenge, and I see how closely I can stick to my shopping list.

Ever wonder why stores send you all the way to the back wall to pick up a gallon of milk? They're forcing you to navigate at least one aisle, passing hundreds of alluring items with bright packaging. Alicia Ross is a syndicated food columnist and the coauthor of *Cheap, Fast, Good!*, a book on maximizing food budgets. She stressed that our home food squandering often stems from poor shopping habits. "Sticking to that grocery list is crucial. It's that impulse buying that leads to waste," Ross warned. "That's food marketers' goal—to tempt you from your list."

Today's shoppers are up against years of studies and consumer research undertaken to prompt buying. Kelley told me that his company, Shook Kelley, has studied shopper psychology for seventeen years. He said that the people in and around the retail food business, his company included, pretty much know how to push our buttons. "I think you'd be shocked, terrified, and impressed all at the same time if you knew how in-depth we studied impulse buying," said Kelley.

All supermarkets feature bright, cheery lighting; it's always sunny in the supermarket. There usually aren't many windows, so neither weather changes nor fading daylight can distract us from commerce. As with casinos, clocks are a rarity. And the music, whether it's subtle or cheery, is mood-enhancing. I recently found myself bopping along to a David Bowie song at Trader Joe's. I'm sure I spent more time there than I'd intended. I know I had some of the free coffee on offer and whatever sample item the store was pushing. And I probably bought a few extra items. Well, maybe one. "Environment affects behavior," Kelley said. "If you enjoy a place, you'll shop it slow, you'll engage in the product. The longer people stay in the store, the more they buy."

Those samples can be another way we essentially buy waste at the supermarket. Waldow said he purchases fresh bread occasionally when they have samples that he likes. The tactic is fine if you know you'll use it, but it can backfire. Often, there's a reason you haven't bought that item before. In addition to directly selling that product, there can be a more latent motive to distributing samples: to keep you in the store. Giving out food eliminates the "I'm hungry" and the "Mommy (or Daddy), I'm hungry" reasons for leaving. Samples keep you and/or your children happy. And happy people buy more food. More food that they might not use.

For every Waldow, who enjoys shopping, there's a Milan, who doesn't. That's why she makes a list—organized by section, no less—and stays true to it. "I try to get in and get out as fast as I can," Milan said. "I just would rather do other things with my time." Stores try to use samples to keep the Milans of the world in the store, buying things that are not on their lists.

In-store specials are another waste inducer. Amanda Hale, whom I observed and interviewed (along with her husband and four children, in Carrboro, North Carolina), admitted to being swayed by the enticing displays at a Super Target. She pointed to an unopened dessert pizza in her cupboard as an impulse buy. Yet, she noted that her husband, Mike, an infrequent shopper, was more prone to be tempted by in-store specials. Mike's children all remembered his legendarily unpopular purchase of Seafood Flakes, which, thankfully, is not a breakfast cereal.

The displays at the end of each aisle, known as "end caps," are often the scene of such temptations, both in the items offered and the deals. And both adults and children are intended targets. On a recent trip to my regular supermarket, the end caps included a rainbow of Pringles cans, gallons of Lipton green and sweet tea, bottles of something called Flavor Splash Water, and a buy-one-get-one-free Lays Potato Chip display with accompanying Lays Dips. Stay strong, friends.

Goods bought just because they're on sale are often wasted. In that light, those supermarket bargains may be anything but. Just ask Benjamin Franklin. Although he lived before the era of 80,000-square-foot supermarkets and discount clubs, he didn't predate bargains. Nor did he mince words: "Nothing is cheap that we do not want," he advised.[14]

Delayed Waste and Unfamiliar Diets

As Waldow was looking through his fridge, he uncovered a couple of relics—two clear containers of pasta primavera that he and Kristina had concocted without a recipe. It was early June at the time, but the leftovers were well past the spring of their lives. They were ten days old.

Waldow walked over to the trash can and emptied the containers, which must have held two pounds of food. The problem: They didn't really like how the pasta tasted. After finishing dinner the night they made it, they still saved the leftovers, but Waldow wasn't sure why. "I knew we wouldn't eat that pasta," Waldow said. "We could barely finish what was on our plates."

I'd bet that an example of this kind of "delayed waste" now lurks in your refrigerator, whether it's dinner leftovers or an unusual purchase. You're likely to find it pushed toward the back or in some nook or cranny. Maybe it's something you didn't want to throw out immediately, as you guessed you'd find a use for it or have a change of heart. So in it went. Depending on the circumstance, waste-delaying is either a form of guilt-assuaging or an act of optimism. Milan guessed that both reasons applied with their pasta primavera: "When we cook something that's kind of so-so, we'll still put it in the fridge even though we know we won't eat it," she said.

I swear I kept a container of homemade walnut pesto in my fridge for at least six months. I didn't really like it, but I *wanted* to. And because it never seemed to go bad, I didn't have the heart to throw it out. That pesto, like the pasta primavera, highlights a dietary truism: Unfamiliar foods cause more waste. For Rathje, this is the First Principle of Food Waste: "The more repetitive your diet, the less food you waste," he said.

Now, I can imagine many of you chafing at the thought of pursuing an especially monotonous diet. I don't mean to inhibit culinary exploration. Yet, if you're not the kind of person who'll find a recipe to use up an item, or who enjoys freelancing a bit, buying and cooking untried foods will likely lead to waste. Grabbing a chayote squash or a Buddha's hand because it looks cool can end badly. Whatever you decide, just know that there's a much greater chance that those whim purchases end up in the trash.

While this doctrine is bad news for foodies and the culinarily curious, it was one of the principles Rathje's student "garbologists" discovered after digging through household trash in Tucson. They noticed that this was especially true with baked goods. The Garbage Project found that homes seldom threw out any slices from the standard loaf of bread. Yet, families wasted 30 to 60 percent of specialty breads like hot dog and hamburger buns, muffins, biscuits, and bagels.[15]

What I call "recipe one-timers" are among the many forsaken foods in our cupboards and fridges. For example, half a can of coconut milk sits in mine as I write this.[16] Waldow and Milan, who frequently make recipes from food magazines, often find themselves with some odd ingredients. As Waldow went through his refrigerator, he found plenty. There was the tube of anchovy paste that I did my best not to smell (he'd purchased it to make a Caesar salad when his mother was in town and hadn't used it since). One shelf of their refrigerator held red chili, green curry, and red curry pastes, all acquired for the same recipe, used once, and now two years past their expiration date. And while Milan said she still hoped to use the buttermilk—bought for a banana bread—to make pancakes, Waldow was doubtful.

For every item Waldow and Milan said they had repurposed, there were three or four that they hadn't. Much like the aforementioned mint, they had a largely untouched and withered package of sage, bought for a chicken with prosciutto dish. "You use it for one recipe and it just sits in the fridge," said Waldow. "I will attempt to use it, but . . ." His voice trailed off, and all three of us knew what would become of that sage.

Kitchen Smarts

Although we discussed Americans' faded foodways in Chapter 4, it's a subject worth reconsidering here. Bill Rathje relayed an interesting and likely apocryphal old wives' tale (pun intended—keep reading): A husband watched his new bride slice away both ends of the roast before putting it in the oven. When he asked her about it, she replied that her mother had always done so. The next time they visited the mother's house, they inquired about her trimming. As you might guess, the mother used to cut the roast so it would fit in her pan. While the story may have been contrived, it symbolizes our loss of food knowhow. That young woman, if she does, in fact, exist, probably has a pan that's twice the size of her mother's (ditto for her oven and kitchen). Yet, she has probably inherited only half of her mother's food knowledge.

While a larger portion of Americans are interested in cooking and food culture these days than, say, fifteen or twenty years ago, fewer know how long you can actually store items in the fridge. In their 1987 study, Shirley Van Garde and Margy Woodburn asked participants to evaluate roasted turkey slices. The participants were presented a container of the meat and asked the question, "This turkey has been stored in the refrigerator for four days. Would you become ill if you ate it today?" Surprisingly, 23 percent of the participants answered yes.[17] Van Garde and Woodburn concluded, politely, that "confident, accurate estimations of food safety were not the norm among householders."

Diminished kitchen smarts mean that fewer Americans know that slightly sour milk is required in many recipes or that stale bread has a million uses (and at the very least can be made into bread crumbs). We're uncertain when foods have gone bad, and when we aren't sure, they're tossed. Unlike in baseball, when a tie goes to the runner, increasingly, close food calls go to the trash can. I once received a restaurant to-go box with a sticker that read, "When in doubt, throw it out." Thanks, guys.

Like manufacturers' expiration dates, the refrigerator shelf-lives listed by the USDA Food Safety and Inspection Service seem a tad cautious.[18] For instance, they advise cooking chicken within one or two days of purchasing it. At that point, many packages have yet to reach their sell-by date.

When listing advice for millions, one can't err on the side of recklessness. That's why USDA estimates have to be cautious. And they also have to account for a range of variables: the guy who leaves the food out too long after eating, the woman who doesn't use sealed containers, and the family whose refrigerator is a tad too warm. As a result, we get a generic three to four days for almost all kinds of leftovers, including pizza.[19] Just three to four days? While I devour my pies long before the fourth day, that seems awfully careful. Heck, I've eaten pizza that's been left out overnight with no ill effects.

We should keep in mind that our foods will likely last longer than the USDA's near-worst-case scenarios. After all, the Food Product Dating USDA Web page noted that "'Use-by' dates usually refer to best quality and are not safety dates."[20] It's too bad the officials don't take their own advice. For sure, there is need for caution here. The line on when to discard food must be drawn somewhere. But it seems we're being advised to draw that line in an exceedingly safe way. This excessive caution has consequences. Just as there are ramifications to eating food that's too old, so are there repercussions for all of our waste.

Strategic Shopping

I've listed the main causes of household waste, but we could probably think of ways we waste food until the milk turns sour. The important question is what to do about it. Since home food loss begins at the supermarket, we'll start there. Our behavior before, during, and after shopping can doom us to waste food. And, as we've discussed, stores often encourage us to waste food. Yet, following these basic steps can prevent much of our food squandering:

Plan meals. Plotting your meals before hitting the store is a crucial step in reducing home food-waste. I recommend only planning dinner, as breakfast and lunch tend to be repetitive and less waste-inducing. Plus, that way you leave lunch open for leftovers! Even with dinners, be sure to build in a little wiggle room. If your life is anything like mine, you may want to leave a few nights per week open for when your plans change at the last moment, or for when it's time for a leftover smorgasbord.

You can jot menu ideas on a scrap of paper, a website, or call on a handheld device, whichever way works best for you. The important thing is not *how*, but *whether* you're planning meals before going shopping.

"Double up" on an ingredient. Finding two recipes that call for the same item can help you avoid that drawer of unused herbs and save you money. For example, two dishes that call for spinach will help prevent a wet green mess in your crisper drawer. One night's eggplant parmesan may lead to another's Asian stir fry with eggplant. Pulling off this maneuver is sort of like plunking down a Scrabble word that garners points both across and down. Double points if you can find two recipes that share two ingredients, and triple for three. But good luck finding two (edible) recipes that employ anchovy paste. (Although, with the Web at your disposal, even that may be possible.)

Take a quick inventory. Before making a grocery list or shopping, take stock of what you do and don't have. At the same time, it's a good chance to play store-keeper and be sure to rotate the older "stock" to the front of your fridge and shelves. Checking supplies will also force you to determine if you're missing any staples. There's nothing worse than returning from the market only to re-alize you now have two tubes of basil paste, and no eggs. The all-stars among us will keep a whiteboard list of perishables near or on the fridge that can be updated at this time.

You guessed it—make a list. When you plan your meals ahead of time, it forces you to make a grocery list. List-making usually means going through recipes to find what ingredients are needed. I've found that the actual process of writing everything down makes me more decisive. Delaying decisions until the super-market can be dangerous, as there are already too many choices required there. And arriving with a solid list makes shopping quicker and less painful. It also keeps you from getting distracted or forgetting an item that may require an expletive-laden return trip to the store.

Stick to the list. This requires remembering to take your list to the store, a feat I often fail to achieve. But mostly, it means avoiding impulse buys. Once you're in the supermarket, it's worth remembering that everything, from the layout to the lighting, is arranged to tempt you into whim purchases. Avoiding impulse buys is essential to reducing waste and saving money, because these purchases often aren't used. As you may have guessed, I've never been called a hedonist.

If you enjoy impulse buying, try coming back to that tempting item later to see if you really want it. After a few minutes, you'll likely have forgotten what it was you thought you needed so much.

Shop for produce last. The less time your fruits and veggies spend in your cart, the less wear and tear they'll experience, and the less time they'll go unrefrigerated. This tactic will also reduce impulse buys common to the produce section, because by the end of your shopping, you'll be ready to get the heck home.

Don't shop hungry. Going to the store on an empty stomach is a real no-no, as an active appetite can derail all shopping restraint. Food columnist and author Alicia Ross warns that this tactical mistake prompts impulse buys and, later, waste. "Don't go hungry—you'll buy everything because it all looks good," Ross said. "You're like Pavlov's dog wandering through the aisles. Often people buy more food than they could possibly consume before it goes bad." I often eat a granola bar before or even while I'm shopping.

Avoid tempting but useless deals. In the spirit of not buying food you can't use, it may not make sense to buy into the three-for-$10 sale. The king of this scenario is the Buy One Get One Free, or BOGOF. While this promotion can help homes save money when it involves shelf-stable items, it ups the ante when they're perishable. For example, getting two containers of strawberries can save you money, but only if you use both before they grow soft or moldy. Splitting items with a friend or another family is one strategy for making use of BOGOF sales, as is using your freezer. Try to consider whether you'll actually use both items before jumping at a two-for-one. For exmple, one BOGOF purchase that never comes close to going for naught in my household: ice cream.

Beware of bulk. Buying in bulk can be as perilous as the BOGOF deals. But as with art, cholesterol, and witches, there are good and bad kinds. The massive bulk deals found at warehouse clubs can steer us to squander food; you can end up throwing away as much as you use. Although these large purchases can be a boon to big families, or event hosts, they are less so for a family of four—or for a couple. Can you really go through a 3-pound tub of sour cream or cottage cheese before it turns green? And you'd probably have to open a hot dog stand to finish that 105-ounce mustard vat. Yet, the bulk food bins found at many healthier grocery stores represent a great opportunity to reduce waste. Customization is the key here. In these aisles, you can actually purchase less than you would with packaged goods.

Be realistic. It's best to shop for your actual habits, not your intended ones. Unless you're in the process of turning over a new leaf, "wishful thinking shopping" ultimately causes waste. If you get out of work at 7 P.M., having all the ingredients to make a mousakka probably isn't all that useful. More often than not, you'll end up eating out or ordering in. If this scenario sounds familiar, keep it in mind the next time you're in the supermarket. Then again, keep it in mind even if it doesn't sound familiar!

Avoid excessive prepared foods. Garbage Project researchers found that the more evidence of prepared foods they found in a home's garbage, the more wasted fresh food appeared in the same trash bag. If you buy a decent amount of prepared food, adjust your shopping to include fewer fresh items. Garbologists found that produce—excluding the peels and rinds—accounted for 35 to 40 percent of total edible food waste.[21] Rathje attributed this to what he called the "Fast Lane Syndrome" caused by busier lives and busier parents. There are now more homes with two or more working parents than there are with one working parent and one parent at home.[22] There's a disconnect between the reality of how we eat and how we wish we ate. "You know what's good for you when you go the store," said Rathje. "You buy fresh fruit, vegetables and meats and you know what your lifestyle is like and you buy a lot of prepared foods. So at the end of the week the prepared foods [packages] are in the trash and the head of lettuce is all gooey in the fridge."

Katy Wolk-Stanley, the Portland blogger who has given up buying new items, voiced Rathje's hypothetical scenario: "A couple years ago I used to be really bad about buying all this food, filling the fridge up and letting it go bad," said Wolk-Stanley. "When you're in the grocery store, you think we really should be eating all these healthy vegetables. . . . You put them in the drawer and then by the time you look at them, they're rotten. Then I'd go back to the store and buy another head of lettuce."

Don't break the cold chain! It seems to go without saying, but it helps to bring perishables home from the store promptly. If that's not feasible, keeping a cooler or insulated bag in the car is a sound idea. When refrigerated items warm to 40 degrees Fahrenheit (or hot items cool to 140), they enter the bacteria "Danger Zone."[23] There, conditions are ideal for bacteria to frolic amongst your food (and reproduce). The time spent in this temperature range reduces the life span of food and, in extreme cases—say, a two-hour yoga class after shopping—ends it.

To give you an idea of temperature vulnerability: A 1992 UK study took temperature readings of groceries before and after the groceries left the refrigerated cases at the store to see what would happen after some time in a car. The products began at 4 to 20 degrees Celsius and finished, after an hour in the boot, er, trunk, at 18 to 38 degrees Celsius.[24] Now consider that the "Danger Zone" begins at 4 degrees Celsius. Plodding shoppers, consider yourselves warned! Also, keep in mind that larger items, such as whole turkeys, stay cold longer than smaller ones, such as sliced turkey breast. And the weather will help or hurt, accordingly.

Use it up. Should you find that meal planning doesn't fit your lifestyle, here's another approach: decide what to eat by seeing what you have. To help here, there are even two books by the same name: *The Use-It-Up Cookbook.* True to her title, Lois Carlson Willand advises that we use up the perishables in our refrigerator before going on our next shopping trip.[25] Willand wrote, "This may mean you change your basic meal-planning process from asking 'What would we like to eat today?' to 'What do we have on hand to eat today?'" If you can make that leap—and not everyone can or wants to—it will mean less shopping and less waste.

Finding a use for tomato paste motivated Catherine Kitcho, a writer and consultant who had previously owned a catering company, to write her version of *The Use-It-Up Cookbook.* Her paste conundrum is the quintessential "recipe one-timer." Like Waldow's anchovy paste, these sauces, condiments, and pastes crowd our fridges. Yet, viewed in another light, they're an arsenal of ingredients.

Finding a recipe with that item in mind can help reduce the odds of throwing away a bottle or tube a year after using a solitary tablespoon.

Once We Get It Home

Store food sensibly. Since the door is the warmest part of the refrigerator, milk and the more perishable items are best stored elsewhere. Vegetables should go in the crisper drawers, where higher humidity levels help keep greens fresher longer. If you have a humidity setting, put it on high for the leafy greens; if you have two drawers, you can set one on high humidity and the other on low for nonleafy vegetables such as carrots and zucchini. And while some fruits and vegetables want to go in the fridge, some don't—tomatoes, for example, are better left out on the counter. For details on other types of veggies, consult your local green-grocer, the Internet, or the appendix in the back of the book.

Keep food visible. This holds true for all foods, but mostly perishable ones in your fridge or freezer. Keeping refrigerators uncluttered always helps, as does using clear containers. Another strategy is to rotate the stock as supermarkets do by placing newer food in the back and pushing the older items to the front. Or create a priority eating shelf, as blogger Angela Barton did. On her blog, "My Year Without Spending," she described writing this command on the shelf: "Eat Me." Making a list of soon-to-go-bad items to keep them in mind is another useful strategy. Giving it a whimsical title, such as "Remember the Alamo," as my wife is wont to do, is optional.

Don't be a fridge filler. Provided you don't have more family members than fingers, filling your refrigerator with food will likely create waste. Having a smaller fridge is another caveat to this rule. Ample refrigerators are not the enemy. In fact, they can save food, by allowing us to fit that entire turkey carcass or stock-pot of stew. The problem is what we often do when faced with so many chilled square feet.

Serve sensible portions. After getting food into our refrigerators and cooked, we can avoid great waste by doing something so seemingly obvious I'm almost embarrassed to bring it up: dish out a reasonable amount of food. There's no need to pile it on, since those who want more can always ask for seconds (or serve themselves seconds, or thirds, for that matter).

Sensible portions are even more important if you're a believer in the "clean plate club." This is definitely delicate ground, but regardless of your take on the "clean plate" ethic, one must admit that serving reasonable portions will cut down on plate waste. Because, after all, the remains on people's plates are seldom saved (even though they can be).

American over-scooping does a real disservice to our waists and our waste. And I'm looking right at you, Grandma! I used the generic term there, but to get specific, my Grandma Abby exhibits another "waste-as-hospitality" behavior. She doesn't dish out heaping amounts, but is prone to pushing a second helping before the first is finished. It's her version of what William Rathje termed the "Good Provider Syndrome," where serving and buying too much food is done in the name of love. In my grandma's defense, who wouldn't want a second slice of kugel? Not even a "sliver?!"

Save leftovers. Discarding leftovers not only means you're squandering the time and effort of cooking, but you're literally throwing away money in the value of that food. If you're going to save leftovers, be sure to refrigerate them promptly in an air-tight container (for most items).

Although I don't quite understand people who categorically deny the left-over, I'll agree that there are some items that don't do as well the next day. Dressed salads are a prime example. That's why I suggest not pouring dressing on the entire serving bowl when at home and ordering it on the side at restaurants. Fried foods tend to be worse in their second iteration, and seafood can be hit or miss. Yet, some items are even better the second or third day. The flavors and constituents of both meatloaf and chili, for example, fully blend in the refrigerator. And some items, such as guacamole, might not look great the day after, but scraping off a microscopic layer of oxidation reveals a flawless interior.

Germophobes won't like this, but, here goes: You might even consider saving food from your loved ones' plates. After all, they are your loved ones, right? Kissing isn't much different, germ-wise, than eating the food that that special some-

one's fork may or may not have touched. While those in the composting industry call this stuff plate waste, I call it "Love Leftovers." Or lunch. Ah, semantics!
Obviously, this formula changes if the person in question is sick.

One argument I often hear from people rationalizing their waste is that the
item was "too small to save." As someone who grew up in a house where all food
was saved, I'm not buying it. I can't say that my mom has thimble-sized Tupperware, but she definitely has the next size up. All food items have another use, if
you want to find one. I also have a term for these smallish leftovers: "remainders."

Eat said leftovers! Once you've saved your leftovers, that's only half the battle.
You have to eat them. If you're not sure whether a food item has gone bad,
chances are it hasn't. When an item has gotten too old, you'll know by its smell,
how it looks, or, in the worst case, that first bite. Foods lose their flavor and texture before they go bad, as Clemson University food-safety expert Angela Fraser
reminded me. There are still bacteria dangers that won't be noticeable; that's
not a result of age, but of mishandling in storage to allow too much time between 40 and 140 degrees Fahrenheit.

Chances are, you're underestimating how long items remain edible in your
fridge. That's not surprising, because, as we discussed, our Department of Agriculture does the same. Although in their case it is intentional, based on the need
for caution because of varying food-handling practices. For most people,
though, this underestimating is just lack of knowledge. I'd like to point out here
that I just ate a six-day-old meatball sub, and not only am I still here, it was pretty
tasty. Of course, it was well wrapped and promptly refrigerated.

If you're simply not a leftover person, try packing them into your child's or
spouse's lunch. Or they can always be used to create another meal. And if that
doesn't work, try to prepare less next time. Halving a recipe or finding cookbooks geared toward one or two diners can help here.

Repurpose. Using up your leftovers does not have to mean eating the same meal
for a second or third time. Sometimes there isn't even enough remaining for another meal, as with "remainders." These leftovers present opportunities to create or enhance any sandwich, salad, or other concoction. Improvising in your
cooking with these remainders can become a food game-show-like experience.

Repurposing is a handy way of ensuring that foods are used. The classic example is making chicken salad from leftover chicken. And the extra hamburgers from the cookout can bring a smoky flavor to the ground beef role in a recipe. Mat Mandeltort, now a restaurant consultant at Technomic, ran a restaurant called Hearth Fare from 1996 to 2001. His advice for restaurateurs and homemakers: Incorporate a few "use-it-up" dishes into your repertoire. "If you have these three things on your menu, you never have waste: Soup, quiche, pizza."

Store leftovers based on your intentions. If you plan to take dinner leftovers for lunch, creating meal-size containers rather than one giant one is a sound strategy. Doing so that night removes a barrier from eating leftovers and helps non-morning people (my hand is raised) get out the door on time. In addition, smaller containers of a dish are better for food-safety reasons because they allow the food to cool down quicker. Just promise me you won't throw away a decent amount of rice merely because there isn't enough to create a third lunch-sized portion, as D. J. Waldow did the night I was observing his habits.

Make friends with your freezer. Freezing leftovers before they go bad is a great way to avoid waste. I like to think of it as throwing out a life preserver. A word of warning: The practice becomes quite addictive and soon you'll have a full freezer. This is a nice way of avoiding the unintended BOGOF waste. And it's nearly universal, as almost everything freezes well.

Leftover night—or week. Planning for a leftover or smorgasbord meal once or twice a week really cuts into your waste. Fridge Fillers the world over will immediately recognize the wisdom of Eating Down the Fridge. Steven Shaw, the cofounder and executive director of the eGullet Society for Culinary Letters and Arts, proposed the idea of not buying groceries for a week. By so doing, he converted a long-practiced strategy in home economy into a Web-shared experience. "Let's all skip a week of shopping. Let's declare national eat the stuff in our freezers and pantries week," Shaw wrote. And former *Washington Post* food writer Kim O'Donnel trumpeted the initiative by issuing a formal "Eating Down the Fridge" challenge on her *A Mighty Appetite* blog.

Regardless of whether participants can last the entire week, Eating Down the Fridge is a worthwhile exercise to see how much excess most of us keep in our refrigerators and pantries. It forces us to find uses for what we have, leaning on recipes and advice from family and friends while eating down your fridge. You'll learn how to get creative with leftovers, and gain insight into your own food habits.

Worst-Case Scenario

Inevitably, there will be some food that won't be used. If you absolutely, positively aren't going to eat a food item, try to keep it out of the regular waste stream, which usually brings a methane-emitting end in the landfill. Rerouting food to animals used to be easy and common when slop buckets were in vogue, or at least in use. Nowadays this will be difficult to pull off unless you have your own pigs, chickens, goats, rabbits, or some other creatures for whom food scraps make a healthy diet. Fido can enjoy the occasional table scrap, but it's probably not a good primary option for him.

Barring those animal ends, it's time to compost. Now, I believe in composting. It's a cheap, green solution for food waste that anyone with a few square feet of outdoor area can do. There are even indoor composting contraptions, such as the NatureMill or the Bokashi method, for those without that space. There are almost as many kinds of compost bins as there are types of foods wasted. The quirkiest is the Roly Pig, a colorful metal bin made to look like a hog, complete with ears and a snout that's lifted to insert food waste. Yet, no matter what kind of contraption we use, composting allows us to avoid the greenhouse gas emissions and produce a useful soil amendment that recycles the nutrients in food waste.

Composting is not something you facilitate as much as let happen. The leaves that fall in a forest eventually break down. Converting food and other organic materials into a nice soil requires a bit more work than simply leaving it alone, but not much more. At its core, you're preventing a pile of food waste from emulating a landfill. That is done by "turning" it to ensure exposure to oxygen; by keeping it from going anaerobic, you keep it from releasing methane. Simple.

In addition to the environmental benefits, composting gives us agricultural wannabes an excuse to use a pitchfork (to turn the pile).

For those unable or unwilling to compost, sending food down the garbage disposal is preferable to the trash. But just barely. Those items will likely be processed at a wastewater treatment facility, avoiding methane emissions. Yet, the environmental impact of dumping food down the disposal is still being debated—(although it's not quite the same hot-button issue as, say, the death penalty). Opponents think it harms the municipal pipes that transport the stuff. And then there's the water and energy usage needed to process the food waste along with other substances humans send down the drain. Until we learn otherwise, I see putting food down the disposal as only slightly better than tossing it in the regular trash.

Unaware of Waste

The first step in reducing home food-waste is admitting that there's a problem. That's always the first step to recovery, right? Though wasting food isn't a disease or an addiction, it tends to be invisible. Not only do folks not pay attention to their waste, they underestimate it. A 1980s study testing methodologies for measuring household food waste found that asking people to recall or approximate their waste "yielded unrealistically low estimates."[26] In fact, 50 percent of low-income participants in one method and 63 percent in another reported having no food waste.

Noticing our food waste can be a real challenge. Because, in addition to sending it *away*—via the trash or garbage disposal—we're taught not to think twice about it. Fortunately, once we do realize how much food we squander, it's a relatively easy habit to minimize.[27]

Chances are, if you're reading this sentence, you've already begun paying closer attention to your food waste. And if so, good for you. If you haven't started, I bet you soon will. To fully grasp how much food is wasted in your home, I challenge you to keep a week's worth of your food waste. You can store it in the fridge or freezer so it doesn't smell. The important thing is to be able to look at your waste in its entirety to get a clear picture of how much loss occurs in your kitchen. If you want to wimp out, you can just keep a record of the items you discard. In either case, though, be sure to include the plate waste you send down the disposal.

Once you've gathered your home's food waste, take a step back. In light of some of the factors raised here, think about why those items ended up not being used. How much of the waste could have been avoided? I'm willing to bet that half of your collection—the edible stuff, not the peels and shells—was preventable. That's why halving your future waste shouldn't be too hard. Mostly, it's about awareness and effort. And you've already got that first one licked.

Senior Gleaners volunteer Eddie Heard gathers grapes from a
backyard arbor in Sacramento, California.

PHOTO BY JONATHAN BLOOM

chapter 9

The Obstacles and Art
of Food Recovery

*Now when you reap the harvest of your land, you shall not
reap to the very corners of your field, nor shall you gather the
gleanings of your harvest. Nor shall you glean your vineyard,
nor shall you gather the fallen fruit of your vineyard; you shall
leave them for the needy and for the stranger.*

—LEVITICUS 19:9–10

arren Shaw parked the banged-up box truck in the fire lane in front of the supermarket and strode inside. He headed straight for the back of the Raleigh, North Carolina, grocery store, walking quickly, and not just for an eighty-year-old. Despite being fifty years his junior, I struggled to keep pace.

Shaw, in jeans, gray sweatshirt, and yellow work gloves, quickly found a deli counter employee. "Anything for the Food Shuttle?" he asked.

Moments later, the woman wheeled out her answer—two shopping carts filled with prepared foods, deli items, and baked goods. The booty included grilled salmon, and smoked baby back ribs, and banana pudding.

Back at the truck, Shaw produced a beat-up, gray utility scale. He stood on the scale a few times while holding the goods. Subtracting his body weight from the haul, he told me that this first stop had netted 87 pounds of food. Amount-wise, it was about a normal pickup.

A former credit-bureau field investigator, Shaw brings a certain skepticism to his collecting. He's convinced that he's only getting a fraction of the potential donations. "I'm sure there's a certain amount going to waste, just like some stores give us produce and some don't," Shaw said. "The stores that don't, I'm sure, have as much as the stores that give, and are just throwing it out."

Yet, when you hit the right supermarket, the quantities from a collection can be staggering. The group for which Shaw has volunteered since 1993, Inter-Faith Food Shuttle (IFFS), collects from this particular grocery store five times a week. Some weeks, the store's donations top 1,000 pounds. He told me of a recent trip to another Raleigh supermarket. "I picked up and then left," Shaw said. "I got a call on my cell phone—they had 65 more pounds of bag lettuce."

After retiring in 1981, Shaw volunteered for the Red Cross for fifteen years. But in 1993, when a friend from his church had an operation, he asked Shaw to cover his shift for the Food Shuttle. He's been volunteering with the food-rescue group ever since. I asked him why he stuck with the unpaid gig for so long. "I liked it," Shaw responded.

What the Heck Is Food Rescue?

Food rescue does not involve sirens or flashing lights, nor do its practitioners wear capes. Rather, food rescue is the custom of collecting edible but unsellable food for distribution to those who need it. It tends to be used interchangeably with the terms "food recovery" and "gleaning." The latter, however, is a bit different because it often connotes recovering unharvested crops. From the urban, basement-level setting of D.C. Central Kitchen to the sprawling exurban Senior Gleaners facility in Sacramento, California, food-rescue groups run the gamut.

The first actual food-recovery group formed during the Great Depression. During that time, despite the widespread hunger, farmers and wholesalers still destroyed crops or let them rot. In 1932, growers in the farm-rich Imperial Valley trashed 1.4 million crates of cantaloupes, 2.8 million watermelons, and 700,000 lug boxes (about a third of a bushel) of tomatoes when they couldn't be sold according to economist Clark Kerr's tabulations.[1] And each week in California's groves, hundreds of tons of unsold oranges were piled up, covered in heating oil to discourage the hungry from foraging and left to rot.[2]

In response to this waste, various civic groups convinced growers to donate their surplus to schools and relief agencies. The first sustained food-recovery group formed in March 1932, when William Downing, owner of a Compton storage and moving company, invited a few army buddies over to discuss L.A.'s food waste. Shortly thereafter, the Compton Veteran's Relief Association formed and began collecting unsold crops from farmers, surplus milk from dairies, excess meat from packing houses, and day-old bread from bakeries.

New York's City Harvest is acknowledged to be the oldest existing food-recovery operation in America. Helen ver Duin Palit founded the group in 1982 after her New Haven Food Salvage Project caught the eye of the New York media and, subsequently, Mayor Ed Koch, who helped Palit bring the idea to the five boroughs. The city's abundant excess food has kept City Harvest busy ever since. Palit got the "Harvest" idea in 1981 while eating potato skins in a restaurant across from the New Haven, Connecticut, soup kitchen where she worked. When Palit asked the purveyor what he did with the potato innards, he told her the daily 30 gallons of unused potato guts were hers if she wanted them.[3]

Today, City Harvest may not do much literal harvesting, but it's definitely of The City. Its list of food donors includes the Plaza Hotel, Yankee Stadium, and Zabar's (Tavern on the Green was a donor, too, until the restaurant closed in 2009). Sometimes the call of duty for a New York food-recovery operation includes recovering ten pallets of cheese from Sargento after a Little Italy festival, or picking up remains from the world's largest fondue, made for *The Today Show*. And the group also has a dedicated truck that only collects kosher foods.

Senior Gleaners, in Sacramento, is one of the nation's largest independent food-recovery groups. Its 144,000-square-foot operation hums like an ant colony, which isn't bad, when you consider that the ants are all retired and most are older than seventy (the ages range from fifty to ninety-nine). Through supermarket recovery, large-scale pallet donations, and field gleaning, the group rescued 13 million pounds of food and household goods in 2007. To keep its 14-acre facility operating, the nonprofit cultivates regular donors and hosts weekend fund-raising events. Games of chance? Bingo.

Yet, one of the more colorful food-recovery groups is the only one that was founded by a restaurant. Food Gatherers, in Ann Arbor, Michigan, started in 1988 as an outcrop of what was then just a deli and specialty foods shop called Zingerman's, now a gustatory mail-order giant. Paul Saginaw, the restaurant's cofounder, got the idea from reading about the donation of foods used in high-end magazine photo shoots. "I thought, every day we have foods that are perfectly edible, but for some reason we weren't going to sell," Saginaw told me. "And I thought, we try as hard as we can not to have any waste, but we do. And there are many places that probably don't try as hard as we do. And then I thought, why don't we go around and collect it?"

Collect they did, making their first run in November 1988 with a van borrowed from a catering company. Saginaw and a few paid staffers picked up both cooked and uncooked remains from their kitchen and those of their fellow Ann Arbor eateries—including vegetables, tofu, milk, and bread—and delivered them to rehab centers, group homes, churches, low-income housing centers, and the Salvation Army. They operated out of Zingerman's, using the deli's offices and phones, while those staffing the operation transitioned from producing food to recovering it.

Saginaw admits that both naïveté and laziness led to Zingerman's funding Food Gatherers. "At that time, I didn't have a lot of experience in the nonprofit sector. What was sad was that there was a lot of red tape," Saginaw said. "I didn't want to deal with that, so we made a commitment that we would just fund the whole operation ourselves," said Saginaw, now the "chief spiritual officer" (no joke!) at Zingerman's culinary empire.

After the group's leaders decided that they wanted to eliminate hunger, not just prevent food waste, Saginaw realized that Food Gatherers needed to become a more professional operation. While still receiving some funding from Zingerman's, Food Gatherers took on other funders and purchased a 10-acre facility at a former slaughterhouse. Saginaw said that Zingerman's has donated between $36,000 and $60,000 annually to the nonprofit (in addition to the donated food), but the group's budget is now about $1.5 million. "In that first year, we recovered 86,000 pounds of food," Saginaw said. "Now they're doing 6 to 7 tons a day, 6 days a week."[4] That's an average of 78,000 pounds per week, for you English majors.

Retail Food Recovery

Our rigid adherence to "sell-by" dates, love of convenience, and insistence on uniform, pretty produce creates an abundance of edible but unsellable items, and food-recovery agencies are happy to swoop in. And swoop in, they do. About 150,000 private organizations help feed hungry Americans. Of these, many are active in securing the food that they donate. Inter-Faith Food Shuttle is one such group.

Sandwiched between North Carolina State University and the Raleigh Farmers Market, the Food Shuttle is the state's leading food-recovery operation. Every day, it sends its fleet of small trucks to grocery stores and restaurants to collect their edible excess and redistributes this bounty to local charities. The Food Shuttle traces its origins back to a 1989 morning when Jill Staton Bullard saw a fast-food worker dumping wrapped breakfast sandwiches into the trash after it had officially become lunchtime. Bullard asked whether she might take them to a soup kitchen, and the regional manager replied that she didn't want the company logo seen in soup kitchens. "She stated that she didn't think that people who paid for her sandwiches would appreciate the fact that people were eating them for free," Bullard said. "Those were her exact words."

Almost twenty years later, in 2009, the Food Shuttle collected more than 6 million pounds of food that would otherwise have met that same 11 A.M. breakfast-sandwich fate.[5] Though my recovery run with the Raleigh group occurred at a Harris Teeter not far from the North Carolina capital, the same process occurs daily in supermarkets across the nation. Unfortunately, there are still many places where it doesn't. Many stores don't have food-recovery organizations in their city or town. And some do have access, but choose not to donate to them.

There are approximately 35,000 supermarkets in the United States and a further 13,000 smaller grocers.[6] And then there are the big box stores that account for about one-third of all food sales.[7] But although all retail food vendors generate heaps of excess food every day, only a fraction donate all types of their unsellable food. Convincing stores to donate their more perishable items is one challenge. A secondary one would then be enabling non-profits to meet the increased collection demand. To a certain extent, the money needed to collect the excess food is a limiting factor. For both reasons, D.C. Central Kitchen founder Robert Egger told me, the group recovers only "a thimble full" of the available food.

There are many reasons why some supermarkets don't donate to food-recovery groups, but few are good ones. First, there's the institutional inertia familiar to anyone who's worked in an organization larger than, say, twenty people. I experienced this phenomenon as a food-sourcing volunteer for Chapel Hill's Inter-Faith Council (IFC) Shelter, where I was tasked with finding new sources of food. I contacted many supermarket managers about the prospect of collecting edible but unsellable food from their stores. Stalling, evasion, and attrition were common.

When one new store from a chain that regularly gave to the IFC opened, we got it to donate, but only after a three-month process that included numerous reminder calls, formal requests sent in on letterhead, and e-mails of approval from the chain's corporate headquarters. And that was for a store with a manager receptive to donating.

Certainly, grocery stores are busy, and it's understandable that donations don't take precedence over day-to-day operations. Still, I would bet that supermarket executives would view food donations as more of a priority if they paused to consider the tax benefits of giving. Stores are allowed to deduct the fair market value of goods donated, which is usually half of the retail price. As a result, most recovery groups weigh what they collect and provide stores with the totals. Yet, a surprising number of stores don't bother to utilize these savings. While I was out with Warren on an Inter-Faith Food Shuttle run, only one of the five stores wanted to know the total weight of its donations, and that was due primarily to that store's manager having a vigilant grip on inventory. In addition to the potential tax deductions, food donors may benefit from savings in their waste-hauling bill.

Donating to food-recovery groups isn't difficult. It just requires a change in mindset. "It's all about shifting that philosophy about excess food," said Paul Eberhart, the kitchen coordinator at the Inter-Faith Council Shelter. "Now it's 'We take the food and put it in the trash.' Well, how about putting it in trays and holding it for us?"

An Irrational Fear

One word makes food recovery much harder than it has to be: *liability*. If you prefer two words, they are *litigious society*. Many supermarkets and restaurants don't donate food for fear that they'll be sued if someone gets sick from those donated items. It's an unfounded anxiety. For starters, they're not going to be sued. And even if they were, they'd win the suit.

As discussed in Chapter 6, the Bill Emerson Good Samaritan Food Donation Act protects all organizations from liability when they donate food in good faith. President Clinton signed the bill into law on October 1, 1996. Congressman Bill Emerson succumbed to cancer after cosponsoring the bill, ensuring that his name would live on in food-recovery immortality. The law extends criminal and civil liability protection to food donors, provided they give what they believe is good food.[8] Only cases of "gross negligence or intentional misconduct" could land donors in trouble.[9] Technically, the bill converted and amended existing "model" legislation from 1990. Yet, in practice, it marked the first time liability protection for food donation existed nationwide.

Prior to 1996, there was a legitimate cause for confusion among supermarket, restaurant, and commercial kitchen managers. Individual states had their own Good Samaritan protections, which created a mishmash of differing liability protections in many states. Chains with locations in multiple states were reluctant to donate. "Corporate lawyers, for, say, a Marriott would have had to go state by state to find out what the laws were for donating food in each location," Egger said.

Leaders of food-recovery groups knew something had to be done, as fear of lawsuits was hindering the recovery of nourishing food. In 1995, 83 percent of food companies surveyed by America's Second Harvest cited "liability concerns" as the greatest factor in determining whether or not they would donate food.[10] With about 25 million hungry people (out of a population of 262 million) at that time, the Good Sam Act made too much sense not to happen.[11] The bill was one of the few pieces of legislation signed by President Clinton, Newt Gingrich, and Strom Thurmond.

Amazingly, more than fourteen years later, many retailers are still ignorant of the Good Samaritan law. As Dan Glickman, who played a role in the law's creation as the U.S. secretary of agriculture at that time, told me, "The fear of liability still acts somewhat as a disincentive, particularly with refrigerated or cooked food as opposed to packaged foods. But it's less so than it used to be."

Even with liability protection, donors usually take some convincing. "There are some grocery stores that are unturned, where it seems like there's a corporate mandate not to give," said Jennifer McLean, vice president of operations at City Harvest. "Getting them to realize that donations are safe and that they're protected from liability isn't easy."

Some potential donors may only pretend to be unaware of the Good Samaritan Act, Eberhart has found. More often, retailers decline to give even though they know they'd win a suit because they're terrified of potential negative publicity. Many who worked to get the bill passed, such as Egger, continue to be surprised and dismayed by this outcome. "That was one of the things that us people who weren't lawyers didn't anticipate—the name thing. That ultimately a company's goal is to never have their name associated with food-borne illnesses," Egger said.

Restaurant and grocery chains alike fear the possible negative publicity more than actual legal trouble. "The donor understands that their name is on the box, and if someone gets sick, they've got a public relations problem," said Peter Clarke, codirector of the Los Angeles–based food-recovery consultant From the Wholesaler to the Hungry. "There are potential donors who fear being subjected to technically frivolous legal suits, but ones that will be potentially embarrassing."

Of course, this fear isn't all that rational. It's like making a business decision based on being afraid of the bogeyman. Why? Because just like the fabled monster, a liability for donation suit has yet to be seen. Nobody I spoke with can recall any such lawsuit. Not Robert Egger, who has run D.C. Central Kitchen for the past twenty years. Nor retired executive director of Second Harvest Heartland Richard Goebel, a man Egger described as "the godfather of food recovery." Neither Dan Glickman, the secretary of agriculture from 1995 to 2001, nor Joel Berg, the USDA's food-recovery coordinator at the time, could think of one when I asked them. Still, this unfounded fear is responsible for letting millions of tons of nutritious food go to waste each year.

Food-recovery groups have instituted stringent food-safety training in response to grocers' and restaurateurs' concerns. All drivers at City Harvest, the Inter-Faith Food Shuttle, and most other food-recovery groups learn the rules of food safety these days. And City Harvest leaders weave a decent amount of caution into their operation. "We like to say we have layers of defense," McLean said. "There are the people in the office taking calls asking the key questions to be sure the food is safe. The next layer is that our drivers who collect the food are trained in food safety. Then we train the [recipient] agencies."

D.C. Central Kitchen is similarly careful—not with what it accepts, but with what it will serve to its clients. "We're pretty methodical," said Egger. "You have to take food safety seriously, that's our business. Sometimes you take food just to keep a donor happy and then you dispose of it when you get back here."

Of course, some of the smaller agencies, especially soup kitchens that collect the food they ultimately serve, question just how necessary some of these measures are. These operations tend to be the ones without the money for refrigerated trucks, and they end up taking a more commonsense approach, rather than a legalistic one. "Give me a break!" Eberhart said, recalling how one supermarket manager voiced concerns about donating on food-safety grounds. "You don't need a food-safety course to drive your groceries home from the supermarket."

A Crack in the Wall

Since beginning this research in 2005, I have seen the food-recovery landscape change in a few ways—more specifically, in one major way—the Walmart way. As the largest food retailer in America, with 2,750 stores and more than three times the sales of its nearest competitor, whatver Walmart does greatly impacts food donations.[12] In January 2006, the retail giant banned the donation of out-of-code goods, a practice that existed at some but not all Walmart and Sam's Club outlets. Instead, they cut a big check to what was then called America's Second Harvest (now Feeding America), playing the old food-safety card. In the meantime, they let all of their nearly expired food go to waste. "We can't guarantee the safety of the merchandise, and consumer safety is our top priority," Walmart spokesman Olan James told the *Sacramento Bee*.[13]

Walmart reversed course in 2009. In encouraging their stores to donate, the chain hasn't set the bar so much as caught up with other leading chains. Given its size, though, the move has been a boon for food banks. By the end of 2009, Walmart's food donation program had reached all Walmart locations, yielding 90 million pounds of food donations to those in need.[14] While the Arkansas-based behemoth's food-safety fears haven't lessened, the company found a way around them—giving millions to facilitate the purchase of refrigerated trucks for transporting donated perishables like meat, dairy products, and frozen foods. Walmart bankrolled Feeding America's purchase of twenty new refrigerated trucks in 2008 and thirty-five the following year.[15]

America's second-leading retailer, Kroger, also has an arrangement with Feeding America. In 2007, Kroger contributed 24 million pounds of food and other products to the national network of food banks. Even more exciting, through its new company-wide food-rescue program, the Perishable Donations Partnership, Kroger donates meat, produce, and dairy products directly from stores to local food banks. According to a company press release, Kroger estimates that the program brings an additional 30 million pounds of food donations to the needy annually.[16]

The Foods That Are and Are Not Given

During my morning food-recovery run with Warren, we received no raw meat or seafood and very few prepared foods. Shaw told me that getting shut out on meat is not unusual. Protein donations vary within the same grocery chain. Some stores give it away on or past its sell-by date and some wouldn't dream of it.

Due to liability fears, donations from stores' butcher department have always been rare. "Early on, meat was one of the things you could not touch," said "the food-recovery godfather," Goebel. "But that has increased some."

Not that meat donation is widespread now. Because they tend to be highly perishable, proteins are the least donated items. That's why food banks are always telling potential donors that their greatest need is for proteins like peanut butter or canned tuna or meat. It's also why food-recovery groups end up establishing a de facto hierarchy of foods. "We can't be everywhere at once," said City Harvest's McLean. "We have to prioritize. We weigh quantity, quality, and type. If it's 20 pounds of meat, I'm interested, because that's the hardest thing to get. Dairy, too. Then quantity."

Similarly, grocery stores are hesitant to donate ready-to-eat items because of food-safety concerns. That's unfortunate, because prepared foods are one of the fastest-growing grocery segments. When it's self-service, as at the Whole Foods hot bar, items can't be donated because consumers certainly aren't trained in food safety. As a result, Lance Parchment, the prepared-foods assistant coordinator for Whole Foods' South Region, estimated that each store throws away 30 pounds of cooked goods—from tofu to turkey (and possibly tofurkey)—daily. "Almost none of the food retailers give away prepared foods—it's too dangerous," said Edward McLaughlin, director of Cornell University's Food Industry Management Program.

Ready-to-eat items that are wrapped, though, or served by employees could and should be donated. The Chapel Hill, North Carolina, Whole Foods doesn't donate items from the display case or even let employees take foods home, as they do with baked goods. Whole Foods team member Lucy Baker told me that they simply let foods sit in the display case for four hours, then dump them. The store could easily put items in the refrigerator to ready them for donation because, at that point, it's not a question of food safety, but one of taste. Jon Kawaguchi, the environmental health supervisor of Oregon's Multnomah County, said that food discard rules vary from state to state and county to county, but that the standard scenario is that a store can sell an item as long as it keeps it at the proper temperature.

Whole Foods sells pre-made sandwiches in the deli departments at most of its locations. In March 2009, Ralph Reese, fifty-seven, an employee at the Union

Square Whole Foods in New York City, decided to set aside one of the thirty tuna-fish sandwiches that he was to throw away as part of his duties. As he told the *New York Times*, he put it on the counter in plain view.[17] When his boss questioned him, Reese said he didn't see the harm in eating something that was going to be thrown out. His boss disagreed and discarded the sandwich. Reese was fired two days later for proposing to eat something that was going to be chucked anyway. The ensuing fallout sparked discussion on how being fired for "misconduct" affects unemployment insurance, but none of the articles or related comments mentioned Whole Foods' habit of throwing out (many!) sandwiches that could be recovered or given away.

As we saw with the tuna tale, food-safety concerns, even when they're unnecessarily cautious, overpower environmental or empathetic ones. If supermarkets wanted to donate all of their unsellable goods, they could do it safely and with minimal effort. They'd simply have to set items aside and chill them to 40 degrees or less by placing them in one of their coolers, as many grocers and restaurants do. But that doesn't always happen. Stores that may be donating less-perishable items are discarding mountains of meat, dairy, and prepared foods. "There are some stores that are just giving bread, but I know they're throwing milk in the trash," McLean said.

A Bevy of Baked Goods

Have you ever been in a bagel shop at the end of the day? The leftovers can be staggering. Stores may bag up a few to sell as "yesterday's bagels," but that's the tip of the iceberg. The Titanic-sinking remainder usually finds its way to the Dumpster.

Not surprisingly, given their New York locale, City Harvest reaps an enormous amount of bagels. Five bagel-specific bakeries are listed as donors on the group's website. At the venerable H&H Bagels (their Midtown East store), I watched as City Harvest's driver, Haisel Vasquez, rapped on the metal bulkhead door down to the basement. The door swung open and clear City Harvest–branded bags of bagels began streaming up a conveyor belt to the sidewalk. Vasquez, a hulking twenty-six-year-old in cargo shorts and a brown City Harvest short-sleeved shirt, lugged the four 50-pound bags back to the truck.

While many folks think shelters are desperate for food, and thus grateful for any kind of donations, that's only partly true. Since the economic downturn of 2008, food pantries have struggled to keep up with the increased demand. Yet, the level of need differs depending on the type of food. The massive volume of available bread and baked goods makes it a low-priority item.

Kae Abel, vice president of the Sacramento-based Senior Gleaners, said that her nonprofit moves more than 25,000 pounds of bread each week. That's more than 12 tons of baked goods. Bread products make up a robust 18 percent of all items that the Inter-Faith Food Shuttle recovers, their CEO Jill Bullard told me.

In its early days, D.C. Central Kitchen found out the hard way that there can be such a thing as too much bread. "We got into these agreements with bakeries to take their leftovers," said Egger. "Then we realized you can't move bread. No agencies need it. We had to go to some people and tell them we couldn't take it because one day it's a baguette, the next day it's a baseball bat."

Food Runners, a San Francisco–based food-recovery organization, has its pick of bread products in the sourdough-centric City by the Bay. Nancy Hahn, Food Runners' CEO, spilled a dirty little secret of the food-recovery world: "Bread and pastry are easy to come by. There's so much excess bread in town that the shelters can't even use it all."

After riding along on a City Harvest pickup run, I went to see the drop-off at the soup kitchen under Harlem's Metropolitan Baptist Church. One of the workers there, who declined to give his name, told me they end up throwing out a large amount of bread and bagels. "It's a shame, but we just get so much," the forty-something, wiry man told me as he divvied up baguettes, rolls, and bagels while wearing surgical gloves.

Some soup kitchens and pantries that are unable to find human takers for their bread find animal ones. Raleigh's Inter-Faith Food Shuttle volunteers collect so many baked goods that they immediately divert the hard bread to the "pig room," where they store loaves for a local pig farmer. The day I visited Senior Gleaners, a cattle rancher happened to be filling up the bed of his beefy Dodge truck with gourmet loaves of slightly unfresh bread, now destined for a bovine end. I wondered whether cows preferred asiago or rosemary ciabattas.

While extra bread is a good problem to have, one has to wonder why the bakeries don't simply make less. Perhaps having their displays look full is part of it, but they could use fake loaves to help accomplish that. At least bread is something that can be nourishing. Many of the other excess baked goods aren't exactly healthy. When I accompanied Warren Shaw on his food-collection route, we received an entire shopping cart full of pies, muffins, and cupcakes, plus the aforementioned store-made containers of banana pudding that caught his eye. Shaw told me that when he collects the excess from Krispy Kreme doughnuts, which he immediately delivers to a nursing home, the usual take ranges from 30 to 100 *dozen* doughnuts. For better or worse, that kind of output isn't unusual. In Portland, Oregon, when I visited Golden Harvesters, a membership food bank, I found more of the same. Cakes and cupcakes occupied more than half of the organization's refrigerator space.

While it's easy for nutritionists to shun the practice of giving out sweets, most of them have the means to indulge in their treat of choice at their leisure (as do most of us). Those struggling to eat may not. In addition, shelter and food-bank operators recognize that their clients look forward to dessert. As the IFC's Paul Eberhart remarked, recipients lead hard lives, so nonprofits should strive to make them a bit sweeter.

Yet, you don't have to be a nutritionist to shudder at the thought of giving poor Americans highly fattening foods. Nobody wants to make food recipients' lives more difficult by adding diet-related health problems to their plate. In an ideal world, aid organizations would serve healthy meals made from fresh, local ingredients. Increasingly, that vision is becoming more of a reality, as ag-oriented food-recovery groups are replacing canned produce with farm-fresh fruits and vegetables.

Rural Recovery

Farm food-recovery, while not as widespread as that from supermarkets and restaurants, is often more bountiful, due to the abundance of unpicked and unsold crops available. Whereas most food-recovery and gleaning groups make the rounds in small trucks or vans, "ag rescue" happens by the tractor-trailer load. Farm Share, a Florida City, Florida ag-recovery group, provides an alarming example. "On an average day when the largest packing house in Homestead, Florida, is processing tomatoes, I can fill a dump truck with 22,000 pounds of tomatoes every 40 minutes," said Patricia Robbins, Farm Share's cofounder and chairperson.

Though the farm-recovery organizations are already picking up food by the truckload, the available edibles far outweighs their ability to collect it. As with all food recovery, farm rescue only recoups a fraction of available food. "We're only able to get .05 percent of what's not used in the South Miami Dade area," Robbins told me. "I usually tell people 5 percent because .05 percent is too hard to explain."

Farm Share falls far short of capturing all that's available even while receiving a gift from the state of Florida: free inmate labor. The Florida Department of Corrections provides as many as twenty-four inmates and two guards five days a week. At Farm Share's facility, inmates in blue short-sleeved shirts and light blue pants mix with volunteers while performing a variety of tasks. While their presence raises eyebrows among fellow volunteers, the inmates have not been convicted of violent crimes and are all near being transferred to work-release programs or simply being freed. The guards don't even carry guns. "They'd have to be stupid to run because they're almost out," said Robbins.

It's cheap to rescue agricultural goods—about 5 cents per pound of food for Farm Share—but it still takes money. Sometimes the cost of recovering farm goods comes from paying a farmer to harvest or process what he'd otherwise plow under. City Harvest reimburses some farmers for the expense of picking what in years past had been squandered. An upstate beet farmer approached the City Harvest booth at a farm bureau meeting near Rochester and told those who were staffing it that he'd love to donate his excess, but he couldn't afford it. He said he threw out about 1 million pounds of beets per year that were too big to process. The following year, City Harvest paid $2,000 to subsidize the harvesting and freight costs and received a tractor trailer full of beets. Without editorializing, I'll just say that's a lot of beets.

Located in the agricultural mecca of Salinas, California, Ag Against Hunger is well-positioned to receive farm donations. Even more so, their storage facility (or "cooler") is within a mile of three major grower/shippers—Green Giant, River Ranch, and Taylor Farms—on a stretch of Abbott Street that locals, including Executive Director Abby Taylor-Silva, call "Produce Row." Ag Against Hunger employs a full-time driver, Henry Arias, who spends his forty-hour weeks making runs between grower/shippers and the nonprofit's cooler. The group recovers and distributes about 10 million pounds of produce per year, the equivalent of more than 250 dump-truck loads. When the group started in 1990, its founders set a goal of 50,000 pounds of food. They got 5 million.

Walking into the Ag Against Hunger cooler is like visiting a wholesaler's warehouse; it's hard to fathom that all of the 10-foot high pallet loads were someone's surplus. The day I visited was an ordinary one for donations, Taylor-Silva said. They had recovered 12 pallets of mushrooms from Monterey Mushroom in Watsonville and 8 pallets of salad mix from River Ranch. They also collected 26 pallets, or one tractor-trailer load of bag salads and shredded "food-service lettuce" from Taylor Farms. Some of the boxes had their intended recipients' names on them—Taco Bell and Burger King. Taylor Farms had two more truckloads that Arias couldn't get and would return for the next day.

Given that there's plenty of low-hanging fruit, farm food-recovery is growing rapidly. Farm to Family, a project of the California Association of Food Banks, pulled in 10 million pounds of mostly peaches, oranges, potatoes, and watermelons in their inaugural year, 2005. Sue Sigler, the association's executive director, said that they had increased that total eightfold by 2009.[18] And Feeding America, the national food-recovery network, planned to bring in 25 percent more farm produce in 2010 than it did the year before.[19]

Virginia's Society of St. Andrew (SoSA) has led the way in agricultural food rescue for the past twenty-five years. Methodist reverends Ken Horne and Ray Buchanan launched the hunger-fighting group in 1979 after they'd moved their families to a farm in western Virginia to live an intentionally simple life. Originally operating out of a converted sheepshed, the group received its first donation—a tractor-trailer load of sweet potatoes—in 1983. The ecumenical Christian group has been redistributing farms' bounties to those in need ever since. "When we started out, nobody salvaged produce and shipped it any distance," said Horne, still the society's executive director. "Now with us, Feeding America, the gleaning operations in Arizona, California, Washington, and Oregon, we probably do a quarter billion pounds per year."

As it grew, SoSA became the first large-scale group dedicated to recovering fruits and vegetables. Today, it runs farm-recovery ministries in twenty states—with a presence in all the forty-eight contiguous states—and has recovered more than 500 million pounds of food to date. In addition to receiving bulk commodity donations, SoSA, like most farm-rescue groups, also runs a more hands-on, albeit less-productive form of food recovery: gleaning.

Picking the Remains

Gleaning, the term for recovering crops that remain after the harvest, is not a new idea.[20] It is an established cultural practice in much of the world and even protected under European law. Gleaning is defended in the centuries-old French penal code as well as by a royal edict from 1554.[21] In nineteenth-century England, gleaning was a legal right for cottagers (tenant farmers).[22] And Jean-François Millet's 1857 painting celebrating the practice—*The Gleaners*—hangs in the Musée D'Orsay.

Going back further, the practice has Old Testament roots. A passage in Leviticus instructs farmers not to reap to the very edges of their field. Deuteronomy 24:21 reads, "When thou gatherest the grapes of thy vineyard, thou shalt not glean it afterward: it shall be for the stranger, for the fatherless, and for the widow." The activity was common in biblical times, as when the destitute Ruth met her future husband, Boaz, while gleaning in his fields, and is still practiced in many parts of the world. These days, much is left in the metaphorical vineyards around the globe, but it's not out of kindness or heeding the word of the Lord. Instead, it's a result of the vagaries of the market, when the price doesn't justify harvesting all of a field.

Since the tradition of leaving crops behind for the destitute never really took hold in the United States, there isn't as much gleaning done in the traditional sense—*by* the poor. It's usually done *for* the poor by volunteers. Whereas the practice of gleaning remains intact in many European countries, the lack of tradition and the taboo of trespassing combine to prevent it here. Plus, more of America's hungry live far from farms, with four times as many Americans living below the poverty line in urban areas as in rural ones.[23] (Although, to be fair, the urban and rural poverty *rates* aren't all that different.)

While the term "gleaning" can refer to recovering food in any manner, it usually implies volunteers hand-picking unharvested crops that remain in the field. It's often called "field gleaning." The work can be demanding, but organizers usually limit the outings to a few hours. After all, they want their volunteers, who come from all walks of life, to glean again. Former Department of Agriculture Coordinator of Food Recovery and Gleaning Joel Berg said the practice is on the upswing, with Arizona, California, Florida, Washington, Oregon, and North Carolina as the top gleaning states.

My introduction to gleaning came when I volunteered on a handful of Saturdays for the North Carolina branch of the Society of St. Andrew. The gleaning events occurred at unharvested fields, usually with crops that hadn't been picked because prices didn't justify the labor of harvesting. Other times, we gathered produce that had been passed over. Except for that gleeful time I picked blueberries, it usually involved stooping—to pick yams, broccoli, or collard greens.

In addition to near-weekly gleaning outings, the Society of St. Andrew holds a larger annual event called the Yam Jam. The name does take some liberties—there's no (musical) jam and they aren't (technically) yams, just sweet potatoes. And lots of sweet potatoes, at that. At the 2009 Yam Jam, 829 gleaners picked 84,010 pounds of potatoes. That yielded more than 252,030 servings spread amongst 46 relief agencies. When I attended the Yam Jam, two tractor trailers parked at the edge of the field communicated the scope and intent of the event. Walking past the trucks and through a clearing, a world of gleaners came into focus, dotting the entire field. There were schools, church groups, families, Cub Scout troops, individuals, and couples.

Gleaning is more enjoyable than grueling. It's a nice excuse to get some fresh air and exercise in a bucolic setting. It's educational—it was the first time I'd seen a broccoli *plant*. And it's awfully gratifying. You know that each sweet potato or collard green you pick will end up on the plate of someone who will appreciate it. Even finding your way to the site can be a pleasant, pastoral challenge. Many times, the designated field has no address, because it's not a farm, just an extra field that the grower planted to be on the safe side. The directions from the organizer once included "Turn right after a very large oak tree," and that's no knock on the directions.

Because organizers crack no whips and free labor isn't abundant, field gleaning is not the most effective way to gather excess. The amount collected pales in comparison to the tonnage received from salvaging already-harvested food. For example, Arizona's Statewide Gleaning Project received just 4 percent of its rescued food from field gleaning in fiscal 2007–2008. Actually picking crops as opposed to picking them up really impedes efficiency. "Field gleaning is a sexier thing to do than recovering food from coolers, but it's really hard to get people to do that," said Cindy Gentry, the project's former director.

On a productive day of field gleaning, Florida's Farm Share reaps 5,000 pounds in five hours. That's by no means shabby, but, not amazing. "We can get that in 10 minutes from a cull line," said Farm Share's Robbins.

Don't tell anyone, but many farm-recovery groups hold gleaning events as much for publicity as for the actual haul. For Salinas's Ag Against Hunger that is certainly the case, as Taylor-Silva estimated that field gleaning only provides about one-quarter of 1 percent of all the food they get. Her predecessor, Patrick Heiman, told me that gleaning's usefulness isn't linked to yield. "It is more an educational and public relations tool," he said.

What's more, gleaning outings only recover a portion of the available crops. There's almost always food remaining in the field at the end of gleaning outings. "Of what's left after harvest, sometimes, we get 50 percent. Some days 10 percent. Some days 5 percent," Taylor-Silva said. "First time gleaners, at the end of the day, they say, 'That's it?' But we can only collect what we can give away."

Because they rely on volunteers, gleaning organizations are familiar with no-shows. But California's Hidden Harvest has found a way of ensuring attendance: paying workers. The Coachella-based group is one of only a few gleaning operations that pays day laborers to pick for the hungry. Perhaps it's no coincidence, then, that Hidden Harvest recovers more food per man- (or woman)-hour than any other gleaning group. Sometimes Founding Executive Director Christy Porter hires an entire crew that has just finished in a field to gather the unsellable fruits and vegetables. Other times, she'll choose out-of-work seasonal pickers or those who may not otherwise be hired because they're disabled or have health problems. For these populations, working for Hidden Harvest is feasible because the pay is by the hour, not based on productivity.

Porter gravitated toward food relief after moving to the Palm Springs area and witnessing a surprising amount of hunger. "Even though we're famous for our golf and beautiful people with flat tummies, we have many empty tummies," Porter said, for what I suspect wasn't the first time.

Having grown up in Kentucky and earned a Ph.D. in English, Porter was familiar with gleaning from the Old Testament and *The Iliad*. "With so many people going hungry, it seemed like a complete obscenity to plow that food under," she said. "It was really just a matter of finding the right grower and asking them how could we do this."

Porter kept hearing from pickers who worked the field by day and were hungry at night. She soon realized that what the working poor needed most was cash—to pay for life's expenses. Yet, that wasn't easy to provide. "In the beginning, the hardest money to raise was for wages because everyone thinks the poor should work for broccoli," Porter said. "But the poor need money."

Knowing that token income wouldn't do, Porter sought to provide a living wage. Porter told me that Hidden Harvest now pays workers $10 per hour. When I asked how the nonprofit can afford that, Porter joked that she and her partner rob convenience stores. In reality, she said, her corporate backers appreciate the group's efficiency and the fact that they give away all that they harvest.

In addition to paying workers to pick food for donation, Hidden Harvest harnesses the goodwill of its neighbors. Citrus trees abound in the Coachella Valley, dotting the landscaped lawns of Palm Springs resorts and homes, with most planted solely for decoration. Every harvest season, Porter couldn't fathom this squandered citrus. She couldn't believe that property owners let lemons, grapefruit, mandarins, and tangerines go to ground and make a juicy mess. It was as if landscapers had created a problem where none had existed. Porter saw a solution: Why not establish collection sites for homeowners to donate unwanted fruit? Today, you can drive up to the drop-spots in seven cities in the valley and deposit bags of citrus into flip-top bins without leaving your car.

Recoverable Food: It Grows on Trees

So-called "tree gleaning" is another way to turn backyard fruit from a nuisance to a blessing. People United for a Better Life in Oakland (PUEBLO) gathers fruit from trees by employing Oakland's teenagers. PUEBLO operates an Urban

Youth Harvest program that pays teens to pick backyard tree fruit and deliver it to seniors. Participants bike themselves and their bounty around town and are paid in conjunction with the Mayor's Summer Jobs Program.

While tree-gleaning groups are usually found in warmer urban areas such as cities in California and Arizona, I visited one in not-so-sunny Portland, Oregon. The Portland Fruit Tree Project (PFTP) stands out in another way, too. At all PFTP outings, volunteers divided the pickings between the food bank and themselves. Unlike other gleaning projects I've visited, PFTP encourages their volunteers to enjoy the fruits of their labor, during and after the event. The participants were more than happy to do so. After all, who doesn't like fresh, delicious, free fruit?

Katy Kolker, the project's director, formed the group in 2006. The idea dawned on her gradually after years of observing so much squandered fruit in a city with its share of unfortunate souls. "I was just walking down the street year after year after year and realizing this fruit was going to waste," Kolker told me. "It just seemed like a really obvious thing to do."

It was a much-appreciated bright Portland morning when I met up with the group in the city's Richmond section. The house whose backyard we were gleaning sat on a street lined with Subarus, Volkswagons, and hybrids, but half of the volunteers arrived by bike. After gathering in a circle for introductions and a quick safety chat, we learned how to collect fruit without harming the tree—or the fruit. Then, the picking began.

Kolker calls these outings "Harvesting Parties," and it sure felt that way, as we picked two Italian plum trees brimming with purple freshness. As volunteers harvested high and low, stationed both on knees and branches, there was a nice mix of participation and plum eating. Using ladders, fruit pickers (basically baskets on a stick), and good old tree climbing, the group reached most of the fruit. In about an hour of work, we collected 280 pounds.

In addition to supplying the hungry and frugal with fresh fruit, the PFTP provides a real service to homeowners. In exchange for putting up with a few hours of hip, eco-savvy strangers in their backyard, they're rid of a potentially smelly, critter-attracting mess. And they get the satisfaction of knowing they've supplied fresh fruit to those who need it most (as well as to a few hard-working frugalistas).

The group moved on to the second backyard, a short drive or bike ride away. The yellow ranch-style home had a sunny backyard with two Asian pear trees waiting to be relieved of their fruit. The picking went quickly, with the harvested fruit divided into three containers: the good, the bad, and the ugly. Okay, fine: the good, the compost-worthy, and the blemished. In a sign that chivalry isn't dead, volunteers were asked to take from the bin of blemished fruit. Their bounty tucked away in backpacks and panniers, a group of recent-college-grad gleaners mounted up and pedaled off as they discussed pear recipes.

Sweet Endings

As Warren Shaw concluded the morning's recovery route, he backed the number-four truck up to Inter-Faith Food Shuttle's loading dock. We unloaded the cardboard boxes of donated food, toting them into the open warehouse dominated by rows of "shelf-stable" goods. Shaw handed in the clipboard with the morning's total—400 pounds.

That afternoon, Shaw would deliver some of those goods along with other recovered food to three locations. First he'd stop at Joseph's Hand, a small food pantry serving mostly elderly folks. Then it would be off to Summit House, a half-way home that keeps families together by enabling convicted women to live with their kids. Finally, Shaw would swing by Darius House, an adult day-care center.

Like many a food-recovery worker, Shaw enjoys seeing the process through: rescuing food that was bound for the Dumpster and rerouting it to those who will enjoy or at least eat it. "The end result is what I believe in: helping homeless, low-income people," he said. "Those in battered women's shelters, recovering alcoholics."

Before those deliveries, it was lunchtime. Shaw snagged a few items from our haul and we headed for the break room. He produced a few Power Bars, individually packaged salads, and, of course, the banana pudding. Shaw divulged that drivers make mental notes of what they collect and usually have their eyes on one or two treats. Cold fried chicken is a popular item, as it can be microwaved back to life in the break room.

We chatted and enjoyed our salads, then ate our banana pudding in silence. To my surprise, the dessert tasted really good. At least, it was much better than I expected a mass-produced pre-made supermarket concoction would be. Maybe it had just been a long morning. After a full four hours of collection, I was tired, and my mind wandered toward home.

Abruptly, Shaw stood up. He extended his hand and told me it had been a pleasure. He had to go load the truck for the afternoon of deliveries. The half-way houses, nursing homes, and soup kitchens needed their food.

Bowls of pasta left uneaten by their original owners and student scroungers at Reed College in Portland, Oregon.

PHOTO BY JONATHAN BLOOM

chapter 10

From Traylessness to Demand Tracking: Ideas and Innovations to Reduce Food Waste

Waste equals food, whether it's food for the earth, or for a closed industrial cycle. We manufacture products that go from cradle to grave. We want to manufacture them from cradle to cradle.

—WILLIAM MCDONOUGH,
ARCHITECT AND AUTHOR OF *CRADLE TO CRADLE*

S tuart Leckie didn't mean to start a movement. He was just trying to reduce waste in his cafeteria.

Leckie is the general manager of dining at Saint Joseph's College in Standish, Maine. Since he began his professional life dealing cards, though, he knows full well that the odds of a lad from southeast England settling in Maine are pretty long. And he's even more amused by the circumstances through which he came to be an innovator in sustainable dining.

Young and looking for a bit of adventure, Leckie put in with a London recruiter seeking croupiers. In 1991, he was placed on the *Scotia Prince*, a ferry that ran from Portland, Maine, to Yarmouth, Nova Scotia. He met an American girl onboard, married during a week-long trip to Vegas, and settled in Maine. The marriage didn't last, but the settling did. He gravitated toward Maine's hospitality industry, working at a resort on Sebago Lake, before answering a classified ad to work for Bon Appetit Management Company in 2001. The institutional caterer had just won the dining contract at Saint Joseph's College, a Catholic school with fewer than 1,000 students.

Less than a decade later, he oversees what is now an exemplar of green dining. With his English accent, frequent smile, and short-sleeved shirt wide open at the collar, Leckie is hard to miss. He is a youthful thirty-nine, which helps explain why the students just call him Stuart. Leckie also sends out a weekly dining update e-mail to the school community, affording a bit of fame. The school's diminutive size doesn't hurt, either.

In 2005, the school held Hunger and Homeless Week, which included a waste audit. In doing so, Leckie learned just how much excess food was left on students' plates. That gave him the idea to compare the results with the waste from a meal without trays. Yet, what gave him the idea to remove trays? Leckie isn't quite sure, but he knows it stemmed from seeing so much excess. "I don't know what inspired that one decision," Leckie said. "I know we'd done some nutritional analysis where we took pictures of students' trays, and the calorie counts were just like outrageous, how much food they had on their trays."

To measure plate waste when students didn't have trays, Leckie and his staff planned a "No Tray Wednesday" for the spring of 2007. Despite flyers promoting the event, the community was caught off-guard. "Everyone was like, 'Where are the trays?' And we're like, 'Well, we're just doing an experiment.'

Then people got used to it after about four or five weeks," Leckie said. It went so well that he continued the weekly trayless experiment for the next few months.

After comparing the amount of waste from the first audit to that from days without trays, Leckie noted that the latter produced 2 to 3 ounces per person, down from 5 or 6 ounces. He was impressed with the findings, but wasn't sure what to do with the information. That summer, he raised the trayless idea during a brainstorming on ways to cut waste at session at a national gathering of Bon Appetit staff. Those at the meeting agreed that removing trays would reduce waste, but nobody thought they could get college administrators to play along. Leckie figured it couldn't hurt to ask and was thrilled when the members of the school's Jesuit administration gave the idea their blessing for the start of the school year in August 2007. And with that "yes," traylessness was born.

After removing the trays from the cafeteria, Leckie was surprised to learn that no other institutions had had the same notion. It seemed like such a simple idea, and in hindsight, it is.

Despite his innovation, Leckie is no crusader on the topic of waste. When I asked him if there was anything in his past that might explain how he came to be a food-waste fighter, he couldn't come up with anything. No childhood poverty or tales of Depression-era grannies. He simply approached the topic with heaps of common sense: "When I used to see the amount we used to waste, the bags of food scraps that went out, it was clearly obvious that we had to make students more aware about the amount of waste they were generating," Leckie said. "Taking the trays away was the idea I had."

The Case for Traylessness

Traylessness, my noun for not having trays in an all-you-can-eat facility, reduces food waste by staggering amounts. Leckie estimates that Saint Joseph's has cut its waste in half in the post-tray era. Reports from other campuses that have pulled trays range from 20 to 50 percent waste reduction. Food-service provider Aramark, in a white paper on the topic entitled "The Business and Cultural Acceptance Case for Trayless Dining," reported that its trayless campuses trimmed 25 to 30 percent of their waste.

Removing trays also reduces water and energy usage. Many schools have had a hard time quantifying the savings, but the University of North Carolina at Wilmington (UNCW) estimates that each tray requires an average of 3.5 gallons of water and 1.5 kilowatts of energy to wash. Having removed trays from Wagoner Dining Hall, UNCW saves 8,782 gallons of water every day. That's about a tanker truck's worth of water. And that's from one medium-sized cafeteria at a school with about 12,000 undergrads. Imagine the potential savings at city-states like the University of Florida or the University of Texas.

When students take less food, it means schools don't have to prepare as much. And that saves money. Using the estimates of 2 to 3 ounces less waste per student without trays, and a cost of $2 per pound of food, Leckie calculated savings of $71,500 for the school year, in addition to the money saved due to fewer trash pickups. Of course, that's at a tiny college. At Virginia Polytechnic Institute (Virginia Tech), a school of about 28,000 students, researchers led by Andy Sarjahani, then studying to be a registered dietician, found that a week without trays at one dining hall yielded 30 percent less total waste.[1] Projecting that amount for the school year and Leckie's $2 per pound estimate, that would mean savings of about $100,000 for the school year.[2]

What happens to those savings would vary from campus to campus. At Saint Joseph's, for instance, Leckie has used the unspent money to keep Bon Appetit's food costs steady despite a dramatic rise in prices from 2007 to 2009. Like many schools, Saint Joseph's lumps room and board costs into one fee. Philip Yauch, Saint Joseph's chief financial officer, said that the savings from traylessness have allowed the school to pursue a backlog of dorm maintenance projects and the occasional kitchen upgrade without increasing the room and board charges too dramatically in one year.

And in case the environmental and economic reasons aren't compelling enough, removing trays also prevents overeating. At a time when obesity is a major issue, and at a place where overconsumption is almost a rite of passage (think "the freshman 15"), why not find a way to trim both waste and waists? Having a tray prompts diners to take more food than they probably should, because they can. And when we're still sitting down and there's food in front of us, chances are we'll eat it—not because we're hungry, but because we often determine when to stop eating based on visual cues.

Leckie's first post-trayless observation was that students were not eating as much dessert as they had before. The kitchen staff realized there was more left over and subsequently began preparing less. More Saint Joseph's students realized after they finished their main course that they were full and didn't bother going up for a slice of pie or cake. Had trays been in use, though, it's more likely that one of those treats would have already been in front of them. And that convenience would likely encourage overeating or, for those with an iron will, squandered sweets.

The Old College Tray

Since Saint Joseph's launched the idea at the beginning of the 2007–2008 school year, traylessness has spread nationwide. As of June 2010, 56 percent of the 600 U.S. campuses served by Sodexo, an international food-service provider, had removed trays.[3] Even better, 75 percent of Aramark's campuses had gone trayless by that same point. The Association for the Advancement of Sustainability in Higher Education predicts that most colleges will abandon trays by 2014.[4]

It's not hard to see why the idea has been popular. Any time institutions have the chance to reduce both their expenses and environmental impacts without any upfront costs, they're probably going to jump at the chance. Traylessness doesn't require any investment. Virtually any other environmental upgrade requires a significant purchase, whether it's a commercial-scale composter, a food pulper (to dewater food waste), or even non-food-related items like solar panels. It's rare to achieve so much simply by removing something.

The Virginia Tech administration certainly was excited by the savings implied in Sarjahani's study. The following school year, the Blacksburg, Virginia, school eliminated trays from one of its two all-you-can-eat cafeterias. It also hired the dynamic Sarjahani to implement this and other changes as the campus's first dining sustainability coordinator.

One thing to keep in mind is that traylessness only works in all-you-can-eat venues, as trays allow customers to pile on the food without paying more. A la carte establishments, where diners pay for each item, already have a barrier to waste—cost. "In college *retail* settings, people tend to not buy more than they need anyway because they can't afford to," Leckie said. "They're not gonna buy an extra burger just because they have a tray."

Cafeteria Conflict

Of course, there are a few drawbacks to traylessness. As students often complain, it is a bit harder to maneuver through the cafeteria. Some would go so far as to call it a nuisance. "It's just a pain not to be able to put all your food on a tray," said Andrew Scott, a Saint Joseph's junior from Worcester, Massachusetts. An editorial in the Princeton University student paper damned the practice as a "silly idea" when the school was considering removing trays in April 2009[5]— though a follow-up article about the popularity of Princeton's traylessness the next fall—"Trayless and Lovin' It"—would seem to render that earlier opinion an outlier.

Students' main gripe is that not having a tray necessitates more trips up to get food. That's true, in theory. Yet, in practice, diners get pretty adept at balancing plates, bowls, and cups. And students with experience waiting tables—a sizeable number—are already used to juggling dishes. Joe Crocker, a junior from Sacco, Maine, whom I spoke with, fit that description, having worked at a Chinese food restaurant, and said he didn't mind applying those skills to his campus dining routine. Those not interested in balancing plates can always just make two trips.

Leckie recalled that the loudest objections to the idea were from the faculty. (Faculty, staff, and students all eat together at St. Joseph's.) During my visit to the school, I spoke with some students who would have preferred to use a tray, but I had a hard time finding anyone vehemently opposed to traylessness. "It didn't take that long to get used to. It was like, 'whatever,'" said Scott, expressing a very age-appropriate sentiment. And if it's no big deal, let's go with the thing that saves money, cuts waste, and reduces greenhouse gas emissions.

In my own trayless lunch at Saint Joseph's, I struggled a bit with strategy and execution. I kept a free hand for my drink by stacking a soup bowl on top of my plate. But in so doing, I pushed my deli sandwich into a pile of (site-made, yummy) applesauce. Pork chops and applesauce, maybe, but I like my turkey on wheat devoid of fruit flavoring (save cranberry sauce). If I ate there thrice daily, though, I'm sure I'd avoid such rookie mistakes.

Plate-stacking aside, limiting what diners can take is kind of the point. It forces diners to choose a few items, rather than piling a few entrées on their tray and eating half of everything. Those who want seconds simply return to the buffet. And considering that the majority of university diners are young adults in the prime of their life, getting up for seconds isn't asking too much. When your argument against something is based on lack of convenience, or—dare I say—laziness, you're not exactly on terra firma.

Of course, when you throw in drinks, utensils, and napkins, you're upping the degree of difficulty. Still, it's no triple axel. Schools can place napkin dispensers on tables and be sure to have cups large enough so one will suffice. Moving utensil stations closer to the tables and leaving room at those stations for diners to rest their plate(s) while snagging silverware, two strategies I observed at Saint Joseph's, also helps.

Another downside to traylessness is that the tables can get slightly messier. There may even be—deep breath—more crumbs. The cafeteria workers I talked to at Saint Joseph's weren't all that concerned with the marginally increased mess (they were probably just wondering why I kept taking pictures of the plate-busing area). A related problem is harder to erase—spills when the aforementioned plate-balancing goes awry. The floor of the main dining area at Saint Joseph's has a carpet that displays a few reminders of these mishaps. Then again, mishaps occur with trays, too.

For those with fond memories of sledding on cafeteria trays or future plans to do so, fear not. Leckie said the school still has its trays and actually hands them out to students by request on snowy days. More importantly, most trayless cafeterias keep some around for diners who are disabled or impaired. In fact, many schools still give them out to anyone who asks. That's a wise policy to minimize complaints, as insistent students can have their tray and eat with it, too.

As my meal at St. Joseph's wound down, I asked the students I sat with if they actually liked traylessness or were just telling me what I wanted to hear. To a student, they seemed sincere. "I think it's better without trays; all you need is one plate," said Crocker. "I know when I had a tray, I'd get a plate, a small plate, a bowl and a cup of something and not end up eating all of it. It was the 'eyes bigger than the stomach' thing."

The Green Path

Whereas trayless dining addresses plate waste in all-you-can-eat settings, Lean-Path, the Portland, Oregon, company we met in Chapter 2, provides a "back of the house" solution for restaurants and institutional kitchens. Their idea—keeping track of what is wasted—isn't all that new. How they do it, however, is.

Launched in June 2006, LeanPath's ValuWaste system has a scale with an attached keypad that allows kitchen workers to enter the type and quantity of food and the reason for disposal. That food-waste data becomes sortable information via ValuWaste's software application. In the end, the customers understand what foods they're wasting and why. As the company's website diagrams, data begets information, which sparks action.

How does the system work in practice? This hypothetical situation should help explain. At the end of dinner service at St. Bloom's Hospital, Joel the sous chef weighs the 10 pounds of American chopped suey that he is about to throw out and then keys in a reason: too much prepared. The ValuWaste system uploads that information to the computer of Susan the executive chef. She notices the entry and pans out to see if there's a trend. Sure enough, she finds that every time the dish falls on a Friday, they throw away more than usual. You might be able to guess where I'm going with this one. Taking a step back, the chef realizes—aha!—that many Catholics don't eat meat on Fridays, so they should prepare less of any meat dish that day.

That's probably an overly simple example, but it illustrates how kitchens—the "back of the house"—can use the ValuWaste system to preserve their resources. Unfortunately, LeanPath can't help its clients trim "front of the house," or customer-caused, waste. ValuWaste isn't aimed at that massive waste stream, but at the low-hanging fruit inside institutional kitchens. Andrew Shakman, the company's president and CEO, told me that the system helps chefs reduce their inventory waste by as much as 10 percent.

Shakman walked me through the ValuWaste system at an American Association of Sustainability in Higher Education conference in Raleigh, North Carolina. LeanPath had a booth in the exhibition hall, and Shakman spoke during a session on greening food-service. As he demonstrated the system's bells and whistles, an intermittent flow of college sustainability coordinators and administrators streamed up to the booth. The product was popular, but the price raised a few eyebrows. Still, the system pays for itself in a few years by trimming that institutionalized fat from college, hospital, hotel, casino, and restaurant kitchens.

When pitching the system to potential clients, Shakman pushes both its environmental and financial benefits. While green concerns are increasingly important, it's not usually the deal maker for the large-scale operations that LeanPath tends to target. "We lead with saving money," said Shakman, who almost became a movie producer in a past life—he holds an MFA from the University of Southern California in motion-picture production. "People today talk about the triple bottom line. But to be truly sustainable as a business, you have to address the real bottom line."

Cloudy with a Chance of Waste

Knowing exactly what you waste is important, as is measuring customer demand.

When restaurants and cafeterias can estimate how much of each item will be ordered from a menu or selected from a buffet, they know roughly how much to prepare. That way, they can eliminate some of their "overs" to reduce the wasted food at the end of the day or meal period. Mostly gone are the days of fast-food establishments dumping loads of breakfast sandwiches once the clock hits 11 A.M. These days, most restaurants have tapered their breakfast prep accordingly so that they don't produce too much more than is needed.

How do they predict demand? Forecasting software. These programs, of which there are many, track orders and cross-tabulate them with several variables, such as day of the week, weather, and season. Armed with a few years' worth of data—and often more—smart managers can determine down to a few sandwiches how many wraps or burgers they'll sell.

It's not as if forecasting is a brand new idea, but demand prediction software has advanced to the point where we can almost see—or at least predict—the future. For centuries, restaurants have known to have more food on hand for a Saturday than for a Tuesday. Yet with the advent of computer-based demand tracking, it is now easier to determine the amount of supplies to order and food to cook. Nowhere has this had more of an impact than in the fast-food industry.

Instead of blindly preparing Egg McMuffins or Whoppers, most fast-food restaurants have adopted somewhat complex demand forecasting that determines how much to make. When I got a job at McDonald's in 2009 for research purposes, there was a printed list of how many beef patties, chicken nuggets, and fish fillets to make for every three-hour period of the day. The data was specific to that particular McDonlald's. Virtually all national chains employ demand-tracking systems. Of course, there are always times when unpredictable events affect demand.

Even having a solid handle on demand doesn't mean there won't be waste, as anyone who's ever been on a cruise or visited Las Vegas can attest. This is especially true at buffets, which prompt waste in two ways. There's the brimming buffet itself that customers demand, and the plate waste when they take too much. Knowing how many diners there will be, as cruise ships usually do, allows the kitchen to determine how much they'll need to prepare. Yet, they still have to provide that heaping abundance—continued through the end of the meal—as that's part of what cruise passengers expect and pay for.

Casinos, cruise ships, hospital cafeterias, and all other large-scale kitchens without a set number of customers are ideal candidates for demand and waste analysis. They don't cook to order and, much like caterers, they're expected to have a bottomless buffet. The stakes are highest for cruise ships, as there's no easy way to resupply out at sea. Erik Elvejord, Holland America's director of public relations told me that the cruise company is quite aware of consumer demand. They have to be, both to trim waste and maintain revenue. And, of course, wasted food cuts into the company's profit margins. "Cooking for a large number of people, one of the largest ways to reduce waste is to know what people eat, how much they consume, and how they order," Elvejord said.

Forecasting has taken on greater importance recently as many restaurants have moved to "on-demand" ordering. This cost-cutting delivery strategy, whereby restaurants receive food more frequently to reduce their need for expensive cold storage space, has become increasingly popular in the past ten years. As a result, restaurants keep less on hand to pad any blips in demand. On the whole, more frequent ordering has helped from a food-waste standpoint.

In addition to "just-in-time" delivery, there's "just-in-time" cooking, another waste-saving tactic in institutional kitchens. This commonsense strategy comes from a simple idea—don't cook everything at once. Colby College, in Waterville, Maine, practices this model in all three of its dining halls. According to Colby's website, "The food is prepared, but not cooked until needed, allowing it to be served at another time, if it isn't used at that meal." The strategy shift yielded 80 percent less preconsumer food waste at Colby.[6] And Babson College, in Wellesley, Massachusetts, has had similar success with the tactic.

Not only does batch cooking reduce preconsumer waste, it means the food is fresher and better tasting; I'd guess that less is left uneaten, too. Under this model, pans of mac 'n' cheese don't sit around for two hours in a warming cart. Another "just-in-time" development is the in-cafeteria cooking exhibition, where stir-fries and fajitas are prepared right in front of students' eyes. While this isn't a new idea—think Japanese steak house or hotel omelet station—it is relatively new in institutional cooking. I'd be lying if I said I wasn't jealous of these undergrad improvements, especially thinking back on my day's version of this demonstration cooking trend—having a sub sandwich made just for you—with lettuce and tomato, if you like! Yet, I appreciate the innovation from a waste-reduction perspective.

Scrounging Up a Meal

One man's trash is another's treasure. That saying is easy to understand when you're talking about a vintage Barcalounger found on the curb, but what about a half-eaten bowl of pasta? "Treasure" may be pushing it, but at Reed College, it's, well, lunch.

To save money, some Reed students "scrounge" by standing in a designated area and eating the leftovers of their board-paying classmates. It's an established custom, so students with meal plans know to drop off uneaten items at the two tall tables near the dish return. This includes food students couldn't finish, or didn't like. For boarders, it's basically another form of recycling. Occasionally, food they bought to donate to the Scrounge (it's not an all-you-can-eat cafeteria). I can only imagine how well scroungers ate in the all-you-can-eat setting that Reed had until 1993.

While saving money, not avoiding waste, is the main motivation of the scroungers, the practice still minimizes the discarded food (and the school composts what isn't eaten by scroungers or others). And some scroungers are particularly proud of their role in keeping food out of the college's waste stream by putting it into theirs.

After hearing about scrounging, it was just a question of when, not if, I'd hit Reed's Portland, Oregon, campus. And there was only one real option: experiencing it firsthand. Before visiting, I had plenty of questions. How did scrounging work in practice? What kinds of foods were donated? What type of students took part? How did the other Reedies view scrounging? What about the administration and campus caterer? Could I hack it?

Delicious Participation

After about 10 minutes of scrounging, it feels completely normal. It's like asking your family member, "Are you gonna finish that?"—only with a family of, say, 1,500. I tried to wade in slowly, taking bites where nobody else had. Yet, nudged by others' examples and my rumbling stomach, my inhibitions faded and I began eating like a veteran scrounger.

I joined the Scrounge for lunch and dinner on yet another sunny Portland day in September 2008. My lunch looked like this: one bite of a quesadilla, two cherry tomatoes from a ranch-dressing-drowned salad, four cucumber slices, numerous bites of pizza crust and one near-whole slice, lettuce from a different salad, half a banana, and the filling from an Asian chicken wrap. On the whole, it was a much more complete lunch than I'd normally eat. And I certainly enjoyed the variety. My compliments to the chef (and the boarders who chose and bought my meal).

There's a reason why the scrounger tables are located on the path to the tray return. Some paying customers drop food off at the scrounging tables; other times, scroungers politely ask if they can have the dinner remains of an approaching student. When an item arrives, the modus operandi is to take a bite and pass it along. When everyone's had their fill, the plate is usually pushed to the middle. Scroungers will go back for a forkful when the donations slow. After items languish for 20 to 30 minutes, though, one of the scroungers usually takes it upon him or herself (and it's often herself, unfortunately) to bring them to the dish return. Believe it or not, even the scrounge table has plate waste. Not much, though.

While I was talking to Russell Mayhew, a junior from Los Angeles who was catching up on some econ reading while scrounging, someone dropped off an apple chewed on all sides. I mentioned that surely nobody would stoop to eating what was essentially a glorified apple core. "Give it time," Mayhew said. "It'll get eaten." And within five minutes, a female scrounger started working on it.

My dinner had an odd beginning: blueberry cobbler. I relaxed my "savory before sweet" rule because, hey, a premature dessert is better than none at all. I then enjoyed a healthy amount of Asian eggplant, a quarter of a garden burger, a few pineapple chunks (in a bowl with another fruit—passion?), and a bite of a turkey, bacon, and Swiss sandwich that was inaccurately touted as "the best sandwich ever" by its donor.

Scrounging is a bit of a grazing process, as it can take a little while to fill up. In a break between plates, I read through "The Principles of the Scrounge," which were hand-written on a massive hanging banner. This was an informal version of the "Scrounge Commandments" that are published annually in the student paper. Dictums such as "Thou shalt not covet the trays of those who have not yet eaten" helps maintain the tradition from year to year.

A rumble of excitement interrupted my reading; someone had dropped off a burger with just two cartoonishly perfect bites missing. Few items create as much excitement as anything with protein and fat. That means that meat, French fries, and pieces of pizza that are more than just crust are quite popular. "Here comes a tray of fries!" one scrounger announced. Four or five students dove in. For the most part, the students' sharing was impressive. Occasionally, though, scroungers' manners faded in the face of a particularly desirable item, or if it had been a particularly lean meal. "At its core, it's a free-for-all for free food," explained Jose Palafox, a junior from Sacramento and an editor of the school newspaper.

Barely Tolerated Behavior

The verdant Reed campus has no shrine to scrounging, just three manila folders of materials, including Scrounger Trading Cards, in the campus archives. Scrounging at Reed dates back to 1965. According to special collections librarian and Reed alumna Gay Walker, what probably happened was that a few broke students just started approaching other undergrads who were about to clear their plates and asked for their leftovers. Walker was a freshman that year and remembers it had grown in popularity by the next year. The practice remains largely the same today.

One could call the custom symbiotic: Boarders are less likely to overeat or feel guilty for throwing away food, and scroungers eat for free. Of course, it's less beneficial for the school's caterer and coffers. If scrounging wasn't tolerated, more scroungers would buy meal plans, which would mean more revenue for Bon Appetit Management Company, and Reed. Debby Bridges, Bon Appetit's general manager, said the company puts up with the practice because they recognize that it's a Reed tradition. Still, given Palafox's estimate that about 100 of the 1,500 enrolled students scrounge, that's a decent amount of unspent money.

The school's administration also accepts scrounging. Michael Leidecker, Reed's associate dean of resident life and the one who manages Bon Appetit's catering contract, said that Reed's leaders stay neutral on the matter: "The administration doesn't have any specific stance on the issue. The students have decided they don't want to waste food and we're fine with that."

When I pushed Leidecker a bit on his answer, he likened it to a harmless, neighborly behavior. "If you and I were sitting next to each other, and I said, 'You want to share my cheesecake?' that'd be okay, right?" No objections here.

On the topic of scroungers' health, the ones I asked said they believed their exposure to a wide variety of germs sharpened their immune systems. And they rely on food donors not to overburden their in-shape natural defenses. One of the Scrounge Commandments aimed at board-paying students reads, "Thou shalt protect the house of the Scrounge from the great plagues." Boarders who are sick convey that message by covering their food with another plate as they head to the tray return, or by simply telling the scroungers that they're sick as they walk by with leftovers. Some scroungers will risk it if it's a really slow meal. Sharing drinks, soups, and cereal is generally avoided, however, because it's easier to transmit germs via liquids.

That informal system didn't cut it for the then campus caterer at that time, Saga, which expressed reservations about liability. Yet, when the Multnomah County Department of Health classified scrounging as a "voluntary food exchange" in 1987, the school and Saga stopped worrying.[7] Today, Leidecker has a downright zen approach to it: "Scrounging—it just is. It has evolved with the institution," he said. Leidecker usually contributes to the Scrounge when he eats lunch in the Commons. "It was here when I arrived and it'll likely be here when I leave. It's a part of who we are."

When I called the Department of Health to get more insight into the practice's legality, Jon Kawaguchi, the county's environmental health supervisor, confirmed that scrounging was legal and possibly not as dangerous as eating after shaking hands with someone. Yet, he certainly didn't encourage the behavior. "I wouldn't recommend it, but there's nothing we can say or do to stop it," said Kawaguchi. When I asked if he'd split a piece of cheesecake with Leidecker and me, he proved just what poor dinner company health-department employees are: "Do you normally sit down and ask your dining companion if they've had any diarrhea or vomiting lately? Without knowing that, I wouldn't be excited about sharing food."

Off-Campus Scrounging

Years of eating others' leftovers is bound to impact how scroungers view food. While the practice illuminates how much food most of us leave uneaten, it's certainly frowned upon just about anywhere off-campus. There have been reports of scrounging at a few other Pacific Northwest schools, but it isn't entrenched at any of them. And Reed has a better chance of becoming a Conservative breeding ground than scrounging does of catching on at restaurants. Yet, some students I spoke with wondered why that was so. It's an interesting question—once you move beyond the health risks and liabilities—especially given that Reedies have experienced a functioning version of the practice.

Laura Bradley, a senior biology major at Reed, put the question to the test at a ski-lodge cafeteria not far from Portland. "I sat down at a table and would ask people if they were done with their food. The manager came out and said, 'That's disgusting, you should be ashamed of yourself.' He threw me out. Some of the people didn't mind, some did. I think one of the people who wasn't pleased told the manager."

Scrounging illuminates not just how much plate waste exists, but also how much of it can be safely consumed. After experiencing that, it's frustrating to watch a waiter take away an untouched plate of a nearby diner. Or even one with some remaining French fries, a few of which many of us would surely eat if it were socially acceptable. At Reed, scroungers have eliminated this particular food waste–inducing social construct.

That's not to say that scrounging is a model for reducing food waste in America. It's unlikely and illegal most anywhere else. But it is useful in reminding us that we have a very narrow definition of what is and isn't fit to eat. If something drops on the floor (and stays there for more than five seconds), it's trash.[8] A piece of cheese with mold on it is discarded. Groceries that surpass a predetermined "sell-by" date are pitched. Bread and butter placed on a restaurant table must be dumped. There's a discrepancy between food's actual condition and the social and legal constraints surrounding its consumption. Few of those restrictions make sense from an objective perspective free of social bounds. (Of course, there are social bounds at Reed, too; they just permit this food sharing.) And it's that contradiction against which scroungers rebel, on and off campus. Then again, maybe they just like free food.

I can attest that scrounging alters your world—or at least your food—view. I often note how eminently edible some discarded foods are. Shortly after returning from Reed, I contemplated eating a few such items. One morning, I broke the barrier. My favorite café is the kind of place where customers bus their own dishes. One morning I was surprised to see an untouched half of a breakfast burrito in one of the plastic dish tubs. Knowing that the restaurant cuts their burritos in half, I was almost certain that the discarded food hadn't been touched by anyone. I had a real George moment, harkening back to the *Seinfeld* episode where George helped himself to a once-bitten éclair that was in the trash, but *"on top."*[9] In taking and eating the burrito, I was accepting a few risks. To me, though, the social stakes—from being seen taking "trash"— were much greater than the health ones (after making an educated guess that the sandwich hadn't been sitting out for hours). After all, that half of a burrito would have been the most pristine food item during my day at Reed. Fortunately, I escaped notice. Of course, poor George wasn't so lucky. He temporarily lost his girlfriend after her mother walked into the kitchen just in time to see him eat the éclair straight from the bin.

I'm not likely to eat any more discards (my mother will be happy to hear), mostly because I doubt I'll find such an immaculate (and tasty) piece of "trash" again. But also because I'm not one to openly flaunt social conventions. Reluctantly, I've made peace with the lack of a mechanism for utilizing untouched food that is deemed "trash." Of course, I do not accept the causes or amount of this waste. Yet, unlike some, I'm not prepared to follow food into the Dumpster.

Dumpsters of Plenty

When scroungers graduate into the adult world, some may become "freegans." Depending on your social, economic, and political leanings, freegans are: (a) food activists drawing attention to America's culture of excess, (b) leeches living off others' hard work, (c) shrewd beneficiaries of America's misused resources, (d) criminals who trespass by going into stores' Dumpsters, or (e) slackers who cheat the homeless out of good food.

One thing is for sure—freegans don't pay for food, but instead eat what others cast off. Freegans practice a kind of food alchemy, turning castaways into cuisine. The practice is often called "Dumpster diving," or even "urban foraging." Semantics-wise, Dumpster divers tend to be more economically motivated, whereas freegan implies that there's a message behind the lack of spending. The name merges "free" with "vegan," and some participants fall into the morally tenuous "vegan unless it's free" category. For others, the term communicates political eating—in the form of protesting American abundance by eating only from its refuse.

Not all Dumpster divers would call themselves freegans. For Sarah Rich, a twenty-nine-year-old magazine editor who recovered food from Dumpsters while at Stanford, use of the term "freegan" connotes a certain mindset. "I don't think I ever used that word, but many of my friends definitely did," said Rich, who now lives in San Francisco. "I'd say the ones who were more self-identified as activists and even anarchists called themselves freegans."

Taking items from someone else's Dumpster is officially considered trespassing. That may seem perverse, but that's how the legal system frames it. Is it possible to steal trash? Dumpster divers prove that it is, but that it's also possible to subsist on it.

Many supermarkets and restaurants lock their Dumpsters, fence them in, or pour bleach on their food waste to prevent Dumpster diving. That last one is particularly sad—grocery stores discarding hundreds of dollars' worth of food every day and then preventing anyone from using it. Joseph Heller couldn't write it any better. Stores seek to make their trash inaccessible because they fear being sued if a Dumpster diver gets hurt. Yet, the fact that procuring Dumpstered food is illegal doesn't bother most freegans, who don't tend to be—how shall we put it—bound by social norms. Besides, a dash of civil disobedience makes a nice companion to message-driven eating. Sure, it's easier to invoke Gandhi when you're fighting for freedom of speech instead of free spanikopita, but the principle is the same.

From an environmental standpoint, Dumpster diving provides a service by keeping food from rotting in landfills and emitting methane. And freegans certainly do a nice job bringing attention to America's waste, as the media loves the sensationalism of turning trash into meals. While freeganism has its charms, it's not above reproach. The main criticism is that many divers are unnecessarily competing with the homeless for food. We'll address this point shortly. Also, while freegans say they're exposing America's disposable culture, I'm not sure they'd be happy in a nation with less free food. I wonder how many of them genuinely want our waste and their gravy train to come to a halt (not that there's much danger of that). On balance, though, I'd say that freegans have a positive impact.

Rechanneling Food

I have to admit that the idea of freeganism intrigues me, partly because I'm a cheap, sorry, practical guy, but also because I've seen how much edible food is thrown out in the United States. The more I've learned about how much is tossed at supermarkets, in some cases doing the actual tossing, the harder it has become to pay full price for produce. In another life, I could be a freegan. As you've seen, I'm not exactly shy with germs. And the "thrill of the hunt" aspect of Dumpster diving appeals to me. It's like a garage sale, except everything's free and, usually, edible.

I'm not ashamed to admit that I've had some freegan moments myself. I once acquired a bag of bagels and salvaged some bell peppers from a farmers market compost box. The bagels were sealed and, yes, George, at the top of the store's wheeled trash hopper. They tasted perfectly fine—just the "day olds" at the end of the next day. The bell peppers had a few bad spots, but weren't unsalvageable. When I asked that particular vendor if I could take a few items from his cull box, he couldn't believe it. Yet, after I carved away the soft spots, the peppers made a great addition to lunch. (I did buy a few items from the stand, too.)

In a perfect world, there wouldn't be a need to peruse Dumpsters. Instead, more stores could give away foods not fit to be sold. I'm not confident that this will ever happen, at least not on a large scale, but it would be a nobler way of enabling the divers and freegans to do what they're already doing anyway— eating from our excess. The store would save on its waste-removal bill and limit the likelihood of those pesky freegans or actual hungry people going through their trash. More "give" might result in less "take." But, one may ask, would that mean fewer donations to food pantries, food banks, and food-recovery operations? It wouldn't have to, as these contributions could be items that food banks wouldn't accept.

This kind of pre-Dumpster diving does happen. In her college days, Rich lived in a cooperative house at Stanford where a few housemates would head to the Palo Alto Whole Foods' loading dock to hunt and gather. Some of the workers there came to expect these students and began setting aside items that were slated to be thrown away. It was mostly culled produce and dry goods that were past their sell-by dates. Yet nearly ten years after the fact, Rich still has fond memories of scoring a prized jar of raw, organic almond butter that was out of her undergrad price range. The practice was not necessarily condoned by store management, but more of an informal arrangement between students and workers.

One local grocery chain in Portland has another way of pre-empting Dumpster diving "donations" by leaving food out for those who might want it. Workers at the New Seasons Market place blemished and slightly bruised fruits and day-old breads in a specific box not far from the Dumpster. I visited the store a few times when I was in the Rose City and was impressed with the quality of what I saw. Sure, there were a few rotten fruits and vegetables of interest to nobody. And some of the tomatoes were too soft for most uses, but they'd be perfect for making a sauce.

When I worked at a supermarket, I tried to start this custom by setting edible but unsellable produce next to the Dumpster (this was before I was able to convince the store to start donating these foods). I'm sure my employers would have frowned on the practice, or even fired me, had they found out. In the end, it didn't work because the store wasn't in a Dumpster-diving-friendly setting. The offerings were like the falling tree in the empty forest.

If stores know that people are going through their Dumpsters anyway, why not make it safer for everyone by putting the food *near* the Dumpster instead of *in* it, along with an "Eat at your own risk" sign? Surely, we can get legal to sign off on that. Sadly, the common reaction to finding that people have been going through the store Dumpster is to fence in or lock it. Or, as mentioned above, even to take the dastardly step of pouring bleach on the discarded food. That possibility, as well as the myriad other contamination threats in Dumpsters, are why I'd caution against eating unpackaged foods from them.

The closest I got to the freegan lifestyle, aside from nabbing those bagels and peppers at the farmers market, was to take an offering from the box at the Portland New Seasons, where I snagged a pineapple whose only visible flaws were the few brown leaves in its crown. With the decorative top lopped off, it looked and tasted like any other pineapple—luscious and juicy. After writing about this undertaking on my blog, a reader objected, saying that I was stealing from the hungry. That raised a valid question—do freegans take food from homeless people who regularly comb through the trash? (And had I done the same?)

I asked Rich for her take on the question and she likened it to shopping at a thrift store. Are thrift-store shoppers with the means to buy new clothes unfairly competing with those who don't? "My instinct is, 'Sure, homeless people need free food more than people with money and shelter,'" said Rich, who occasionally sourced food from Dumpsters while living in Oakland after graduating. "But I don't view it as a grave transgression that both parties participate in mining that source."

The critique that freegans steal food from the homeless seems a bit troublesome. True, in some cases, the actual food that freegans take might have found its way to a homeless or truly hungry person. From what I've seen, though, there's *plenty* of good food to be had in Dumpsters. Yet, when there is a shared source, I do think freegans should give way. And from what I hear, most do. Whether they're acting on their beliefs or acquiring their daily bread, freegans play a vital role in shedding light on our cornucopia of food waste. I'm just dubious of Dumpster diving as a life strategy.

In Digestion We Trust

Regardless of how many people want to subsist off it, there's always going to be food waste. We can reduce the amount of edible food that's squandered, but it can't be completely, or even mostly, eliminated unless we're prepared to do away with restaurants, supermarkets, and the concept of convenience. And furthermore, there will always be inedible food scraps like peels, skins, ends, and rinds.

The question then becomes: What to do with this waste? Traditionally, composting has been the answer. But—and you knew that "but" was coming—why make dirt when you can make energy? Anaerobic digestion is a waste-to-energy technology that harnesses bacteria to consume (or digest) organic waste in an enclosed tank (hence, anaerobic). The byproduct of this bacteria feast is methane, which is quite a versatile, useful gas when it's controlled. Methane can power a generator in order to create electricity. It can be compressed into natural gas (CNG) to run a vehicle or turbine. And it can be cooled and used as a liquefied natural gas.

In the United States, anaerobic digestion (AD) has long been a popular solution for human and animal waste. Digesters are located at progressive wastewater treatment plants and in livestock-laden areas, mostly in the Midwest. Not shockingly, though, substances that haven't already been digested have a higher energy content than stuff that has—manure. That reality, combined with the push for renewable energy, has prompted a push to use anaerobic digestion to create energy from food waste.

For all of 2008, I worked for Orbit Energy, a company with ambitious plans to spread the food-waste-to-energy idea nationwide. The Raleigh-based outfit has a proprietary technology for a high-solids variety of anaerobic digestion that was developed at the National Renewable Energy Labs in the 1990s. It currently operates a 5-ton-per-day demonstration site in rural Clinton, North Carolina, just south of Spivey's Corner, home of the National Hollerin' Contest.

When I stopped working there, we still hadn't broken ground on a commercial anaerobic digestion project, which was frustrating for everyone involved. Because the equipment and licensing fees for the technology are expensive, capital is a major barrier. Finding investors proved a whole lot harder than locating available food waste, as you might guess after reading the previous chapters.

Anaerobic digestion plants don't smell that bad, perhaps surprisingly, because the waste is processed in giant, enclosed containers. Unfortunately, the truckloads of food waste being delivered do. For that reason, finding a suitable site for anaerobic digestion projects is another challenge. Nevertheless, the technology's day seems to be coming. Energy companies will be increasingly interested, as many states have deadlines—known as the Renewable Portfolio Standards—that will require power companies to acquire a certain amount of energy from renewable sources (such as AD). While the percentages mandated and the deadlines vary by state, this nudge will speed AD adoption, as will the lure of selling renewable energy credits (RECs) and, potentially, carbon credits.

Onsite Power Systems (OPS), of Davis, California, is an anaerobic digestion company. Its facility looks like the set of a science-fiction movie, with color-coded tubes running between its four main tanks. The setting of the plant seems even more fictional after having driven by the neighboring stables of the Center for Equine Health, run by the University of California at Davis, to enter the plant. OPS has operated its digester intermittently, doing tests and demonstrations. One such demonstration processed food waste from San Francisco's green bin program. The company is hoping to become the end point for San Francisco's food waste, in which case OPS would build a commercial-scale facility closer to the Bay Area, roughly 100 miles from Davis.

Onsite Power is the brainchild of Dr. Ruihong Zhang, a professor in the Biological and Agricultural Engineering Department at UC Davis. She improved upon existing AD technology by dividing two kinds of bacteria into separate tanks to speed up the process. Zhang, who came to AD after studying organic waste for more than twenty years, originally worked with agricultural waste. She gravitated toward food-processing excess through a rather personal connection: Her husband is a food-processing engineer who also teaches at Davis. Through exposure to food processing, she saw how much waste existed. Similarly, doing consulting work for trash companies shed light on the environmental dangers of food in the waste stream.

Zhang envisions a future where most municipalities have their own digester. And we're talking about the near future; she estimates that within five years, we'll see municipally owned digesters in operation. She espouses a sort of anaerobic digestion "domino theory." Once that first city builds a digester, municipalities won't want to be caught dead without one. One can hope.

The beauty of anaerobic digestion is that the technology can be scaled up or down depending on need. Zhang sees a use for small digesters at supermarkets and maybe even some restaurants. Yet, she stopped short of endorsing my "digester in every home" pipe dream (motto: "In digestion we trust!"). That's probably wise, as it's doubtful that there would be enough waste to justify building a digester in *every* home. But, what if money was no object? And if your home did create energy from food waste (and other organic waste—use your imagination), wouldn't that necessitate a new LEED certification—perhaps a "diamond" level?

Continuing her skeptical ways, Zhang is pessimistic about Americans adopting the simple, neighborhood-level microdigesters found in China and India. Zhang said China has more than 10 million of these contraptions, often shared by a few families to supply biogas for heating and cooking in rural areas. She doesn't think they'd fly in the United States, because Americans are used to sending their trash *away*. She's probably right, although that could change.

Yet, AD and shipping our waste off could coexist; it would just require us to separate it first. Once the food waste is isolated, rolling it out to the curb is easy. That's happening throughout Europe, where permitting and developing landfills has long been a challenge because there is just less available real estate. As we'll see in the next chapter, using anaerobic digestion to process food waste is now thriving in the United Kingdom. British AD development has had two advantages to help jumpstart it—the British government's financial backing, and the massive economic stimulus of an escalating European Union landfill tax. The Landfill Directive mandates that by 2016, the disposal of organics in landfills by member nations must be below 35 percent of 1995 levels (although some nations have received special dispensation on the timing).

In addition to Orbit and Onsite Power, a handful of other U.S. companies are pursuing anaerobic-digestion projects. And the dominoes may have started to fall. Municipalities' wastewater treatment facilities have long used AD to process human waste and are looking at food waste as an energy source. Oakland's East Bay Municipal Utility District was the first U.S. facility to turn postconsumer food waste into energy through an anaerobic digester. The plant has been treating wastewater with AD since 2004 but has added food waste from San Francisco and Contra Costa County restaurants.

Companies utilizing anaerobic digestion may differ in their approach and in the exact technology, but they all agree that the food-waste market is plentiful. Americans produce enough food waste to keep commercial composters and anaerobic digestion companies quite busy, provided we get better at separating it from the regular waste stream. That will likely be the hardest part.

It is not surprising that Onsite Power's CEO, Dave Konwinski, is bullish on the potential market for anaerobic digestion. Yet his vision is an evocative one. "Our goal, primarily, is to take all the organic waste we're burying and make it into energy," Konwinski said. "You hear all the news about dependence on foreign oil. We're burying enough stuff to probably offset 20 percent of our oil use. I don't know if we're trying to make ourselves the Saudi Arabia of the next century, but we're burying what would equate to millions of gallons of gas per day."

One of the Charity Run vans that Pret A Manger employs to collect
excess food from the sandwich chain's London shops.

IMAGE COURTESY OF PRET A MANGER

chapter 11

Great, Britain! A Kingdom United in Hating Waste

Wilful waste makes woeful want.

—SCOTTISH PROVERB

The waste of plenty is the resource of scarcity.

—THOMAS LOVE PEACOCK,
NINETEENTH-CENTURY ENGLISH SATIRIST

*e*xiting the tube station at Westminster, I was in no danger of forgetting where I was. The tableau included Big Ben, Parliament, Westminster Abbey, the Thames, double-decker buses, and, seemingly everywhere, bobbies.

I walked past the iconic stretch on a brisk, overcast December morning en route to meet with Hilary Benn, a member of Parliament (MP), and, at the time, a cabinet minister and the secretary of state for the environment, food and rural affairs. As such, Benn led the Department of Environment, Food and Rural Affairs (DEFRA), which is like America's EPA and USDA rolled into one. Given that, it makes perfect sense that the head of the British department tasked with these two areas has latched onto food waste.

After I arrived at DEFRA's Smith Square headquarters, a friendly staffer deposited me in what the sign identified as the SOS (secretary of state) Waiting Room. A pocket-sized *Food Stats 2009* book provided the only reminder of where I was, until I was led into Benn's office and overheard another visitor tell his well-dressed companion, "We need to sort out this Spanish asparagus business."

Benn greeted me in the sitting room portion of his office, along with two close advisers. The room had massive windows peering out onto the Thames and rich wood-paneled walls leading the eye to the gymnasium-height ceiling. The vast square footage was similarly conducive to basketball. It seemed like an odd place to talk about food waste. But that was the point. That was precisely why I had come to Britain—because everyone from the supermarket managers to senior government ministers was discussing wasted food. I wanted to experience what it felt like to be in a country where the secretary of state rails against the cultural and climate-warming impact of food waste in public statements.

I visited the United Kingdom in December 2009 to peek into what I hoped would be America's future. If the U.S. government eventually recognizes the importance of food waste, it might look a little like the Britain of today. Like virtually all nations, developed or not, Britain still squanders a sizable portion of its food—that is why they are now focusing on waste. There are countries with a better record at recycling food waste, but none trying harder to reduce it. Certainly, no English-speaking nation (and English just happens to be the only language in which I'm fluent) has taken on the issue with such gusto.

So there I was, discussing ways to minimize the confusion between "sell-by" and "use-by" dates with a cabinet minister. Benn, a Labour Party MP representing Leeds, is a fourth-generation politician. While I never forgot his trade, Benn's pulse seemed to rise when discussing how much sense it made to keep food out of landfills. In snippets that couldn't quite be called sound bites, he asserted that wasting less food is essential for our fiscal and environmental health. "When food is chucked away, and of course, some of it does have to be, then what do we do?" Benn asked rhetorically. "Sticking it in landfill is a really bad idea. Doing something else with it—a much, much better idea. There are two really good reasons why you should do this—save money, save the planet."

DEFRA has raised the issue of food waste with grocers and brought it to the public's attention. Yet, the department's most effective move in prompting enlightened food-waste handling has been making it really expensive not to recycle food. DEFRA has achieved that through the landfill tax, or levy. Enacted in 1999, the landfill tax installed annual increases of £3 per tonne (that is, per metric ton) for all waste sent to landfills. Starting in April 2008, DEFRA expanded these "landfill tax escalators" to an £8 per tonne increase each year.[1] As a result, the price of landfilling essentially doubled from 2007 to 2010.[2] The twin goals of making food-waste recycling more economically feasible and landfilling less so have certainly worked. Household waste totals decreased by 12 percent from 2005 to 2007.[3] And they fell by about 25 percent in less than ten years, while composting and anaerobic digestion rates have increased.[4]

DEFRA didn't act on its own but was spurred into action by the European Union. The Landfill Directive, or Council Directive 1999/31/EC, in Euro-bureaucrat-speak, became law in April 1999. It requires Britain to reduce the biodegradable municipal waste it sends to landfills to 35 percent of 1995 levels by 2020.[5] And that's with a four-year extension that Britain received because of its weak history of recycling.

Britain's Climate Change Act of 2008 also sparked food-waste reduction. The law set firm targets for reduce greenhouse gas reductions, through action in the United Kingdom and abroad, of at least 80 percent by 2050. It also requires that CO_2 emissions be trimmed by at least 26 percent by 2020, against a 1990 baseline.[6] Given the greenhouse gas emissions of landfilled food, the act has created further impetus to recycle this waste instead.

Taken together, the landfill tax, the Landfill Directive, and the Climate Change Act have meant less buried waste: A mere 16.5 percent of food waste and packaging waste is now landfilled, according to the Food and Drink Feder-ation.[7] To be fair, some of the non-landfilled food is merely incinerated—not the most environmentally benign process. By contrast, 97 percent of U.S. food waste is sent to landfills.[8] It's not a perfect comparison, because the UK figure includes packaging, but it still illustrates the massive gap between British and American food-waste handling. Heck, even the UK Food and Drink Federation, which represents UK food manufacturers, set a goal of sending zero waste to the landfill by 2015.[9]

During my visit, I was reassured to see that DEFRA puts its money where its collective mouth is. As one would hope, at the Department of Environment, two large gray bins—for paper and mixed recycling—loomed in the hallway. In the fine print on these bins, however, I read that one could "recycle food waste at tea points." After my interview with Benn, I paid a visit the floor's tea point. While that's just another way of saying kitchen, I was disappointed to learn, the room had a small countertop bin containing organics to be composted. The green Aardvark Recycling kitchen caddy had a biodegradable bag liner, and in-side that, I'm guessing, many, many tea bags.

In researching the British response to food waste, I got a true sense of how little the U.S. government has addressed the issue. America and Britain certainly share strong ties and a fairly similar culture. With food waste, however, we're coming from two very different places. Britain has embraced the role of reduc-ing food waste to halt climate change, while America has not. That distinction is all the more impressive, considering that the United States should have *more* impetus to stem the tide. After all, the average American creates 4.6 pounds of overall solid waste per day, compared to 3.7 pounds per day for each Briton.[10] But even that doesn't show how far America lags behind Europe when it comes to food waste, because Britain's recycling and composting rate was below the E.U. average in 2007.[11]

Numbers Game

Speaking to Benn was nothing if not refreshing. To hear a person with the power to effect change talk about altering how Britain buys, uses, and disposes of food was heartening. And perhaps most importantly, Benn recognizes that

Britons need to do all three. If DEFRA has exhibited one shortcoming on the matter, it's in focusing most of its attention on household and retail waste and not enough on farms, food manufacturers, restaurants and other segments of the food chain. In all, though, DEFRA is doing a sound job in making the British public aware of the harmful effects of food waste—53 percent of UK households were aware of the problem as of 2008.[12]

Statistics like the one cited above have been vital to DEFRA. They have allowed the department to focus the British media's gaze, and consequently, the public's, on food waste. For example, in July 2008, a study called "The Food We Waste" came out with the finding that Britons throw away one-third of the food they buy.[13] It also found that 18 million tonnes of carbon dioxide are used to produce the food squandered in the United Kingdom, the equivalent of the CO_2 spewed into the air by one-fifth of the cars on the UK roads.[14] With that kind of data being published, the British media and public were almost forced to take notice. The subsequent media attention has been impressive. While having a politician of Benn's stature rallying attention to waste has helped, the media also had firm numbers and concrete examples on which to peg articles. For example, there was the tidbit that Britons throw away 4.4 million untouched apples every day.[15] That statistic, like many of the others in the United Kingdom, came courtesy of the Waste & Resources Action Programme (WRAP), a not-for-profit company that's a major player in Britain's efforts to reduce waste.

According to its own description, "WRAP helps individuals, businesses and local authorities to reduce waste and recycle more, making better use of resources and helping to tackle climate change." Established in 2000, WRAP is a private operation, but one with a rich public-sector uncle. WRAP is often called a semi-governmental group, as it's backed by £80 million in government funding annually, DEFRA being one such benefactor.[16] This seems to be a happy arrangement, as WRAP receives steady support and has access to government decisionmakers. At the same time, though, WRAP's principals can do things like suggest behavioral changes related to food that would earn elected officials the "nanny state" charge.

Banbury, halfway between Oxford and Birmingham, is an odd place for a UK-wide group to be based, but that's where WRAP has its headquarters. I visited their office in what's called The Old Malt House, where aged wooden beams hang over the open cubicles, and, you'll be glad to hear, the bathrooms have dual flush toilets and eco cleaning products. While I'd imagined, perhaps dreamt, that every WRAP employee worked on the food-waste problem, in reality it was about ten out of 200. Mark Barthel, WRAP's special adviser on food waste, heads the unit. Barthel worked in London as a commodities trader for eleven years before earning a master's degree in environmental management and a Ph.D. in sustainable systems for businesses. He's held jobs on Wall Street, in the oil industry, and in the retail sector, and now he's focusing on food waste.

The statistic Barthel kept returning to was that British homes waste 8.3 billion tonnes of food and drink. And 64 percent of that is "avoidable," meaning it was edible at some point prior to being chucked. WRAP came to that conclusion after combing through the trash of more than two hundred households. Given that finding, Barthel's next task was figuring out *why* Britons squander so much food. The research went well. Too well, actually. "When we looked at the different behavioral drivers, we found about seventy-four quite complex, interrelated human behaviors leading to food being wasted," Barthel said. "And that left us with a bit of a problem because trying to tackle seventy-four behaviors is pretty tough."

Boiling those reasons down to their essence, WRAP identified two main causes of waste: Britons leave food unused (for a variety of reasons); and they cook, prepare, or serve too much. With those targets determined, WRAP sought to reach these squanderers. In November 2007, the group launched a campaign to raise awareness on food waste and limit its occurrence: Love Food Hate Waste. "It says it all, really," Barthel said of the name. "You're engaging those that are really interested in food with the 'love food' piece. And you're engaging people that are really frustrated by the amount they're wasting with the 'hate waste' piece."

WRAP now teams with local councils to spread its message of (waste) hate. This campaign includes radio and print ads as well as information booths at events. Yet, the campaign centers on the fabulous Love Food Hate Waste website, which provides hints to help visitors trim their waste. The tips—many user-submitted—center on planning meals, shopping smarter, and learning about expiration dates and storing food properly. A portion calculator assists home cooks, and a party-food planner helps hosts plot out their nibbles, with options based on the number of guests and the length of the party. One page features the Arctic Aunt character, who encourages visitors to use their freezers to avoid waste. And, of course, there are boatloads of recipes. "Rescue Recipes" help Britons use up old ingredients, and "Cook Once, Eat Twice" ones convert leftovers into new meals. Plus, there's a handy feature that spits out recipes in response to your selection under "What Food Needs Using Up?"

The Love Food Hate Waste campaign calls on humor, or at least a bit of whimsy, with its "food lovers," actors who resemble certain food items. As Alana Godley, the site's administrator, explained it to me, WRAP had casting agencies put out a call for models or actors who looked like an apple, a fish, an egg, a crown of broccoli, and—my favorite—a lamb. One of the resulting ads pairs the words "Potato Lovers Hate Waste" with the image of a downright spud-like (spuddish?) man.

In addition to its online viral marketing, WRAP aimed to combat waste through a partnership with the Women's Institute (WI). Toward that end, WRAP funded a program in 2007 and 2008 that created a series of Love Food Groups to communicate the significance of food waste and teach practical ways it could be avoided. The WI was a natural choice, as the charity was created in 1915 to encourage women to produce and preserve more food during World War I. The more recent Love Food Groups were like book clubs mixed with home economics classes. The centrally planned lessons tackled portion sizes, meal planning, food storage, and using leftovers. The Love Food Groups certainly worked: Participants in the pilot project ended up cutting more than half of their edible food waste.[17]

Oxfam, the world-renowned charity, has even dabbled in publicizing food-waste reduction. The organization produced a series of You Tube videos in 2008 and 2009 in which an English septuagenarian dubbed "the Green Granny" dispensed household environmental tips, including how to use leftovers. When I found out that this granny, who goes by the name of Barbara Warmsley, lived only a short distance from London, I asked if I could pay her a visit. When she responded that she'd even bake the same bread pudding she'd made for the video, I was ecstatic. Over tea and pudding, she charmed me with her strategies for using up bread, potatoes, and a variety of other items.

Most impressive, though, was the Green Granny's tiny refrigerator. Warmsley's lone means of refrigeration only comes up to her chest, and she's not a tall woman.[18] The compact size of the appliance, and many others like it in Britain, helps reduce waste. It limits the amount of perishables she can buy at one time and encourages her to use what she has to minimize the overcrowding. Warmsley was kind enough to indulge my food-waste voyeurism when I asked if she'd show me what was in her fridge and if anything might go for naught. "I shan't throw anything away," Warmsley reassured me, saying she'd put some leftover vegetables into a soup and use up old fruit in smoothies for her grand-children.

Yet, the meager volume of these smaller fridges can also prompt waste. Es-pecially when people buy too many groceries and then must purge some of the older goods instead of using them. For the humble and huge fridge owners alike, there's a great opportunity to reduce food waste by encouraging them not to buy more than they need. Fortunately, many UK supermarkets are spreading this message to their shoppers.

Super Markets

My fascination with British supermarkets and their attention to food waste began in July 2008, when Prime Minister Gordon Brown chided retailers for cre-ating "unnecessary demand."[19] In other words, supermarkets were to blame for tempting shoppers into buying more than they needed. Hearing a head of state address food waste was scintillating (at least in these quarters). To have said leader scold a business for pursuing what was, in effect, a major part of its busi-ness model was fascinating.

Brown's primary target that day—the main "unnecessary demand" creator—was the promotional tactic of buy-one-get-one-free, or BOGOF. The Prime Min-ister's questioning of the sales strategy prompted great focus on it. Critics such as Hilary Benn and the WRAP crew derided BOGOF as a waste-enabler with per-ishables, saying it enticed shoppers, especially single people, to take home more than they could possibly consume (or fit in their fridge). In October 2009, mega-retailer Tesco announced it would shift to "buy-one-get-one-free—later" (BOGOF-L). This idea, which Benn praised in our meeting as "a really, really smart policy," would give shoppers a voucher to collect the free item on a subsequent visit.

Tesco tried the BOGOF-L scheme for two weeks in February 2010. If the chain is pleased with how it went, the sales scheme will become a regular feature at the UK's largest food retailer, said Ruth Girardet, Tesco's corporate responsibility director. She also specified that shoppers could take the free item that same day if they so desired, and that it would only be used with produce.

Girardet listed BOGOF-L as just one of many changes Tesco has made in the effort to cut waste in stores and shoppers' homes. The retailer has also begun selling half-loaves of bread and more items in resealable packaging to better serve smaller households. Bananas are now displayed in a padded "hammock" to protect them from bruising and keep them fresher longer.[20] And under the unfortunate promotion name "Eat me, keep me," the store sells shrink-wrapped packs of bananas with some yellow ones (eat me) and some green (keep me). In addition, Tesco includes food-storage tips, recipe ideas for leftovers, and date-label advice in stores and on its website.

While in England, I spent a few happy hours browsing through supermarkets. Unfortunately, BOGOF-L hadn't been implemented yet, as exemplified by the four-pack of oranges under a two-for-one sign. Indeed, a Tesco manager, in London's two-story Kensington store, told me that food-waste changes were coming, but they were "in process." Yet, I saw some positive signs. Simply selling items for "half price" is a better way of reducing waste than BOGOF-L. And there were plenty of 50-percent-off items, including honeydews, smoked salmon, parma ham (prosciutto), and a box of Christmas pudding, the British equivalent of the survive-the-apocalypse fruitcake that nobody wants.

Following these developments from afar, I sensed that UK grocers really understood the importance of food waste and were committed to helping shoppers trim their home squandering. Nothing I saw in person made me believe otherwise. The mere fact that most British supermarkets have pages on their websites devoted to the topic puts them ahead of their American counterparts. In particular, supermarket giant Sainsbury's "Love your Leftovers" campaign is quite useful. It features a section on why food waste matters, and a top-ten leftover list, which pairs each item with a use-it-up recipe.

Morrisons has joined the parade by launching a "Great Taste, Less Waste" campaign. After finding in a survey that 90 percent of those polled were keeping fresh foods in the wrong places, the Bradford-based retailer decided to create "Best Kept" labels. This sticker-based storage advice now adorns the majority of fresh produce, telling shoppers that it's best to keep apples, for example, inside the fridge, and tomatoes out of it. The chain has also conducted "Keep it Fresh" tests to determine which fruits and vegetables need packaging and which do not. Few will be surprised that bags or trays reduced in-store grape waste by 20 percent. Yet, other findings were interesting. Cucumbers, for example, lasted for fourteen days with a plastic wrap and only three without it.[21] The Co-operative, Britain's fifth-largest food chain and a functioning, yes, co-operative, was the first retailer to put fruit and vegetable storage advice on its plastic produce bags, which were branded with the "Love Food, Hate Waste" logo. The company also held forty-five "Watch Your Waste" demonstration events in the fall of 2009.[22]

While many grocers independently launched efforts to reduce waste in shoppers' homes, others weren't as proactive. DEFRA and WRAP impressed upon the less progressive stores the importance of spreading this anti–food waste message. Whether they jumped in or had to be nudged, almost all UK grocers signed on to the July 2005 Courtauld Commitment—a voluntary agreement between WRAP and virtually all UK grocers to reduce the amount of food and food packaging in household waste.[23] The Courtauld Commitment lacks the teeth of mandatory reduction targets. Instead, it focuses on the retail sector's contribution to waste in private homes, with the goal of getting UK households to waste 155,000 fewer tonnes of food in 2010 than they did in 2008. The food-waste-reduction tactics proposed include improved packaging, in-store waste-reduction guidance, and the Love Food Hate Waste campaign.

The Courtauld Commitment mirrors the waste strategies of UK supermarkets. While they lavish attention on helping shoppers reduce food waste in their homes, grocers could do more to reduce their in-house waste. And there certainly is plenty of the latter. According to WRAP, retailers in the United Kingdom generate 1.6 million tonnes of food waste annually.[24] Like their U.S. counterparts, British supermarkets prioritize appearance, which prompts superficial culling both before and during retail display.

When I saw a cart in Tesco's vegetable section promoting the store's thrice daily "Freshness check," I was amazed by its overtness: "If it's not good enough for us, it's not good enough for our customers. It goes straight into the bin."

Prepared sandwiches are found in almost every UK supermarket, with an array of choices so vast and English that it's frightening. I counted eighty-six different prepared sandwiches at one Tesco, all, thankfully, devoid of Marmite, the British yeast-extract spread that's an acquired taste.[25] Stocking that many sandwiches, in addition to twenty-seven varieties of cut fruit and twenty-eight types of salads and pastas, means more will go unsold. Thankfully, the top shelf at that London Tesco had a section for reduced-price sandwiches whose "display-until" date was that day.

There is plenty to applaud in British supermarkets. Marking down items nearing their sell-by dates appeared to be quite common. I found sale racks in the produce sections, bread aisles, and prepared-food coolers. The level of frugality at some stores was impressive. At a London Sainsbury's, two egg-stained boxes of, yes, eggs sat on the discount shelf. All of their contents were whole, but they'd likely been next to a damaged box. Had an employee in a U.S. supermarket seen this, the item would've been discarded immediately for contamination fears. The epitome of the British grocers' thrift, however, was a taped-up box of puff pastry roll. The repair job was sloppy and it featured obtrusive gray tape on the red package. I'd wager a hundred boxes of puff pastry that this would never happen in the United States. Yet, I loved it, because, after all, the flattened dough inside was identical to one in a pristine box.

Meanwhile, Morrisons has its own waste-avoiding strategies. It supplies its own meat and some produce. The resulting lack of middle men—or a vertically integrated supply chain, if you're business-y—helps reduce in-store waste, as is described on the store's website. Since the buyers send large cuts to each store, they can customize the offerings to suit shoppers' preferences. This tactic also affords flexibility to avoid weather-related waste. As Morrisons' site says, "So if the sun decides to come out, our butchers can switch their attention from stewing and braising meat cuts to kebabs and barbecue-ready products." Similarly, by buying and packing its own produce, the store can adapt rapidly to shifting demands and inventory levels. A hot day means more salads are packed, whereas cold, wet weather brings more root vegetables.

Morrisons claims it can get products from soil to store in twelve hours. The chain offers to give cauliflower trimmings to customers—rabbit owners, in particular—and to *sell* their salmon heads and bones to those who want to make stock. If goods at or near their use-by or best-before dates don't sell at a discount, Morrisons actually uses them in meals they cook for their staff to serve in their in-store canteens.[26]

Going Anaerobic

While these supermarket waste-avoidance strategies are progressive, they're necessary, as British grocers don't donate as much unsold food to charities as their American counterparts. In addition to implementing waste reduction strategies, UK retailers are getting quite handy at recycling their food waste. Many supermarket chains now send it to anaerobic digestion plants. AD is one of the solutions that Sainsbury's is using to reach its zero-waste (to landfill) goal by the end of 2010. As of May 2010, 250 of the chain's 800-plus stores were diverting their food waste to AD plants, said Jack Cunningham, environmental affairs manager for the company. And that number will grow, he hopes, when more AD plants are constructed. "If and as developers build more plants, we're keen to enter partnerships with them," Cunningham said. "It's our preferred route, but the availability is the limiting factor now."

Waitrose is among the leaders in this supermarket food-waste-to-energy movement. As of the spring of 2010, roughly half of its 222 stores were sending their food waste to digesters. Their motivation is evenly split between the cold reality and the warm, fuzzy stuff, as Arthur Sayer, manager of recycling and waste, told me. "Quite clearly, landfill costs are going up, so that is a motivation," he said. "But the equal driver is the sort of desire to be doing the right thing. Following our corporate social responsibility. We really don't want to be putting food into landfill if we can avoid it."

The tonnes of food waste being sent to AD plants will quickly mount as participants and capacity increase. Sayer estimated that each Waitrose store produces 1 tonne of food waste per week. And through a waste audit, Morrisons found that each store created 1.6 tonnes weekly in a trial of food-waste segregation. Yet, using AD to process food waste does not excuse the sheer volume of it. Nor does it erase the environmental impact of food waste. The energy created is useful, but not nearly as environmentally beneficial as preventing waste.

Environment Secretary Hilary Benn and his DEFRA colleagues have made a massive push to increase the use of anaerobic digestion in Britain. The title of a February 2009 DEFRA study, "Anaerobic Digestion—Shared Goals," communicated the department's support for the technology. WRAP has a page on its site promoting and explaining AD, and DEFRA created an anaerobic digestion website, "England's Official Information Portal on Anaerobic Digestion."[27] In February 2009, Environment Minister Jane Kennedy announced a joint government/private-sector anaerobic-digestion task group to speed its adoption. That July, the task group published an implementation plan recommending— count 'em—forty-six steps that government and industry could take to speed the widespread adoption of the technology.[28]

During our discussion, Benn repeatedly praised anaerobic digestion. Calling it "a technology I'm very keen to encourage," he pointed to AD as a way to keep food out of landfills and help meet zero-waste and carbon-emission goals. He also mentioned another driver for AD growth: using the technology to diminish the problem of animal waste in concentrated livestock facilities (and the National Farmers Union agreed, saying it envisioned 1,000 farms with digesters to process their animal waste).[29] "It's a very important answer to the problem of what do you do with the food waste that you've got," Benn told me.

Part of the impetus for AD came from the need to meet the binding EU goals on landfill tonnage, greenhouse gas emissions, and renewable energy creation. Today, the demand for AD outstrips the capacity. When I met with Benn at the end of 2009, there were eleven food-waste-processing digesters in operation and many more in the works.[30] Nina Sweet, a WRAP technical specialist in organic waste, told me that Britain had the capacity to process 280,000 tonnes of food waste at the end of 2009, but that the capacity would double over the next two years. "I think it's on the point of taking off," Benn said. "I'm confident we're going to see a big growth over the next ten years in anaerobic digestion."

Under Benn, DEFRA has encouraged local councils to implement separate food-waste collection in whatever manner they prefer. Yet, they've communicated that they'd prefer to see it go to an anaerobic digester. Of course, to do so, a nearby AD facility needs to exist. To speed the process and illustrate how collection would work, DEFRA funded demonstration sites. In the West Midlands county of Shropshire, the Ludlow plant was the first in the UK to use anaerobic digestions to process solely food waste.

BioBags, Badgers, and a Box of Condoms

Driving from London to Ludlow, a medieval market town near the border with Wales, is best done in the daylight. That way you can see the rolling green hills, the hedgerows crowding the road, and the minuscule sign for the A443. And when you near the town of 10,000, you'll be able to spot the medieval castle and Tudor-style half-timbered buildings and get a decent photo of the "Don't Feed the Sheep" road sign. Alas.

I arrived at the Veolia Environmental Services facility in the Ludlow Business Park on the outskirts of town on a cold, damp Monday morning that did nothing to dispel my stereotype of British weather. I'd arranged to tag along on a food-waste collection run with a couple of Veolia workers. Or at least, I'd arranged it in principle. The manager I spoke with said to call that morning and we'd "sort it out."

After experiencing decidedly less cooperation from American waste-industry executives, I was surprised by the Veolia executive's nonchalance. Yet, it made sense after having talked a bit with driver/loader Charlie Tolley. The fifty-five-year-old former plasterer told me how they'd had quite a few visits from the media recently because food waste and anaerobic digestion had become prime news topics. Tolley, who looked like an older version of Daniel Craig, was so comfortable being observed that he asked if I was getting good enough photos, offering to pose as he emptied a bucket of food waste into the truck. (No Cartier-Bresson, I took him up on his offer.)

The food-waste collection I observed in Ludlow was fairly straightforward. Tolley and his taciturn partner, Brian Saunders, pulled up to a row of homes, disembarked, and grabbed the 25-liter blue bins at the curb. They dumped each bin's contents into the open back of the collection vehicle, which was more of a van than a garbage truck. Each knee-high bin held one or two green, corn-based BioBags. The whole process was fairly neat and odorless, as the local council pays for the distribution of the biodegradable bags that line participants' kitchen caddies. Tolley and Saunders kept a roll of bags in the backseat and resupplied those who had left a note in their bin asking for more.

In Ludlow, this voluntary participation reached 77 percent in the spring of 2009, three years after food-waste collection began. Ludlovians who participate receive a gray kitchen caddy with a reminder sticker on what they can and can't compost, along with the larger blue bin. Normally, the Veolia workers on the food-waste route use a media- and environmentally-friendly electric vehicle. When I visited, though, it was out of commission. We made the rounds in a van borrowed from the nearby town of Shrewsbury. On the passenger side of the dashboard sat a pair of sunglasses, which seemed inconceivable on such a drizzly day, and a box of Trojan condoms. To be fair, it was a borrowed vehicle.

Tolley, who lives in Ludlow and participates in food waste collection at his home, told me that the pick-ups usually run smoothly. There's the occasional feline or canine attention, which can make a mess. And once in a while, there's a reminder that Ludlow sits in a fairly rural area. "One lad told me a badger kept visiting the back of his yard," Tolley said. "He'd knock over the bin and get at it. They're quite strong, badgers."

Yet, untidy bins aren't much of a problem, as the contents are just dumped in the back of the truck, bag or no bag. A larger obstacle in the first few years was getting customers to understand what "food waste" meant—that they were just collecting food, not the waste associated with it. Tolley said he still sees the occasional cutlery mixed in, or an out-of-date yogurt in its container. When that happens, the loaders can decide not to collect the waste, leaving a sticker with the reason and jotting the address so the council can get in touch with the offending party to clarify the definition of "food waste."

The average participating household in Ludlow produces 2.5 kilograms per week, which is more than 5 pounds. Tolley said he's been surprised by how much food waste exists, calling it "a massive amount." Yet, he felt that having residents segregate their food waste is raising awareness and lowering the tonnage. "I think it's probably decreased a little, as we're in a recession now. People separating it helps, too. Before, when you just threw it in the black bin with everything else, you didn't notice it," Tolley said.

Yet, Tolley has been surprised by the goods—both inedible and edible— he's seen discarded in his six years of waste-collection service. He lamented the array of electronics that is regularly cast away instead of repaired. And he recalled seeing Christmas cakes and fruits tossed in bins whole. "I've noticed some fruit in the back [of the truck] that's been better than what I've brought for the lunch break," Tolley said, singling out grapes as being prematurely discarded.

Ludlow's food waste accumulates, but it doesn't go very far. The food waste that Tolley and his Veolia co-workers collect ends up at the South Shropshire Biodigester less than 100 yards from the Veolia depot. The anaerobic digester, run by BiogenGreenfinch, receives 70 tonnes of waste weekly, primarily from households in Ludlow and a few smaller towns in the area. Surprisingly, from an odor perspective, BiogenGreenfinch's corporate offices are under the same roof as the food-waste collection.

At the facility, I met Lucy Lewis, BiogenGreenfinch's innovation manager. Lewis, dressed casually in a gray zip-up top, jeans, and sneakers, walked me through the AD process in a boardroom before we headed downstairs to the loading dock. Entering the enclosed area where food waste arrives, I was taken aback by the stench. I've been to quite a few places that handle food waste, but none that were inside. The facility's proximity to other businesses necessitates that the receiving happen indoors (with the giant bay door closed). Yet, this enclosement only exacerbates the stench. Inside, a pile of food waste with half-broken bags lay on one side and a maze of conveyor belts and tanks took up the other side. Flies gathered on the equipment as I pondered whether it was good or bad that I hadn't yet eaten lunch.

What amounted to a large garage door opened and a collection van from the small Welsh company Cwm Harry drove up. The driver had a load of commercial food waste from restaurants. He said something to me that the hum of machinery and his accent made incomprehensible, but with a little help, I learned that he was warning me to stand back—the materials would make a good splash when he dumped them.

Once the load payload was deposited, a Bobcat scooped the material into a macerator, which broke the bags and pulped the waste. The food waste, by then a grayish stew, journeyed up a conveyor belt to a holding tank, from which it would be piped to another macerator and outside to the first of four large green cylindrical tanks, where it would be consumed by bacteria. Behind those sat a white globe about two stories tall that holds the methane—the whole point of this fifty-day process.

AD awareness has spread rapidly in Ludlow. Lewis told me that, in comparison to a few years ago, Ludlovians now have a much better understanding of just what the heck anaerobic digestion is. "People know what I mean when I say 'biodigester' now. I don't dread people asking me what I do anymore. It used to be 'Oh, no, this is gonna be a long conversation,'" Lewis said.

And that public familiarity on AD has gone hand-in-hand with increased attention to food waste. As separation and collection have continued into a fourth year, participation and effectiveness have increased. Lewis confirmed what Tolley suspected: Participating homes now put less food waste in their blue bins each week. "There has been a drop in amount produced per household," Lewis said. "They're seeing what they're throwing away, and so they're reducing the amount of food that they buy maybe, or that they waste. Maybe they're eating more leftovers."

Though that dip in food waste is generally good news, it makes it harder to produce a steady amount of biogas. Lewis said the plant has the capacity to accept more material and is exploring receiving more commercial waste from nearby towns or industrial food-waste from large processors. There are many cider makers in the area, so apple pulp is one possibility. At present, the plant receives whey from a local cheesemaker every so often. And when I was there, the digester had just received a one-off shipment of—horror of horrors—waste chocolate from Cadbury's. The chocolate maker milled the product too fine and didn't have a use for what was essentially cocoa powder.

Anaerobic digestion in the United Kingdom has progressed to the point where some food processors are building dedicated biodigesters on their property. Branston, one of Britain's largest potato suppliers and distributors—and that's saying something—has contracted with BiogenGreenfinch to build a 300-kilowatt facility to handle its "outgrade potatoes."[31] Construction on the digester at the company's Lincoln facility began in late 2009.

With full government backing, anaerobic digestion is becoming a widespread, viable destination for UK food waste. WRAP's Barthel believes it will help the United Kingdom meet its renewable energy requirements. Barthel told me that if 60 percent of UK food waste went to AD plants—a reasonable goal, in his view—it would create enough electricity to power two major cities. And though domestic food-waste collection is growing by the day in Britain, the United Kingdom isn't near the top of the European AD food chain. "England is pretty low down on the hierarchy in terms of actually applying the technology itself. Germany, Austria, Sweden are leaders," Lewis said. "There's a lot in planning and development now in England. I'd say in three years time, there'll be a lot of digesters."

A Labour of Love

While UK retailers are much more attuned to reducing waste and disposing of it in environmentally friendly ways, they lag behind their American counterparts in donation of retail food that would otherwise be discarded. There is some recovery of goods that are edible, but unsellable, but it is largely done by local charities and in a less formal manner than in the United States. There is no national organization that rescues these perishable foods; nor are there local groups like those found in most major U.S. metropolitan areas to swoop from supermarket to restaurant, recovering food that would otherwise be wasted.

Yet, that doesn't mean there isn't a sizable redistribution of food in the United Kingdom. In fact, there is a national organization bringing this food to those in need—they just don't collect the food themselves. FareShare, a London-based charity, has a different model. It receives surplus food from manufacturers and retailers and then delivers it to hunger-relief groups. It's not as much food recovery as food reception and redistribution. (American food-recovery groups also receive similar donations.)

FareShare CEO Tony Lowe figured that the food industry already had the infrastructure in place to deliver food across the country, so why waste resources doubling their efforts? And since FareShare only has three vans at its London operation, and some of its depots in other cities do not even have one, they try to use them mostly for deliveries, rather than pickups. FareShare does collect some goods. For instance, the London depot retrieves food from the head offices of Marks & Spencer and Sainsbury's. Yet the majority of food arrives by the pallet-load, on lorries from food manufacturers such as Nestlé, Kraft, and Cargill. These massive donations add up. In 2009, FareShare redistributed 3,100 tonnes of food. That amounts to 7.4 million meals. "It's a lot—not enough—but it's a good start," Lowe said.

When I toured the London headquarters at the industrial Tower Bridge Business Complex in the southeast borough of Southwark, colossal stacks of goods that my guide called "ambient food" (hard groceries) filled the main room of the warehouse, along with two delivery vans. Many of the brand names were unfamiliar, but their reason for being there—damaged packaging—was not. As in any U.S. food bank, there were bashed boxes, dented cans, and torn cellophane. How FareShare sources the majority of its food is quite different, though. Through its FareShare First program, the charity offers to process all of a food company's waste for a fee. They sort through it, distributing what's edible and arranging for the disposal of what isn't. Lowe told me that FareShare First is doubly nourishing, yielding 70 percent of the charity's food supply and a source of revenue that Lowe hopes will eventually fund their operations.

Food companies will pay FareShare for this service partly because it allows them to donate without having to sort the good from the bad. It also helps them become aware of their inefficiencies. But mostly it's because it still saves food manufacturers money. Due to the dearness of landfill dumping and other disposal methods, that's not difficult to do. Since it started using FareShare First, Nestlé's disposal costs, for example, have decreased 40 percent. FareShare prices its service to undercut the cost of regular disposal, Lowe said. While boardroom motivations are shifting, the bottom line will always remain essential. "In the last three years, FareShare First being cheaper was the driver," explained Lowe. "In the recent years, though, the fact that it's socially beneficial and environmentally friendly and creates carbon credits is definitely rising in importance. But if I told a company 'It will cost you more money,' they'd still say 'No thanks.'"

Lowe said that one obstacle to donation is getting food manufacturers to realize that they have food to donate. And even the most efficient companies still have food to donate because of the sheer volume of their operations. As an example, Lowe pointed to Gerber, which imports juices from Europe and packages them for UK supermarkets. The company is extremely prudent, with waste of only 0.04 percent—"naught point naught four percent." But that still equates to 300,000 liters, or 1.2 million servings of juice, that they (now) donate to FareShare.

That's why Lowe's main priority is getting the food companies to recognize their excess and automate their donations. Toward that end, FareShare issued a challenge to food makers: "It's a challenge to them to complete their ethical supply chain," Lowe said. "Most businesses source ethically, but don't have an ethical disposal method. We have to make it so if they can't sell it, it's systematically donated. Without that, they're too busy, there's no process, so it's all going to be destroyed. And that's sad."

Ready to Recover

It's not often one finds oneself sitting in a sandwich shop waiting for it to close. Yet that's where I found myself on a chilly night in London's hip West End. More precisely, the shop was a Pret A Manger, the chain which, as its name indicates (in French), specializes in sandwiches ready to eat. That strategy works well in the harried environment of London's lunch hour but it virtually guarantees a surplus of food at the end of the day. Fortunately, the chain is determined to ensure that these leftovers don't go for naught.

I'd seen restaurants, supermarkets, and other retail operations donate their leftover or unsellable food. But I'd never seen or heard of a retailer, British or otherwise, that went shop to shop within its own chain to collect and then donate its excess (at a significant expense). That is, I hadn't before I met up with Andy Cuthbert inside the Albemarle Street store. Cuthbert is the driver/loader on the "West End Route" of Pret's Charity Run, a program the chain started in 2007 to redistribute its leftover food (it had delivered food to charities by foot before then). Cuthbert was unmistakable in a "Pret delivers" black fleece jacket and Pret baseball cap with a "Charity Run" button pinned on it. The equally conspicuous Pret Charity Run van was parked right outside. I sat down with Cuthbert, who told me about the job and had the barista make me a latte as we waited for the store to officially close. At exactly 6 P.M., the clerk motioned to the open wall of refrigerated foods and told Cuthbert, "It's all yours."

The end of the store's retail day marked the start of our evening collection. Cuthbert leaped into motion, a fifty-one-year-old in Mizuno running shoes swooping toward the chrome shelving. He stacked the boxed sandwiches, from ploughman's to coronation chicken, into a gray, hard-plastic bin. The triangular boxes—packaged so the two sandwich halves (cut diagonally) face the consumer through clear wrapping—fit neatly together. He loaded a few baguette sandwiches and then filled one paper bag with pretzels and another with croissants from a case near the register. All told, there were twenty-four items.

In its tallying, Pret doesn't distinguish hot wraps from cold sandwiches from baked goods—they're all just considered "items." In total, the retail chain collects 1.7 million of these items from its London locations annually. And that's only about half of the stores, as the remaining locations have charities collect their daily excess.

When Pret started selling sandwiches in 1986, there wasn't a viable food-recovery group in operation. As a result, at the first Pret shop, located near Victoria Station, employees handed out the leftovers to the homeless at the end of the day. In a chat at the company's funky Victoria headquarters, Pret Sustainability Director Nicky Fisher told me how the original solution came about. "The area is known as an area with many homeless," she said. "So we took one problem—hunger among the homeless—and another problem—having all this extra food—and we solved both by putting the two together."

As Pret expanded, its leaders looked for a more systematic way of getting the excess to the hungry and turned to FareShare, which collected the sandwiches for a few years until they deemed the arrangement too costly. Although some stores had individual arrangements with charities, Pret's leaders realized that if they didn't want to throw away massive amounts of food, they would have to create their own solution. What began in 2007 with one vehicle has morphed into a five-van fleet, complete with five hired drivers to collect and distribute the day's leftovers among the city's homeless shelters and other charities. That led to a line of cute electric vans and, at present, more reliable Citroën liquefied petroleum gas (LPG) vans, like the one I rode in with Cuthbert. As of December 2009, Pret had six vans collecting from fifty of its London stores. As a result, the vans salvage 250 tonnes of food each year, and that then feeds people instead of landfills.

Pret aims to reduce waste by letting the available foods taper off toward the end of the day. Yet, the stores also want to have some food to sell right up to closing, like their fellow Francophiles at Au Bon Pain. To balance those competing desires, Fisher said that Pret aims to have the ten top-selling foods on the shelf at closing time. From what I saw and from what Cuthbert told me, it was clear that the amount varies from store to store. We collected 72 items at the Tottenham Court Road store, 32 at Sicilian Avenue, and 23 at Goodge Street. Cuthbert told me he had recently recovered 300 items at one Pret, not far from his personal high of 400. Yet, about once a week, he will arrive at a location to find that they've completely sold out and have no items to donate.

Although nobody wants to miss a sales opportunity, knowing that most of their leftovers will be donated must relieve some of the karmic pressure in the closing-time stock question. I say "most" because Pret doesn't donate all of its foods. Soups and sushi aren't redistributed, due to food-safety concerns. Pret only has two rules for its recipients—keep the food refrigerated, and use it by 2 P.M. the next day. After collecting, Cuthbert and I delivered our haul to the Simon Community, a charity that drives food around in a van, giving it to the "rough sleepers" it finds on the streets. Cuthbert knocked on the unmarked red door of the group's Kentish Town rowhouse and exchanged one bin of food for some empty containers.

Part of the reason Pret has so much stock to donate is that it doesn't use anything the next day. Unlike the pre-made sandwiches that populate almost every supermarket, Pret's offerings don't have sell-by dates, because they'll only be sold on the day they're made. The only exceptions are packaged yogurts, cut fruit, and desserts. Fisher said that not having dates also prevents objections from donation recipients who don't quite understand what "sell-by" means. It allows for common sense to prevail over excessive caution. "It's a ridiculous situation to be in where you're throwing away food that's perfectly edible just because of a number on a sticker," Fisher said.

Action on Expiration Dates

In addition to prompting Pret A Manger to recover its own leftovers, the lack of retail food redistribution in the United Kingdom means that a steady stream of edible yet unsellable food goes untapped. Some see the discarding of these items near or at their "best-before" date as unfortunate or even disgraceful. Dan Cluderay saw it as an opportunity.

The United Kingdom boasts a vibrant secondary market in goods that are approaching or past their "best-before" dates. After being laid off from his job as a software developer at Sony Ericsson in 2000, Cluderay entered the world of discount food. He sold out-of-date foods with his father-in-law at markets and car-boot sales. He zipped from Leeds to Hull to Doncaster in his green Mercedes Sprinter van, selling items that retailers had no use for, and quickly learned that there were plenty of Britons who knew that an item at its best-before date was still good. Instead of meaning the food had spoiled, it just meant it could be had for a song at stalls like the one Cluderay ran. "I know we were giving people quality goods because they kept coming back," Cluderay said. "We were just working that gray area. If someone puts a date on a can of soup and it's good for two years, does it matter if it's a week past that?"

Calling on his technology background, Cluderay spotted an opportunity to transform his in-person success to the Internet. He launched Approved Food & Drink (then just Approved Food) in 2007 and, thanks partly to what was for him a fortuitous economic downturn, the site's sales boomed. Working out of a warehouse the size of a football, sorry, soccer pitch, Sheffield-based Approved Food & Drink now ships 30 tonnes of goods per day. They don't sell perishable items, instead focusing on dry goods.

In our conversation, Cluderay uttered the phrase "value for money" often, and after perusing his site, it's easy to understand why. In December 2009, when I browsed through Approved Food & Drink, the site was selling a box of Special K with Red Berries for £0.99 ($1.60), whereas online retailer Tesco had it for almost three times that much, £2.89.[32] It listed £0.59 tins of tuna and £0.99 six-packs of Coke Zero. And Cluderay is betting that customers will pay £1 for a Cadbury bar four days past its "best-by" date, though a fresher one would retail for £1.79.

Cluderay's years of selling to the public and his later experience as a wholesaler supplying other vendors gave him a sense of the value of expired foods. "If you've got a good idea of what the general public wants and how much they're willing to pay for it, you're in good shape. That's my expertise," Cluderay said. "It was, 'Here's the date, here's the price, do you want to pay it?' You soon learn what the price of a short-dated can of beans is. Or what an out-of-date can of custard costs."

Cluderay estimated that 40 percent of the goods he sells are past their "best-before" dates, while the rest are nearing it, or "short-dated." Approved Food & Drink doesn't sell anything past the "use-by" date, as that would be illegal. In the United Kingdom, there is a clear distinction between these terms, with the former more about a food's quality and the latter referring to food safety. Here's the official take on the terms from Paul Cook, head of microbiological safety at the Food Standards Agency, who wrote by e-mail that "best before is an indication of quality rather than safety; eating food past the best before date doesn't necessarily put someone at risk from food poisoning as long as the food is handled/prepared properly. Use by is the important one to look at, as the date relates to the safety of the food."[33]

Unfortunately, as often as not, that distinction is lost on consumers. WRAP has surveyed Britons on these terms and knows they yield a great deal of confusion. "Half the UK population doesn't understand the meaning of what 'best before' means. And neither do they understand the meaning of 'use-by,'" Barthel said. "And even worse, just about 36 percent of the population get the two confused. They're eating food past the use-by date when they shouldn't be because they're treating it as a 'best-before' date. Or they're throwing food away after a best-before date because they're treating it as a use-by date."[34]

Given the unnecessary waste that this confusion causes, government agencies such as DEFRA, the Food Standards Agency, and WRAP are attempting to educate people, and in a June 2009 speech, Environment Secretary Benn urged the food industry to clarify date labels. In our interview, Benn told me that DEFRA was encouraging supermarkets to examine the issue and working with WRAP and the Food Standards Agency to possibly require changes in 2010. A spokesperson at the Food Standards Agency told me that WRAP is taking the lead on the matter. WRAP has pushed for reform with supermarkets and sought to help individuals understand expiration dates through its Love Food Hate Waste site.

Further muddling the issue, some items have a "sell-by" or "display-until" date. These dates are meant to tell retailers when to pull the item, but they confound shoppers. It's a problem WRAP is hoping to address. "We are looking at a few opportunities to see if we can actually make that display-until date invisible to consumers," Barthel said. "To either encrypt it, or use a bar code or a data matrix or something like that on the pack, rather than a date that people can recognize and confuse with another form of date labeling."

What's more, I found that many perishables in UK supermarkets had the same date listed for both "display until" and "use by," even though they have different meanings. Britons who understand the terminology can avoid plenty of waste and take advantage of deals at Approved Food & Drink and a similar site, Nearly Out of Date. Those who aren't clear on the terms may end up throwing away a lot of good food. Cluderay exhibits a sense of humor about this divide on his website. "Some people believe consuming food & drink that has passed its 'best before' date is unacceptable and these people might be better off shopping at www.tesco.com," the site reads, linking visitors to the massive UK retailer.

Bringing It All Back Home

Letting food go unused because of a lack of knowledge or effort used to be quite rare in Britain. The workbook for the now defunct Love Food Groups had a section on leftovers. It reminded readers that "leftovers have often been associated with the Sunday roast followed by shepherd's pie on Monday and/or bubble and squeak." While I included that line partly because I wanted "bubble and squeak"—the name of a dish made with leftover potatoes, vegetables, and (sometimes) meat, fried together—to appear in this book, it has a larger meaning. It signifies that food-waste reduction was once part of the pattern of life. The leftovers from the Sunday roast went into the next day's meals—it was just how you did things. Nowadays, you can buy frozen bubble and squeak, which is ironic, since it sort of loses its meaning unless the company selling it is somehow using the industrial leftovers from other frozen vegetable dishes. It's the equivalent of manufacturing brand new jeans with a worn-out look.

In England, as in most developed nations, busier lives, socioeconomic changes and urbanization have minimized these traditional waste-avoiding routines and habits. Yet, as we've seen, Britons, more than Americans, have come to recognize that they have a food-waste problem. To some extent, that may be a result of the poverty and devastation that Britain faced after World War II, compared to the postwar boom experienced in the United States. Labor and capital were in short supply, as was government intervention.[35] Accordingly, Britons don't have to look quite as far into their past to recall food shortages and rationing. Although Americans experienced both during World War II, the rationing of some British items stretched well past the war's end. Rationing didn't fully cease until the stroke of midnight on July 4, 1954, when meat and bacon were finally sold freely.[36] It's equally improbable that the first restrictions weren't lifted until 1948, three years after the war was over.[37] And even more astounding was that limitations on tea didn't cease until 1952. That's right, *tea*. England's national drink was rationed for seven postwar years.[38]

Barbara Warmsley, the Green Granny, remembers rationing. She was born right before the war and recalled how plain all the food tasted, because there was little shortening or meat to impart flavor. "My father died when I was five," she said. "I lived with my two sisters, grandmother, and mother. We didn't have much money. I've never been used to having a lot of money, so I've never wasted stuff. When I have to throw food away—and sometimes you have to—it really hurts."

When I asked Warmsley about her nickname, she seemed a bit unsure whether she deserved it. Yesterday's normal is today's sustainable. "I think it's what I've always done is now green," Warmsley said. "I never connected rationing and being green until Oxfam said we need a 'Green Granny.'"

As in the United States, more recent British generations have become less frugal and more inclined to consume and squander. "I think the war generation have probably always lived like I've lived," Warmsley said. "But after the war, in the 60s and 70s, it was very much a consumer society, which it still is."

Environment Secretary Benn concurred, lumping food waste in with all forms of consumption. "I would say society has been living in this bubble, a fifty-year bubble, in which we thought that we could just take, use, dispose without thought of the consequence. And we've come to realize now, for a whole host of reasons, that we can't do that anymore," Benn said.

Yet, extended rationing and a delayed postwar boom can't be the only explanation for why the average Briton is more waste-aware than his or her American counterpart. While I kept tossing out questions about the prolonged rationing and its effect on British character in interviews and phone conversations, nobody really took the bait. Then again, that shouldn't be shocking—most of the people now leading the anti-food-waste charge weren't around when rationing last was (Hilary Benn had lived all of seven months by the time the final rationing restrictions were lifted). Still, nobody wanted to attribute the current receptiveness to food-waste reduction to anything sociological. I can only conclude that Britain's mid-twentieth-century legacy has aided its current food-waste reduction binge, but not nearly as much as mandated targets to reduce waste and carbon emissions and increase renewable energy.

Though the Climate Change Act is British law, the EU Landfill Directive should receive more credit for effecting change in the United Kingdom. It brought increased emphasis on recycling, which led the government and others to the problem of food waste. And it prompted the landfill tax as a means of reaching the prescribed waste levels. From that perspective, there isn't much room for optimism about America, or other non-EU countries, paying increased attention to their food waste. And America's sheer size also hinders our awareness of waste. Although it's becoming increasingly difficult to site a new landfill, there's still plenty of available land and landfill capacity. Some states even compete to import other states' trash. That's quite different from the situation in Britain and most of Europe generally, where room for landfills just doesn't exist.

What does provide hope, though, is the sheer momentum of food waste reduction in Britain. The attention on the issue spread from researchers to government to media to businesses to households. Detailed statistics prompted awareness, as when you're looking for food waste, it is hard to miss. That attention brought action. When people learn about the adverse impact of food waste and see how easy it is to avoid, sending it to the landfill seems so foolish. That's why there's room for optimism, America. Once food waste has our attention, our shortcomings are obvious. And once we see how easy it is to avoid waste, we'll act. Because few learn about the problem and decide not to seek solutions. As Benn put it, "I haven't met anyone who said 'Yeah, food waste—that's a good thing, not a problem, stop worrying about it.' Because it's self-evidently a problem that we ought to do something about."

Heeding this simple message would likely mean less food waste.

IMAGE CREATED BY AMRIT VATSA

chapter 12

If I Were the King of the Forest: Big Changes

Demonstrate thrift in your homes and encourage thrift among your neighbors…. Make economy fashionable lest it become obligatory.
—DAVID HOUSTON, U.S. SECRETARY OF AGRICULTURE 1913–1920

*I*f I had three wishes—and wishing for more wishes was not allowed—here's what I'd do: Establish a national food-recovery coordinator, create a national public-service campaign to raise awareness about food waste, and ban food from landfills. These three changes, in concert with a host of smaller ones, would help end our long national food-waste nightmare.

A National Food-Waste Czar

We need to establish a federal caretaker to advocate for food recovery and against food waste. Often, these kinds of roles seem to involve czars, be it for drugs, energy, or intelligence. What's one more? No matter what we call this person, he or she must have access to the decision makers in the White House and the Capitol. If this official were able to present the bare facts on food waste to the right people, I'm confident he or she could convince lawmakers that a more efficient, and possibly more ethical, distribution of our food has no downside.

The federal government employs 2 million Americans, not counting the military or the postal service.[1] Adding one measly employee who focuses on food waste doesn't seem like too much to ask. In the 1990s, Joel Berg filled this role and fared well, spreading the word to farmers about food donation and gleaning, discrediting the fallacy that schools couldn't donate excess food, and naming state gleaning coordinators. He even convinced President Clinton to sign an executive memo encouraging all federal agencies to cooperate with food-recovery efforts. Yet, today, these responsibilities are left untended. When I asked the USDA's Jean Buzby, author of a few food-waste-related studies, if someone at the Department of Agriculture specifically focused on food waste, she said she didn't know of anyone. Neither do I.

Having someone champion food-waste reduction would be a major help in fighting hunger. We desperately need this role created, as we have near-record harvests and hunger. It would also help stem environmental and economic losses. When Berg held it, the position was at the USDA, largely because the secretary of agriculture, Dan Glickman, believed in food recovery. Reestablishing it at the USDA would work. I could also imagine this person serving as part of the Food and Drug Administration. No matter where the job is located, it should exist. In addition to raising awareness and lobbying for potential legislative changes, this official would encourage growers, grocers, and restaurateurs to donate their excess goods. In effect, it would be like having a national Lorax—someone to speak for the food.

Spreading the Word

Who thinks about food waste these days? Based on their behavior, the majority of our fellow citizens do not. That's why we need to spread the word. In the tradition of past public-service campaigns, a national food-waste awareness effort campaign is long overdue, especially considering that the best way to reduce food waste is to get people thinking about it. Such a campaign would prompt us to do just that. Few of us are okay with wasting food; it's just that it's not foremost in our thoughts.

Getting the message out could take a variety of formats. We could do a lot worse than to emulate the Litter Bug campaign. Created in 1952 by the Pennsylvania Resources Council, it was used widely in the second half of the twentieth century, notably by Keep America Beautiful, Inc.[2] The trash-spewing Litter Bug character used in the campaign not only helped reduce littering, but introduced a term into our lexicon. The recycling movement provides another example. I'd argue that the practice wouldn't have caught on as thoroughly as it has if it had not been for its prominent message and that ubiquitous triangle of arrows.

Yet, when I think of public-service announcements, I think of television spots, and, in particular, Smokey the Bear and Woodsy the Owl. In addition to providing generational touchstones for my peers, these campaigns worked. I know I've yet to start a forest fire or litter in the woods. That's why I think we need to create a character or symbol to represent or promote food-waste reduction. Though we can figure out the specifics later, I'd suggest the noble worm as a mascot. As anyone who's ever seen a worm composting bin can attest, these creatures don't waste any food—not even the peels or rinds!

Getting this kind of campaign to work will require an effective slogan. While we're not likely to top Woodsy's owl-centric, rhyming play on words—"Give a Hoot, don't pollute"—we can try. Since gaining traction on the Web is essential—because the TV audience is more diffuse these days—simple is probably best. That's why I'd vote for something like "Respect (Your) Food."

While we're starting campaigns, I'd like to see one aimed specifically at promoting acceptance of nonhomogeneous produce. After all, our drive for perfect, uniform fruits and vegetables causes so much waste. A pro-"ugly" produce campaign could communicate that taste is more important than appearance. If consumers let it be known that they'd buy curved cucumbers and skinny squash, that demand would trickle down from stores to wholesalers to growers. If Uglydolls can flourish, why not ugly fruit?

Food Is Not Trash

Banning landfill food-disposal would alter the waste landscape, spurring many changes. Such a prohibition would create pressure throughout the food chain to reduce waste. Since this pressure doesn't seem to be occurring organically, it's time to provide a push with one simple stroke of policy.

A landfill food-waste ban would essentially blend the best of the public and private sectors. One legislative swoop would prompt innovation. We'd be forced to seek out and develop environmentally friendly ways to process food waste. Composting operations would love it, as landfills could no longer undercut them on price. And some large waste-generators would appreciate it, too, as it's difficult to justify composting to shareholders when landfilling is the cheaper option (at least it is in the short term).

Dawn Harris, manager of environmental sustainability at Harris Teeter, would love to have all stores in her supermarket chain compost, but she told me that she's boxed in by the low cost of landfill dumping. "Increased tipping fees would help us promote composting," she said. "North Carolina has some of the cheapest tipping fees in the region. Forty dollars per ton would make composting a very easy sell for me to the board because that's what we're paying now. Although we try to be as good of a corporate citizen as we can to the environment, it really, truly does come down to a business decision."

If municipalities weren't allowed to dump food at landfills, they'd be forced to make residents separate food from their other trash, like many of them already do with recycling. From that point, municipalities would either collect it or ensure its collection. In addition to the environmental benefits, towns or cities might even see economic ones. While every municipality's situation is unique, Seattle saved more than $250,000 in 2009 by composting, said Seattle Public Utilities senior planning and development specialist Brett Stav. And Seattle, which made household composting mandatory in 2009, will continue to benefit the more food waste is diverted from the waste stream. Stav said that it costs the city about 20 percent less to haul a load of food waste to nearby Cedar Grove Composting than it does to send its regular trash to landfill in Oregon.

If they're large enough, it may make financial sense for cities or counties to run their own composting or anaerobic digestion operations. The former wouldn't require as much capital initially, but it wouldn't have nearly the pay-off as an AD plant. Still, facilities of either type would eliminate the expense of long-distance shipping and the associated dumping fees while creating a usable soil amendment for local parks. Although I haven't heard of too many towns or counties running their own composting operations, that would quickly change if landfilling food was forbidden.

We should remember that this kind of landfill ban isn't unprecedented. As of 2008, twenty-three U.S. states had made it illegal to throw out another organic material—yard waste.[3] (Although a federal ban on food in landfills would be more effective than state bans, and, hence, is the better wish to make, a more practical approach would be to push for state bans.) The European Union's Landfill Directive requires member nations to reduce biodegradable municipal waste sent to landfills to half of 1995 levels by 2013.[4] The massive undertaking is inspiring, as are the daily fines of as much as £500,000 for noncompliance. Not content with that initiative, Norway banned food and all biodegradable waste from its landfills, effective July 1, 2009,[5] and the United Kingdom has *pledged* to do the same. Secretary of State for the Environment Hilary Benn told a waste-industry conference in October 2009 that banning food from the landfill would happen in the near future. "As a world, we're using the resources as if we had three planets to call upon," Benn told me. "When I last checked, there aren't another two hidden in the cupboard somewhere."

Sweeping change that would once have been laughed off as ludicrous can happen. In case we need inspiration closer to home, there are now rules prohibiting us from smoking just about anywhere, from restaurants to bars to *entire* college campuses. How ridiculous would that have sounded fifty years ago?

Rolling Up Our Sleeves

Trading my wishful-thinking cap for a slightly more realistic one, I'll admit that banning food from U.S. landfills won't be easy. We would need to overcome the status quo inertia of our national waste habits and the lobbying might of the ever-growing food industrial complex. We could probably get the waste haulers on board, but not if they're also landfill owners (and, sadly, that's often the case). If, for some reason, a landfill ban doesn't fly, there are other ways to minimize food waste.

When I ran this conundrum by economist Amartya Sen, he pondered the problem out loud and it was a beautiful thing to behold. "You can't stop all waste," Sen said. "There's no chance of a zero-waste food situation. The question is: How much can you prevent? Can you reduce the waste? What mechanism do you use for that? Making food dearer—economists tend to think of prices. Making food more expensive will reduce waste, but it will also increase hunger. The discriminating thing would be if you could increase the cost of disposal."

In light of Sen's deduction, if we're not ready for an outright ban, I'd settle for an EU-style landfill tax. This would only help if businesses and individuals were made to feel this increased cost. The thinking here is that municipalities would institute some kind of "pay as you throw" system. We pay for the amount of water, gas, and electricity we use. Why not our garbage, which also taxes natural resources? Some cities have adopted this approach. For better or worse, economic incentives are the surest way to get our attention and prompt changes in behavior. A law requiring garbage haulers to charge by the ton, rather than per pickup, would be a more targeted way to induce policy-based change.

Making waste disposal more expensive or charging by the ton would have a ripple effect through the food chain. A renewed sense of food conservation would likely bubble up from the suddenly-more-conscientious public.

Still, there's no simple answer for reducing food waste. Barring a food-waste ban, we'll likely need a blend of incentives and disincentives, and possibly date-pegged mandates. Yet, our nation's burgeoning environmental awareness is encouraging. The next trick will be getting Americans to link reduced food waste with sustainability. Our public-service campaign had better be good!

Dream On

Just because I've exhausted my three wishes is no reason to stop dreaming of ways we can slow our squandering. A certain amount of food waste is inevitable, but there are many possibilities for making a significant dent in the problem. With that in mind, here are some suggestions on what we can do prevent food from going uneaten:

Waste Measurement

Commission a new, all-inclusive food-waste study. A fond wish of mine is to see an up-to-date analysis of exactly how much food we waste. It's difficult to fix anything until you know the extent of the problem. We need to know exactly how much food is being lost, where that's happening, and, if possible, why. As we saw in the United Kingdom, that's the first step toward garnering media attention for the issue that then prompts awareness and action. If a thorough, government-backed study came out finding that we wasted 40 or 50 percent of our food, we'd have no trouble getting a czar or two appointed.

At present, the USDA has no plans to release another chain-wide study to update 1997's "Estimating and Addressing America's Food Losses." Even worse, that report used data that had been collected in 1995. Sadly, as of 2010, that's still the most recent federal study on the topic, and it's frequently cited by academics and journalists writing on waste. While I can't fault the authors, every time I read an article citing the fifteen-year-old statistic that we waste 96 billion pounds a year, a little more steam comes out of my ears. But I am looking forward to celebrating the data's sweet-sixteen next year.

I used the term "all-inclusive" in pleading for a new study because "Estimating and Addressing America's Food Losses" didn't even address the entire food chain. The authors recognized this shortcoming in noting that "preharvest, on-the-farm and farm-to-retail losses were not measured."[6] They also lumped household waste (called "consumer level," in the study) together with restaurant loss. Lead author

Linda Scott Kantor has retired, passing her data and the mantle of food-waste research on to Jean Buzby. In talking to Buzby, I got the sense that she's genuinely interested in the topic. She told me that she'd like to write an all-encompassing report on waste, but that she has numerous responsibilities and the department doesn't quite have the right data.

Another woman at the USDA, who preferred to remain anonymous, told me that funding for food-waste studies has not been forthcoming. Food waste, or even the slightly more encompassing term "loss," is not a huge priority for the department. "There's a lot of different things to study—it's a complex economy," she told me. "If it was the most important thing, maybe it would have been studied."

Set a goal! It's much easier to prompt change when you have a set target. That way, you can know how difficult a task you face, set an appropriate strategy, and determine how much it will cost. After we learn how much food we currently waste, we'll have a better sense of how much room for improvement exists. My guess: plenty. Based on what I now know, I'm comfortable with the estimate of Swedish researcher Jan Lundqvist, who said that industrialized nations can halve their food waste. "It's not realistic to reduce waste by 100 percent. We're saying it would be realistic and would produce many benefits to reduce it by 50 percent," Lundqvist told me. "That could be the target goal."

I'd be content with a goal of 25 percent, which is probably more realistic and, most importantly, would still enable us to feed all of America's hungry, as discussed in Chapter 3.

Track it or lose it. I propose requiring any institution that accepts federal funds to track its food waste, at least for a specified period of time. That includes farms, state universities, and schools that serve meals under the National School Lunch Program (94 percent of public and private schools).[7] This requirement would yield hard data that would improve the sure-to-come all-inclusive study. It would also prompt these institutions to reform their wasting ways. Once they became aware of how much food they squandered, all but the most inert would make changes. For example, a state university might start using smaller plates, go trayless, and hold a waste weighing to raise student awareness.

Farm Plans

Incentivize farmers to harvest all that they grow. Whatever the means—whether it's through tax breaks, fines, or reduced subsidies—we have to make this happen. There's no sense having 15 percent of Americans living with hunger while millions of tons of healthy produce aren't even harvested. This happens when that commodity's prices aren't great, labor isn't available, or the crops are the wrong shape for the market. These occurences are understandable from the individual farmer's perspective, but not from a societal standpoint. Whether this farm-level waste is a result of price drops, labor problems, limitations of cross-country shipping, or the market's preference for homogeneous items, we can't keep letting this perfectly good produce go to waste.

Encourage farmers to donate excess food. Once we figure out how to get farmers to reap all of what they sow, the next step is prompting them to donate what they can't, won't, or don't sell. Currently, incorporated farms can take deductions for the fair market value of their donated goods, but unincorporated ones cannot. We should provide an incentive for all farms—large and small—to go through the trouble of giving. And because these tax deductions are difficult to realize, many farms don't bother with them even when they would qualify. It has reached this point: "The majority of people who donate don't get a tax credit," Berg said.

We should amend and simplify our tax code (not the first time that's been suggested) to encourage all farmers to give. Otherwise, the path of least resistance is to not harvest that extra field. In addition to simplifying the current tax benefits of donating, we need to do a better job of publicizing them. Many growers aren't even aware that they can receive tax breaks for passing along edible food. In 2000, Senators Dick Lugar (R-IN) and Pat Leahy (D-VT) introduced a Good Samaritan Tax Bill, to no avail.

More gleaning! Gleaning is as much an awareness tool as a food-recovery strategy, but we're not using it for that purpose as much as we could. Let's get citizens, institutions, and policymakers thinking about hunger, food recovery, and farm excess by promoting more gleaning participation. The food-recovery czar could encourage growers to contact gleaning organizations when they have crops they're not going to harvest. In addition, why not channel the AmeriCorps program in this direction to let enthusiastic, energetic young Americans recruit volunteers and help recover crops that would otherwise go to waste? This already occurs in a few locations, but could be much more widespread.

From hard time to farm time. Part of the reason gleaning is more of a marketing tool than anything is that it's not terribly productive. It's hard work. We have a great source of cheap labor already performing work that's not nearly as useful. I'd rank feeding the hungry above weeding or highway litter patrol. Inmate labor is already used in food-recovery operations elsewhere in Arizona in addition to Texas, Florida, and Idaho. Why not promote this nationwide?

Yet, far more effective than gleaning would be harnessing already-harvested crops from growers and packers. Thousands of pounds per day are tilled under or discarded because this produce doesn't meet the specifications of the market. And that brings us to the next suggestion.

Bring hungry people to the excess. The majority of food-recovery groups rescue fresh foods for those who need it. That model is certainly admirable, but can deprive food-pantry customers of a sense of independence. To encourage self-reliance and foster food appreciation, why not bring urban food-bank clients to the excess farm food? Since the majority of these folks may have difficulty getting to these excess crops, one idea is to arrange transportation to participating farms. Such outings could also include some gardening training and be paired with an urban or community garden program.

AmeriCorps could organize these gleaning trips. Alternately, religious or civic groups could facilitate harvest outings where poorer members gleaned for their own pantries, not a soup kitchen's. These groups could organize buses or carpools from urban areas to agricultural ones. Gleaning would be difficult for the working poor who are too busy to participate, and the community members who are not able-bodied. Yet, most families would be able to send a representative on a Saturday—even if it was a teenager, considering that there would be supervision. And introducing poor children to gardening and getting them more closely connected to their food would be a neat by-product.

Certainly, hunger is not just an urban problem. Fifteen percent of those in rural areas live below the poverty line. We could also encourage the rural poor to glean for their families' food supply. The logistics would definitely be easier.

Create a database of food donors and recipients. One goal of any increased federal attention on food waste should be to build a national database of food recipients and donors. Sortable by state and county, this Web-based application would allow potential donors—be they farmers, wholesalers, grocers, or restaurateurs—to find groups that might collect and use their products. And food-recovery organizations would have leads for finding potential farm excess. I've heard many a farmer talk about how they hate to see the food they've produced go to waste. At the same time, many aren't sure how they can avoid it. Through listings or even regional forums on this new site, farmers could communicate what was available to gleaning groups.

There would be other uses, too. For example, a trucker who found her cargo rejected and wanted to find a non-profit to salvage the goods could go online and browse this database. The site could also include listings for nonprofits that would buy food at a discount. Today, sharing information about available food is mostly done—inefficiently—by e-mail or phone. An online listing site—a kind of Craigslist for food recovery—would expedite the process. There are already fledgling online exchanges, such as Veggie Trader, Ample Harvest, and Shared Harvest.[8] The USDA should either build its own or throw its weight behind one of these existing sites so it can attract the critical mass needed to thrive.

A farm bill for food usage. Our next farm bill should represent the interests of all Americans, including the hungry. That would include goals for pounds of food recovered and percentage of crops harvested. It would also extend the donation incentives to all farms, not just incorporated ones. To further promote giving, I'd even explore making the donation of excess crops mandatory for farms that receive federal funds. And, as mentioned earlier, this farm bill would include the precondition that federally funded entities track their waste.

In our next "food bill," as Michael Pollan, the acclaimed journalist, would have it, we must reconsider what foods the government funds. Subsidizing commodity crops has made them artificially cheap, which encourages waste or harmful exporting. Diverting federal funding from the production of crops like corn, soybeans, and wheat to smaller farms is sorely needed. Because this harmful, full-speed-ahead commodity crop farming has dominated U.S. ag policy for more than thirty years, this change won't be easy. It will require political backbone. But shifting strategy will only get harder over time, so the sooner the change, the better.

While it's nice to have extra, our abundance is excessive, especially given its accompanying strain on the environment. To grow double the needed food, only to waste nearly half and dump a sizable portion of the rest on foreign markets—undercutting local growers there—makes little sense.

Larger Changes

Change school lunch. In addition to prioritizing *what* we serve, I'd like to improve *how* we do it. Let's push schools to have lunch after recess. As we've seen, this boosts food consumption, and thus afternoon academic performance while limiting waste. This schedule change would not cost school districts a dime. Lengthening lunch periods, while a little harder to implement, would bring similar results. At present, the allotted lunch time at some schools, particularly at the junior and senior high levels, is shamefully short.

In addition, I'd like to link reduced food waste to the growing movement to bring students closer to their food. Whether it's called the Edible Schoolyard or simply the school garden, helping kids know where their food comes from creates healthier, heartier eaters. Staff involved with these projects have observed that when children help grow veggies like spinach and swiss chard, they're less likely to shun or discard it. And with better nutrition, students are better equipped to learn. We can link schools that lack the staff or space for a garden (remember, rooftops are in play, too) to nearby farms. At worst, field trips there could have a similar effect to gardening.

Implement regional food systems. Moving away from a national food-distribution model would eliminate great amounts of food waste inherent in long-distance shipping. As I imagine it, a regional food system is related to the local food movement but is just a little more forgiving (i.e., realistic) in terms of food miles. Because many Americans wouldn't likely accept a return to true seasonal eating (with long parsnip-laden winters), what I'm suggesting is that we develop regional food systems that promote greenhouse use to create warm-weather crops year-round.

Alternately, we could split the country into regions based roughly on time zones. In this scenario, lettuce and oranges are shipped north from Florida with a return cargo of potatoes, seafood, and maple syrup. In that way, eating regional would incorporate America's longitudinal variety. While "Eat Regional" may never become a bumper sticker, minimizing the intra- and intercontinental food chain would reduce waste. We'd utilize more items that are perfectly good but aren't shipped because they wouldn't be in prime shape after the long journey.

Retail Level Changes

Start a Green Grocer program. Supermarkets tend to keep their waste habits—both the good and the bad—to themselves. Yet, how will consumers know which stores are taking the sensible, virtuous path by donating unsellable food and composting inedible remains? That's where the Green Grocer program would come in. Such an independent entity would verify environmental responsibility (in areas separate from waste, too) and provide a seal that supermarkets could display on their doors and websites to broadcast their conscientiousness. If restaurants have two standards to communicate environmental bona fides, surely supermarkets deserve one. That way, consumers would know just what kind of store they were supporting.

Bye Bye, Sell-By. It's ridiculous that expiration dates, created to help consumers know how long to keep food items, are confusing consumers. Here's a simple solution: Eliminate the "sell-by" label on packaging. Because this "pull date" is intended for retailers, it can be communicated through closed-date markings, the coded messages undecipherable to you and me that are already common with some groceries. This solution would go a long way toward reducing the expiration-date uncertainty. Although it won't address the waste that occurs when perfectly edible foods are tossed because they've reached their "use-by" or "best-before" dates, it's a start.

Encourage supermarkets to discount soon-to-expire and blemished goods. Who wouldn't want to get some value from an item that's about to lose all of it? It would seem to make sense for stores to discount goods that are approaching their expiration or "sell-by" dates. Yet, the practice isn't nearly as common as one would expect, probably because it requires keeping a careful eye on the dates. Grocers that can pull it off, though, trim their waste while increasing sales. I know my interest is always piqued by these discounted items.

If there are millions of people struggling to pay their bills and millions of pounds of edible food being discarded at supermarkets, why not join the two together? There are plenty of people—both old and young—who would happily pay less for less perfect goods. Charlie Edwards, a salesman for North Carolina's Nash Produce, took up the idea in the context of produce: "We as a people have demanded these perfectly shaped, perfectly colored items so many times that we are the ones who are responsible for paying these higher prices. At the same time, you might buy that less attractive item at a lower price."

Did you catch that, supermarket execs? Many grocery managers are wary of displaying anything less than perfect, especially with produce, because they fear it would undercut that desired image of utter freshness. But I think it would do the opposite; it would communicate just how fresh the produce on the regular shelves is. Besides, everyone loves a bargain, and some people still remember how to use a paring knife.

Create an acceptable waste range. Supermarkets would have more incentive to sell discounted items if they had a hard cap on food waste. Since reducing food waste tops the EPA food-waste recovery hierarchy, we need a way to incentivize supermarkets to do just that. Establishing a standard range of food waste per square foot would suffice. In that scenario, stores that didn't exceed the lower threshold of acceptable waste would receive tax breaks. Those that surpassed the upper threshold would have to pay a fine. Just to make sure stores' vigilance didn't plateau, we could lower the range of acceptable waste every few years. I can almost see the sale produce racks now!

Fund supermarket composting. There would be a certain beauty in a program (state or federal) that funded composting facilities at every grocer or supermarket larger than a certain size. Yet, it would be really beautiful if the money came with the stipulation that the store must also accept customers' home food scraps. That way, the food you didn't use and the accompanying scraps would return from whence they had come. Or at least from whence you had seen them come.

To facilitate consumer participation, funding could also provide stores with compostable bags distributed at the checkout. After this practice became established, the new checkout question would be: "Paper, plastic, or green bag?" Maybe we could even get BioBag, the compostable-bag maker, to sponsor the whole thing. Grocers in towns that have curbside food-waste collection would be exempted. And supermarkets could also opt to send their food waste to a nearby composting facility instead. Simple.

Study and promote anaerobic digestion. How effective is anaerobic digestion in reducing greenhouse gas emissions? I'm not quite sure. Where does this waste-to-energy process rank on the food-waste-recovery hierarchy? Don't know; it's not on it. I think AD is a fantastic use of our inevitable food waste, but I'd love to hear the EPA's take on it. Just how beneficial is it compared to feeding animals and composting? If it's found to be as useful as I think it might be, then we should provide incentives to jump-start the creation of an AD infrastructure.

This would include making land available, providing funds to prompt counties or municipalities to build digesters, and encouraging separate collection of food waste (a wise practice regardless of AD's status). Tax breaks for sending your food waste to an AD plant, or, to be fair, a compost facility, would be an enlightened use of public funds, in my mind. After all, the practice would curtail future environmental problems.

Canning Our Old Food Culture

Less for less. Another noble goal would be to get more restaurants to offer smaller portions for a smaller price. To encourage this practice, I'm thinking we need a branded campaign with a catchy name. "Smart Sizing" would work and might even reverse the negative impact of super-sizing. Customers could lower both their calorie intake and potential waste by telling the waiter to "Smart Size it."

Alter the catering equation. When I look at our food culture, one of the things that astounds me is the relentless feeding at catered events. What if we all agreed to make it acceptable for the food to not be endless? I'm not proposing that some guests not get fed, just that we lose the expectation that buffets are to be refilled until the event is over. If you show up ten minutes from the end, well, you might not get a pig in a blanket. Also, the de facto requirement of bringing an extra 15 to 25 percent, "just in case," needs some rethinking.

While we're thinking of caterers, let's pass legislation giving their customers the right to decide what to do with their leftovers—donate them to food-safety-trained nonprofits or take them home. California State Senator Jenny Oropeza introduced such a bill in 2008 that would have let catering customers write donation into their contracts. Unfortunately, restaurant-industry groups shot it down, largely because of liability fears. It's time to write this commonsense solution into law—federal law.

A few more changes. It's a massive step, but we need to start moving away from abundance as the standard operating procedure. In addition, piggybacking on the "ugly produce" campaign, how about a return to valuing taste over appearance? That would greatly reduce the culling of imperfect or nonuniform foods throughout the food chain. That idea will be difficult to implement, but I'm hoping our culture reverts to this bit of common sense.

I'd also like to see doggie bagging become the presumed outcome for leftovers. We shouldn't have to ask to take our meal remains home. Instead, we should have to specify that we don't want to do so. Restaurants should be thankful for this cultural shift—it'll save them thousands on their waste-disposal bills.

Why I'm Not Worried

Food-waste reduction will succeed because it will become second nature. A look at recycling provides a window into how that might look. Only twenty years ago, recycling was the domain of Volvo-drivers and PBS-watchers—both fine traits—not the majority of Americans. Today it is widespread. We recycle one-third of our waste stream, and 60 percent of us can do so at the curbs in front of our homes.[9] Just as many of us can hardly believe how nonchalantly we used to throw soda cans into the trash only a few years ago, future generations will find it unbelievable how much food we threw away. If the consequences of our waste weren't so sad, they would be laughable.

Personally, I've never known what it's like to not recycle, as I grew up in a town where we brought our trash and recyclables to a very progressive, very un-smelly recycling center. Today, well, Wednesdays, I wheel a blue bin filled with all sorts of glass, paper, and plastics to the curb, and the materials are magically whisked away to be processed in an environmentally friendly way (or at least in a manner more enlightened than landfill dumping). While the story might be a bit more complicated than that, it's hard not to feel a tinge of green pride as we gaze at the bins lining the streets like Monopoly houses, content that the recycling fairies will minimize the carbon footprint of our consumption. At least in theory.

There's no magic solution, no easy answer. Curbside food-waste collection won't reduce the amount of actual food waste we create. Accomplishing that will require changes in behavior. That's a hard ask, I realize, and one that takes time. Yet, it's vital. These changes may take years or decades. In the meantime, we need to keep food out of the landfill by any (well, almost any) means necessary.

I asked Andrew Shakman, the founder of LeanPath—the company that sells a waste-tracking system—what he would do if he could snap his fingers and have any wish granted. His gut-reaction answer was predictable, as he admitted. "If I could wave my hand and make a change it would be to make food-waste tracking routine in every commercial food-service and hospitality operation, just as hand washing is an expected and required behavior today. I know this simple step would lead to broad-based and substantive reform."

Then he seemed to switch lenses and answered from a broader perspective. His e-mailed response was poetic:

> We come to value that which is scarce and expensive. Food is neither in America right now, and yet it's one of our most fragile resources. We do not have sufficient respect for the precious plants and animals that sustain us because the concept of not having them doesn't enter our consciousness. If we had less abundance and less reliability in our food system, we would value food more and waste less. Of course, I do not want to shock the system through scarcity. However, I would love to see better awareness of this topic—perhaps we need a national day where we all pledge to skip one meal—just one meal—to remind ourselves of how good things are.

Great idea, Andrew. Let's *establish* National No Lunch Day as the final item on this chapter's wish list. If Christians can forswear something for the forty days of Lent, Muslims can forgo food from sunup to sundown for a month during Ramadan, and Jews can fast for twenty-four hours on Yom Kippur, Americans of all stripes can skip one lunch. After all, many struggle daily to find enough to eat. If every healthy American skipped lunch once and donated that unspent money or the time from that unneeded lunch break to a hunger-related cause, we would all benefit.

How We'll Know We've Succeeded

We'll never end food waste. There won't be any "Mission Accomplished" banners hung from the USDA headquarters. Still, a few indications will tell us when we've effected change. The day it is normal to bring a take-home container to a restaurant, my sense is that we'll have food waste under control. When school cafeteria waste barrels aren't full of milk, fruit, and cookies, and when restaurant portions aren't sized for three, we'll know we have made progress. And we'll be nearing our goal when supermarket Dumpsters don't look like salad bars.

On Thanksgiving, we celebrate abundance. Yet, we'll know a cultural shift has occurred when "holiday Tupperware" is part of that day's tradition. By dispersing that plenty to all in attendance, instead of having half of it go bad in the host's refrigerator, we truly honor the higher power, the land, the sun, turkeys, or whomever or whatever we choose to thank. Many families already pursue this strategy, but we'll have made great headway when the divvying of leftovers becomes nearly universal (and as special as the carving of the turkey).

These changes are well within our reach. The question is whether we'll make them voluntarily or have them forced upon us. Because the current rates of waste and population growth can't coexist much longer. Our planet's demographics will force us to be more respectful and efficient with our food sooner or later. Sooner seems like the wiser choice. An increased respect for our food will keep our planet and its inhabitants physically and morally healthy. If we set our minds to it, we can minimize food waste and distribute our abundance to those in need. And we better. Because if we don't, it will be a real waste.

ACKNOWLEDGMENTS

There are many people to whom I am eternally grateful and owe many thanks. My agent, Lynn Johnston, was essential in helping me turn a blog into a book deal. I truly appreciate her help in shepherding me through the process.

Renée Sedliar, my editor, was instrumental in helping me turn a book proposal into the real thing. She really "got it" from day one and continually impressed me with her creativity, smarts and gameness. Working with her was nothing if not pleasant. The same is true for Collin Tracy, the book's project editor. She was masterful at pulling everything together and gracious in tolerating my last-minute changes.

D.C. Central Kitchen has a special place in my heart, as it's where this book began. Seeing the what—so much food recovered that would otherwise go to waste—prompted me to start researching the where, why, and how. In particular, Robert Egger, has been both inspirational and helpful. This research formally began at the School of Journalism at UNC–Chapel Hill. There, Barbara Friedman encouraged me to find the narratives within the subject of food waste and Chris Roush pushed me to follow the money. Both made for excellent thesis advisers as I launched the research that eventually produced this book.

In my early, J-school days exploring the subject, Dianne Bittikofer at the Society of St. Andrew was a great assistance on the topic of gleaning, as was gleaner-extraordinaire Les Williams. Jill Staton Bullard and Don Eli at the Inter-Faith Food Shuttle were similarly supportive in the context of food recovery. And Chris Moran and Paul Eberhart at the IFC Shelter helped me see a food bank's perspective.

Gary Smith's insight on the publishing industry was a real asset early in the process. As was the advice of Cori Princell, who was an invaluable source of ideas on how best to write this book. Brian Rosa, in addition to becoming a friend, helped me understand all things composting. He launched the North Carolina Food Diversion Task Force that has helped divert food from the landfill and brought many of us waste avoiders to the same table. In addition, he also gave me worms (the composting kind—red wigglers).

I'm indebted to Jack Rosenthal, the president of the New York Times Foundation, for uttering two words: 'So what?' In asking why he should care about food waste, he pushed me to strengthen my argument in Chapter 2. Thanks to *Garbage Land* author Elizabeth Royte for talking trash with me and Blair Pollock for showing it to me at the Orange County Landfill.

Thanks to Brian Williams and Andy Rankin at Viget Labs for office space at the right price, web hosting, and sound advice. Also, apologies for the significant dent I put in the office coffee supply! Thanks as well to the guys at Rue Cler for the good cheer and occasional cup of milk (to go with the coffee). Writing above a French restaurant and bakery is a challenge, but they made it less of one.

Hodan Farah Wells was gracious in walking a history major through the maze of agricultural statistics. Brian Quinn gets a hearty thanks for helping me think through economic ideas and for living across the street from Berkeley's Martin Luther King, Jr. Middle School, site of the original Edible Schoolyard. And a tip of the hat to Syrah McGovern for her epigraph assistance.

LeanPath's Andrew Shakman has been a warm and insightful resource in restaurant and institutional food waste. Katy Kolker took me tree gleaning in Portland, Oregon, and showed me the waste-avoiding and milk-producing powers of goats. Thanks to Jeanne and Jeff Becker just outside of Portland for gamely opening their home to me as a potential representative couple. Sorry guys, you were just too green (food scraps to pigs, chickens and goats!).

My brother Seth has been a source of strength and a vital brainstorm-partner and publicity strategist throughout this process. Matt Taylor was a game buffet-restaurant companion and an attentive listener. Andy Sarjahani's enthusiasm on the topic was indeed contagious and provided a much-needed boost in the middle of this process.

I owe David Maxwell for his occasional, yet insightful thoughts on supermarket economics and for being a great friend. Eleanor Hicks has been very generous in letting me stay at her place in San Francisco, even when my visits coincided with her birthday. Bill McMorran was clutch in providing non-couch lodging and supermarket contacts in London. Thanks to Ben Wolford and family for further London housing and the all-important Arsenal ticket. Kudos to Kabir Sen for arranging my interview with his father and for his steady encouragement.

Thanks to all the people who've chipped in to help facilitate my work at its hairiest, close-to-deadline stages. Chief among them are Adena Williams, Linda Williams, Ashley and Alex Quigley, and Katherine Siu. And thank you to the many folks that I didn't have space to mention individually.

I'd like to thank my mother, Susan, for demonstrating that no leftover is too small to save and that sometimes the best lunch comes from last night's dinner. She also taught me that food can communicate love. I'm grateful for her love, devoted ear, and encouraging words. My father, Joel, shares some of the blame for my passion, too, as he's the master of the cold sandwich, be it meatloaf or Thanksgiving. He has my deepest gratitude for passing along a love of letters and encouraging me not to go to law school. And for taking us to Arthur Bryant's in Kansas City and just about every other restaurant of note—high and low—in our travels.

Finally, my sincerest thanks to my own family for absorbing the effects of this book project, especially in my absences. For all of his young life, my son, Bruce, has been an inspiration. Knowing that his smiling face would greet me every morning motivated me to have productive nights and provided perspective after bad ones.

My wife, Emily, has been an advisor, editor, ear-lender, fort holder-downer, frustration-soother, brunt-bearer, and all-around goddess. Her list of roles could continue for pages, but suffice it to say there's no way I could have written this book without her help and companionship. Words can't express my gratefulness, Em.

NOTES

NOTES TO INTRODUCTION

1. My calculations. First, I found that the Rose Bowl holds 84,375,000 gallons from Pasadena.com (http://www.rosebowlstadium.com/RoseBowl_general-info.htm). I applied the conservative 27 percent waste rate, from Linda Scott Kantor, Kathryn Lipton, Alden Manchester, and Victor Oliveira, "Estimating and Addressing America's Food Losses," *FoodReview*, January–April 1997, 3, http://www.ers.usda.gov/Publications/FoodReview/Jan1997/jan97a.pdf, to the most recent estimate of total food produced—591 billion pounds. That means 159.6 billion pounds wasted. I then converted that to cubic yards by dividing by 1,000, then divided by 365 to get the per day waste. Since 1 cubic yard = 201.97 gallons, I found that we waste 88,536,558.9 gallons per day. The (Rose) Bowl overfloweth. The authors of this study were all employees of the U.S. Department of Agriculture. For the liberal estimate that we waste half of our food, I got 295.5 billion pounds wasted per year, which translated to 295 billion cubic yards per year. That meant 809,589 cubic yards per day, which converted to 163,515,957 gallons per day. Given that the Rose Bowl holds 84,375,000 gallons, we would fill it once, then 97 percent on the second time through.

2. At the Economic Research Service's suggestion, I tallied the total agricultural output from the U.S. Department of Agriculture, Economic Research Service, Publications, "Agricultural Outlook: Statistical Indicators," Table 39, updated March 2010, http://www.ers.usda.gov/publications/Agoutlook/AOTables/.

3. Kantor et al., "Estimating and Addressing America's Food Losses."

4. U.S. Environmental Protection Agency, "Municipal Solid Waste Generation, Recycling and Disposal in the United States: Facts and Figures for 2008," November 2009, 1, http://www.epa.gov/osw/nonhaz/municipal/pubs/msw2008rpt.pdf (accessed January 8, 2010).

5. Kevin D. Hall, Juen Guo, Michael Dore, and Carson C. Chow, "The Progressive Increase of Food Waste in America and Its Environmental Impact," PLoS ONE, November 25, 2009, 4, http://www.plosone.org/article/info:doi%2F10.1371%2Fjournal.pone.000 7940.

6. The average American male weighed 195 pounds and the female average was 165, according to the Centers for Disease Control and Prevention (CDC), FastStats, "Body Measurements," http://www.cdc.gov/nchs/faststats/bodymeas.htm (accessed January 9, 2010); CDC, "Anthropometric Reference Data for Children and Adults: United States, 2003–2006," 8, 10, http://www.cdc.gov/nchs/data/nhsr/nhsr010.pdf.

7. The oldest U.S. food-recovery group is New York's City Harvest. But since the people who started City Harvest don't work there anymore, and Egger is somewhat of a visionary on food recovery, he's the senior spokesman for the topic. Plus, he calls people "Dude," which has its charm.

8. Pennsylvania Department of Transportation, "History of the Litter Bug and PennDOT," http://www.dot.state.pa.us/Internet/pdKids.nsf/HistoryofLitterBugand PennDOT?OpenForm.

9. This idea of trash flowing away comes from a show I saw by the Blue Man Group more than ten years ago in Boston. Although the material flowing away in that show was sewage.

10. U.S. Census, "State and Country Quick Facts," listed 2008 housing units at 129,065,264. See http://quickfacts.census.gov/qfd/states/00000.html (accessed March 22, 2010).

NOTES TO CHAPTER 1

1. Rich Pirog and Andrew Benjamin, "Checking the Food Odometer: Comparing Food Miles for Local Versus Conventional Produce Sales to Iowa Institutions," Leopold Center for Sustainable Agriculture, July 2003, http://www.leopold.iastate.edu/pubs/staff/files/food_travel072103.pdf (accessed October 24, 2009).

2. Monterey County Agricultural Commissioner's Office, "Monterey County Crop Report 2007," http://www.co.monterey.ca.us/ag/pdfs/CropReport2007.pdf.

3. Linda Scott Kantor, Kathryn Lipton, Alden Manchester, and Victor Oliveira, "Estimating and Addressing America's Food Losses," *FoodReview*, January–April 1997, 3, http://www.ers.usda.gov/Publications/FoodReview/Jan1997/jan97a.pdf.

4. U.S. Department of Labor, Bureau of Labor Statistics, "Consumer Expenditures in 2007," http://www.bls.gov/news.release/cesan.nr0.htm.

5. Food wastage is 50 percent of available food for Jan Lundqvist, Charlotte de Fraiture, and David Molden, "Saving Water: From Field to Fork—Curbing Losses and Wastage in the Food Chain," SIWI Policy Brief, May 2008, 5, http://www.siwi.org/documents/Resources/Policy_Briefs/PB_From_Field_to_Fork_2008.pdf. I clarified

this finding by phone with the study's lead author, Jan Lundqvist. He said the estimate was not specific to any country; rather, it was meant to apply to all nations, including the United States. The study places great importance on the verbs. In the developed world, more food is wasted, and in the developing world more food is lost, owing to poor technology. The study's 50 percent estimate includes a sizable leap, though, as it assumes that the inefficient conversion of grains to protein in livestock is a waste of food. In other words, that we'd be better off eating these grains than feeding them to hogs and cows. According to Timothy Jones, in "The Corner on Food Loss," *BioCycle*, July 2005, we waste 40 to 50 percent of our food.

6. Kevin Hall, Juen Guo, Michael Dore, and Carson C. Chow, "The Progressive Increase of Food Waste in America and Its Environmental Impact," PLoS ONE, November 25, 2009, 4, http://www.plosone.org/article/info:doi/10.1371/journal.pone .0007940.

7. Kantor et al., "Estimating and Addressing America's Food Losses," 6.

8. Ibid. It was estimated at 32 percent.

NOTES TO CHAPTER 2

1. This data comes from the Orange County Solid Waste, "2005 Waste Characterization Study," April 2005, http://www.co.orange.nc.us/recycling/docs/WasteSort2005/Summary2005.pdf. Yet, there's no county-wide total, as the individual columns represent the county's towns, UNC, and the unincorporated portions of Orange County.

2. Orange County Solid Waste, "2005 Waste Characterization Study—Comparison of Residential Waste Compositions," April 2005, http://www.co.orange.nc.us/recycling/documents/WasteSort2005/ResidentialComp.pdf; Orange County Solid Waste, "2005 Waste Characterization Study—Comparison of Commercial Waste Compositions," April 2005, http://www.co.orange.nc.us/recycling/documents/WasteSort2005/CommercialComp.pdf.

3. U.S. Environmental Protection Agency (EPA), "Municipal Solid Waste in the United States: 2007 Facts and Figures," http://www.epa.gov/waste/nonhaz/municipal/pubs/msw07-rpt.pdf, 46.

4. Carol Diggelman and Robert Ham, "Life-Cycle Comparison of Five Engineered Systems for Managing Food Waste," University of Wisconsin–Madison, 1998, 2, http://warrr.org/418/1/Life-Cycle_Comparison_Report.pdf.

5. EPA, "Municipal Solid Waste Generation, Recycling, and Disposal in the United States: Detailed Tables and Figures for 2008," 3.

6. Ibid. As far as the landfill food-rate doubling, it increased from 9.5 percent to 18.6 percent—close enough!

7. EPA, "Municipal Solid Waste in the United States: 2001 Facts and Figures," 65, http://www.epa.gov/osw/nonhaz/municipal/pubs/msw2001.pdf. The composting rate dropped from 2.6 to 2.2 percent.

8. EPA, "Municipal Solid Waste EPA, "Municipal Solid Waste Generation, Recycling, and Disposal in the United States: Detailed Tables and Figures for 2008," 3.

9. Ljupka Arsova, Rob van Haaren, Nora Goldstein, Scott M. Kaufman, and Nickolas J. Themelis, "The State of Garbage in America," *BioCycle* 49, no. 12 (December 2008): 22, http://www.jgpress.com/archives/_free/001782.html.

10. Food is 12 percent of all waste "generated," according to EPA, "Municipal Solid Waste in the United States: 2007 Facts and Figures." On average, every American sends 0.55 pounds of food waste to the landfill each day. Here's the math: 0.12 (12 percent of what we discard is food) times 4.62 (the average daily weight of all our trash) equals 0.55.

11. I'm borrowing a line from the wonderfully horrible Adam Sandler vehicle *Billy Madison*.

12. U.S. Environmental Protection Agency (EPA), "Inventory of U.S. Greenhouse Gas Emissions and Sinks: 1990–2007,"U.S. Environmental Protection Agency (EPA), "Inventory of U.S. Greenhouse Gas Emissions and Sinks: 1990–2007," http://www.epa.gov/climatechange/emissions/downloads09/GHG2007-ES-508.pdf (accessed June 15, 2010), 28.

13. Ibid., 33.

14. Ibid., 43.

15. U.S. Environmental Protection Agency (EPA), Office of Air and Radiation, "Frequently Asked Questions About Landfill Gas and How It Affects Public Health, Safety, and the Environment," June 2008, http://www.midland-mi.org/government/departments/utilities/faqs_about_LFG.pdf, 3.

16. Cliff Chen and Nathaniel Greene, "Is Landfill Gas Green Energy?" Natural Resource Defense Council, March 2003, vii, http://www.nrdc.org/air/energy/lfg/lfg.pdf.

17. Diggelman and Ham, "Life-Cycle Comparison," 2.

18. Salinas Valley Solid Waste Authority, "Fact Sheet: Crazy Horse Landfill Closure," http://www.svswa.org/facilities/Crazy%20Horse%20closure%20sheet.pdf (accessed October 10, 2009).

19. Citizens Waste Info, "Environmental Problems from Municipal Solid Waste," 2004, http://www.citizenswasteinfo.org/A559CA/ccwm.nsf/5155d8f53ce25d2785256cc300567828/c050375504a2a75085256e7d005a325f?OpenDocument (accessed October 10, 2009).

20. Martin Heller and Gregory Keoleian, "Life Cycle–Based Sustainability Indicators for Assessment of the U.S. Food System," 2000, 42, http://css.snre.umich.edu/css_doc/CSS00-04.pdf.

21. Institute of Science in Society, "Current Food Production System Due for Collapse," April 6, 2005, http://www.energybulletin.net/node/5173.

22. David Pimentel and Marcia Pimentel, "Energy Use in Food Processing for Nutrition and Development," Cornell University, http://www.unu.edu/unupress/food/8f072e/8f072e06.htm.

23. Leo Horrigan, Robert S. Lawrence, and Polly Walker, "How Sustainable Agriculture Can Address the Environmental and Human Health Harms of Industrial Agriculture," *Environmental Health Perspectives* 110, no. 5 (May 5, 2002), http://www.ehp online.org/members/2002/110p445-456horrigan/horrigan-full.html (accessed August 29, 2009).

24. Pimentel and Pimentel, "Energy Use in Food Processing."

25. Heller and Keoleian, "Life Cycle–Based Sustainability Indicators," 42.

26. Pimentel and Pimentel, "Energy Use in Food Processing."

27. Heller and Keoleian, "Life Cycle–Based Sustainability Indicators."

28. Monica Bruckner, "The Gulf of Mexico Dead Zone, Microbial Life Educational Resources," Montana State University, http://serc.carleton.edu/microbelife/topics/deadzone/.

29. David Pimentel and Mario Giampietro, "Food, Land, Population and the U.S. Economy," *Carrying Capacity Network*, November 21, 1994, http://www.dieoff.com/page55.htm (accessed October 24, 2009).

30. Institute of Science in Society, "Current Food Production System Due for Collapse."

31. John Barton, "Transportation and Fuel Requirements in the Food and Fiber System," Agricultural Economic Report No. 444, 1980, U.S. Department of Agriculture, Economic, Statistics, and Cooperative Service.

32. U.S. Department of Agriculture, Natural Resources Conservation Service, "Energy Management," Conservation Resource Brief, February 2006, 5.

33. U.S. Department of Agriculture, Economic Research Service, "Briefing Room: Water and Irrigation Use," November 22, 2004, http://www.ers.usda.gov/Briefing/WaterUse/.

34. Pimentel and Pimentel, "Energy Use in Food Processing."

35. Phone interview with Jan Lundqvist, June 2008.

36. David Pimentel, "Soil Erosion: A Food and Environmental Threat," *Environment, Development and Sustainability* 8, no. 1, February 2006, 119–137.

37. Tristram Stuart, *Waste* (London: Penguin, 2009), 86.

38. James McCarthy, "Interstate Shipment of Municipal Solid Waste: 2007 Update," CRS Report for Congress, 5, https://www.policyarchive.org/bitstream/handle/10207/18953/RL34043_20070613.pdf?sequence=2 (accessed September 2, 2009).

39. Ibid. It went up 147 percent!

40. Ibid.

41. Commonwealth of Pennsylvania, Department of Environmental Protection, "County Waste Destinations," http://www.depweb.state.pa.us/landrecwaste/lib/land recwaste/municipal_waste/reports/county_2008.pdf (accessed September 17, 2009).

42. EPA, "Municipal Solid Waste in the United States: 2007 Facts and Figures," 46.

43. Diggelman and Ham, "Life-Cycle Comparison," 5.

44. Heather Rogers, *Gone Tomorrow: The Hidden Life of Garbage* (New York: New Press, 2005), 199.

45. Deborah Gordon, Juliet Burdelski, and James Cannon, "Greening Garbage Trucks: New Technologies for Cleaner Air," INFORM, 2003, 4, http://informinc.org/reportpdfs/st/GreeningGarbageTrucks.pdf.

46. EPA, "Municipal Solid Waste in the United States: 2007 Facts and Figures," 23.

47. William Rathje and Cullen Murphy, *Rubbish! The Archaeology of Garbage* (New York: HarperCollins, 1992), 107.

48. The California Energy Commission's Consumer Energy Center provided this fact: For every 2 minutes a car is idling, it uses about the same amount of fuel that it takes to go about one mile. See "Should I Shut Off the Motor When I'm Idling My Car?" http://www.consumerenergycenter.org/myths/idling.html.

As of August 29, 2009, with the price of gas roughly $2.50 per gallon, and estimating that an average car gets 25 miles per gallon: If 2 minutes of idling uses the same amount of fuel as going 1 mile, that's 1/25 gallon, which costs a dime. Thus, 20 minutes of idling costs $1.00. Assuming $1.64 in food wasted per day: 20 x 1.64 = 32.8 minutes of idling.

49. The USDA's low-cost plan, the second of four levels, estimates that a family of four would spend $174.20 on weekly groceries. Multiplied by 0.25—William Rathje's estimate for home food-waste (whether thrown out or put into the garbage disposal), this means $43.55 in food waste for that average family every week, and thus $2,264.60 per year.

50. Here's the math: 0.15 x $174.20 = $26.13 x 52 weeks= $1,358.76.

51. General Accounting Office, "Food Waste: An Opportunity to Improve Resource Use," September 16, 1977, 46.

52. U.S. Department of Agriculture, Economic Research Service, "ERS Per Capita Consumption of Major Food Commodities," http://www.ers.usda.gov/publications/agoutlook/aotables/2009/07Jul/aotab39.xls. Kudos to Hodan Farah Wells at the ERS for walking me through this process.

53. Keep in mind that the 1997 poundage estimate was a conservative one because the authors didn't consider preharvest, on-the-farm, or farm-to-retail losses. And in the areas they did study, they erred on the side of caution. They wrote: "Estimates of retail, foodservice and consumer food losses are likely understated due to limitations in the published studies on which these estimates were based." Linda Scott Kantor, Kathryn Lipton, Alden Manchester, and Victor Oliveira, "Estimating and Addressing America's Food Losses," *FoodReview*, January–April 1997, 6, http://www.ers.usda.gov/Publications/FoodReview/Jan1997/jan97a.pdf.

54. World Bank, "Gross Domestic Product 2008," http://siteresources.worldbank.org/DATASTATISTICS/Resources/GDP.pdf (accessed September 5, 2009).

55. U.S. Department of Agriculture, "National School Lunch Program Fact Sheet," http://www.fns.usda.gov/cnd/lunch/AboutLunch/NSLPFactSheet.pdf (accessed September 8, 2009).

56. Stephanie Wentworth, "Sinai Weighs In on New Plan to Cut Hospital Food Waste," *Baltimore Business Journal*, September 22, 2006, http://www.leanpath.com/lpweb/Docs/Sinai_Baltimore.pdf.

57. John Lauritsen, "North Memorial Health Care Reduces Food Waste by Tracking It," WCCO-TV, July 17, 2009, http://www.youtube.com/watch?v=44UTgmH4vCo.

58. WasteCap of Massachusetts, "Roche Brothers Supermarkets Recycle Organics and Cut Waste Costs Up to 40%," February 2003.

59. Massachusetts Department of Environmental Protection, "2001 Progress Report on the Beyond 2000 Solid Waste Master Plan," December 2003, http://www.mass.gov/dep/recycle/priorities/swpr01.doc (accessed September 16, 2009).

60. Jewish Nature Center, "Bal Tashchit, a Radical Solution to Environmental Problems," http://jewishnaturecenter.org/html/bal_tashchit.html (accessed September 5, 2009).

61. Berachot 52b.

62. Rabbi Samson Raphael Hirsch, Horeb, Chapter 56, Section 401. Via Richard Schwartz, "Jewish Values vs. Realities Related to Use of Resources," http://www.all-creatures.org/articles/jvresources.html.

63. Kiddushin 32a.

64. Rabbi Samson Raphael Hirsch, Horeb, Chapter 56, Section 399. Via Schwartz, "Jewish Values vs. Realities."

65. Jewish Nature Center, "Bal Tashchit."

66. Koran, Al-Araf, Chapter 7, Verse 31. Via http://searchtruth.net/search.php?keyword=waste&translator=2&search=1.

67. Koran, Al-Anaam, Chapter 6, Verse 141. Via http://searchtruth.net/search.php?keyword=waste&translator=2&search=1.

68. Jayaram V, "The Concepts of Hinduism," Hindu Website, http://www.hinduwebsite.com/hinduism/concepts/annam.asp.

69. Global Oneness, "Hinduism and Food," http://www.experiencefestival.com/a/Hinduismand_Food/id/54150.

70. Okinawa Diet, "Hara Hachi Bu," http://www.okinawa-diet.com/okinawa_diet/hara_hachi_bu.html (accessed October 29, 2009).

71. Garr Reynolds, "One Secret to a Healthy Life," *Presentation Zen*, June 29, 2007, http://www.presentationzen.com/presentationzen/2007/06/one-secret-to-a.html (accessed October 29, 2009).

NOTES TO CHAPTER 3

1. Mark Patinkin, "Goodbye to an Old Soldier," *Providence Journal*, May 8, 2007, http://www.projo.com/lifebeat/markpatinkin/LB-Mark08_05-08-07_9E5HUV5.1e74cac.html.

2. Mark Nord, M. Andrews, and S. Carlson, "Household Food Security in the United States, 2008," U.S. Department of Agriculture, November 2009, 15, http://www.ers.usda.gov/Publications/ERR83/ERR83.pdf

3. U.S. Department of Agriculture, "Food Security in the United States: Measuring Household Food Security," Briefing Room, http://www.ers.usda.gov/Briefing/Food Security/measurement.htm.

4. Nord et al., "Household Food Security in the United States, 2008."

5. Ibid., 7.

6. Ibid.

7. Mark Rank and Thomas Hirschl, "Estimating the Risk of Food Stamp Use and Impoverishment During Childhood," *Archives of Pediatrics & Adolescent Medicine* 163, no. 11 (November 2009): 994–999. They found that 49 percent of kids live in a home that uses food stamps at some point in their childhood.

8. Kevin Hall, telephone conversation with author, March 31, 2010. The calculations were also part of a presentation Hall made to the Union of Concerned Scientists on March 11, 2010, called "The Push Effect: Why America Is Fat, Hot and Wasteful." Hall explained that he used a conservative estimate of 2,500 calories needed per day to fully feed someone. And he used the figure of 250 calories to lift someone out of hunger.

9. Ibid.

10. United Nations, Food and Agriculture Organization, "High Level Conference on World Food Security: The Challenges of Climate Change and Bioenergy," June 3, 2008, http://www.fao.org/foodclimate/hlc-home/en/ (accessed October 30, 2009).

11. Jan Lundqvist, Charlotte de Fraiture, and David Molden, "Saving Water: From Field to Fork—Curbing Losses and Wastage in the Food Chain," SIWI Policy Brief, 2008, 4, http://www.siwi.org/documents/Resources/Policy_Briefs/PB_From_Field_to_Fork_2008.pdf (accessed January 13, 2010).

12. An explanatory video of the FoodBox is on YouTube at http://www.youtube.com/watch?v=JwY0qXFkQ0U.

13. Judy Putnam, Jane Allshouse, and Linda Scott Kantor, "U.S. Per Capita Food Supply Trends: More Calories, Refined Carbohydrates, and Fats," *FoodReview*, Winter 2002, 3, http://www.ers.usda.gov/publications/FoodReview/DEC2002/frvol25i3a.pdf (accessed September 22, 2009).

14. United Nations Population Division, "The World at Six Billion," October 12, 1999, 3, http://www.un.org/esa/population/publications/wpp2008/pressrelease.pdf (accessed January 15, 2009). The document actually projects we'll be at 8.9 billion in 2050 and hit the 9 billion mark in 2054, but that's close enough.

NOTES TO CHAPTER 4

1. Annie E. Casey Foundation, "Kids Count Data Center," Mississippi page, http://datacenter.kidscount.org/data/bystate/StateLanding.aspx?state=MS.

2. Henry Hampton and Steve Fayer, "Voices of Freedom," February 1991, excerpt available online at http://www3.niu.edu/~td0raf1/1960s/PoorPeople'smovement 1968.htm.

3. Jennifer Smith Richards, "Cost Constraints and Students' Palates Often Make School Lunches Unhealthful," July 5, 2009, *Columbus Dispatch*, http://www.columbus dispatch.com/live/content/insight/stories/2009/07/05/schoolfood_cheap.ART_ART_07-05-09_G1_RIEBQNS.html?sid=101.

4. Mary Jane Getlinger, Carol V.T Laughlin, Elizabeth Bell, Christine Akre, Bahram H. Arjmandi, "Food Waste is Reduced when Elementary-School Children Have Recess before Lunch," Journal of the American Dietetic Association 96, no. 9 (September 1996): 906–908.

5. Jean Buzby and Joanne Guthrie, "Plate Waste in School Nutrition Programs: Final Report to Congress," E-FAN No. (02-009), U.S. Department of Agriculture, Economic Research Service, March 2002, 3,
http://www.ers.usda.gov/publications/efan02009/efan02009.pdf.

6. Ibid.

7. GAO, "School Lunch Program."

8. Mary Jane Getlinger, "Food Waste Is Reduced When Elementary School Children Have Recess Before Lunch."

9. U.S. GAO, "School Lunch Program."

10. Ibid.

11. Alice Jo Rainville, "Recess Before Lunch, It Does Make a Difference!" slideshow presented to the School Nutrition Association, Annual National Conference, July 17, 2006.

12. GAO, "School Lunch Program."

13. Ibid.

14. U.S. Department of Agriculture, Census of Agriculture, 2007. http://www.agcensus.usda.gov/Publications/2007/Full_Report/usv1.pdf

15. Growing a Nation, "A History of American Agriculture: Farm Machinery & Technology," http://www.agclassroom.org/gan/timeline/farm_tech.htm (accessed August 11, 2009).

16. Michael Pollan, "Unhappy Meals," *New York Times Magazine*, January 28, 2007, http://www.nytimes.com/2007/01/28/magazine/28nutritionism.t.html?ref=magazine.

17. Technomic, Inc., "For the Love of Leftovers," *American Express MarketBrief*, October 2009, 5.

18. Lisa Young and Marion Nestle, "The Contribution of Expanding Portion Sizes to the US Obesity Epidemic," *American Journal of Public Health* 92 (February 2002): 246–249.

19. National Heart, Lung, and Blood Institute, "Portion Distortion I Slide Show," http://hp2010.nhlbihin.net/oei_ss/PD1/slide1.htm.

20. National Heart, Lung, and Blood Institute, "Portion Distortion II Slide Show," http://hp2010.nhlbihin.net/oei_ss/PDII/slide1.htm.

21. I visited the Durham, North Carolina, Costco on August 13, 2009.

22. Brian Wansink and Koert Van Ittersum, "Portion Size Me: Downsizing Our Consumption Norms," *Journal of the American Dietetic Association* 107, no. 7 (July 2007): 1103–1106.

23. Brian Wansink, *Mindless Eating* (New York: Bantam Books, 2006), 52.

24. The Small Plate Movement, "Learn More," http://smallplatemovement.org/learn_more.htm (accessed August 22, 2009).

25. Technomic, Inc., "For the Love of Leftovers."

26. Adrienne Carter, "Slimmer Kids, Fatter Profits," *BusinessWeek*, September 5, 2005, http://www.businessweek.com/magazine/content/05_36/b3949101.htm.

27. Wikipedia, "Jamestown Settlement," http://en.wikipedia.org/wiki/Jamestown_Settlement.

28. Ibid.

29. Michael Duffy, "Propaganda Posters—United States of America (2)," First WorldWar.com, August 22, 2009, http://www.firstworldwar.com/posters/usa2.htm.

30. Maine Historical Society, "Food—Don't Waste It, World War 1 Poster," Maine Memory Network, http://www.mainememory.net/bin/Detail?ln=15116.

31. D. R. Eberhart & Associates, "Crop Harvests at Home in America During World War II," Fruit from Washington, September 8, 2009, http://www.fruitfromwashington.com/History/harvest.htm.

32. Leah Zeldes, "Waste Not (Want Not)," *Chicago Sun-Times*, January 21, 2009, http://www.suntimes.com/lifestyles/food/1388298,FOO-News-depress21.article (accessed July 31, 2009).

33. Mary MacVean, "Food Lessons from the Depression," *Los Angeles Times*, December 10, 2008, http://www.latimes.com/features/food/la-fo-depression10-2008dec10,0,1456860.story.

34. Wikipedia, "United States Home Front During World War II," http://en.wikipedia.org/wiki/United_States_home_front_during_World_War_II#Rationing.

35. Ames Historical Society, "Rationed Goods in the USA During the Second World War," http://www.ameshistoricalsociety.org/exhibits/ration_items.htm.

36. Travel & History, "Wars and Battles, The Home Front," http://www.u-s-history.com/pages/h1674.html.

37. New Hampshire State Library, "Save and Sacrifice" category, "Unifying a Nation: World War II Posters from the New Hampshire State Library," http://www.nh.gov/nhsl/ww2/sacrifice.html.

38. D. R. Eberhart & Associates, "Can Vegetables and the Kaiser Too," Fruit from Washingon, http://www.fruitfromwashington.com/History/images/07-0151.jpg.

39. Ohio Historical Society, "Am I Proud, I'm Fighting Famine by Canning Food at Home," Ohio Pix: Picturing Ohio's History, http://ohsweb.ohiohistory.org/ohio pix/Image.cfm?ID=3179.

40. New Hampshire State Library, "Use It Up—Wear It Out—Make It Do!"poster, Unifying a Nation: World War II Posters from the New Hampshire State Library, http://www.nh.gov/nhsl/ww2/ww15.html.

41. Katy Wolk-Stanley, "Waste No Food Challenge—An Update," The Non-Consumer Advocate, November 19, 2008, http://thenonconsumeradvocate.wordpress.com/2008/11/19/waste-no-food-challenge-an-update-ix/.

42. U.S. Environmental Protection Agency, "Municipal Solid Waste in the United States: 2007 Facts and Figures," 9, http://www.epa.gov/waste/nonhaz/municipal/pubs/msw07-rpt.pdf.

43. Ljupka Arsova, Rob van Haaren, Nora Goldstein, Scott M. Kaufman, and Nickolas J. Themelis, "The State of Garbage in America," *BioCycle* 49, no. 12 (December 2008), 22, http://www.jgpress.com/archives/_free/001782.html.

44. Technomic, Inc., "For the Love of Leftovers," 4.

45. Debra A. Aleksinas, "Restaurant Leftovers Aren't for the Dogs Anymore," *South Coast Today*, April 9, 2009, http://www.southcoasttoday.com/apps/pbcs.dll/article ?AID=/20090409/ENTERTAIN/904090350/-1/rss49.

46. Technomic, Inc., "For the Love of Leftovers."

47. A large portion of pasta weighs 2 pounds and is served on a 15.5-inch plate. See David Zinczenko and Matt Goulding, "16 Secrets the Restaurant Industry Doesn't Want You to Know," *Men's Health*, December 2007, http://www.menshealth.com/16secrets/secrethigherups.html.

NOTES TO CHAPTER 5

1. Linda Scott Kantor, Kathryn Lipton, Alden Manchester, and Victor Oliveira, "Estimating and Addressing America's Food Losses," *FoodReview*, January–April 1997, 3, http://www.ers.usda.gov/Publications/FoodReview/Jan1997/jan97a.pdf.

2. Timothy W. Jones, "The Corner on Food Waste," *BioCycle*, July 2005, 3.

3. Rhonda Bodfield Bloom, "UA Researcher Wants Not for Waste Theories," *Arizona Daily Star*, January 5, 2005, http://www.azstarnet.com/sn/related/55407.

4. Jan Lundqvist, Charlotte de Fraiture, and David Molden, "Saving Water: From Field to Fork—Curbing Losses and Wastage in the Food Chain," SIWI Policy Brief, SIWI, 2008, http://www.siwi.org/documents/Resources/Policy_Briefs/PB_From _Field_to_Fork_2008.pdf.

5. Food Marketing Institute, "U.S. Grocery Shopper Trends 2008," 88, available for purchase at http://www.fmi.org/forms/store/ProductFormPublic/search?action=1 &Product_productNumber=2266.

6. Douglas McGray, "California's Food Banks Go Locavore," *New York Times Magazine*, October 7, 2009, http://www.nytimes.com/2009/10/11/magazine/11banks-t .html?_r=1&ref=magazine&pagewanted=all (accessed October 16, 2009).

7. Justice Potter Stewart wrote that phrase into his concurring opinion in *Jacobellis v. Ohio*, 378 U.S. 184, June 22, 1964, in regard to whether or not the film *The Lovers*, directed by Louis Malle, should be considered obscenity.

8. U.S. Department of Agriculture, "Dietary Guidelines for Americans," March 2002, http://www.cnpp.usda.gov/Publications/DietaryGuidelines/2000/2000DG BrochureHowMuch.pdf.

9. U.S. Department of Agriculture, North Carolina School Nutrition Action Committee (NC SNAC), "What's in a Serving Size?" March 2003, http://www.fns.usda .gov/tn/healthy/Portions_Kit/serving_size.pdf.

10. Oxbo Corporation, "Oxbo Citrus Harvester Features," 2007, http://www.oxbo corp.com/citrusfeatures.php.

11. These would be the robots from *Lost in Space*, *Star Wars*, *Short Circuit*, and *Wall-E* respectively. And while I'm sure C-3PO could pick fruit just fine, I'd be willing to bet that he'd whine the entire time.

12. Food Marketing Institute, "Supermarket Facts: Industry Overview 2008," http://www.fmi.org/facts_figs/?fuseaction=superfact (accessed August 3, 2009). The actual number of supermarkets (with sales of more than $2 million) was 35,394.

13. Kelly Cobiella, "Salmonella Scare Rocks Tomato Country," CBS News, July 2, 2008, http://www.cbsnews.com/stories/2008/07/02/eveningnews/main4229216 .shtml (accessed August 2, 2009).

14. Dan Chapman, "Tomato Farmers See Prime Crop Go to Waste," *Atlanta Journal Constitution*, July 28, 2008, http://www.ajc.com/business/content/metro/stories/ 2008/07/27/tomato_losses.html (accessed August 2, 2009).

15. Calculations based on data for each crop from the National Agricultural Statistics Service (NASS), Quick Stats page, http://quickstats.nass.usda.gov/. For each "crop," I compared "national" figures. The percentages come from dividing results for "acres harvested" by acres planted.

16. Comptroller General of the United States, "Food Waste: An Opportunity to Improve Resource Use," September 16, 1977, 11.

17. N. B. McLaughlin, A. Hiba, G. J. Wall, and D. J. King., "Comparison of Energy Inputs for Inorganic Fertilizer and Manure Based Corn Production," *Canadian Agricultural Engineering* 42, no. 1, 2000, http://engrwww.usask.ca/oldsite/societies/csae/ c9915.pdf (accessed October 24, 2009).

NOTES TO CHAPTER 6

1. City of Albany, California, "The History of Albany," http://www.albanychamber.org/about_albany-history.php (accessed August 3, 2009).

2. North Carolina Division of Environment and Natural Resources—Division of Pollution Prevention and Environmental Assistance, "A Fact Sheet for Licensed Garbage Feeders," February 2000, http://www.p2pays.org/ref/04/03991.pdf (accessed August 11, 2009).

3. WasteCap Wisconsin, "Business Food Waste Briefing Paper: Options for Grocers, Restaurants, and Food Processors," http://www.wastecapwi.org/documents/food waste.pdf (accessed August 11, 2009).

4. Tom Miner, analyst and principal at Technomic, telephone conversation with author, August 14, 2009.

5. The Cheesecake Factory, Menu-Welcome Page, http://www.thecheesecake factory.com/menu/welcome/Welcome (accessed August 22, 2009).

6. Chili's, "Chili's Nutritional Information," http://www.brinker.com/gr/nutritional/chilis_nutrition_menu.pdf (accessed August 8, 2009).

7. Some states, counties, and cities require nutritional information to be made available, but a national bill introduced in 2009, the Labeling Education and Nutrition (LEAN) Act of 2009, hadn't made much progress in Congress as of May 2010.

8. Lisa Young, *The Portion Teller* (New York: Morgan Road Books, 2005), 244–245.

9. Marge Condrasky, Jenny H. Ledikwe, Julie E. Flood, and Barbara J. Rolls, "Chef's Opinions of Restaurant Portion Sizes," *Obesity* 15 (August 2007): 2086.

10. Brian Wansink and Koert Van Ittersum, "Portion Size Me: Downsizing Our Consumption Norms," *Journal of the American Dietetic Association* 107 (July 2007): 1106.

11. Ibid.

12. Lisa Young and Marion Nestle, "The Contribution of Expanding Portion Sizes to the Obesity Epidemic," *American Journal of Public Health* 92, no. 2 (February 2002): 247.

13. Young, *Portion Teller*, 21.

14. Carlson, "T.G.I. Friday's Restaurants Make 'Right Portion, Right Price' Permanent Part of Menu," May 1, 2008, http://www.carlson.com/media/article.cfm?id=561&group=restaurants&subhilite=4&terhilite=1.

15. Brian Wansink, *Mindless Eating* (New York: Bantam Books, 2006), 34.

16. "Big Chain Restaurants' New Small Portions," *Time*, May 10, 2007, http://www.time.com/time/magazine/article/0,9171,1619548,00.html (accessed August 17, 2009).

17. "Eat'n Park Debuts Smaller Portions at Smaller Prices," Reuters, March 12, 2008, http://www.reuters.com/article/pressRelease/idUS223135+12-Mar-2008+PRN20080312.

18. Lisa Baertlein, "Restaurants Go Small to Boost Sales," Reuters, April 3, 2009, http://www.reuters.com/article/smallBusinessNews/idUSTRE5322X420090403.

19. Condrasky et al., "Chef's Opinions of Restaurant Portion Sizes," 2089.

20. Nanci Hellmich, "Survey: Restaurants Dishing Out Extra-Large Portions," *USA Today*, October 21, 2006, http://www.usatoday.com/news/health/2006-10-21 -portions-restaurants_x.htm (accessed August 21, 2009).

21. I averaged the diameter of Amazon's ten top-selling dinner plates, as listed in the specs.

22. Brian Wansink and Collin Payne, "Eating Behavior and Obesity at Chinese Buffets," *Obesity* (June 5, 2008): 1958, http://www.nature.com/oby/journal/v16/n8/ full/oby2008286a.html.

23. Thomas John, telephone conversation with author, December 2009. While Au Bon Pain does allow each store to toss $80 worth of leftovers at the end of each day, the stores do sell their baked goods for half-price during the last hour.

24. U.S. Environmental Protection Agency, "Generators of Food Waste," March 24, 2010, http://www.epa.gov/osw/conserve/materials/organics/food/fd-gener.htm.

25. Green Seal, "Green Seal Environmental Standard for Restaurants and Food Services, GS-46 Requirement Checklist," 2009, http://www.greenseal.org/certification/ standards/GS-46_Restaurant_and_Food_Service_Requirement_Checklist.pdf (see section 3.4).

26. Green Restaurant Association, "Waste Reduction and Recycling Requirements," http://www.dinegreen.com/standards/Waste.html.

NOTES TO CHAPTER 7

1. Food Marketing Institute, "Grocery Store Chains Net Profit," http://www.fmi .org/docs/facts_figs/NetProfitPercentof0Sales2008.pdf.

2. Food Marketing Institute, "Median Average Store Size, 2008," http://www.fmi .org/facts_figs/keyfacts/?fuseaction=storesize.

3. Technomic Information Services, "The Retailer Meal Solutions Consumer Trend Report," 2007.

4. WasteCap of Massachusetts, "Roche Brothers Supermarkets Recycle Organics and Cut Waste Costs Up to 40%," February 2003. This case study listed food waste as 35 percent of the organic waste (which also includes flowers, wood, paper, and cardboard) produced by the Roche Brothers stores. Organic waste, in turn, makes up 75 percent of the total waste produced at the stores. That means that of the total 565 tons of waste per store per year, 148 tons were food waste.

5. Food Marketing Institute, "Industry Overview 2008," http://www.fmi.org/ facts_figs/?fuseaction=superfact. The actual number of supermarkets (with sales of more than $2 million) was 35,394.

6. I used 850 pounds and multiplied it by 35,000. I then divided that sum by the weight of the Hummer H2, 6,614 pounds. The result was 4,498 Hummers.

7. Jean Buzby, Hodan Farah Wells, Bruce Axtman, and Jana Mickey, "Supermarket Loss Estimates for Fresh Fruit, Vegetables, Meat, Poultry and Seafood and Their Use in the ERS Loss-Adjusted Food Availability Data," Economic Information Bulletin 44, March 2009, http://www.ers.usda.gov/Publications/EIB44/EIB44_ReportSummary .pdf.

8. Ibid.

9. Food Marketing Institute, "U.S. Grocery Shopper Trends 2008," 88. Available for purchase at http://www.fmi.org/forms/store/ProductFormPublic/search?action =1&Product_productNumber=2266.

10. The notion of pastoral, farm-themed supermarket decorations appears in the documentary *Food, Inc.*, but Kevin Kelley voiced the importance of that visual cue to me in a phone interview on February 16, 2010.

11. William Rathje and Cullen Murphy, *Rubbish! The Archaeology of Garbage* (New York: HarperCollins, 1992), 61.

12. I should say that the items I took home were solely foods that were intended for the Dumpster. I didn't cull anything with the purpose of taking it home. But that's why stores don't let workers take home any food—because it would be very easy to pull a "rotten" avocado then slip it into your bag. That's an aspect of what store managers call "shrink." What I did was akin to Dumpster diving, but occurred one step before the Dumpster.

13. "Sell-by Dates Could Be Scrapped to Stop Food Waste, Says Hilary Benn," *The Telegraph*, June 9, 2009, http://www.telegraph.co.uk/foodanddrink/foodanddrink news/5485574/Sell-by-dates-could-be-scrapped-to-stop-food-waste-says-Hilary-Benn .html.

14. Shirley Van Garde and Margy Woodburn, "Food Discard Practices of Householders," *Journal of the American Dietetic Association* 87, no. 3 (March 1987): 329.

15. U.S. Department of Agriculture, Food Safety and Inspection Service, "Safe Food Handling Fact Sheet," February 8, 2007, http://www.fsis.usda.gov/Factsheets/ Food_Product_Dating/index.asp.

16. Food Marketing Institute, "Supermarket Facts," 2008, http://www.fmi.org/ facts_figs/?fuseaction=superfact.

17. U.S. Department of Agriculture, Food Safety and Inspection Service, "Food Product Dating Fact Sheet," February 8, 2007, http://www.fsis.usda.gov/Fact _Sheets/Food_Product_Dating/index.asp.

18. Catherine Jacob, "Labels Revamp to Tackle Waste Food Mountain," Sky News, June 9, 2009, http://news.sky.com/skynews/Home/UK-News/Food-Labels-Review -To-Combat-Landfill-Waste-Creating-Greenhouse-Gases-Contributing-To-Global

-Warming/Article/200906215298864?lpos=UK_News_Second_Home_Page_Feature
_Teaser_Region_0.

19. Waste and Resources Action Programme (WRAP), "The Food We Waste," July 2008, http://www.wrap.org.uk/document.rm?id=5635.

20. METRO Group, "METRO Group Future Store Initiative," http://www.future -store.org/fsi-internet/html/en/375/index.html.

21. U.S. Census Bureau, "2006–2008 American Community Survey 3-Year Estimates." The figure of 2.6 people per family is from the U.S. Census Bureau's estimates for 2006–2008, http://factfinder.census.gov/servlet/ADPTable?_bm=y&-geo_id=01000US& -ds_name=ACS_2008_3YR_G00_&-_lang=en&-_caller=geoselect&-format=.

22. Debra Chanil and Meg Major, "Shaking the Tree: 2008 Produce Operations Review," *Progressive Grocer*, October 2008, 68. Available for purchase at http://store.vnue media.com/digitalmall/store/product_view.jsp?product_id=20601&category_name=. I calculated this statistic by adding the higher-value categories in the "Produce Sales by Segment" table.

23. Ibid., 7.

24. Gary Lucier and Biing-Hwan Lin, "Factors Affecting Carrot Consumption in the United States," Outlook Report from the Economic Research Service of the United States Department of Agriculture, March 6, 2007, 3, http://www.ers.usda .gov/publications/vgs/2007/03Mar/VGS31901/VGS31901.pdf.

25. Food Marketing Association, "Food Marketing Industry Speaks," 2008. Available for purchase at http://www.fmi.org/forms/store/ProductFormPublic/search?action =1&Product_productNumber=2265.

26. Teri Karush Rogers, "Turning Supermarkets into Restaurants, Too," *New York Times*, August 28, 2005, http://query.nytimes.com/gst/fullpage.html?res=9D01E5 DD1F3EF93BA1575BC0A9639C8B63&pagewanted=all.

27. International Dairy-Deli-Bakery Association, "IDDBA's What's in Store Reports: Deli Trends," December 10, 2008, http://www.iddba.org/prwisdeli.aspx.

28. From Whole Foods Market, "Prepared Foods," http://www.wholefoodsmarket .com/products/prepared-foods.php.

29. In-store conversation at Harris Teeter, Martin Luther King Parkway, Durham, North Carolina, June 18, 2009.

30. The rotisserie chickens sold for $6.99, and all were marked as 28 ounces. I arrived at a per-ounce-price of 24.9 cents.

31. Food Marketing Institute, "FMI Survey of Supermarkets and Food Banks," 2005.

32. Peter Clarke, telephone interview with author, March 2006.

NOTES TO CHAPTER 8

1. Jennifer Cheeseman Day, "Projections of the Number of Households and Families in the United States, 1995 to 2010," in U.S. Bureau of the Census, *Current Population Reports* (Washington, D.C.: Government Printing Office, 1996), 3.

2. I'd observed other families without telling them why I was watching them and it was always a bit awkward. I'm not sure I got the best information because the subjects behaved as Jane Goodall's chimps might have if they knew she was writing a book on their every feces toss. With Waldow and Milan, I was up-front about my research and they promised to act as they normally would.

3. Cornell University Food and Brand Lab, "Consumers FAQ," http://foodpsychol ogy.cornell.edu/faq/consumer.htm (accessed August 23, 2009).

4. Food Navigator, "US Wastes Half Its Food," November 26, 2004, http://www .foodnavigator-usa.com/Financial-Industry/US-wastes-half-its-food.

5. Comptroller General of the United States, "Food Waste: An Opportunity to Improve Resource Use," Report to Congress, September 16, 1977, 22.

6. William Strutz, "A Brief Summary and Interpretation of Key Points, Facts and Conclusions for University of Wisconsin Study: Life-Cycle Comparison of Five Engineered Systems for Managing Food Waste," April 1998, http://warrr.org/418/1/Life -Cycle_Comparison_Report.pdf (accessed August 22, 2009).

7. Shirley Van Garde and Margy Woodburn, "Food Discard Practices of Householders,"*Journal of the American Dietetic Association* 87, no. 3 (March 1987): 322.

8. Comptroller General, "Food Waste," 20.

9. Van Garde and Woodburn, "Food Discard Practices of Householders," 326.

10. Sub-Zero, "The Science of Fresh," video, http://www.subzero.com/ (accessed August 7, 2009).

11. Mark Bittman, "So Your Kitchen Is Tiny. So What?" *New York Times*, December 13, 2008, http://www.nytimes.com/2008/12/14/weekinreview/14bittman.html (accessed September 30, 2009); Tara Parker Pope, "Mark Bittman's Bad Kitchen: An Interview," Well blog, November 20, 2008, http://well.blogs.nytimes.com/2008/11/ 20/mark-bittmans-bad-kitchen/ (accessed September 30, 2009).

12. Lisa Young, *The Portion Teller* (New York: Morgan Road Books, 2005), 22.

13. Web search done June 16, 2009.

14. Benjamin Franklin's quote taken from: Lydia Maria Francis Child, *The American Frugal Housewife*, 27th ed. (New York: Samuel S & William Wood, 1841), 5 (accessed via Google Books).

15. William Rathje and Cullen Murphy, *Rubbish! The Archaeology of Garbage* (New York: HarperCollins, 1992), 62.

16. We bought the can of coconut milk for a recipe that required a half cup.

17. Van Garde and Woodburn, "Food Discard Practices of Householders," 328.

18. U.S. Department of Agriculture (USDA), Food Safety Inspection Service, "Cold Storage Chart," http://www.foodsafety.gov/~fsg/f01chart.html.

19. U.S. Department of Agriculture, Food Safety and Inspection Service, "Kitchen Companion: Your Safe Food Handbook," February 2008, 13, http://www.fsis.usda .gov/PDF/Kitchen_Companion.pdf (accessed October 2, 2009).

20. USDA, "Cold Storage Chart."

21. Rathje and Murphy, *Rubbish!* 64.

22. U.S. Census Bureau, "Current Population Survey, 2005," in *Annual Social and Economic Supplement,* http://pubdb3.census.gov/macro/032005/hhinc/new05_000.htm.

23. U.S. Department of Agriculture, Food Safety and Inspection Service, "Safe Food Handling Fact Sheet," http://www.fsis.usda.gov/Factsheets/How_Temperatures _Affect_Food/index.asp.

24. Stephen J. James and Judith Evans, "Consumer Handling of Chilled Foods: Temperature Performance," *International Journal of Refrigeration* 15 (1992): 290–306.

25. Lois Carlson Willand, *The Use-It-Up Cookbook* (Minneapolis: Practical Cookbooks, 1979), x.

26. Gail G. Harrison and William J. Rathje, "The Food Loss Project: Methodologies for Estimating Household Food Loss, 1981–1983," Chapter 9 of *USDA Methodological Research for Large-Scale Dietary Intake Surveys, 1975–88,* Home Economics Research Report no. 49, 228, http://www.ars.usda.gov/SP2UserFiles/Place/12355000/pdf/meth/ methods1989_herr49.pdf.

27. Ibid., 241.

NOTES TO CHAPTER 9

1. T. H. Watkins, *The Hungry Years* (New York: Henry Holt, 1999), 97.

2. Ibid.

3. Story from Palit's America Harvest bio, http://www.americaharvest.org/our _people.html.

4. Food Gatherers collected about 4.8 million pounds in 2009, according to an information sheet that Food Gatherers CEO Eileen Spring sent me on February 4, 2010.

5. Inter-Faith Food Shuttle, 2008 Annual Report, http://www.foodshuttle.org/2008 annual_report.pdf.

6. U.S. Department of Labor, Bureau of Labor Statistics, "Career Guide to Industries," http://www.bls.gov/oco/cg/cgs024.htm. The estimate of the number of grocery stores is according to 2006 data.

7. Steve Martinez and Phil Kaufman, "Twenty Years of Competition Reshape the U.S. Food Marketing System," *Amber Waves,* April 2008, http://www.ers.usda.gov/ AmberWaves/April08/Features/FoodMarketing.htm (accessed March 3, 2009).

8. Community Food Bank of New Jersey, "America's Second Harvest: Ending Hunger. The Bill Emerson Good Samaritan Food Donation Act, P.L. 104-210. Background Guide," http://www.njfoodbank.org/site/DocServer?docID=177.

9. Public Law 104-210, 104th Congress. See http://fdsys.gpo.gov/fdsys/delivery/getcontent.action;jsessionid=57e82421428fbda4a3b7f3dc6853fa50e437052a952edcf00b14971c6903c85c.e38Kb3eQa30Nby0QbNiQahuOahn0?filePath=http%3A%2F%2Fwww.gpo.gov%2Ffdsys%2Fpkg%2FPLAW-104publ210%2Fhtml%2FPLAW-104publ210.htm.

10. Community Food Bank of New Jersey, "America's Second Harvest."

11. U.S. Census Bureau, "Population Profile of the United States: 1995," July 1995, http://www.census.gov/population/www/pop-profile/title.html. The January 1, 1995, population estimate was 261,638,000.

12. "SN's Top 75 Retailers of the Year," *Supermarket News*, January 2009, http://supermarketnews.com/profiles/top75/walmart_stores09/.

13. Brian Kline, "Waste Not, Wal-Mart," *Wal-Mart Watch*, January 6, 2006, http://walmartwatch.com/blog/archives/waste_not_wal_mart/ (accessed October 10, 2009).

14. Walmart.com, "Feeding America," http://walmartstores.com/Community Giving/8803.aspx (accessed October 10, 2009).

15. The Walmart Foundation, "Hunger Relief Fact Sheet," http://walmartstores.com/download/3396.pdf.

16. Kroger.com, "Feeding America," http://www.kroger.com/company_information/community/Pages/feeding_america.aspx (accessed October 10, 2009).

17. Jennifer 8. Lee, "Fired Over a Tuna Sandwich, and Fighting Back," City Room blog, New York Times Online, http://cityroom.blogs.nytimes.com/2009/03/16/fired-over-a-tuna-sandwich-and-fighting-back/.

18. Sue Sigler, telephone interview with author, February 5, 2010.

19. Douglas McGray, "California's Food Banks Go Locavore," *New York Times Magazine*, October 11, 2009, http://www.nytimes.com/2009/10/11/magazine/11banks-t.html (accessed October 11, 2009).

20. Note: For the sake of clarity: When I use the term "gleaning," I'm not talking about digging through the trash for food.

21. *Les Glaneurs et La Glaneuse*, film directed by Agnes Varda, 2000.

22. L. W. Cowrie, *Dictionary of British Social History* (London: Wordsworth Reference, 1996), 130.

23. U.S. Census Bureau, "Current Population Survey: POV41: Region, Division, and Type of Residence," 2009 Annual Social and Economic Supplement, 2009, http://www.census.gov/hhes/www/cpstables/032009/pov/new41_100_01.htm.

NOTES TO CHAPTER 10

1. Andy Sarjahani, Elena L. Serrano, and Rick Johnson, "Food and Non-Edible, Compostable Waste in a University Dining Facility," *Journal of Hunger and Environmental Nutrition* 4, no. 1 (January 2009): 95–102, http://www.informaworld.com/smpp/content~db=all?content=10.1080/19320240802706874. There was 30 percent less edible waste, called "Edible Compostable Waste" in the study. Virginia Tech had an enrollment of 28,432 in 2009–2010, according to "Factbook: Student Overview," on the school's website, http://www.vt.edu/about/factbook/student-overview.html.

2. Sarjahani et al., "Food and Non-Edible, Compostable Waste." The exact amount of the savings would be $99,846, but with rounding, we'll call it $100K.

3. Sodexo spokesperson Monica Zimmer, e-mail correspondence with author, April 21, 2009.

4. Bon Appetit Management Company, "Bon Appetit Management Company Leads Food Service Industry in Reducing Greenhouse Gas Emissions from Food Waste," June 9, 2009, http://www.bamco.com/news.40.htm.

5. Kevin Halenda, "Going Trayless and Brainless," *Daily Princetonian*, Opinion, April 3, 2009, http://www.dailyprincetonian.com/2009/04/03/23257/ (accessed October 5, 2009).

6. Colby College, "Green Dining," Green Colby, http://www.colby.edu/green/dining.htm (accessed October 5, 2009); Babson College, "Social Responsibility," Babson Dining, http://www.babsondining.com/social.html (accessed October 5, 2009); University of Vermont, "University Dining Services Sustainability Initiatives," 12, http://uds.uvm.edu/documents/social/sustainability_07.pdf (accessed October 5, 2009).

7. Newsweek On Campus, March 1987.

8. PR Newswire, "New Study Takes Bite Out of '5-Second Rule,'" January 29, 2010, http://www.prnewswire.com/news-releases/new-study-takes-bite-out-of-5-second-rule-83020877.html.

9. Alec Berg and Jeff Schaffer, "The Gymnast," *Seinfeld*, November 3, 1994.

NOTES TO CHAPTER 11

1. UK Department for the Environment, Food and Rural Affairs (DEFRA), "Landfill Tax Factsheet," May 24, 2007, http://www.defra.gov.uk/environment/waste/strategy/factsheets/landfilltax.htm (accessed January 3, 2010).

2. BBC News, "Landfill Tax 'Costing Homes £30,'" March 18, 2009, http://news.bbc.co.uk/2/hi/uk_news/7949761.stm (accessed January 3, 2010).

3. Letsrecycle.com, "UK Must 'Radically Overhaul' How It Deals with Waste," November 16, 2009, http://www.letsrecycle.com/do/ecco.py/view_item?listid=37&listcatid=5413&listitemid=53912.

4. DEFRA, "Landfill Tax Factsheet."

5. UK Department for the Environment, Food and Rural Affairs (DEFRA), "Anaerobic Digestion—Shared Goals," February 2009, 3, http://www.defra.gov.uk/environment/waste/ad/documents/ad-sharedgoals-090217.pdf (accessed January 3, 2010).

6. Ibid.

7. Nick Morley and Caroline Bartlett, "Mapping Waste in the Food Industry," Prepared by Oakdene Hollins for the Food and Drink Federation and the Department for the Environment, Food and Rural Affairs, August 20, 2008, 6, http://www.fdf.org.uk/publicgeneral/mapping_waste_in_the_food_industry.pdf (accessed January 4, 2010).

8. U.S. Environmental Protection Agency, "Municipal Solid Waste Generation, Recycling, and Disposal in the United States: Detailed Tables and Figures for 2008," November 2009, http://www.epa.gov/epawaste/nonhaz/municipal/msw99.htm.

9. Food and Drink Federation, "Waste: Promoting Resource Efficiency," http://www.fdf.org.uk/environment/waste.aspx (accessed January 5, 2010).

10. Center for Sustainable Systems, "US Environmental Footprint," University of Michigan, http://css.snre.umich.edu/css_doc/CSS08-08.pdf.

11. For EU landfill/recycling rates, see Letsrecycle.com, "UK Achieves Ninth Best Recycling Rate in Europe," March 10, 2009, http://www.letsrecycle.com/do/ecco.py/view_item?listid=37&listcatid=2787&listitemid=31212. For U.S. landfill/recycling rates, see Ljupka Arsova, Rob van Haaren, Nora Goldstein, Scott M. Kaufman, and Nickolas J. Themelis, "The State of Garbage in America," *BioCycle* 49, no. 12 (December 2008): 22, http://www.jgpress.com/archives/_free/001782.html.

12. Mark Barthel, interview with author, Waste & Resources Action Programme, December 8, 2009.

13. Waste & Resources Action Programme, "The Food We Waste—Executive Summary," July 2008, 2, http://www.wrap.org.uk/downloads/Summary_v21.1c418321.5460.pdf.

14. Ibid., 3.

15. Waste & Resources Action Programme, "An Apple a Day Gets Thrown Away," April 7, 2008, http://www.wrap.org.uk/wrap_corporate/news/an_apple_a_day_gets.html (accessed December 31, 2009).

16. Alice Miles and Helen Rumbelow, "How to Save the World? Use Up Those Leftovers Just Like Mum Did," *The Times*, December 29, 2007, http://www.timesonline.co.uk/tol/news/environment/article3105640.ece.

17. The amount increased from 37 percent to 69 percent. Julia Falcon, Sarah Gray, and Noelle Virtue, "Love Food Champions: Final Report," October 2008, 14.

18. You can see the Green Granny's teeny (or should I say sensible?) fridge on You Tube at the 30-second mark of this video: http://www.youtube.com/watch?v=H6IWTS3JAZ4&feature=channel.

19. James Hall, "Gordon Brown Puts the Spotlight on Supermarket Food Waste," *The Telegraph*, July 8, 2008, http://www.telegraph.co.uk/finance/newsbysector/retail andconsumer/2792884/Gordon-Brown-puts-the-spotlight-on-supermarket-food-waste .html (accessed January 3, 2010).

20. Rebecca Smither, "Tesco Launches 'Banana Hammock,'" *The Guardian*, June 12, 2009, http://www.guardian.co.uk/money/2009/jun/12/tesco-banana-hammock (accessed January 12, 2010).

21. Morrisons Press Office, "Morrisons Launch 'Great Taste, Less Waste' Campaign to Save Families Up to £600 Per Year," http://www.morrisons.co.uk/Corporate/Press -office/Corporate-releases/Morrisons-launch-Great-Taste-Less-Waste-campaign-to -save-families-up-to-600-per-year-/ (accessed January 4, 2010).

22. The Co-operative, "Watch Your Waste," http://www.co-operative.coop/ membership/events/changetheworld/Watch-your-waste/.

23. The twelve retailers involved represent 92 percent of the UK supermarkets. Waste & Resources Action Programme, "The Courtauld Commitment," http://www .wrap.org.uk/retail/courtauld_commitment/ (accessed January 3, 2010).

24. Waste & Resources Action Programme, "Non-Household Food Waste," http://www.wrap.org.uk/retail/food_waste/nonhousehold_food.html (accessed January 3, 2010).

25. To be fair, Marmite is an efficient use of food resources, as it repurposes yeast extract, a byproduct of beer breweries. Unfortunately, it tastes like it does, in many folks' view, prompting Marmite's "Love it or hate it" marketing slogan.

26. Morrisons, "Great Taste, Less Waste: Food Waste Factbook," 15, http://www .morrisons.co.uk/Documents/Great_Taste_Less_Waste_Final_Draft.pdf (accessed January 13, 2010).

27. Waste & Resources Action Programme, "Anaerobic Digestion," http://www .wrap.org.uk/recycling_industry/information_by_material/organics/anaerobic _digestion.html; UK Department of Environment, Food and Rural Affairs, "Anaerobic Digestion," http://www.biogas-info.co.uk/.

28. Anaerobic Digestion Task Group, "Developing an Implementation Plan for Anaerobic Digestion," July 2009, http://www.defra.gov.uk/environment/waste/ad/ documents/implementation-plan.pdf (accessed January 14, 2010).

29. UK Trade & Investment, "UK Forms Anaerobic Digestion Taskforce," February 18, 2009, http://www.ukinvest.gov.uk/OurWorld/4042439/en-GB.html (accessed January 4, 2010).

30. UK Department of Environment, Food and Rural Affairs, "Anaerobic Digestion," www.biogas-info.co.uk. This was as of December 2009. This site has an interactive map of AD plants at http://www.biogas-info.co.uk/maps/index2.htm. Of the plants, eleven are classified as "off farm."

31. Branston, "Branston Commits to 1.4m Environmental Investment," September 7, 2009, company press release, http://www.branston.com/news/ad_water_plant/ (accessed on January 4, 2010).

32. These prices come from online research done December 30, 2009.

33. Paul Cook, e-mail to author, December 31, 2009.

34. Tom Quested and Hannah Johnson, "Household Food and Drink Waste in the UK," Waste & Resources Action Programme, November 2009, http://www.wrap.org .uk/downloads/Household_food_and_drink_waste_in_the_UK_-_report.ae34bc6d .8048.pdf (accessed December 20, 2009).

35. W. E. Alford, *British Economic Performance, 1945–1975* (Cambridge: Cambridge University Press, 1995), 12 (accessed via Google Books).

36. BBC Online, "1954: Housewives Celebrate End of Rationing," July 4, 1954, http://news.bbc.co.uk/onthisday/hi/dates/stories/july/4/newsid_3818000/3818563 .stm (accessed on January 2, 2010).

37. BBC Online, "1952: Tea Rationing to End," October 3, 1952, http://news.bbc .co.uk/onthisday/hi/dates/stories/october/3/newsid_3122000/3122485.stm.

38. I'll hear arguments that beer is the national drink, but am confident that they'll be brushed aside. While coffee may be making inroads on the "cuppa," the same has long been true with wine and hard alcohol on beer. Besides, I was asked if I wanted tea before every interview conducted in England. Not once was I offered a beer!

NOTES TO CHAPTER 12

1. U.S. Department of Labor, Bureau of Labor Statistics, "Career Guide to Industry, 2010–2011 Edition," http://www.bls.gov/oco/cg/cgs041.htm.

2. Pennsylvania Department of Transportation, "History of the Litter Bug and PennDOT," http://www.dot.state.pa.us/Internet/pdKids.nsf/HistoryofLitterBugand PennDOT?OpenForm (accessed October 8, 2009).

3. Ljupka Arsova, Rob van Haaren, Nora Goldstein, Scott M. Kaufman, and Nickolas J. Themelis, "The State of Garbage in America," *BioCycle* 49, no. 12 (December 2008), 22, http://www.jgpress.com/archives/_free/001782.html.

4. European Community, "Council Directive 1999/31/EC of 26 April 1999 on the Landfill of Waste," *Official Journal of the European Community*, July 16, 1999, 5, http://eur-lex.europa.eu/LexUriServ/LexUriServ.do?uri=OJ:L:1999:182:0001:0019 :EN:PDF (accessed October 7, 2009).

5. Tonje Pareli Gormle, "New Landfill Ban on Biodegradable Waste," International Law Office, http://www.internationallawoffice.com/Newsletters/Detail.aspx?g=ec 416e86-c533-46c0-9502-040d6b24da5c (accessed October 7, 2009).

6. Linda Scott Kantor, Kathryn Lipton, Alden Manchester, and Victor Oliveira, "Estimating and Addressing America's Food Losses," *FoodReview*, January–April 1997, 6, http://www.ers.usda.gov/Publications/FoodReview/Jan1997/jan97a.pdf.

7. Katherine Ralston, Constance Newman, Annette Clauson, Joanne Guthrie, and Jean Buzby, "The National School Lunch Program: Background, Trends, and Issues," U.S. Department of Agriculture, Economic Research Service, Economic Research Report no. 61, July 2008, 1, http://www.ers.usda.gov/Publications/ERR61/ERR61 .pdf.

8. For full disclosure—I once spoke with Shared Harvest's creators about potentially working for the company in some capacity.

9. U.S. Environmental Protection Agency, "Municipal Solid Waste in the United States: 2007 Facts and Figures," 9, http://www.epa.gov/waste/nonhaz/municipal/ pubs/msw07-rpt.pdf.

RESOURCES

MEAL PLANNING

Meals Matter (www.MealsMatter.org)
- Plan meals, create shopping lists, and customize your own cookbook at this free site. Note to technophobes—you can print your menu or shopping list after doing them online.

E-Mealz (http://e-mealz.com)
- At this subscription-based site, you choose the diet type, store and number of people and they supply the shopping listz and menu planz.

DinnerPlanner (http://dinnerplanner.com)
- After signing up for this subscription-based service, you'll receive a weekly e-mail with seven dinner menus with recipes and corresponding shopping list.

USE-IT-UP RECIPE SITES

All Recipes (http://allrecipes.com/Search/Ingredients.aspx)
- Select as many as three ingredients you have and three ingredients you don't want included and the site provides recipe choices.

BigOven Leftover Wizard (www.bigoven.com/leftoverwizard2.aspx)
- Choose items from up to three pulldown menus—everything from abalone to zucchini—and the Wizard spits out recipe options that you hopefully won't spit out.

Not Beans Again (www.notbeansagain.com)
- Type in as many as five ingredients and the site lists recipes containing all of them. Since it's a UK site, beware the aubergine factor, and see if you can elicit the Posh Spud recipe.

Love Food, Hate Waste (www.lovefoodhatewaste.com/recipes)
- On the site's recipe page, you choose "what food needs using up" and the UK site supplies recipes.

FOOD SAFETY/STORAGE

Still Tasty (www.stilltasty.com)
- Helps determine how long foods stay safe to eat. Now with an iPhone app, too!

FoodSafety.gov (www.foodsafety.gov)
- "Your Gateway to Federal Food Safety," not surprisingly, errs on the cautious side.

Greenling Produce Storage Guide (www.greenling.com/community/newsletters/files/produce_guide.pdf)
- Helps you store your produce properly. Also found in this book's appendix.

DONATING FOOD

Food Bank Finder (http://feedingamerica.org/foodbank-results.aspx)
- This Feeding America resource helps individuals and commercial donors locate their nearest food banks.

A Citizen's Guide to Food Recovery (www.usda.gov/news/pubs/gleaning/content.htm)
- This USDA site has some good and some outdated information. The saddest part is the link to the defunct "USDA Gleaning and Food Recovery Home Page." Sigh.

Ample Harvest (http://AmpleHarvest.org)
- Links backyard gardeners with food pantries so individuals can donate their excess.

Veggie Trader (www.veggietrader.com)
- Trade backyard produce so it doesn't go to waste! Facilitates trading, buying, or selling.

America's Grow a Row (http://americasgrowarow.com)
- The non-profit matches farmers willing to donate land to grow food for the hungry with volunteers who will tend to the crops.

SCHOOLS

School Composting . . . The Next Step in Recycling (www.ct.gov/dep/cwp/view.asp ?A=2718&Q=325392)
- This manual helps schools establish and maintain a composting program.

Composting in Restaurants and Schools: A Municipal Tool-Kit (http://www.cetonline .org/Publications/res-schools-online.pdf)
- Another step-by-step guide, this one with budget estimates and case studies.

The Worm Guide: A Vermicomposting Guide for Teachers (www.calrecycle.ca.gov/Publi cations/Schools/56001007.pdf)
- Instructions for worm composting, it includes classroom activities and materials.

Composting with Worms (http://dnr.wi.gov/org/caer/ce/eek/earth/recycle/compost2 .htm)
- A practical guide for kids in how to compost using worms.

FOOD RECOVERY/GLEANING

Food Donation Connection (www.foodtodonate.com)
- Links food service donors with hunger relief groups.

Food Rescue (http://foodrescue.net)
- This growing food recovery network has chapters in 18 states and is looking for people to start more.

The Society of St. Andrew (www.endhunger.org)
- To glean food from farms, this ecumenical group is likely your best starting place. They operate in all 48 contiguous states, but their presence is larger in some.

RESTAURANTS AND COMMERCIAL KITCHENS
Donations

Perishable Food Donation Guide (http://feedingamerica.org/partners/product-partners/perishable-food.aspx)
- Guidelines for restaurants and supermarkets donating fresh or perishable food.

Food For Thought: Restaurant Guide to Waste Reduction and Recycling (http://www.calrecycle.ca.gov/Publications/BizWaste/44198016.pdf)
- A must for all restaurateurs interested in reducing waste and/or donating food.

Food Donation: A Restaurateur's Guide (www.p2pays.org/ref/12/11907.pdf)
- A fairly extensive manual for restaurant operators considering donating food.

Putting Surplus Food to Good Use (www.epa.gov/wastes/conserve/materials/organics/pubs/food-guide.pdf)
- A short guide on keeping food from the landfill, featuring the EPA food waste recovery hierarchy.

Waste Diversion and Composting

Food Waste Management Cost Calculator (www.epa.gov/wastes/conserve/materials/organics/food/tools/index.htm)
- Allows commercial kitchens and grocers to see the financial benefit of diverting food waste from the landfill. Happily, it lists reducing waste as an option and enables users to enter results into the . . .

WAste Reduction Model (WARM) (http://epa.gov/climatechange/wycd/waste/calculators/Warm_home.html)
- Calculates greenhouse gas emissions for solid waste, including one catch-all category for food waste.

Find-a-composter, (www.findacomposter.com)
- An invaluable tool for those who need to locate a commercial composting facility.

Supermarket Composting Handbook (www.mass.gov/dep/recycle/reduce/smhandbk.pdf)
- Teaches grocers how to divert and compost food waste and other organics, while providing resources and publicity ideas.

A Guide to Commercial Food Composting (http://www.epa.gov/wastes/conserve/materials/organics/food/fd-guide.htm)
- Helps supermarkets, restaurants and institutions begin and sustain a composting program.

Miscellaneous

Banana Guard (www.bananaguard.com)
- Avoid fruit waste in the form of squished or bruised bananas and other fruit.

Banana Saver (http://bananasaver.com)
- Slightly different design from the above, but the same idea.

Feeding America (http://feedingamerica.org)
- It's good to know that these folks run the nation's largest network of food banks. Previously called America's Second Harvest.

BioCycle Magazine (www.jgpress.com/biocycle.htm)
- As the leading (and only?) magazine on organics recycling, it's *the* source for composting and anaerobic digestion news. The December "State of Garbage in America" issue is an annual must read (but makes the post-holiday trash even more sobering).

APPENDIX:
PRODUCE STORAGE GUIDE

ABBREVIATIONS

FR = Fridge

RT = Room temperature

GUIDELINES

Apples	**FR**—Loose
Artichoke	**FR**—In plastic bag or in crisper
Asparagus	**FR**—Keep tips moist, standing
Avocadoes	**RT**—Refrigerate after ripening
Bananas	**RT**—Freeze after ripe for B-bread
Beets	**FR**—Ventilated plastic bag in crisper
Bell Peppers	**FR**—In plastic bag or in crisper
Blackberries	**FR**—In crisper
Blueberries	**FR**—In crisper
Broccoli	**FR**—In crisper
Brussels Sprouts	**FR**—In crisper
Cabbage	**FR**—In crisper
Cantaloupe	**RT**—Refrigerate after ripening
Carrots	**FR**—Ventilated plastic bag in crisper
Cauliflower	**FR**—In crisper
Celery	**FR**—Ventilated plastic bag in crisper
Cherries	**FR**—Covered. Store soft ones separately. Rinse when ready to eat.
Corn	**FR**—In crisper, in husk

Cucumbers	**FR**—In plastic bag or in crisper
Garlic	**RT**
Grapefruit	**RT** or **FR**—Never in plastic bag
Grapes	**FR**
Green Beans	**FR**—In plastic bag or in crisper
Green Peas	**FR**—In plastic bag or in crisper
Herbs	**FR**—In plastic bag or in crisper
Honeydew Melon	**FR**—Ventilated plastic bag in crisper
Jalapenos	**FR**—In plastic bag or in crisper
Kiwi	**RT**—Refrigerate after ripening
Lemons	**RT** or **FR**—Never in plastic bag
Lettuce	**FR**—Plastic bag. High humidity and cool temps.
Limes	**RT** or **FR**—Never in plastic bag
Mangoes	**FR**—Ventilated plastic bag in crisper
Mushrooms	**FR**—Plastic bag. High humidity and cool temps.
Nectarines	**RT** or **FR**—Never in plastic bag
Okra	**FR**—Plastic bag. High humidity and cool temps.
Onion	**RT**
Oranges	**RT** or **FR**—Never in plastic bag
Peaches	**FR**—Ventilated plastic bag in crisper
Pears	**FR**—Ventilated plastic bag in crisper
Pecans	No particular storage needs
Pineapple	**RT**—Refrigerate after ripening
Plum	**FR**—Ventilated plastic bag in crisper
Potatoes	**RT**—Cool, dark area; no plastic bags
Raspberries	**FR**—In crisper
Salad Greens	**FR**—Plastic bag. High humidity and cool temps.
Snap Peas	**FR**—Ventilated plastic bag in crisper
Spinach	**FR**—Plastic bag. High humidity and cool temps.
Squash	**FR**—In plastic bag or in crisper
Strawberries	**FR**—In crisper
Sweet Potatoes	**RT**
Tangerines	**RT** or **FR**—Never in plastic bag
Tomatoes	**RT**—Refrigerate after ripening
Watermelon	**FR**—Ventilated plastic bag in crisper
Zucchinis	**FR**—In plastic bag or in crisper

Source: Greenling.com, "Produce Storage Guide," http://www.greenling.com/community/newsletters/files/produce_guide.pdf.

INDEX